BOATS ON THE MARNE

BOATS
on the
MARNE

JEAN RENOIR'S CRITIQUE
of
MODERNITY

PRAKASH YOUNGER

INDIANA UNIVERSITY PRESS

This book is a publication of

Indiana University Press
Office of Scholarly Publishing
Herman B Wells Library 350
1320 East 10th Street
Bloomington, Indiana 47405 USA

iupress.indiana.edu

© 2017 by James Prakash Younger

All rights reserved

No part of this book may be reproduced or utilized in any form or by any means, electronic or mechanical, including photocopying and recording, or by any information storage and retrieval system, without permission in writing from the publisher.

The paper used in this publication meets the minimum requirements of the American National Standard for Information Sciences—Permanence of Paper for Printed Library Materials, ANSI Z39.48–1992.

Manufactured in the
United States of America

Cataloging information is available from the Library of Congress.

ISBN 978-0-253-02901-0 (cloth)
ISBN 978-0-253-02926-3 (paperback)
ISBN 978-0-253-02942-3 (ebook)

1 2 3 4 5   22 21 20 19 18 17

*This book is dedicated to
Jocelyn, Leela, and Meenakshi.*

CONTENTS

Preface: The Enigma of La règle du jeu   ix
Acknowledgments   xxiii

Introduction: Jean Renoir, Cinephilosopher   1

1. Genesis and Style of the French Renoir   23
2. Escaping from Flaubert; or, Reflecting on Romanticism   77
3. Loving the Distance; or, Historical Experience and the Fruits of Reflection   164
4. *La règle du jeu*; or, Putting Modernity in Question   224

   Conclusion: Why *La règle du jeu* Matters   295

Bibliography   315
Index   319

PREFACE: THE ENIGMA OF *LA RÈGLE DU JEU*

To articulate the past historically does not mean to recognize it "the way it really was." It means to seize hold of a memory as it flashes up at a moment of danger. Historical materialism wishes to retain that image of the past which unexpectedly appears to man singled out by history at a moment of danger. The danger affects both the content of the tradition and its receivers. The same threat hangs over both: that of becoming a tool of the ruling classes. In every era the attempt must be made anew to wrest tradition away from a conformism that is about to overpower it.

Walter Benjamin, "Theses on the Philosophy of History," 1940

When I made *La Règle du jeu* I knew where I was going. I knew the malady that gnawed at the contemporary world. That doesn't mean that I knew how to give a clear idea of that malady in my film. But my instinct guided me. My awareness of danger furnished the situations and the lines, and my comrades felt like I did. How anxious we were! I think the film is good. But it's not so difficult to do good work when the compass of anxiety indicates the true direction.

Jean Renoir, "Interview," 1952

THOUGH I FIRST SAW *La règle du jeu* a long time ago, during my first year in college, I have never forgotten the astonishment of the experience. I was not far into the film when I caught a glimpse of something vital, the key to a mystery of human relations I had been wondering about in real life, and the expectation that this magical something was about to be revealed riveted my attention to every detail of events onscreen, carried me all the

way to the end, when I realized that I had absolutely no clue whatsoever—only the vivid memory of having glimpsed one, blissful confirmation that the magical something existed. That glimpse felt like proof of something because, as far as I could tell, the film had just made me more *intimate* with a civilization that was completely strange to me than I had ever been with anything or anyone; since I could not have imagined such intimacy on the basis of past experience, could not even have colluded with the film to produce it, I figured it could only be, had to be, *real*—grounded in some deeper strata of existence that my world and the strange world of the film had in common. But what the magical something was, or by what incredible mechanism I had become intimate with an entire foreign civilization, I hadn't the slightest idea.

I know that as I watched the film I became acutely sensitive to what I might now call its ontological effects. As the intricate narrative unfolded, every detail and nuance of events seemed to add to a complex, ellipsis-ridden backstory, which I imagined in the form of a vast baroque coral reef, teeming with life; I sensed that this rapidly expanding enigma was never going to be resolved by the film and—somewhat logically—came to believe its source could only be located somewhere just behind the fiction, in the historical realities of the time when the film was made. But much stranger, I came to feel that this invisible Event behind the film's events had *not yet finished happening*, that, like the light and sounds that still travel to us from long-vanished stars, it was desperately trying to make itself manifest now, as I watched the film. Every shot in the film was alive and teeming with unfinished business, as if I was always just a moment too late (because it was too close, too distant, too fast, too slow, too loud, or too soft) to catch what was essential, which I nonetheless felt was somewhere right in front of me, patiently waiting to be seen and heard. A unique historical world was flaring up and vanishing before my eyes; everything had an unsettling poignancy, to the point where I could feel the cool, damp air of the hunt sequence against my skin, feel the heavy gray lid of that sky, imagine that I was somehow the first person—and might be the last person—to see all these strange and wonderful people alive. One catalyst for this weird way of watching the film must have been the indelible death spasm, the languid stretching and folding gesture of the rabbit at the end of the hunt; for reasons that are either obvious or impossible to explain, the patch of ground on which that rabbit dies always seems to be imperceptibly moving, a documentary evocation of the immense size and rotation of the planet at that very moment. In any case, I must really have dwelled on—or in—this wormhole in Time, for I came to believe the actors always knew their ultimate fate, exactly how ephemeral their world was in the grand scheme of things; beyond all reason, I thought I could see the actors knowing *then* that people like me would be watching them *now*, and because they kept this and their other secrets so perfectly, they made the entire film glimmer with an uncanny ironic familiarity, like a glistening eyeball.

Of course, when my brain cooled I realized I had it all backwards, that my hallucinations about the actors' secrets were the result of having imbibed more uncanny ironic familiarity than I, as a cocky but naive undergraduate, was used to. But at the time, and as a sort of reflex to my time-traveling contemplations, I became starkly aware of the arbitrariness of the location to which I had returned, been thrown, when the film ended, that is, a university auditorium in Queen's Park, the leafy center of

Toronto, Canada, planet Earth, in the early 1980s.[1] I sat for a while after the lights came back on, trying to secure all the pieces of the experience, and then walked in blissful lucidity through the cosmic dusk of the campus to the dining hall, where I got my supper and sat down with a few guys from my dorm. Our usual banter seemed totally absurd, and I must have been abnormally quiet because they looked at me strangely—and looked strange to me; I had a brief but agonizing moment of existential panic, as if seeing the film had permanently defamiliarized my world.

Back then there was nobody I could discuss the film with, and I would not in any case have known how to discuss it, with the same hyperbolic phrases— "an infinite, teeming world" or "the precise flow of life" or "completely *adult*" (meaning "deeply experienced, flawed, human, conscious of mortality")—bouncing around in my head. Absorbing my professors' passion for Foucault and Barthes, I was learning that any film is only a machine of culture designed to reproduce ideological effects, yet no amount of skeptical head-shaking could erase the impression that this particular film was somehow more real, or at least *better digested*, than real life itself:

in no detail did it resemble my own experience of life, but in every detail I could see that it had thoroughly digested the life it had been given to digest. To me it was as complex and multifaceted as life but more intense and more distilled, infinitely fresh and surprising and yet, with each surprise, somehow more familiar; it was faster than anything I had ever experienced, like a raging mountain torrent, and yet, at the same time, crystal clear, a deep and limpid pool one could, in principle, see through to the very bottom. I had the sense that if I ever did get to the bottom of it I would also have caught up to my own life, grasped some of the logic behind the meandering routes it had taken.

Sharing this personal story is obviously not the most prudent way I could have started to explain what this book is about, but it seems relevant to disclose its roots in what, several decades later, still feels like a gift of chance, a message in a bottle that dropped into my lap from a starry night sky. Beyond its extravagance, my encounter with the film put me on a hook, created a void that was only aggravated by further screenings and amateur research, and I soon learned that both elements, the extravagance and the hook, were common to the experience of others, including the filmmaker Alain Resnais:

> It remains, I think, the single most overwhelming experience I have ever had in the cinema. When I first came out of the theatre, I remember, I just had to sit on the end of the pavement; I sat there for a good five minutes, and then I walked the streets of Paris for a couple of hours. For me, everything had been turned upside down. All my ideas about the cinema had been changed. While I was actually watching the film, my impressions were so strong physically that I thought that if this or that sequence were to go on for one shot more, I would either burst into tears, or scream, or something. Since then, of course, I've seen it at least fifteen times—like most film-makers of my generation.[2]

In my attempts to get off the hook, I watched all the Renoir films available on video in the university library, and I remember obsessively replaying short clips from Boudu sauvé des eaux (1932) and A Day in the Country (1936) as if they might, on the umpteenth try, yield the magic key, that undeniably real thing I had first glimpsed in La règle du jeu. I also read what I could find on and by Renoir, in search of a sentence or phrase that would somehow explain the film's effects.[3] Most of the critical consensus on the film was in place, and it all made good sense: the magisterial, Bazin-approved style of long takes, composition in depth, and camera movements; the parallel arrangement of characters and intrigues among masters and servants; the vexed issues of class, gender, and nation; the unique "dancing-on-a-volcano" fluctuation between comedy and drama; and the volatile synthesis of classical sources (Marivaux, Beaumarchais, Mozart, and Musset) with contemporary references (to the Anschluss, Munich accords, anti-Semitism). But nobody seemed willing to take the final step and say how these elements added up, what was at stake in all the well-coordinated mayhem, what the film was ultimately about; years later I discovered I was not alone in thinking there was a mysterious lacuna in the writing on the film, and the critic who flagged the issue, the late great Robin Wood, did not himself attempt to resolve it:

> I have never read a *satisfying* account [of La règle du jeu], an account which gives one the sense (though it may in the long run prove illusory) that the writer has probed to its heart. There are two possible explanations for this: either (as most would have it) the film is so complex and multifaceted that,

like life itself, it repels all attempts at definition; or, despite the almost universal (and I think justified) acclamation, it is itself on some deep level unsatisfactory, confused, evasive. It has always seemed to me a question whether it is a film about people who go too far or a film about people who can't quite go far enough, and I think Renoir himself may have shared this uncertainty.[4]

As I had found to be the case with other great films, I expected repeat viewing would allow me to discover nuances that would progressively enrich my understanding and enable me to resolve the enigma; but with *La règle du jeu* the magic moments I thought I knew were often quite different from what I remembered, and though new details would always rise to prominence, these too would seem slightly *off* the next time I watched the film. In my experience there is only one other film that conveys a comparable sense of uncanny, mutating aliveness, and, as different as they otherwise are, everything Peter Lehman says about that film is, for me, equally true of *La règle du jeu*: "I have always felt that in *The Searchers* [John Ford, 1956] what happens and why is so ambiguous that all the repeated viewings in the world won't fully clarify it.... With most films, the more we see them the more clear they become for us and repeated viewings, however pleasurable, confirm our essential understanding of the film. My experience with *The Searchers* is nearly the opposite; the more I see it, study it, read about it, and edit essays on it, the less sure I am about anything."[5] As my amateur investigation lost steam, I could not help but wonder if all the strange phenomena—my original ontology-fueled time-traveling, the evasiveness and ambiguities in the scholarship, the hermeneutic black hole of repeat viewing—were not all effects of the same cause: that the film *did* mutate or behave slightly differently every time one watched it, that it *was* animated or alive with a restless energy or spirit. This was such an obviously crazy idea that I was not happy, even a bit scared, to have arrived at it: how could any film—which is, after all, only an *object*, albeit a complex aesthetic object—behave or act like a *subject*? As far as I can recall, arriving at that bizarre question was when I decided to drop my initial quest for the key to *La règle du jeu*. I had no further clue how to figure the film out, and there were, of course, other things going on: the film drifted down to the bottom of the river, became another in the scattered collection of unforgettable experiences trying to make sense of each other in the gloom.

Much later, after more than a decade in which I was engaged in very different pursuits, the film and the idea for this book resurfaced in my life. Coming of age during the historical and intellectual tumults of the late 1980s and early 1990s—the spectacular sunset of Theory, the dawn of Postmodernity and Globalization, the end of History, and so on—I spent a lot of time pondering issues of political philosophy that had become, for me and a few friends, inescapable.[6] Under the influence of a diverse group of thinkers and artists (for example, Simone Weil, George Grant, George Steiner, Hannah Arendt, Walter Benjamin, André Bazin, Fredric Jameson, Eugenio Montale, D. H. Lawrence, Leo Tolstoy), I had come to view the experience of modernity as governed by the tension between two opposed paradigms, the modern assumptions that generally underlie public discourse and that we implicitly live by (which I followed Grant in tracking from Rousseau through Kant, Hegel, and Nietzsche to Heidegger and Foucault) and older ethics-oriented assumptions that I had come to believe were more vital and fundamental (articulated in a Platonic tradition carried forward by Weil, Grant, Arendt, Emmanuel Levinas, and Stanley Rosen). Despite the differences between philosophers in the modern lineage, from the standpoint of the Platonic tradition they all tend to reduce the human experience of time to that of history; that is, they assume that meaning and truth are created by human action and that thought is ultimately only a mode of action. This stress on time-as-history reflects a model of human nature in which traditional distinctions between desire and will are lost and concepts of desire, ethics, and rationality get subsumed under the instrumentality of the will (as in Heidegger's concept of Technology or Foucault's concept of Power). In contrast with these modern assumptions, the model of human nature put forward by the Platonic tradition and exemplified in the myth of the charioteer in the *Phaedrus* is rooted in the capacity of attention and ethical receptivity to the Good, which reason uses to guide the soul into proper relationships with other people and the world (the precise *distance* from the Other at which his or her beauty or reality becomes visible). The concept of will in this model (the good horse) is basically the same as that developed by the Stoics, an ally of reason (the charioteer) in its effort to restrain or tame the blinding force of passion (the bad horse); in contrast to the absolute forms of freedom found in Hegel and Nietzsche, freedom in the Platonic model is relative to the self-mastery/effacement of a human life oriented by the cognate faculties of attention and love.

As I became increasingly convinced and conscious of the reality of the tension between these two paradigms—one so pervasive as to be invisible and unquestionable, a self-fulfilling tautological prophecy epitomized by the then-contemporary slogan "Just Do It," and the other quasi-taboo, tainted by religious affiliations, and generally subject to misunderstanding—I fell into the habit of reading the world through a bifocal lens. Making sense of the cultural and political events that concerned me at the time (for example, films, literature, painting, and music; ethnic violence in India and Sri Lanka; Canadian debates over Native rights, Quebec, and free trade; Tiananmen Square; the Gulf War, and so on) meant recognizing how modern assumptions shaped discourse and events and how traditional assumptions registered their deeper ethical significance, their ultimate consequences, and how they played out in the long run. To take a well-known example, I could see how the "universal homogeneous state" or "postmodern condition" that came into view during the years 1989–91 was both the emancipation celebrated by Hegel, Alexandre Kojève, and Francis Fukuyama (universal access to social recognition and the possibility of better life via participation in the globalized market economy) and the tyranny that concerned Grant, Rosen, and Jameson (the growing incapacity to imagine the totality of the world or register the deprival of human needs beyond consumer capitalism's will to power) and how both emancipation and tyranny were illuminated by the issue of technology as analyzed by Heidegger and Grant.

Within the context of such concerns, my long-delayed epiphany about *La règle du jeu* was that the film understood this philosophical predicament, brought it to life or, more precisely, was itself brought to life by the degree to which we, its audience, were enmeshed in that predicament. It occurred to me that all the film's enigmatic effects—my original time-traveling, its comparable impacts on Alain Resnais and others, the bizarre tumults of its Parisian premiere, the unconscious evasiveness in the scholarship—could perhaps be traced to a common cause in *our* subjectivities, *our* contradictory responses to an endemic philosophical danger. This intuition about the philosophic powers of *La règle du jeu* led to the question as to how and why the film's author had come to engage with such issues, and it seemed logical to consider the possibility, first raised at the time of the film's release, that it represented the "distillation" of the "entire body of filmic experimentation" that preceded it, that it was the logical culmination of a career motivated, at least in part, by Renoir's reflections on the world around him.[7] I decided to explore the possibility that Renoir's films of the 1930s articulated an inadvertent but nonetheless coherent narrative of philosophical response to the historical dangers of the times.

The key idea guiding my research was that *La règle du jeu*'s pronounced anachronism, its return to what Renoir called "a classical spirit" and sources—its strange evocation of pre-revolutionary modes of life and traditions of thought as a means of depicting contemporary French society—was by no means an expression of nostalgia or political conservatism; instead, I saw this "radical anachronism" to be the key to the film's provocative effects.[8] Taking seriously Renoir's claim that the film embodied his "desire to escape from naturalism, even to escape from Flaubert," I recognized its relation to his perennial critique of phenomena he groups under the label of *romanticism*, and I began to see the extent to which these phenomena had already been examined in his earlier films of the 1930s.[9] As Renoir characterizes it, romanticism is more than a once-prominent-but-now-extinct movement in the high arts; it is, rather, a pervasive element of modern life, a dangerous hydra-headed malady that intimately shapes our personal lives, society, culture, and politics, blinding us and binding us into unhealthy relationships and agonistic conflicts. As I began to reconstruct a cultural genealogy that cohered around the ideas and influence of Jean-Jacques Rousseau, I also began to discern the distinctive articulations of a counter-attitude, an alternative to romanticism with philosophical roots in the Enlightenment, Montaigne, and traditions of thought that reach back, ultimately, to Plato.

Making narrative sense of these two philosophical tendencies in Renoir's work was daunting, for to reconstruct their dialogical relations and properly assess their significance, I had to engage with two distinct approaches to, and domains of, history. On one hand, to appreciate *how* Renoir staged this philosophical confrontation, I had to venture into what is, by general consensus and the opinion of those who seem qualified to judge, the most labyrinthine jungle in all cultural history—*romanti-*

cism—and emerge with an account of the topic relevant to Renoir's work, tracking its dissemination in literature, art, and the assumptions of modern philosophy while also trying to identify and understand the cultural genealogy and counter-assumptions relevant to Renoir's articulations of premodern philosophical traditions.[10] On the other hand, to understand *why* Renoir found romanticism to be such a critical problem, and why he therefore might have sought to revive premodern traditions of thinking, I had to examine the social and cultural climate of France in the 1930s and identify the pathological role romanticism played there. The dramas and dangers of the time brought the philosophical narrative of Renoir's filmmaking during the 1930s into focus; over the course of the decade, as France slid ineluctably toward social disintegration and political collapse, the dialogical conflict between romanticism and its pre-modern Other in Renoir's films can be seen to grow more explicit, complex, and intense, culminating in the final battle of *La règle du jeu*.

Having reconstructed the intertwined back stories of *La règle du jeu*, I realized the anachronistic aspect of the film backs up to a point before the origins of romanticism and modern political philosophy in the work of Rousseau and that this backing-up establishes a hermeneutic center of gravity—a view of Renoir's target—from a vantage point outside the ideological force field, the Platonic Cave, of modern assumptions. Developing the metaphor, one might say that the aesthetic mechanisms governing the film's radical anachronism function in the manner of a slingshot or crossbow, whereby the greater the distance we travel into and inhabit—become unconsciously convinced of—the unfamiliar philosophic assumptions of the past, the greater the critical, defamiliarizing force that is brought to bear on our modern assumptions when the projectiles are released. This complex, ever-mutating aesthetic figure combines an imperceptibly slow gathering of power and thematic significance with unpredictable lightning-flash releases of that power and significance and governs the fictional events of *La règle du jeu* from behind the scenes, like an invisible hand or ghost in its machine. At once too slow and too fast to be visible to the naked eye of inductive critical analysis, the subliminal effects of this figure serve, among other things, as my in-a-nutshell explanation for the paradoxes of the film's reception and reputation. Assuming the film is neither confused nor a free-standing epitome of Life itself, Robin Wood's equivocation between "people who go too far" and "people who can't quite go far enough" can derive only from his own uncertainty regarding human potential and limitations, that is, contradictions the film exposes within his own assumptions, and it is precisely by tapping into such uncertainties that the film generates the uncanny sense of being alive. As in the films of Chaplin that first inspired Renoir, *La règle du jeu* uses gags, interlocking devices of cognitive dissonance that, fractal-like, operate at different scales of magnitude, in order to expose the contradictions in our assumptions. The film has remained an enigma because we have yet to catch up to the thoughts its gags provoke in us, because the interpretive protocols we have hitherto used to understand it (for example, auteurist or historicist conceptions of Renoir as a director, ideological notions of Right and Left) are themselves based on romantic beliefs, modern conceptions of human desire, will, freedom, personal identity, community, history, and time that are the targets of Renoir's critique. We recognize that something of tremendous significance happens in the film but have found it impossible to define what that something is because the truths the film shows us remain, to our modern and postmodern ears and eyes, *incredible*. The fundamental goal of this book is to make those incredible truths credible and to thus enable the light and sounds from *La règle du jeu*'s long-vanished star to come home to rest where they began, in our own experience.

NOTES

1. A feeling I was later stunned to reencounter in a philosophy class that discussed Heidegger's vision of humanity brutally "thrown" into the arbitrary facticity of creation. The concept of "thrownness" is introduced in Heidegger, *Being and Time*, 127.

2. Cited in Sesonske, *Jean Renoir*, 440. The first impression of the critic Nino Frank is also worth quoting: Nino Frank, in *Premier Plan* (Lyon, 1962), nos. 22–24, ed. Bernard Chardère, 29, quoted in Harcourt, *Six European Directors*, 90.

3. It is perhaps a testament to the authenticity of my obsession that my copy of Christopher Faulkner's *The Social Cinema of Jean Renoir* is inscribed as a twenty-fifth birthday gift from my future parents-in-law.

4. Wood, *Sexual Politics and Narrative Film*, 60–61.

5. Though I can't pause to elaborate on the significant difference between the two films' technique in creating this effect, I could telegraph my general impression by saying that with *La règle du jeu* the spectator can't keep up with changes, whereas with *The Searchers* the spectator can't slow down enough to register them. Peter Lehman, "Preface: A Film That Fits a Lot of Descriptions," in Eckstein and Lehman, *"The Searchers,"* xiii.

6. My thumbnail periodization of postmodernity starts in the global tumults of 1968, achieves a locked-in sense of momentum in 1975 (experienced, conversely, as the locked-in *stasis* of modernity), and culminates with the end of the Cold War paradigm and corollary triumph of the market economics/globalization/End of History paradigm after Tiananmen Square and the other momentous events of 1989–91. The significance of 1975 in this narrative was originally derived from Fredric Jameson's article "Reification and Utopia in Mass Culture," which I read as saying the Event of postmodernism happens right in the middle of *Jaws* (Steven Spielberg, 1975) and articulates the events of Watergate and the end of the Vietnam War, but this date has since also been solidified by my own allegorical reading of the Hindi film *Sholay* (Ramesh Sippy, 1975) in relation to the crisis of the Emergency period in Indian history (1975–77).

7. "*La Règle du Jeu* is a film of the utmost importance for the career of its author—even, I would say, for the history of French cinema. It is the product of an entire body of filmic experimentation. Renoir, who shot many films and in all sorts of genres, seems to have produced, this time, the distillation of what, to his mind, cinema must be. *La Règle du Jeu* is a kind of manifesto." From a review by Marcel Lapierre in *Le Peuple* (July 15, 1939) and quoted in Phillips and Vincendeau, *Companion to Jean Renoir*, 144–45.

8. Renoir, *Renoir on Renoir*, 237.

9. Ibid.

10. Berlin, *Roots of Romanticism*, 1.

ACKNOWLEDGMENTS

THIS BOOK WAS WRITTEN during research leaves from the University of Western Ontario and Trinity College; I am most thankful for the free time and material support of those institutions and also for the encouraging camaraderie of my colleagues in the film studies department at Western and the English department at Trinity. Preston Browning, director of Wellspring House, allowed me to finish the book in the most conducive setting imaginable. For that, and much more, I can never thank him enough.

I am grateful to the super-efficient but also patient team at Indiana University Press who helped me make this book the best it could be. I owe a unique debt of gratitude to the IUP's anonymous reviewers who gave so much of their time and attention to earlier drafts of the book. My editors Raina Polivka, Janice Frisch, and Darja Malcolm-Clarke have guided me carefully through every stage of the process, and it has been a genuine pleasure to work with them.

I discovered the art of film in an introductory film studies course I took with Cam Tolton at the University of Toronto. Seeing great, unimaginable films every week for a year and listening to Cam's enthusiastic, horizon-expanding lectures, I was, as Susan Sontag aptly describes the cinephile rapture, kidnapped; Cam was the first in a series of inspirational film teachers without whom this book or my career as a film professor would never have come to fruition.

I arrived at the philosophical and theoretical background for this book while doing an MA at York University. I am thankful for a course with

Peter Morris that introduced me to the work of George Grant and am especially grateful for the dialogues I had with Evan Cameron, who taught me to have the courage of my Platonic-Grantian-Bazinian convictions.

When I decided to get my PhD and write a book on Jean Renoir, I realized that Dudley Andrew was perhaps the only person who might appreciate what I was trying to do. Dudley's own writing on film is designed to generate a reverence for the subject, thoughtfully exploring it in all its aesthetic, cultural, and historical dimensions but also subtly pointing out deeper enigmas for readers to explore for themselves. In my own way I tried to do something comparable in this book, and writing it with Dudley in mind as its ideal reader shaped my thinking at its roots and hopefully improved the expression of my thoughts as well. Other teachers at the University of Iowa also had a huge influence on my thinking, opening up rich paths of discovery that I expect to follow for the rest of my career; I can't call them to mind without a feeling of deep affection and gratitude: Rick Altman, David Depew, Philip Lutgendorf, Lauren Rabinovitz, and Angelo Restivo.

The passion, camaraderie, and wonderful discussions I have had with friends are also relevant to what I have tried to do in this book and are something I'm deeply grateful for. The following are interlocutors with whom I have gotten real, real gone over the years: Robert Abate, Stacey Donen, Christian Keathley, John McLellan, Geoff Shaw, Chris Smit, and Donato Totaro. Thanks also go to Tim Barnard, Jay Beck, Ashok Chaddah, Chander Chaddah, Angela Della Vacche, Mark Eagles, Chris Gittings, Chika Kinoshita, Zoran Maric, Michael Meneghetti, Sasa Milic, Dylan Mosenthal, Kelly Ann Oleksiw, Henry Owh, Gerald Peary, Brian Plungis, Milla Riggio, Louis-Georges Schwartz, Jocelyn Sealy, Gerald Sim, Jennifer Tramble, Greg Walker, Ray Watkins, Jennifer Wild, and Joe Wlodarz.

At the very deepest level, whatever I have been able to accomplish in this book has been shaped by the love and support of my family. My parents, Paul and Susanna Younger, did everything in their power to help me and my brother, Ajit, to thrive and strive to be the best we could be. Though I never thought to become a professor like my father, my parents expected a level of family discussion that was deeply educated, principled, and engaged with the wider world; this eventually took its toll and carried me into a profession that I have come to love. My expanded family now includes Cathy, Miriam and Nathan, Linda, Joey and Liam, and my wife's family, especially her parents, Maurice and Heather, all of whom, along with Aunt Chinna Oommen, a brilliant educator whom I have looked up to all my life, inspired and supported the writing of this book.

In trying to express my gratitude to Jocelyn, Leela, and Meenakshi, I don't know where to start and will never know where to end. For thirty years Jocelyn has been my soul mate, cheering me up, motivating me to be better, and beautifully modeling how to make the elements of our life together—work, children, traveling, friendships, family, books, music, films, cats, dogs—a lifelong Adventure. It has always been a joy to collaborate and share in each other's work, and she has been there with me at every stage of the writing of this book. Leela and Meenakshi make my life complete, every day, in every way; Leela made one sentence in this book perfect—though she can't remember which one—and Meena provided the *je ne sais quoi* and Fred Astaire flair. This book is dedicated to these three lovely and indispensable characters.

BOATS ON THE MARNE

Introduction:
Jean Renoir, Cinephilosopher

THIS BOOK'S CORE PREMISE is that Renoir's films of the 1930s articulate a narrative of reflective engagement with issues of political philosophy made pressing by the historical circumstances of the time. As such, it entails new approaches to film history and film-as-philosophy that need to be explained before we begin our reconstruction of that narrative. The first two sections of this introduction will address each of these approaches in turn, and it concludes with a sequential overview of the topics to be covered in the rest of the book.

A DIALOGICAL/DIALECTICAL APPROACH TO THE AUTEUR AND HISTORY

Boats on the Marne is an extended essay in what I call dialogical auteurism, one of the many possible approaches to film history underwritten by the paradigm of cinephilosophy I have put forward elsewhere and will briefly review in the next section of this chapter.[1] Among other things, I believe dialogical auteurism offers one way beyond a theoretical quandary or impasse that has had a long-standing impact on the discipline of film studies. Writing in 1957, Roland Barthes considered the relation between aesthetic artifacts such as films and the historical contexts in which they operate and found it impossible to imagine an approach that would do justice to the complexities of both:

> This is a difficulty pertaining to our times: there is as yet only one possible choice, and this choice can bear only on two equally extreme methods: either to posit a reality which is entirely permeable to history, and ideologize; or, conversely, to posit a reality which is ultimately impenetrable, irreducible, and in this case, poetize.... The fact that we cannot manage to achieve more than an unstable grasp of reality doubtless gives the measure of our present alienation: we constantly drift between the object and its demystification, powerless to render its wholeness. For if we penetrate the object, we liberate it but we destroy it; and if we acknowledge its full weight, we respect it, but we restore it to a state which is still mystified.[2]

Prescient of tendencies that were to become dominant within the discipline of film studies, the tension or choice between aesthetic analysis and historical understanding is still an unresolved issue for contemporary approaches to film authorship. As the discipline emerged during the 1960s and 1970s, the tendency that Barthes labels poetry became dominant first and treated the works of an auteur as autonomous, either self-identical or governed by principles of stylistic and thematic development understood to be independent of contextual factors (for example, industrial practices, cultural shifts, political events), while for the past forty years the tendency that Barthes calls ideology has held sway in three successive waves, from the feminist/psychoanalytic condemnation of all narrative films as artifacts of a status quo of power relations, through the cultural studies model of contested and mobile power relations, to the recent focus on what one might describe as politically neutral microhistoricism, the assumption that any film is best understood as an artifact of its most immediate historical contexts. Though the strongest work in the discipline has in fact always struggled to overcome this impasse, tacitly reading aesthetic structures through or onto historical contexts, or visa versa, it remains the case that scholars typically make their allegiance to one set of methodological assumptions explicit, while at the same time implicitly attempting to express their loyalty to the other set.

Dialogical auteurism is based on what I believe is a sensible rejection of the options that Barthes argues we are forced to choose between, either traditional auteurism (the auteur above history) or radical historicism (both auteur and films rendered comprehensible as artifacts of their immediate historical contexts); as I see it, what the proponents of both tendencies fail to recognize is that the auteur exists in *time* before he or she exists in *history*. What I mean by "existing in time" is simply that all human beings reflect on the world around them and that this process of reflection necessarily disengages us to a certain extent from immediate historical determination, tracking out as it were to an indeterminate, open, unfinished engagement with memories (the past, what has happened) and imagination (the future, what might happen) as a means of gaining a better understanding of the present, the only world within which we act as historical agents: as Hannah Arendt and others have shown, reflection necessarily entails a temporary suspension of action, and hence of history, insofar as history is the realm of intentional activity and reflection is a moment of contemplative attention—a pause—that suspends that activity.[3] Building on these assumptions, dialogical auteurism proposes that it is possible to interpret a group of films so as to recognize patterns that reflect an auteur's recurring habits of thought, the issues that he or she pauses over, and the figures or tropes he or she commonly uses to make sense of historical experience. Why do Renoir's style and use of cultural idioms change in the specific ways they do? What accounts for the pattern of dramatic ruptures and surprising, differential returns—the profound restlessness—that characterizes his career? Can one identify the urgent, danger-driven questions that Renoir keeps coming back to? Can one make narrative sense of the sequence of different answers he tries out? Once one abandons the idealist constants found in traditional approaches to the auteur, the stylistic and thematic diversity of Renoir's work presents itself as the main critical-historical issue that any account of that work needs to address. Though auteurists may have failed to speak to this diversity, the historicism that dominates contemporary film scholarship is no better at accounting for it; each approach excessively reduces one term of the auteur-history equation to the other. Neither attempts to recover the movements of thought making sense of events, the processes of existential reflection and cultural memory that are an inescapable part of any human response to historical experience.

As the dialogical intersection of cultural discourses mediated by an auteur's reflection, the work of film art can be defined as a focal point, a lens that brings certain issues into focus, the burning questions that in Walter Benjamin's vivid formulation "flash" between the living contradictions of the present (the specific political and social dangers that Renoir faced) and the contradictory testimony of the past (the cultural heritage he used to think through those dangers). In this context, the auteurist conception of "Jean Renoir" is of value only because his concerns are, as Peter Wollen once expressed it, the "catalyst" that brings the past and present into a charged, often desperate, dialogue; neither the self-identical will of traditional auteurism nor the plaything of circumstances who staggers through historicist scholarship, the auteur reappears as a moving target, someone more like us, trying his best and changing his mind as he struggles to keep track of the moving targets in the world around him. By virtue of the modest hypothesis that "the auteur reflects," the dialogical auteurism of this book proposes to bring Renoir's process of reflection to life via a Benjaminian mode of film history, an image of his life and art inevitably shaped by the endemic dangers that link it to our own lives and times; just as Renoir's relations with his cultural heritage and the past were shaped by the urgent need to resist and escape the ideological conformism of his time, so must our own deepest concerns inevitably determine what we as film scholars are capable of seeing in his films today.

With these dialectical conditions in mind, it should be evident why this study will not attempt to reconstruct the causality linking specific films to their immediate contexts, as if one could track the manifestation of Renoir's thoughts against historical events of the 1930s via a kind of point-by-point parallelism. Despite the fact that Renoir is on record and sometimes very explicit in identifying his concerns when making a given film, I do not think films or other works of art disclose their true significance when viewed as immediate reactions to events, for such analysis inevitably depends on and reinforces existing ways of understanding those events and does not allow for the possibility of delayed, reflection-based responses. Instead, the auteurist and philosophical commitment of this project will lead me to focus first on the aesthetic and diachronic dimensions of Renoir's work, reconstructing the thematic and narrative structures of each film as a whole in relation to those before and after them, and only then will I try to explain how and why the extended cinematic narrative makes sense as a coherent response to the intertwined political, social, and cultural narratives of the decade. The notion of time as distinct from history, reflection as distinct from action, is thus integrated into the way this book's argument is presented; just as Renoir needed time to think through the dangers that concerned him, we need time to weave Renoir's cinematic stories into the Big Story of France and the world in the 1930s, to see it the way he saw it, through the filter of hopes and anxieties we share.

CHRONOTOPES: CLIMATES OF POSSIBILITY IN 1930S FRANCE

The theoretical framework I will use to organize those hopes and anxieties, to make them palpable and comprehensible in thematic and narrative terms, is Mikhail Bakhtin's concept of the *chronotope*, which can for our purposes be treated as synonymous with Raymond Williams's idea of structures of feeling or Fredric Jameson's dynamic conception of allegory.[4] Given the importance of this concept to our explorations, it makes sense to quote Bakhtin's definition at length prior to explaining how I intend to use it, but for starters, I would argue that everything Bakhtin says about chronotopes in literature should be understood to make as much sense, and even better sense, when applied to film:

> We will give the name *chronotope* (literally "time space") to the intrinsic connectedness of temporal and spatial relationships that are artistically expressed in literature. This term (space time) is employed in mathematics, and was introduced as part of Einstein's Theory of Relativity. The special meaning it has in relativity theory is not important for our purposes; we are borrowing it for literary criticism almost as a metaphor (almost but not entirely). What counts for us is the fact that it expresses the inseparability of space and time (time as the fourth dimension of space). We understand the chronotope as a formally constitutive category of literature; we will not deal with the chronotope in other areas of culture. In the literary artistic chronotope, spatial and temporal indicators are fused into one carefully thought-out, concrete whole. Time, as it were, thickens, takes on flesh, and becomes artistically visible; likewise space becomes charged and responsive to the movements of time, plot and history. This intersection of axes and fusion of indicators characterizes the artistic chronotope. The chronotope in literature has an intrinsic *generic* significance. It can even be said that it is precisely the chronotope that defines genre and generic distinctions, for in literature the primary category in the chronotope is time. This chronotope as formally constitutive category determines to a significant degree the image of man in literature as well. The image of man is always intrinsically chronotopic.[5]

For me, the sentence that establishes how different the chronotope is from superficially similar concepts like genre is the following: "Time, as it were, thickens, takes on flesh, and becomes artistically visible; likewise space becomes charged and responsive to the movements of time, plot and history." When one speaks of "thickened time" and space, an entire diegetic world that is "charged and responsive," one indicates the way a work of art can give us a sense of being inside its world, its climate of possibilities. The chronotope's open, unpredictable climate of possibilities can be contrasted with the concept of genre and its predictable climate of probabilities, just as time, the experience of reflecting on immediate possibilities in the present, can be contrasted with history, the retrospective recognition of fated necessities; in saying the chronotope defines genre and generic distinctions (and not the other way around), Bakhtin reminds us that time precedes history, just as a full awareness of possibilities logically precedes an accurate determination of probabilities and necessities.

In proposing to categorize Renoir's films of the 1930s in terms of distinctive chronotopes, I am forced to assert something now that I hope the consideration of style and narrative structure in chapter 1 will demonstrate, that in the experience of watching a Renoir film from the 1930s we maintain a quasi-subliminal awareness of the era's wider climate of possibilities—the historically bounded infinity of what might have happened and what still might happen—even as the genre-determined and genre-determining fatality of what has happened on-screen closes in on the characters. As awkward as the metaphor may seem, I want to say that the story and characters resonate differently—have a very different thematic resonance—because of their presence within a specific chronotope. The elusive quality I'm trying to get at can perhaps be better understood by evoking specific audiovisual effects—the singular way people on-screen dress and talk; the one-of-a-kind-for-all-eternity background sounds of the city of Paris on a particularly cold, cloudy, gloomy day in 1937; the languid tumble and twist of a river's current—that can defamiliarize the fictional narrative we are watching and make us aware of the film as a documentary, its events in fact determined by a completely different network of motives and causes at work on a given day in 1937. Though we can by chance experience such moments of defamiliarization watching any film, my invocation of the chronotope in relation to Renoir posits that in his 1930s work it remains a constant, a deliberately invoked subconscious dimension of our experience that puts us in a very special relation to the historical world of which the film is also a generic artifact: we are, as it were, living inside that world vicariously, open to possibilities that existed *then* but which the film had no intention of representing to us *now*.

Raymond Williams's formulations on structures of feeling home in on this uncanny sense of inhabiting a historical moment from the past in the present, and they also illuminate the distinction between time-as-thought and time-as-history that will be relevant to every aspect of our exploration: "For structures of feeling can be defined as social experiences *in solution*, as distinct from other social semantic formations which have been *precipitated* and are more evidently and more immediately available. Not all art, by any means, relates to a contemporary structure of feeling. The effective formations of most actual art relate to already manifest social formations, dominant and residual, and it is primarily to emergent formations (though often in the form of modification or disturbance in older forms) that the structure of feeling, as *solution*, relates."[6] Though I doubt my interpretation would pass muster as orthodox Marxist theory, what I nonetheless believe Williams's chemistry class metaphor is getting at is the distinction I have been making between a climate of possibilities—a clear, open, to-be-determined *solution* that represents human freedom as the pause of open-minded reflection considering a range of invisible possibilities in the present—and the visible ("evident," "available") judgment and valuation manifest in the narrative events *precipitated* on-screen (already in the past). Another passage makes the connections between time-thought-the-present and history-action/events-the-past explicit, and the very hesitations (that is, "pauses") in Williams's writing perform the sense of living inside a moment, thinking it through, that we are attempting to define: "An alternative definition would be structures of *experience*: in one sense the better and wider word, but with the difficulty that one of its senses has that past tense which is the most important obstacle to recognition of the area of social experience that is being defined. We are talking about characteristic elements of impulse, restraint, and tone; specifically affective elements of consciousness and relationships: not feeling against thought, but thought as felt and feeling as thought: practical consciousness of a present kind, in a living and interrelating continuity."[7]

To bring this section of the introduction to a close, and to hopefully make the idea of the chronotope-as-climate-of-possibility more vivid and concrete, I would like to use an anecdote of Bernstein's from *Citizen Kane* (Orson Welles, 1941) as the pretext for a thought experiment:

> Well, you're pretty young, Mr. Thompson. A fellow will remember a lot of things you wouldn't think he'd remember. You take me. One day back in 1896 I was crossing over to Jersey on the ferry. And as we pulled out there was another ferry pulling in. And on it there was a girl waiting to get off. A white dress she had on. She was carrying a white parasol. I only saw her for one second. She didn't see me at all. But I'll bet a month hasn't gone by since that I haven't thought of that girl.

When examined in the context of Bernstein's role in the film as a whole, the girl on the ferry story is more than just an example of a romantic memory that Bernstein is suggesting to Thompson might be behind Kane's dying word "Rosebud," yet another section of the "trail of whiteness" leading back to the snow globe scene and Kane's lost childhood; part of the poignant effect of the anecdote is that it briefly reveals a side to Bernstein's character that is quite different from the Bernstein we know. The Bernstein we know is a street-smart, middle-class Jew, a pragmatic hustler who caught the rising tides of New York City in the Gilded Age to retire as a rich and successful business executive. Ever loyal to his boss, Kane, both on principle (it's part of what he thinks he's being paid for) and through a natural affinity (he admires Kane's bold, anarchic creativity and sense of humor), we might assume that he enjoyed his job so much that he never had time for a private life or family; in any case, we never hear of a private life or family, never see or hear him express any desire for either. The image of him transfixed by his one-second glimpse of the girl on the ferry is one for which we have no precedents—however we might imagine it, the expression on his face always has a striking freshness, in part because the measured and detached way in which he tells the story indicates that he has himself remained surprised by the power of the encounter for more than forty years. It is only fair to describe the anecdote as archetypal; the triangle sketched by the three vectors of looking in the image (old Bernstein looks at young Bernstein, young Bernstein looks at the girl, the girl looks elsewhere or offscreen) traces one of the classic figures of romantic love, while the urban location and motion of the ferryboats bringing Bernstein and the girl together (briefly) and then carrying them apart (forever) infuse it with the characteristic resonance of nineteenth century modernity, full of promise yet bittersweet: the flaneur's eternal search for the lightning-flash romantic epiphany.[8] But to start to sketch a concrete example of a historical climate of possibility, we need to bracket off the retrospective view with all its romantic effects, return to the moment itself, and add a few things to Bernstein's description of "the girl." Begin by imagining her to be a voluptuous, working-class Irish redhead in her early twenties, in the middle of a group of friends, laughing at a raunchy joke. Then picture her as an elegant, upper-class blonde WASP in her late fifties, standing alone at the railing, wistful. Now try a dignified black woman in her mid-thirties, with a pair of children, a boy and a girl, all in their Sunday best. Try and imagine all of these variations and then assess the extent to which you find one or more of them difficult to imagine. In any of these cases the retrospective historical "climate of probability," the in-principle-semi-predictable-thanks-to-statistics disposition of social, cultural, and political forces in New York on a given day in 1896, would determine the odds of Bernstein actually getting together with "the girl": whether or not he could approach her, what they would have to say to each other if he did, where they could spend time together, and the social obstacles to a possible marriage between them. What we need to be clear about, however, is that the single most important factor determining the historical probability of anything happening between Bernstein and the woman is what *he* can imagine happening in the wake of his lightning-flash epiphany moment on the ferry, and this in turn would be determined by what we have defined as a chronotope, a historical climate of possibility of the era: whatever the limitations of our own imaginations may be, each of my three variations would have been equally possible for Bernstein and just as possible as a fourth variation that featured a Jewish woman of the same class and age as he was in 1896. The stories and characters in Renoir's 1930s films only precipitate, take on flesh, after they have germinated and grown to term in the invisible life-giving thought solution of their chronotopes.

CINEPHILOSOPHY: A BAZINIAN APPROACH TO FILM AS PHILOSOPHY

RENOIR: People are not convinced by arguments. They are convinced by the sound of a voice. For example, I'm sure the people who followed Hitler weren't convinced by what he told them. I'm sure it was the little man's strange personality.

CAHIERS: The magical side?

RENOIR: The magical side! I think that convincing people is magic. People think that one convinces with arguments, with logical reasons. It's not true. Logic never convinced anyone. Absolute truth is absolutely invisible.

CAHIERS: And Socrates' dialogues?

RENOIR: Ah! I'm sure it's the same thing. There was a magical side. Because Socrates' reasons are excellent, but the truth is that if one cares to, one can respond to them, one can oppose them. But I'm sure that the element that convinces us, in what we have of Socrates' dialogues, is probably a kind of magic in the writing. It's in every writer in fact. It's by means of the magical side that one can reach the reasonable, or the reasoning side. Of course it's a paradox, but paradoxes are true. In any case, they have as much chance of being true as logical truths do.[9]

I arrived at this book's approach to treating films as philosophy by way of a close analysis of one of André Bazin's best-known essays, "The Ontology of the Photographic Image." In trying to reconcile the then-prevailing understanding of that essay's argument with the totality of Bazin's work, I stumbled on several passages that manifestly echoed passages from Plato, and in searching out and then pondering these striking similarities, I came to the conclusion that Bazin's philosophical conception of the art of cinema was more or less the same as Plato's art-dependent conception of philosophy.

In reaching that conclusion I knew I was placing myself directly at odds with the general consensus that Plato and Bazin were, in one sense or another, "idealists" and "rationalists" in the worst possible way. At the time, the dominant reading of Bazin's Ontology essay was that it argued for a cinema based on "realism"—understood to be an objective, quasi-scientific revelation of pro-filmic reality based on the automatic transcription of visible appearances realized by photographic technology. In contrast to the standard reading of Bazin as holding a naive faith in science and reason, I read him to follow Plato in being deeply skeptical of rational discourse precisely because he was mindful of the philosophic benefits and ideological dangers inherent in art. In both cases the writers make clear that the goal is not objective knowledge in the scientific or historical sense but, instead, true belief, the product of an aesthetic experience dependent on the erotic-ethical capabilities of the spectators or readers; only by means of what Renoir and his Cahiers interlocutors call "the magical side" can a work of art engage and defamiliarize the spectators'/readers' entrenched habits of thinking and convince them of the truth. Beyond its usefulness in connecting Bazin, Plato, and Renoir, it is worth noting that this relationship between truth and erotic-ethical responsibility addresses a question about the justice of human existence that we all ponder as we grow up. It makes clear that understanding the world depends on one's loving attentiveness to the world and people in it and not on unjustly distributed variables such as material wealth, cultural capital, social privilege, education, and/or intelligence. However we happen to stumble upon this Platonic truth, it is, I think, deeply reassuring to know that a poor, deprived, mentally challenged person who understands the world is better off, actually has a better-because-more-meaningful-and-real life, than a rich and privileged genius whose experience is structured by self-centered illusions and fantasies.

With this general conception of art-as-philosophy in view, I would introduce my own approach to treating films philosophically in terms of a very simple two-step process, one that is designed to make explicit whatever philosophic capabilities they may already have as art. The first step focuses on film analysis in the inductive manner, reconstructing the elements of style, aesthetic, narrative structure, and so on, so as to mobilize the effects of a film for the reader; this step may entail recourse to specific theories of film and art, not as reiterated dogma but only as heuristic devices that can illuminate the critical issues at hand. The second step clarifies the philosophical stakes at issue, situating the effects of a film in terms of their cultural genealogies and historical contexts so as to isolate and clarify the specific complexes of belief being challenged (ideology/false assumptions) or promoted (philosophy/truer assumptions). In the case of both steps, the methods involved are generic or common, critical analysis plus cultural genealogy and history, and as such the practice of cinephilosophy distinguishes itself from brand-name approaches to film and philosophy—for example, the specific theoretical traditions associated with Deleuze, Stanley Cavell, David Bordwell, cognitivism, or psychoanalysis. That said, the practice of cinephilosophy can be situated as in the lineage of André Bazin insofar as its understanding of film-as-philosophy is grounded in the Platonic assumptions he outlines in the Ontology essay. A brief review of that essay's argument should therefore be an efficient means of clarifying what this or any other essay in cinephilosophy takes for granted.

As with Plato's poetically expressed ban on poetry in *The Republic*, or Renoir's comments about the equivocal magic employed by Hitler and Socrates, Bazin's ontological argument is built around the recognition of the cinema's equivocal propensity to engender both true and false belief, philosophy and ideology: "The quarrel over realism in art stems from a misunderstanding, from a confusion between the aesthetic and the psychological; between true realism, the need that is to give significant expression to the world both concretely and in its essence and the pseudorealism of a deception aimed at fooling the eye (or for that matter the mind); a pseudorealism content in other words with illusory appearances."[10] Bazin here identifies "two essentially different phenomena that any objective critic must view separately in order to understand the evolution of the pictorial."[11] This distinction between the aesthetic and the psychological is crucial to understanding Bazin's use of the term "reality," which is here explicitly connected to art and the aesthetic. Bazin organized the essay into six distinct sections separated by asterisks. Consideration of this structure reveals that he establishes the distinction in the first section of the essay, explores the psychological genealogy of photography in the second, third, and fourth sections, examines the aesthetic potentials of photography in the fifth section, and concludes with the famous reversal of the sixth and last section (a stand-alone one-sentence paragraph): "On the other hand, the cinema is a language" (my translation of "D'autre part le cinéma est un langage").[12] In a loose accord with this structure, my review of his argument will deal first with psychology, next with aesthetics, and will conclude with an examination of the reversal and its implications.

The first section of the essay traces the psychological function of art from the mummies of ancient Egypt up to the present and closes with the following conclusion: "If the history of the plastic arts is not only a matter of their aesthetic but *in the first place* a matter of their psychology, it is essentially the story of resemblance, or if you will, of realism" (my translation and italics).[13] For our purposes it is essential to note that Bazin reaches this conclusion after acknowledging that "the evolution, side by side, of art and civilization, has relieved the plastic arts of their magic role."[14] Without denying the processes of desacralization, rationalization, and historical understanding that have characterized the development of modern civilization, he nonetheless affirms the inescapable power of resemblance over human psychology, bluntly asserting that the suggestibility we associate with the primitive ideologies of the past remains at work today: "How vain a thing is painting if underneath our absurd admiration for all its works we do not discern man's primitive need to have the last word in the argument with death by means of the form that endures."[15] For the sake of clarifying what verges on being a confusing or paradoxical affirmation, I will restate what Bazin is saying here as a series of propositions:

1. Whether they are aware of it and acknowledge it or not, human beings are attached to mortal beings and the world by an erotic or ethical relation.
2. The development of scientific rationality and modern beliefs notwithstanding, this attachment always takes the form of an irrational attraction to the appearances of those beings and the world.
3. Its stated motives and historical justifications notwithstanding, art derives its initial motive and orientation from this irrational attachment to appearances.

In light of what has often been written about Bazin's irrational faith in reality, it is essential to emphasize the skeptical aspect of his affirmations about psychology and his manifest awareness of human vulnerability to illusion and ideology. For Bazin, our receptivity to the world in which we live is inevitably conditioned by the desire we carry with us and by the ideologies that have shaped that desire, and this vulnerability is presented as a constant relevant to the consideration of all art, including photography and the cinema. In this context, his point is that the photograph represents a powerful and ambiguous illusion that defies the critical power of the modern rationality that created it:

> The essential factor in the transition from the baroque to photography is not the perfecting of a physical process...; rather does it lie in a *psychological fact*, to wit, *in completely satisfying our appetite for illusion* by a mechanical reproduction in the making of which man plays no part.... *In spite of any objections our critical spirit may offer*, we are forced to accept as real the existence of the object reproduced, actually *re*-presented, set before us, that is to say, in time and space.... A very faithful drawing may actually tell us more about the model, but *despite the promptings of our critical intelligence* it will never have the *irrational* power of the photograph to bear away our faith.[16] (all italics mine)

In these quotes and others we might consider, Bazin's point is to recapitulate with regard to the photograph the general argument about the psychological basis of art that he made in the essay's first section; his discussion of the photograph extends his general point that the irrational power of resemblance persists within our enlightened and disenchanted modern civilization. Far from disclosing a pseudo-scientific or religious-mystical "axiom of objectivity" as some of his interpreters have suggested, Bazin's argument in the first four sections of the essay assumes that all the theoretical edifices of our knowledge—all "the promptings of our critical intelligence"—are as powerless to discriminate between truth and illusion in the photograph as they are in everyday life.[17]

Though it may satisfy our constant craving for resemblance-based illusion, the photograph does not in itself satisfy our deeper appetite for reality or truth. According to Bazin, only art can satisfy this deeper desire, though the truths revealed by art paradoxically depend on the primary psychological fact of resemblance and illusion.[18] To understand this paradox we need to retrace its articulation in the essay's first section. The section closes with Bazin's adaptation (already quoted above) of a quote from Pascal: "How vain is painting, which attracts admiration by the resemblance of things, the originals of which we do not admire!"[19] This reference is designed to remind of the point earlier in the section where Bazin defines the function of art as "sauver l'être par l'apparence" or "to save Being by means of Appearances."[20] If the task of art is to satisfy our erotic desire and ethical concern for the mortal beings that inhabit our world, the quote from Pascal underlines the ambiguous value of resemblance in allowing us to accomplish this task. For Pascal this ambiguity is an inescapable determinant of the human imagination, and like Bazin he recognizes the extent to which it defies rationality. As he puts it in another pensée: "It is that deceitful part in man, that mistress of error and falsity, the more deceptive that she is not always so; for she would be an infallible rule of truth, if she were an infallible rule of falsehood. But being most generally false, she gives no sign of her nature, impressing the same character on the true and the false. I do not speak of fools, I speak of the wisest men; it is among them that the imagination has the greatest gift of persuasion. Reason protests in vain; it cannot set a true value on things."[21] Recasting this ambiguity in terms of the aesthetic/psychological distinction, we might say that in itself the psychological power of photographic resemblance leads us to imaginative relations with both truth and illusion and that the aesthetic is that faculty which allows us to discriminate between these relations, to distinguish between true and false beliefs. But when viewed in the context of their common root in desire and the inability of reason to discriminate between them, Bazin's repeated distinction between the aesthetic and the psychological forces us to track it into another dimension: we are led to posit a qualitative difference in the heart of desire itself—the suspension of our (own) will in a moment of lucid and loving attention (to others)—that allows us to distinguish aesthetic achievement and philosophical truth from gratifying illusions.

This difference is articulated only later in the essay, in the quote with which we began. Unpacking the full sense of this quote, we find that it distinguishes between a base psychological desire that is "content with illusory appearances" and a higher, stronger, purer, more ethical form of desire that is satisfied only with true realism, defined as a union of "the Concrete" and "the Essential." Seen as the process of reflecting on and discriminating between true and illusionary relations, Bazin's model of aesthetic production presupposes a simultaneous double-mimesis that puts the sensual power of contingent appearances to work in the service of an invisible or offscreen reality that only a higher or purified quality of desire allows access to. Thus, in the history of painting: "The great artists have always been able to combine the two tendencies. They have allotted to each its proper place in the hierarchy of things, holding reality at their command and molding it at will into the fabric of their art."²² It is this process of double-mimesis that is expressed in the phrase "the form that endures" (*la pérennité de la forme*), which refers at the same time to the persistence of resemblance itself, the formal qualities of art, and the Platonic notion of forms.²³ The work of art thus fuses together two realms, a realm of sensuous immediacy grounded in the power of resemblance and an invisible realm of Necessity grounded in Being or Truth. With this model in mind, Bazin's affirmations concerning the aesthetic potentials of photography lose their hyperbolic appearance and simply acknowledge the paradox that the cinema's singular capacity to produce reflection is grounded in both the irrational power of conviction provided by photographic contingency and in the artist's/spectator's erotic-ethical capacity to care: "Only the impassive lens, stripping its object of all those ways of seeing it, those piled-up pre-conceptions, that spiritual dust and grime with which my eyes have covered it, is able to present it in all its virginal purity to my attention and consequently to my love. By the power of photography, the natural image of a world *that we neither know nor can see*, nature at last does more than imitate art: she imitates the artist" (my italics).²⁴ At the root of Bazin's ontological argument is the assumption that ethics is always at work in the heart of human life and culture, bringing into being both the philosophical illuminations of art and the skeptical awareness of ideology. All photographic images have an immediate claim on our desire through the power of resemblance, but a photography-based art such as the cinema effects a qualitative transformation of desire that allows us to discriminate between reality and illusion.²⁵

"On the other hand, the cinema is a language." The Janus-faced closing sentence of the Ontology essay is meant to remind the reader that the processes of spiritual struggle and discrimination we have outlined take place not in some abstract realm but in the historically specific languages and cultures from which the art of the cinema emerges. In one sense, it indicates that the aesthetic achievements of the cinema can be registered only by attending to the historical changes they effect in cinematic language—the unique configuration of their style, thematic figures, narrative design, and so on—while in another sense, its blunt qualification of what preceded it reminds us not to misunderstand Bazin's poetic affirmations, which are nothing more than a set of inferences about cinematic potential drawn from the realized facts of cinematic art: the truths revealed by art are the *source* of all definition or difference and therefore cannot themselves be defined.

Bazin's ontological argument is the theoretical basis for the cinephilosophical approach that this book is an essay in. On one hand, his conception of reality references the irrational conviction that specific patterns of audiovisual contingency can have, a power that we can only infer to be the product of existential contradictions in the spectator's experience. Considered in isolation, this conviction is what Bazin calls pseudorealism, the irrational and ephemeral allure that as-yet-unexamined contradictions give the photographic image through the power of resemblance; reality in a basic sense refers both to the ground of historical experience that is the root cause of cinephilia and to "the reality of the human condition" as always engaged in the process of discriminating between truth and illusion, as stuck in Plato's Cave and trying to get out. On the other hand, Bazin's use of the term also references the new world outside the cave that appears after one has responded philosophically to an encounter with aesthetic truth, a world that remains to other eyes and ears (governed by lazier minds and/or weaker qualities of desire) identical to the first but that has been transfigured from within by the liberating effects of true realism, cinematic art as philosophy. If philosophy is a mysterious movement of eros that carries us between two invisible and unknowable worlds, the art of the cinema registers that movement in a way that allows us to see it, hear it, and reflect on what it might mean:

> The word "realism" as it is commonly used does not have an absolute and clear meaning, so much as it indicates a certain tendency toward the faithful rendering of reality on film. Given the fact that this movement toward the real can take a thousand different routes, the apologia for "realism" *per se*, strictly speaking, means nothing at all. The movement is valuable only insofar as it brings increased meaning (itself an abstraction) to what is created. Good cinema is necessarily, in one way or another, more realistic than bad cinema. But simply being realistic is not enough to make a film good. There is no point in rendering something realistically unless it is to make it more meaningful in an abstract sense. In this paradox lies the progress of the movies. In this paradox too lies the genius of Renoir, without doubt the greatest of all French directors.[26]

CHAPTER-BY-CHAPTER SUMMARY

Boats on the Marne culminates in the close reading of *La règle du jeu* in the fourth chapter. With the Platonic/Bazinian conviction that, beneath all their historically variable alibis, the core vocation of both philosophy and art is simply to make incredible truths credible, the topics examined in the first three chapters of the book—how Renoir's style works, how that style was articulated into four distinctive chronotopes during the 1930s, how and why those four chronotopes evolved in response to historical events and resulted in a Fifth chronotope—weave a dialogical narrative designed to make the aesthetic mechanisms of *La règle du jeu* fully manifest and effective for the reader. This book does not purport to offer a better or more comprehensive account of Renoir's films, French culture or politics in the 1930s, the philosophical legacies of Plato or Rousseau, or any of the other subjects it examines along the way, though it should, I hope, offer a different and liberating way of looking at all of these things: the modest but sincere ambition of this book is to recognize the specific philosophical differences the films are capable of making and to carry these forward into a variety of domains and contexts.

Chapter 1 provides a critical analysis of Renoir's style during the 1930s, with the goal of providing a general sense of his creative problematic, his way of using the medium to address philosophical questions. This chapter begins with Renoir the cinephile-spectator and shows how the influence of Griffith, Chaplin, and von Stroheim shaped his ideal of the cinema as a modern popular art. It then turns to the issue that consistently shaped his reflections on style, the dialectical tension between what he calls "internal truth" (an effect of the actors' performances) and "external truth" (an effect of historical verisimilitude, but also a function of deep-focus cinematography, camera movements, certain sound and editing practices, and the like). The basic stylistic formulas recovered here—the construction of characters as layered, contradictory types; the deployment of what I call pictorial space and the dispassionate camera—provide the context needed to situate the philosophical figures that will be examined in the chapters that follow.

Chapter 2 treats the stylistic and thematic development of Renoir's work during the 1930s as a whole. The chapter begins with an analysis of the interrelations between narrative and style in *Une partie de campagne*. Adapting Bakhtin and other theorists of philosophical art, we see how the film's dialogue of chronotopes (climates of possibility that cohere around distinctive figures and themes) produces a reflective engagement with the problem of romanticism. We then examine four major chronotopes that Renoir works with during the 1930s, four climates of possibility in which the effects of romanticism are made manifest in very different ways: a Flaubertian genre (*La chienne, Madame Bovary*), Cytherean tragicomedy (*Boudu sauvé des eaux, Une partie de campagne*), naturalist melodrama (*Toni, Les bas-fonds, La bête humaine*), and a genre focused on revolutionary communities and popular culture (*Le crime de Monsieur Lange, La Marseillaise*). Detailed analysis of these eight important films illuminates the microscopic (that is, psychological) and macroscopic (that is, cultural, social, political) dimensions of romanticism, exploring phenomenological models and cultural genealogies as we trace their connections to a modern philosophical tradition that originated in the work of Jean-Jacques Rousseau.

Chapter 3 begins by outlining the complex but cohesive pattern created by the historical occurrence of these four chronotopes and reads this pattern as Renoir's reflection on the cultural-ideological climate and experience of the 1930s; when one considers this pattern in light of historical developments, Renoir's work discloses a desperate search for a solid philosophical basis for human community. Each film can be seen to pose the question "how to meet" by testing its imaginative purchase on the contemporary situation, and as the political climate worsens over the course of the decade we are prepared to understand why a Fifth chronotope now emerges in Renoir's work, incipient in *Les bas-fonds* and then fully articulated in *La grande illusion*. A product of the dialectic of films and contexts that preceded it, this Fifth chronotope is the fruit of profound reflection on the movements of political history and culture that led to the crises of the 1930s: its invocation of an anachronistic pre-revolutionary ideal of Civilization effects a bold and thorough critique of romanticism, nationalism, impulses of reaction and revolution, and concepts of Culture and History that governed the ideologies of the time.

Chapter 4 offers a close reading of *La règle du jeu* that draws on the critical analyses of Renoir's style in chapter 1, the chronotopic figures and philosophical issues identified in chapters 2 and 3, and the historical and political concerns that were considered in chapter 3. After a brief overview of the film's design, I work through a segmentation of the film designed to reactivate its intricate structures of philosophical violence, the mortal combat it stages between the paradigms of Civilization and Culture. By means of a complex narrative structure and gags that reproduce the experience of anachronism on every level of magnitude (moments within scenes, scenes, sequences, the film as a whole, larger narratives of world history within which the film situates itself), Renoir develops engagements with his characters and their unstable society that articulate a dialogical critique of modern understandings of human nature, human relations, and historical time. Having identified and elaborated the cultural genealogies that support this articulation, we can now reconstruct a process of reflection on the post-Enlightenment opposition between technological rationalism and romanticism—between "reasons" and "desires"—that serves to recover and validate certain premodern categories and concepts. Our exploration of Renoir's cinephilosophical odyssey during the 1930s comes to rest in a conclusion that attempts to explain what the results of the odyssey might be.

NOTES

1. Younger, "What Is Cinephilosophy? A Bazinian Paradigm, Part One" and "What Is Cinephilosophy? A Bazinian Paradigm, Part Two."

2. Barthes, *Mythologies*, 159.

3. The fundamentally different relationship to time entailed by the activities of thinking and willing is given a thorough and clear treatment in Arendt, *Life of the Mind*.

4. Williams uses the concept in *A Preface to Film* (1954), *The Long Revolution* (1961), and *Marxism and Literature* (1977). Though Jameson's most controversial use of the term "allegory" was in an essay on Third World literature, the concept is in fact used extensively throughout his work. In my opinion, the most extended and convincing explanation of what Jameson means by allegory is found in Imre Szeman, "Who's Afraid of National Allegory? Jameson, Literary Criticism, Globalization," *South Atlantic Quarterly* 100, no. 3 (Summer 2001): 803–27.

5. Bakhtin, *Dialogic Imagination*, 84–85.

6. R. Williams, *Marxism and Literature*, 133–34.

7. Ibid., 132.

8. The centrality and complex function of triangular figures in classical Greek philosophy and poetry is examined at length in Anne Carson's *Eros, the Bittersweet* (Champlain, IL: Dalkey Archive Press, 1998); Baudelaire's poem "To a Passer-by" in Charles

Baudelaire, *Selected Poems* (New York: Penguin Books, 1986), 171, deals with an encounter similar to Bernstein's; and the image of "boats against the current" in the last line of F. Scott Fitzgerald's *The Great Gatsby* (New York: Scribner's, 1953), 182, condenses the tension between modern aspirations and the eternal currents of human mortality in a similar manner.

9. Renoir, *Renoir on Renoir*, 121. Plato provides the paradigmatic articulation of this paradox in his employment of poetic discourse to ban the poets from his ideal Republic in Book X of *The Republic*, 239–52. The central role ethical and political exigencies play in shaping this paradox is discussed in Stanley Rosen, "Plato's Quarrel with the Poets," in Cook, *Philosophical Imagination and Cultural Memory*, 212–26.

10. Bazin, *What Is Cinema?*, 1:12.

11. Ibid., 11.

12. Bazin, "Ontologie de l'image photographique," *Qu'est-ce que le cinéma?*, 19.

13. Ibid., 12.

14. Bazin, *What Is Cinema?*, 1:10.

15. Ibid.

16. Ibid., 12–14.

17. The notion that all of Bazin's work can be reduced to such an axiom seems in general to emanate from a misreading of Eric Rohmer's argument in "André Bazin's Summa" in *Taste for Beauty*, 93–104.

18. Undergraduates presented with the received view of Bazin's ontological argument often wonder why Bazin does not privilege the documentary; the account I'm presenting here recognizes that aesthetic or ideological concerns always structure our perception of real events in the same way aesthetic or ideological artifacts structure our perception of fictional events.

19. Pascal, *Pascal's Pensées*, 38.

20. Bazin, "Ontologie de l'image photographique," 11.

21. Pascal, *Pensées*, 24.

22. Bazin, *What is Cinema? Volume I*, 11.

23. Bazin, "Ontologie de l'image photographique," 12.

24. Bazin, *What Is Cinema?*, 1:15.

25. This process of discrimination is referenced throughout Bazin's writings, as in this passage from "An Aesthetic of Reality," which illustrates all the main points we have considered so far:

> Reality is not to be taken quantitatively. The same event, the same object, can be represented in various ways. Each representation discards or retains various of the qualities that permit us to recognize the object on the screen. Each introduces, for didactic or aesthetic reasons, abstractions that operate more or less corrosively and thus do not permit the original to subsist in its entirety. At the conclusion of this inevitable and necessary "chemical" action, for the initial reality there has been substituted an illusion of reality composed of a complex of abstraction (black and white, plane surface), of conventions (the rules of montage, for example), and of authentic reality. It is a necessary illusion but it quickly induces a loss of awareness of the reality itself, which becomes identified in the mind of the spectator with its cinematographic reproduction. As for the film maker, the moment he has secured this unwitting complicity of the public, he is increasingly tempted to ignore reality. From habit

and laziness he reaches the point when he himself is no longer able to tell where lies begin or end. There could never be any question of calling him a liar because his art consists in lying. He is just no longer in control of his art. He is its dupe, and hence he is held back from any further conquest of reality. (Bazin, "An Aesthetic of Reality: Neorealism," in *What Is Cinema?*, 2:27)

In a general sense, the production of aesthetic experience and philosophic insight can be said to depend on a process in which we purify our desire in a manner modeled by Plato's myth of the charioteer in the *Phaedrus*, and the Platonic origins of Bazin's film theory emerge quite clearly when one compares the passage above with one from that dialogue:

> PHAEDRUS: What is all this leading to?
> SOCRATES: We shall see, I think, if we ask the following question. Is a great or a slight difference between two things more likely to be misleading?
> P: A slight difference?
> S: So if you proceed by small degrees from one thing to its opposite you are more likely to escape detection than if you take big steps.
> P: Of course.
> S: Then a man who sets out to mislead without being misled himself must have an exact knowledge of the likenesses and unlikenesses between things.
> P: That is essential.
> S: If he does not know the true nature of any given thing, how can he discover in other things a likeness to what he does not know, and decide whether the resemblance is small or great.
> P: He cannot.
> S: Now, when people's opinions are inconsistent with fact and they are misled, plainly it is certain resemblances that are responsible for mistakes creeping into their minds.
> P: Yes, that is how it happens.
> S: Is it possible then for a man to be skilled in leading the minds of his hearers by small gradations of difference in any given instance from truth to its opposite, or to escape being misled himself, unless he is acquainted with the true nature of the thing in question?
> P: Quite impossible.
> S: It seems then, my friend, that the art of speaking displayed by a man who has gone hunting after opinions instead of learning the truth will be a pretty ridiculous sort of art, in fact no art at all.
> P: It looks like it. (Plato, *Phaedrus and Letters VII and VIII*, 75–76)

26. Bazin, "The French Renoir," *Jean Renoir*, 85.

Genesis and Style of the French Renoir

THE GENESIS OF THE FRENCH RENOIR: THE IDEAL OF MODERN POPULAR ART

"*Contact* with the public, you see ... that's the thing I would have liked to experience. That must be overwhelming, eh? When I think that it's passed me by, well, it does something to me. Then I try to rack my brains, to work out what happened ..."

Octave confesses his deepest anguish
to Christine in La règle du jeu

THOUGH RENOIR'S POINT OF DEPARTURE as a cinephile has been obscured by the originality of his own achievement, it can be seen to have played a crucial role in his formation as a filmmaker. Of central importance is the ideal of the cinema as a modern popular art that he derived from silent American films, especially those of D. W. Griffith, Charlie Chaplin, and Erich von Stroheim.[1] In describing his growing interest in the cinema, Renoir consistently draws a sharp contrast between the American filmmakers he loved and the French cinema of the time, which he found to be pretentious and boring.[2] The first defining moment of this narrative is "the revelation of Charlot" that took place during World War I.[3] This episode begins with the enthusiastic report of a friend in Renoir's bomber squadron whose father, a Nobel Prize–winning scientist named Richet, had asserted that Charlot was a greater actor than Sarah Bernhardt and that through such films as his the cinema was going to play an important role in the development of nations. Back in Paris and determined to see a Chaplin film, Renoir had scarcely taken off his hat and coat before his elder brother, Pierre, asked him, "Have you seen Charlot?"

> I told him what Professor Richet had said. "That doesn't surprise me," said Pierre. "Greatness attracts greatness"—and we went to see a Charlot "short" in a little theatre near the Place des Ternes. To say that I was enthusiastic would be inadequate. I was carried away. The genius of Charlot had been revealed to me.... I saw every film of his that was shown in Paris again and again, and my love of him did not grow less. I began to be interested in other films and became a fanatical cinema fan. Charlie Chaplin had converted me. I reached the point of seeing three feature films a day, two in the afternoon and one in the evening. The cinema was beckoning to me.[4]

Inspired by Charlot and American films, Renoir initially felt his future profession was beckoning to him from across an unbridgeable gulf.

> The idea of working in the cinema did not occur to me. It seemed to me impossible to do anything worthwhile in France. Weren't the American films I loved so much, and the actors who transported me, scorned and even totally ignored by most of our critics? How could I, who dreamed timidly of following in their footsteps, but never hoped to equal them, how could I have conceived of having the slightest chance in this pedestrian country of mine?[5]

At the time, the gulf between Renoir's aesthetic values and those of the French society he inhabited was embodied in the fact that the American films he loved played only in the smaller, cheaper theatres, while the "pretentious nonsense" of French cinema and "totally ridiculous" Italian films played in the prestigious larger theatres.[6] He quotes the professional assessment of the theatre-actor Pierre:

> "The cinema doesn't suit us [French]," he said. "Our burden of literature and drama is too heavy for us to follow that particular line. We must leave cinema to the Americans... the American cinema is essentially working-class. Between ourselves, I envy my colleagues over there who have that kind of public to work for—Irish or Italian immigrants who scarcely know how to read."[7]

Though from a historical perspective these judgments may now seem rather sweeping, for our purposes they serve to introduce the political dimension of Renoir's aesthetic ideals:

> An essential element in the quality of any work of art is simply the quality of the public from whom the artist gets his living. Mack Sennett's was an ideal public, a working-class public largely composed of newly arrived immigrants. Many of them knew very little English: the silent cinema exactly suited them. Today's public is composed of the children of those primitive audiences. They come from the university; they live in a world of advertising, newspapers and weekly reviews; they behave according to the principles instilled in them by the most effective publicity media, the most "artistic" and the most entertaining. For their benefit the film factories churn out heroism or love or, worst of all, psychology.[8]

Though most of these remarks were first published in 1974, they ostensibly refer to critical judgments that Renoir and his brother made almost sixty years earlier; as such, they appear prescient of issues that critics and film historians would address much later. During the 1980s the rediscovery of a "cinema of Attractions" and the heated debates over the working-class composition of its audience all took place in the context of an existing consensus that the classical Hollywood cinema was essentially an apparatus of ideological conditioning.[9] Many of these scholars drew their theoretical inspiration from Walter Benjamin's seminal 1935 article "The Work of Art in the Age of Mechanical Reproduction."[10] As a result of their corrosive impact on traditional aesthetic categories, Benjamin argued that photography and the cinema could play two very different roles in modern life. On the one hand, they offered a means for the masses to liberate themselves through an aggressive defamiliarization of existing cultural values; throughout the essay Benjamin refers to Chaplin as a prime example of this revolutionary potential.[11] On the other hand, the control of these technologies by the forces of capitalism and fascism tends to "violate" this potential, putting it to the task of reconstituting "ritual values" that alienate the masses from their own experience; in place of the lost aura of traditional culture, capitalism and fascism substitute "the phony spell" of stars and other commodities, using the new technologies as an unprecedentedly intimate means of ideological domination.[12]

It should be clear what Renoir's comments share with this analysis. He contrasts the direct bond between an art and its public, exemplified by the aggressive defamiliarizations of Mack Sennett, with a cinematic apparatus that works in tandem with other technologies of ideological conditioning ("the most effective publicity media") to reconstitute ritual values ("the most 'artistic'") by extracting a surplus from the distracted state of the audience ("the most entertaining"). In place of real love and heroism, this type of cinema offers an ersatz based, in the worst instances, on a false notion of human "psychology" that alienates the public from its own most intimate experiences. As a consequence, in what Renoir calls the "over-developed" nations, the "bourgeois way of life has made the worker himself into a bourgeois. A genuine proletariat is now only to be found in the under-developed countries. The Brazilian peon is a proletarian, but the worker for General Motors is not."[13]

Renoir made this distinction between an authentic popular culture and one that is false or alienating throughout his life, and denunciations of the latter can be found throughout the range of his published writings. From his disgust with the debilitating myth of the *poilu* that flourished during World War I, through his scathing critiques of "bourgeois manias," fascist rhetoric, and pornographic music hall spectacles during the 1930s, to his complaints about Hollywood, American Christmas celebrations, the "immense childishness" of post–World War II culture, and even the work of his *nouvelle vague* disciples, one gets the sense of a pronounced and persistent discontent with the political and cultural state of the world.[14] Though an understanding of the reasons for this discontent will only start to emerge in later chapters, it is important to note the extent to which he felt it before his career even started and to preview the fact that his aesthetic and philosophic agenda would often be defined by an agonistic relation with existing tendencies in French culture.[15]

What exactly was it about silent American films that attracted Renoir? If part of the answer resides in their power to render contemporary experience through a defamiliarization of alienating cultural values, then another part can be grasped by recognizing the links between the American cinema and earlier popular traditions: "Old-fashioned melodrama was cunningly undermining its conquerors, the discursive plays and drawing-room comedies, the boulevard-theatre in general. Literary theatre occupied the centre of the road, but the cloak-and-dagger heroes were not done for and only awaited their chance to come out of hiding. This chance was what the American cinema gave them."[16] In Renoir's view, the success and value of the silent American film derived from the fact that it resurrected old-fashioned melodrama and reconstituted the popular audience for that form; again, the implications of this view can be illuminated by briefly reviewing a relevant trend in film scholarship. Though interest in melodrama was already manifest in the rediscovery of Douglas Sirk during the late 1960s, Thomas Elsaesser's 1972 article "Tales of Sound and Fury: Observations on the Family Melodrama" was the first comprehensive attempt to identify a genealogy that linked cinematic manifestations of the form with roots going as far back as medieval morality plays and popular *gestes*.[17] Published four years later, Peter Brooks's study of the melodrama hidden beneath the realist surface of nineteenth-century fiction defined it as a reaction to the "desacralization" of modern life, the popular symptom of "a renewed thirst for the Sacred" that had an integral kinship with romanticism.[18] This work provided a broad context and support for the model that feminist and Marxist film scholars then used to recover the social contradictions masked by the ideological function of classical Hollywood narration.[19] Working in a formalist and structuralist tradition, Rick Altman's 1992 article "Dickens, Griffith, and Film Theory Today" put forward a dialogical model of classical Hollywood cinema that showed how its affective power derives from a tension between the historical time and practical concerns of linear narrative and the mythical time and moral concerns of melodrama.[20] Taking Altman's argument one final step further, Linda Williams in "Melodrama Revised" (1998) and *Playing the Race Card* (2001) jettisons the surface/depth hermeneutic that has generally governed the scholarly recovery of the form, arguing instead that melodrama is the fundamental *mode* through which Americans make moral sense of their historical experience.[21] Drawing on evidence from a wide variety of domains (films, novels, stage plays, popular songs, television shows, and news coverage), she defines it in terms of familiar figures (a space of innocence, victim-heroes whose virtue requires recognition) and characteristic affects (produced by a dialectic of pathos and action); melodramatic texts are only artifacts of a pervasive process whereby the historical experience of marginalized groups—women, African Americans and other ethnic minorities, the lower classes—achieves cultural and political recognition.[22]

Though these scholarly concerns are only latent in Renoir's comments on melodrama, they illuminate the cultural politics underlying his enthusiasm for American genre films. In addition to their powers of aggressive defamiliarization, these films provided their audience with the compelling figures it needed to make moral sense of contemporary experience; like scholars of melodrama, Renoir recognized that their social and aesthetic achievement is obscured by notions of literary quality and psychological realism and is grounded instead in the familiar relations they reestablished with the audience: the cloak-and-dagger heroes emerged from historical oblivion, vanquished the stale bourgeois culture that had presumed to supplant them, and triumphantly reunited a popular art and its audience.

From the time of his earliest cinephile enthusiasms on, the ideal of a modern and popular art shaped Renoir's obsessive concern with the quality of his contact with the public. Few major directors have reflected as often and explicitly on this issue or assigned the audience as central a role in their creative process. Renoir generally identified different periods in his career in terms of paradigm shifts in his relations with the audience; as we shall see, the genesis of the "French Renoir" (André Bazin's term for the films of the 1930s) was mainly a matter of discovering the cultural idioms and aesthetic strategies he believed would link him to the French audience of the time. This concern also shaped Renoir's work within periods/paradigms, as the reception of his films explicitly influenced his creative decision making going forward.[23] Renoir relied on previews in a way that was exceptional, driven by the belief that the audience could recognize something that he could not:

> In every successful film there is one scene to which its success may be attributed; but it is impossible to tell in advance which scene this will be. It is a sort of key that opens a locked door. The key itself may be rusty or badly finished, but no matter; for me it opens that particular door. Without the film-maker realizing it, the scene puts the audience in touch with every character in the film, and thanks to it they come to life and become recognizable people. Their words and gestures, from being matters of indifference, become passionately interesting and the audience wants to know more about them.[24]

As the notion of the key scene suggests, the desired quality of immediate contact, of being in touch or meeting, is understood to elude the exact predictions and control of the filmmaker; this quality can be discovered only through a dialogue that entails creative priorities that differ from the traditional top-down, high-art ideals of self-expression, coherence, or perfection:

> I've basically shot one film, I've continued to shoot one film, ever since I began, and it's always the same film. I add things, I see things that I haven't said before and that I have to say, but the truth is it's the same conversation that I began with the audience. There are weak points and strong points in these conversations, but what counts is the contact, the establishment of a bridge. Perfection is an insane joke.[25]

Rather than a form of market research or pandering, Renoir's use of previews and notion of the key scene indicate an effort of synchronization in which the self-expression of the auteur and the self-recognition of the audience could, in principle, coincide. His remarks clearly suggest a dialogical context whereby the evolving circumstances of the broader conversation precede and shape the individual films that occur within it and a certain quality of relation with the audience is a prerequisite for understanding one's own intentions going forward; as Renoir wrote to his actor and friend Radha Shri Ram, "This terrifying contact with them is like a drug which helps you to understand yourself."[26] Though they might seem idealistic, the possibilities of mutual self-understanding outlined by Renoir's remarks reflect a conception of the auteur-audience relation that is more plausible than the unidirectional ones that film studies scholars have generally used. With a continuing conversation as a common aspiration, Renoir's films are neither top-down expressions of the auteur's vision nor commodities produced bottom-up to satisfy the immediate demands of audiences; instead, both auteur and audience are themselves evolving creations of a dialogue that precedes them.

By Renoir's own account, the films from *La fille de l'eau* (1924) up to *On purge bébé* (1931) represent an apprenticeship during which he learned the craft of filmmaking while struggling to assimilate and then free himself from his American models.[27] As he acknowledges, his initial attempts to follow in the footsteps of his American heroes were made without understanding the importance of his own cultural inheritance and experience: "Naively and labouriously, I struggled to imitate my American masters. I had not yet learned that, even more than his race, man is shaped by the soil that nourishes him, by the living conditions that fashion his body and mind, and by the countryside that parades before his eyes day in and day out. I did not yet know that a Frenchman, living in France, drinking red wine and eating Brie cheese against gray Parisian vistas, can only create a work of merit if he draws on the traditions of people who have lived as he has."[28] The cinematic encounter that served to remind him of his irreducible "Frenchness" was with von Stroheim's *Foolish Wives* (1924): "It was a great stroke of luck that in 1924 brought me into a theater which was showing Erich von Stroheim's *Foolish Wives*. This film astounded me. I must have seen it at least ten times. Destroying my most cherished notions, it made me realize how wrong I had been. Instead of idly criticizing the public's supposed lack of sophistication, I sensed that I should try to reach the audience through the projection of authentic images in the tradition of French realism."[29]

These comments identify the point at which Renoir's critical values were synthesized into what we might call a creative ideal. In one sense, von Stroheim's synthesis of comic irony and naturalist melodrama allowed Renoir to recognize a continuum of modern popular art linking his American idols with European traditions. But in another sense it did something far more important: *Foolish Wives* allowed him to step back from the existing achievements of the cinema and recognize the broader cultural matrix within which they took shape, to move past Griffith, Chaplin, and his other American exemplars toward a more open horizon of creative possibilities. Though the prospects ahead were in part imagined as a return to older French traditions such as Impressionist painting and Naturalist literature, this reflex on Renoir's part should not be interpreted as a form of cultural conservatism; on the contrary, in this case and in others we will examine it can be described as an attempt to recover and revive vital cultural resources obscured by the existing ideological climate. Here, at the outset of his career, the experience of *Foolish Wives* can be said to have carried Renoir back to the general principles of a robust modern popular art first articulated in Baudelaire's "The Painter of Modern Life": he saw *types*, he saw *realism*, and he began to imagine everything he could create using those principles.

Baudelaire's formulations are valuable because they illuminate Renoir's encounter with von Stroheim and, far more important, the theoretical terms he consistently used to discuss his own work. Baudelaire's basic critical insight was that the modernity of modern art was realized in two distinct ways. First, it was achieved through what he calls "mnemonic art," the way an artist's powers of observation and memory capture and "resurrect" the contingent details of contemporary experience, saying to every object, "Lazarus, arise."[30] Second, it was manifest in specific human *types* characteristic of modernity (for example, the Soldier, the Dandy, the Woman), each of whose external appearance and behavior derives from an internal "form of beauty" defined by the "moral laws that govern it."[31] For Renoir, *Foolish Wives* was an object lesson in the cinema's ability to realize these two aesthetic mandates, combining an unprecedentedly realistic recreation of a contemporary diegetic world (its massive yet precisely detailed sets, portrait of a multilayered international society, use of long takes and composition-in-depth) with a dramatic structure built around an ensemble of familiar but complex human types (von Stroheim's Karamazin as "Military Man/Dandy/Villain," the "Idle, Foolish Wife," the "Busy, Blind Husband," the "Deceived Maid"). After the revelation of Charlot, this was the second defining moment for Renoir as a cinephile and soon-to-be-filmmaker; from this moment on the relation between these two aesthetic mandates was to become the "big question which I am asking myself constantly" and "the most important preoccupation regarding filmmaking I've had in my life."[32] His discussion of his own work is dominated by the distinctions he makes between "interior realism" and "exterior realism," "internal reality" and "external reality," or "internal truth" and "external truth," and in reviewing his career he often describes turning points in it as "realism crises," moments when he had to rethink the relations between these categories.[33] Though Renoir's terms have often been assimilated to those in the auteurist scholarship by, for example, rendering external reality as "Nature" and internal reality as "Theatre," I believe such assimilation obscures their meaning, which can be more clearly elaborated with reference to Baudelaire's formulations.[34]

In Renoir's usage, external realism corresponds loosely with certain approaches to mise-en-scène that can be said to create an effect of verisimilitude: authenticity of dress, setting, and speech, the precise articulation of social differences, synchronized and natural sound, and the use of deep-focus cinematography and the long take. These strategies are the cinematic equivalents of what Baudelaire calls mnemonic art and have always received considerable attention and emphasis in the criticism and scholarship on Renoir. In contrast, his concept of internal realism has never been given the central place it has in his own reflections on filmmaking. In this context the concept does not function as one term of a thematic binary such as Theatre-Nature but is always represented as the *primary* fact of aesthetic creation, one that precedes and determines one's approach to external realism. He uses Chaplin as an example to make the distinction between these two categories:

> I often make use of the following example to explain my approach to the basic question of interior as opposed to exterior truth. An actor is cast in the role of a fisherman. In his concern for realism he decides to use no make-up. He pays a visit to a small Brittany port and takes part in fishing trips out to sea. He has procured the worn clothes of a real fisherman, and he acquires a genuine sun-tan; passing him in the street one may detect no difference between him and the genuine article. After this meticulous preparation he plays the part, some of the sequences being shot on a real Brittany fishing-boat. The director does not even use a stand-in for a scene of real storm. And the end of it all is that our actor, unless he is a genius, looks like a ham. Indeed, the real scene surrounding him seems to have the effect of emphasizing his own lack of reality.
>
> But now let us suppose that Charlie Chaplin is playing the sailor. The sequence will be shot in the studio, against a painted backcloth. Chaplin will not even trouble to wear a genuine sailor's get-up. We shall see him in his usual tailcoat, complete with bowler-hat, enormous boots and cane, but after a few minutes we shall accept the eccentricity of his attire and believe we are watching a real sailor.[35]

What Renoir is arguing here is that the internal truth or credibility of Chaplin's performance and character precedes and determines our impression of external truth or historical verisimilitude. He voices the same thought in saying, "I believe that artistic creation must be centripetal before it becomes centrifugal."[36] In his own view, *La chienne* (1931) was a turning point in his career, the beginning of the conversation *Foolish Wives* had made him dream of, because the possibilities of sound and total freedom of the production allowed him to arrive at an equation between internal and external realism that had hitherto eluded him; he claims that only when his actors began to talk did he recognize the possibilities of "genuine characterization" in film:[37]

After all, the purpose of all artistic creation is the knowledge of man, and is not the human voice the best means of conveying the personality of a human being? Details, details, that's what counts the most. I heard his voice, you see, I heard Michel Simon interpret this character with a slightly monotonous voice, with the voice we hear in the film now, a voice that avoid outbursts, highs and lows. This question of Michel Simon's voice was one of the driving forces in the film.[38]

Having identified the two aesthetic mandates that governed Renoir's approach to filmmaking, I will now outline some of the stylistic strategies that Renoir used to realize each of those mandates.

INTERNAL TRUTH: THE INNER LIFE OF HUMAN TYPES

"*The Rules of the Game* was the result of a dream, of something I had inside myself, deep down. I believe that many authors, and certainly myself, tell one story all our lives, the same one, with different characters, different surroundings. My preoccupation is with the meeting: how to belong, how to meet."[39] According to this comment, which this study takes seriously, the question that governed Renoir's ongoing dialogue with the audience was "how to belong, how to meet." This quote has often been read to suggest that Renoir's films tell one self-identical story and as such has been a bone of contention with auteurists using it to demonstrate the unity of his work and revisionists attacking it in order to recognize the diversity of Renoir's work in different historical contexts. Against both positions I would argue that a more careful reading of the quote would recognize that it discloses two related questions—"how to belong, how to meet"— and does not in any sense suggest that Renoir's films offer any consistent answers to those questions. In taking Renoir seriously as a philosopher, one needs to recognize the degree to which these questions exert a destabilizing force along a number of different axes. How do the characters in a film meet each other? How, and to what extent, do those on-screen meetings allow the filmmakers to meet their audience? How, and to what extent, do they allow the spectators to meet each other and belong as an audience/community? How does a film allow all concerned—characters, filmmakers, spectators—to meet themselves, that is, achieve self-knowledge or wisdom? Each of these questions is implicated in the others, and considered as a whole they serve to identify human isolation or alienation (not-meeting) as Renoir's ongoing preoccupation and the stable bases for human community (belonging) as his ultimate goal. How to meet or belong is problematic for Renoir because all the other aspects of his filmmaking, the external truth of his mise-en-scène and the design of his narratives, are built around his loyalty to the uniqueness and diversity of his characters and actors; in a sense, their internal truth as singular human types constitutes a network of challenges, the smaller questions or driving forces laid out for the director in his attempts to address his larger, governing questions.

The concept of type requires elucidation if we are to understand the impact of internal truth on Renoir's filmmaking, and Baudelaire's original hypotheses still offer a clear and compelling model of how types function to engage our attention. On the one hand, a type is determined from within by the specific "moral laws" that govern it, a unique complex of values and affective reflexes that regulate its external behavior and appearance; because of its unchanging consistency, it is apt to define this as the *nature* or *form* of the type, something that we do not see or hear directly but arrive at by drawing an inference: "The specific beauty of the dandy consists particularly in that cold exterior resulting from the unshakeable determination to remain unmoved; one is reminded of a latent fire, whose existence is merely suspected, and which, if it wanted to, but it does not, could burst forth in all its brightness."[40] In addition to their inner natures, the Dandy and other types can also be located within specific historical contexts:

> Dandyism appears especially in those periods of transition when democracy has not yet become all-powerful, and when aristocracy is only partially weakened and discredited. In the confusion of such times, a certain number of men, disenchanted and leisured "outsiders," but all of them richly endowed with native energy, may conceive the idea of establishing a new kind of aristocracy, all the more difficult to break down because established on the most precious, the most indestructible faculties, on the divine gifts which neither work nor money can give. Dandyism is the last flicker of heroism in decadent ages; and the sort of dandy discovered by the traveler in Northern America in no sense invalidates this idea; for there is no valid reason why we should not believe that the tribes we call savage are not the remnants of great civilizations of the past.[41]

What this description suggests is that we apprehend a type such as the Dandy as the product of certain conditions that can in principle be recognized or reimagined in a potentially infinite variety of specific historical contexts. Put differently, the *nature* of the Dandy leads us to infer, however dimly, a sense of the historical experience and specific *culture* that formed him or her and his or her backstory. In recognizing a Dandy, we move from the initially opaque details of his or her appearance and behavior, to the internal consistency of the moral laws that explain these, and from these laws to the historical experiences and mythical moment of self-determination that seem to have shaped the Dandy's responses to the world once and for all. In Renoir's terms, these "centripetal" or inward movements of inference regarding the thoughts and emotions of a type establish our stake in following the Dandy's "centrifugal" movements, that is, his or her behavior, actions, and ongoing narrative: every detail of an actor's face and body, every inflection of voice or movement become legible as a testimony to ways in which the type acts in and responds to the world. The contingency of photographic images and recorded sounds is infused with meaning by our imaginative engagement with types, and in this sense the external realism in any film—the meaningfulness we attribute to its contingent audiovisual surfaces—can be logically said to depend on its internal realism, that is, the recognizable subjectivity of its types.

The work of Stanley Cavell contains some of the strongest theoretical statements concerning the function of types in the cinema; drawing directly on Baudelaire's insights, his discussion of the concept in *The World Viewed* clarifies some points essential to understanding Renoir's notion of internal realism. Most important, he directly addresses the common misunderstanding of the term, which opposes types to well-rounded characters, and views the former as simplistic and reductive clichés in contrast with the individuated specificity of the latter: "What makes someone a type is not his similarity with other members of that type but his striking separateness from other people. . . . One gesture or syllable of mood, two strides, or a passing mannerism was enough to single them out from all other creatures."[42] What Cavell means here can, I hope, be illustrated by a simple example. Humphrey Bogart's Sam Spade or Philip Marlowe, Basil Rathbone's Sherlock Holmes, and Clint Eastwood's Man with No Name can all be described as forms of the Dandy. But what *makes* them Dandies for the audience is not anything they have in common but the qualities each character exhibits as a unique human specimen. While each character impresses us with his own "unshakeable determination to remain unmoved," the contingent details that give us this impression—the death-mask set of Bogart's mouth, Rathbone's bird-of-prey expression and mannerisms, Eastwood's intense squint of anger and disbelief—are unique or incommensurable. It is these singular qualities that we recognize, and it is only through an inference from these qualities that we know them as types. Cavell thus argues for a fundamental reversal of what is often meant by the term "type"; far from destroying an actor's individuality by restricting his or her performance to the display of certain common attributes, the inferred "nature" (fixed moral laws) and "culture" (mythical history) of the type are what make the unique contingency of the human being on-screen effective as a complex and meaningful figure. Once again, in Renoir's terms, internal realism logically precedes and animates our interest in external realism, and with this generic model of the type established, we can turn to consider the specific aesthetic strategies Renoir uses to create the types in his films.

Bazin's essay "The French Renoir" begins by noting the impression of a casual, amateur sloppiness in Renoir's films, manifest most clearly in a lack of synchronization or fit between the characters and the narrative: "The most immediately noticeable paradox in Renoir's style, and the one which almost always trips up the public, is his apparent casualness toward the very elements of the cinema which the public takes most seriously: the scenario and the action. The casting is tangential to the roles, but more than that, the style of acting seems irrelevant to the dialogue and the dramatic situation. Renoir directs his actors as if he liked them more than the scenes they are acting and preferred the scenes which they interpret to the scenario from which they come."[43] Bazin is saying that the performances of Renoir's actors, the unique sets of contingent details through which we know them as types, do not cohere with the dramatic functions and roles assigned to them by the narratives of the films; this impression is, as he puts it, "immediately noticeable." By implication, however, he is suggesting that this incoherence is only a first impression, something that then gives way to a different impression. Combining these two thoughts, he is saying that to understand the style of a Renoir film, one needs to consider the ultimate effects of such apparent sloppiness on the spectator: "If Renoir is enjoying himself, if he entertains us by pushing his actors to the limits of parody, if he seems to linger over apparently incidental attractions, it is only the better to impress with a sudden revelation of truth when we are no longer expecting it.... We say to ourselves that the actor is definitely not the character up until the instant when all falls into place and he becomes the perfect incarnation of that character. In this way Renoir moves from an original discordance to an incomparable human harmony."[44]

How, in a practical sense, do the techniques that generate these effects work? Vaclav Havel's analysis of the structure of the silent comedy gag provides us with a simple theoretical model that can, I believe, fruitfully illuminate the more complex and intricate development of gag structures in Renoir's films.[45]

The Gag

Havel treats the gags in silent comedy as moments of performance that produce an effect of defamiliarization and models them in terms of "two basic phases which in themselves need not be either comical or absurd, but which begin to evoke the sense of absurdity and laughter at the moment of their encounter": "Crying over the death of one's wife does not constitute a gag. Mixing a gin-fizz for oneself is also not a gag. However, when Chaplin receives news that his wife has died, turns away from us shaking with grief, and then, as he slowly turns back to us, we discover that he was not shaking with grief but rather shaking a cocktail shaker—that is a gag."[46] Havel defines the first phase of the gag (crying over the death of one's wife) as what is initially assumed in the narrative exposition of the situation and describes it as "passively awaiting" its defamiliarization by the "active" second phase of the gag (mixing a gin-fizz). Our narrative understanding of each phase depends on what Havel calls an "automatism," an unconscious perceptual reflex governed by conventional assumptions regarding the character's response to a given situation; considered in isolation, each phase represents an equally valid narrative interpretation of the same on-screen event (Chaplin's shaking body) insofar as Chaplin's performance makes the movements equally credible as either sobbing or mixing a drink.[47] The basic cognitive effect of the gag derives from the abrupt shift from one automatism to another, which itself entails an even more abrupt (because retrospective) shift in the unconscious inference that the spectator makes with regard to the character's response to the situation (the death of his wife). Recognizing the simple fact of this shift is not, however, sufficient to understand how the gag produces humor or engagement with the character, both of which depend on a qualitative difference between the two phases.

Havel argues that to understand what distinguishes the two phases in any gag, one needs to recognize that the motives governing the first phase are always determined by what are "weak" or insincere emotions (in retrospect and relative to those in the second), while the motives governing the second phase are always determined by what are (relative to those in the first) "strong" or sincere emotions. Weak emotions tend to be enlarged or acted out precisely because they are insincere and are trying to hide or compensate for that fact; they are thus "centrifugal" and "extensive," whereas the sincerity of strong emotions produces a corresponding restraint or moderation in their expression, and they can be described as "centripetal" and "intensive."[48] When defamiliarized by the comic shock of the gag, the insincerity of the weak emotion in the first phase, what we take to be the overstated pathos of the Tramp's performance of grief, gives way to reveal emotions in the second phase that are taken to be a more authentic or sincere reflection of the character's feelings toward his wife.

Havel's model helps us make sense of Bazin's account of the spectator's shift from an originally discordant understanding of Renoir's characters to a deeper, more harmonious one. The performance of a gag forces the spectator to make the transition between two distinct interpretations of an event, but this transition can only happen, can only make sense, after the spectator has, by a retrospective inference, already made the transition between two distinct conceptions of a character's motives. Though we shall see that Renoir also uses a variety of other devices to develop and inflect the basic effect of the gag, Havel's model demonstrates how a moment of interpretive ambiguity at the most basic level of narrative comprehension—"What am I seeing/hearing?"—can be used to focus our attention centrifugally, inside the human subject on-screen. The perceptual and cognitive disparity, the shimmering contingency or excess that the gag produces, can be resolved only by a movement of inference into the consciousness of the character who performs it, a process in which we abruptly see through the insincere and clichéd motivation of the first phase (revealed to have been the product of our own assumptions) to the relatively sincere and realistic motivation of the second phase. Our final impression of internal truth or realism is dialectically produced by our experience of a failure in external realism—the interruption of the unconscious reflexes, the default automatisms we use to interpret the surfaces of everyday life—and grounds itself in a differential recognition, at once surprising and familiar, of the character/performer being "true to type."[49] Considered in terms of its final effect, the gag is a device that establishes closer contact between spectator and character insofar as it creates an understanding of the character's motives mediated by a revelation of the spectator's own unconscious assumptions. As Bazin puts it: "Renoir does not choose his actors, as in the theater, because they fit into a predetermined role, but like the painter, because of what he can force us to see in them."[50]

This brief elaboration of Havel's model of the gag serves to introduce three critical hypotheses that I will develop and apply to Renoir. The first is that his notion of internal realism refers to a certain depth in the performances of actors, a carefully constructed ambiguity of intention capable of sustaining processes whereby spectators question and revise their understanding of types. The second is that Renoir's mise-en-scène is, like that of Chaplin, designed primarily to develop the spectator's engagements with types, though Renoir's more complex approach to external realism typically functions to articulate the rapidly shifting relations between an ensemble (rather than focusing on a central protagonist). The third hypothesis is that internal realism requires a narrative that is multistranded and dialogical; just as a gag depends on at least two distinct interpretations of a single event, the central effects of Renoir's films derive from the spectator's hesitation or equivocation between several distinct ways of organizing the events on-screen into narratives.

The remainder of this chapter and the first section of chapter 2 will outline each of these three hypotheses in turn. This section will conclude with a consideration of how Renoir's direction of actors and approach to recording dialogue serve to create internal realism, the following section will identify two strategies of Renoir's mise-en-scène that focus and help articulate our engagement with types/characters, and finally, the first section of chapter 2 offers an account of *Une partie de campagne* (1936) that shows how the film creates dialogical relations between the chronotopes of neoclassical comedy and romanticism.

The Italian Method and Marivaux

Renoir's own writings and interviews, the recollections of his collaborators, and other forms of evidence testify to the consistency of his approach to directing actors, his faith in what he calls "the Italian method." Renoir claimed to have learned about this method through his friendships with Jean Giraudoux and Louis Jouvet and believed its survival in their theatre work to be a remnant of what was once a widespread influence on European drama (he claims that it was known and practiced by, among others, Molière and Shakespeare):[51]

> It [the Italian method] consists of reading the text in the same way that one reads a phone book, forbidding yourself all expression. When an actor reads a text and gives meaning to it immediately, you can be sure that he's giving it the wrong meaning. It has to be wrong, it has to be a cliché, it has to be banal, because you don't find something original like that immediately. You pull out a file, take out something already used, and apply it to this line, to the words you're speaking. If you don't let yourself do that, if you reread, reread, reread a text, at some point—I don't know how it happens, I can't explain it physiologically—at a certain moment there is a kind of spark [that] springs from the actor, or from the actress, and sometimes it's the beginning of discovering a role.[52]

At first glance, this description might misdirect one towards an incorrect conception of the quality Renoir is seeking in his actor's performances; more specifically, it may recall Method acting with its goal of revealing psychological depths and thus lead one to imagine that the representations of strangled animal anguish and violated id in the voices of Montgomery Clift or Marlon Brando are examples of the spark Renoir speaks of. But this false impression is useful because it identifies two things Renoir uses the Italian method to deliberately *avoid*. In the first place, this method is designed to avoid reproducing clichés of any sort, especially those derived from romantic belief systems such as psychoanalysis (which Renoir particularly detested).[53] In the second place, the method is designed to avoid *expressiveness*, that is, anything that seems to come to the surface from the depths of the actor, in favor of a *flatness* or *opacity* of surface that forces the spectator to actively infer or imagine a depth within the type. Renoir assumes that any deliberate expressiveness or intention in acting is bound to be false because it inevitably reduces the internal truth of the type to a clichéd interpretation of a particular moment in the dramatic narrative:

> Acting out the moment is always contrived. You're in a dramatic scene, and you have a man whose mistress has just left him, he wants to kill himself, and so obviously, if you act out the moment, you'll have him do it with a trembling voice, which is very false, and which will probably remind us of things we've seen or heard before, which do not correspond to the true character.[54]

In this passage Renoir takes pains to oppose the truth of the character to the truth of the narrative moment. But can we really grasp a character apart from a consideration of his or her relation to a narrative? I believe one way to make the distinctive qualities of Renoir's characters manifest and illustrate his conception of "the true character" is to briefly consider the theatrical lineage of the Italian method and identify specific aspects of style that can be said to have survived via modern analogues in Renoir's films.

The historical influence of the Italian method within French culture originated with the actors of the Italian commedia dell'arte who began performing in France in the middle of the sixteenth century.[55] During the early period of their career in France, members of the main Italian troupe in Paris were forced to perform in Italian because French troupes had a monopoly on performing in French. The obligation of performing in a language that only a small fraction of their audience could understand reinforced the form's existing emphasis on a very physical style of acting and the use of familiar personae (Harlequin, Columbine, Pantalone, the Doctor, the braggart soldier, and so on), most of which were defined by characteristic masks and costumes. Treated as a coherent system, these aspects of commedia dell'arte performance can be said to present the audience with a well-defined collection of characters-as-masks whose facial expressions, postures, and gestures function as immediately legible indexes of the familiar complex of intentions that define their respective types.[56] One quality we can isolate and apply as relevant to Renoir's concept of "true character" would be the idea of a performance as mask, something that seems fixed, opaque, immobile, and relatively illegible as a psychologically plausible response to a given dramatic moment but that is legible and comprehensible as the expression of a type.

The second quality I would like to recover and apply to Renoir derives from the eighteenth-century collaboration between the Comédie-Italienne and Marivaux.[57] While he adopted many of the commedia dell'arte types and his writing of their roles often maintained their familiar characteristics, Marivaux developed a form of dialogue that greatly enhanced their complexity. In contrast to his predecessor Molière's focus on self-identical stereotypes (the miser, the religious bigot, the womanizer, and the like) and a solidly constructed plot, Marivaux "created plays in which the action takes place in the mind of the character and in which dialogue is of primordial importance."[58] As Frédéric Deloffre puts it: "In Marivaux's plays the stress is above all on the word itself, not on what the word represents. But in each repeated word we are aware of different nuances of interpretation, quibbling over meaning, arguing, sudden unexpected twists—in a word, dramatic progression. Language is no longer the sign of the action, it becomes instead its very substance."[59] This autonomy of the dialogue in Marivaux is, in his own words, meant to give the impression that "the actors do not seem aware of the value of what they are saying."[60] Renoir's friend and collaborator Louis Jouvet states that to produce this impression of unconsciousness the actors must highlight the spectator's awareness of artifice by self-consciously "playing at playing" the various "games" that Marivaux's narratives are usually built around; thus while the characters generally believe themselves to be playing a role in a game that they control, they typically find themselves involved in another very different game that is beyond their understanding: it is in this context of overlapping games that the words of the dialogue take on a multivalent life of their own.[61]

Marivaux's *Le jeu de l'amour et du hasard* presents a simple example of how narrative situations can be designed to focus a certain quality of attention on the dialogue as being the very substance of the action. The plot concerns two noble-born romantic leads, Dorante and Silvia, both of whom decide to disguise themselves as servants in order to size the other up before agreeing to the marriage being arranged by their fathers, while at the same time forcing their respective servants, Harlequin/Bourguignon and Lisette, to impersonate them while they conduct their investigations. As Claude Schumacher explains, "The four characters are aware of the role they are playing but when they unexpectedly fall in love, they are forced to play a role they had not bargained for and for which they are not prepared. What this means is that throughout the play the actor, without shedding the identity of the character he played at the outset, has to superimpose a second character on the first; and this second character has to convey the impression that he is improvising without knowing where all this will lead him."[62] Once a narrative structure such as this is up and running, it allows for the dialogue to be interpreted with reference to three distinct conceptions of character and levels of knowledge: the false character each plays for the other (for example, Bourguignon, as played by Dorante, for a woman he thinks is the maid Lisette; Lisette, as played by Silvia, for a man she thinks is the valet Bourguignon); the self-aware character who does the playing and who wrongly thinks he or she understands the game being played (Dorante and Silvia as each understands himself or herself to be); and the true character revealed by the semiconscious attraction to one another that neither understands (the *real* Dorante and Silvia, which only the spectator recognizes). With these three levels in view, one can appreciate how dialogue such as the following can have the effects identified by Deloffre:

> DORANTE: Since we are on a friendly footing and have foresworn formality, tell me, my little Lisette, is your mistress your equal? She is very bold to dare to have a personal maid like you.
>
> SILVIA: Bourguignon, that question tells me that, in accordance with custom, you have come intending to murmur sweet nothings to me. Is that not true?
>
> DORANTE: My word, I came with no such plan, I must tell you. Valet as I am, I have never become very intimate with ladies' maids—I have no taste for below stairs wit. But in your case it is a quite different matter. Why, great heavens you subdue me! I am almost shy. My friendliness is afraid to be tame with you. I keep wanting to take my hat off to you, and when I try to be free and easy with you, I feel as though I am acting. In short, I long to treat you with marks of respect which would make you laugh. What kind of servant are you then, who seem like a princess?
>
> SILVIA: Well, all you say you have felt on seeing me is precisely the story of all the valets who have seen me.
>
> DORANTE: Upon my word, I should not be surprised if it were also the story of all the masters.[63]

Though it may at first seem awkward, the analogy I would propose for such dialogue is the commedia dell'arte mask. The analogy may seem inappropriate because the mobile play between the levels on which the dialogue can be interpreted ("different nuances of interpretation, quibbling over meaning, arguing, sudden unexpected twists") seems at odds with the image of a fixed, opaque, and immobile mask. What I mean is that the mask offers an analogy for Deloffre's concept of "the word itself" as distinguished from any predetermined or default representational function. Representation—what is actually happening in terms of narrative causality—is always put in question because Marivaux's dialogue maintains a "straight face" or ambiguity that does not allow the spectator to secure it as an event on any one of the three levels of character and narrative; whatever inferences we make about the reference of the dialogue are always being put in question by other, equally plausible inferences. The word itself thus functions as a fixed and opaque surface that generates and allows for the mobile play of the spectator's imaginative engagement with different dimensions or levels within types.

It should be evident how these two earlier deployments of the Italian method line up with our previous hypotheses concerning internal realism. The commedia dell'arte mask and its extension in Marivaux's dialogue are the functional equivalents of the silent comedy gag insofar as all three involve the projection of an opaque and ambiguous surface that allows for multiple interpretations and processes of imaginative inference that focus the spectator's attention on points of depth within characters.[64] The masklike flatness that our genealogical detour brought to light should also help clarify why the Italian method involves reading the dialogue like a telephone book; Renoir's method of rehearsing is designed to flatten or resist the actors' efforts to express the conventional senses of the narrative moment and to thus flatten them into discovering the inherent contradictions in their types, into a semiconscious enchantment with the characters that expresses both more than they are consciously aware of and more than the auteur could have anticipated: "When the mysterious marriage of the personality of the actor and personality of the author takes place, something unexpected comes out, something that even the actor doesn't expect. If the actor knows in advance how he's going to say a word, it's bad, it's conventional. He shouldn't know. It has to come by itself, and the only way is to ask monotony to help you, the monotony of repeating sentences and words."[65]

Son Direct

To characterize Renoir's aesthetic ideal of internal truth, we began with the concept of character-as-type and have considered how gag structures, multivalent dialogue, and rehearsals with the Italian method might all work in tandem to create characters of depth and complexity. I would like to close this theoretical detour by modeling the material qualities that Renoir sought in his actors' reading of the dialogue, for these singular qualities of the human voice, highlighted by the comments above regarding Michel Simon's voice in *La chienne*, seem to be the core of internal truth around which he built all the other aspects of their performances. One way of isolating this quality is to consider the specific mobilization of technology that enabled its reproduction, and in this regard Charles O'Brien's study of sound technology and film style in France during the 1930s provides us with hypotheses that are also relevant to other aspects of Renoir's use of sound, to be examined in the next section of this chapter.[66]

O'Brien integrates film analysis with a consideration of economic factors, cultural discourses, and production practices to argue that filmmaking in France and the United States during the 1930s utilized sound in ways that were fundamentally different. He argues that from early in the decade, Hollywood filmmaking adopted an approach to film sound that privileged the immediate intelligibility of dialogue as a narrative event. Insofar as Hollywood's main imperative was the creation of a strong causal narrative and seamless fictional diegesis, American filmmakers took advantage of technological developments that allowed them to separate sound into a number of different tracks (for example, the standard breakdown of dialogue, sound effects, and orchestral accompaniment) that were then modified (volumes adjusted and noises filtered out) and recombined with each other and the image to produce a story-world with no necessary reference or fidelity to the actual conditions in which they were recorded.[67] In contrast to Hollywood's tendency to separate, modify, and recombine sounds and images, French filmmakers valued the naturalism of what they called direct sound (*son direct*), the simultaneous recording of sound and image.[68] Despite the technical difficulties that this practice gave rise to—the difficulty of recording during lengthy camera movements and/or with the action articulated in deep space, jump-cuts in volume or room tone, overlaps between dialogue and noise that affected intelligibility—the French industry nonetheless celebrated direct sound's fidelity to "thousands of prosaic sonorities of real life" over "the anonymous character, the absence of soul of American film sound."[69]

This basic difference of approach to sound reproduction has implications regarding the actor's voice that can illuminate what Renoir was able to accomplish using the Italian method. Hollywood during the 1930s focused on delivering dialogue with immediate intelligibility, and the general maxim was that all sounds had to be accompanied by a visual depiction of their source; actors were framed so that their facial expressions were clearly visible and allowed for unambiguous interpretations of the dialogue as a narrative event.[70] In contrast to Hollywood's ideal of "telephonic clarity," "French films, with their direct recorded soundtracks, capture the phenomenal characteristics of actor's speech—dimensions of voice quality and timbre—together with the spatial characteristics of the recorded environment. While vocal characteristics can be said to define recorded speech in American films as well—and indeed in sound films made virtually anywhere—in French films their salience, the way they compel the viewer's interest, may exceed the role of dialogue as the conduit for a film's plot development, to instead substantiate the materiality of a scene's setting."[71] In contrast to Hollywood dialogue's ideal of being transparent to the immediate concerns of the fictional narrative, what Renoir refers to above as "acting out the moment," direct sound can be said to allow for the production of opaque or resistant relations, vocal resonances that express ambiguity or mixed emotions. By using the Italian method within the context of French sound practices, Renoir was able to isolate certain unique qualities of aural contingency that his actors were capable of producing, qualities whereby their social and cultural experience, the personal history sedimented in their voices, resonated with the contradictions that defined their fictional types. As it leads us from dialogical narratives to ambiguous dialogue to fragile contingencies of timbre and inflection, the Italian method is designed to systematically focus our attention on types that are both familiar and mysterious; at the very heart of internal realism, the singular voices of Renoir's characters are designed to function as opaque and fragile surfaces, trapdoors that give way to reveal depths and contradictions in their types.

In terms of its production, the internal truth of the true character is the result of the mysterious meeting of actor and director in the rehearsal process: it is a complex and contradictory construct the precise elements and organization of which no one could have anticipated but which it is the director's job to recognize and fix in place when it appears. In terms of its reception, internal truth is reproduced by a process in which spectators rediscover it for themselves by revising their inferences concerning types; it is not true because it corresponds to existing criteria of realist representation (for example, historical accuracy of costume or *argot*, strangled animal anguish or violated id) but because of a deliberately engineered failure of such criteria. Internal truth is simply the dialectical consequence of seeing through a false-because-simplistic notion of the character: it is a flash of contingency that carries the realization that there is more to the character than one had thought.

The Opening of La chienne *as an Initial Illustration of Internal Truth*

In the preceding I have drawn on Renoir's own critical reflections and other sources to develop several genealogical hypotheses concerning the concept of internal realism that was by his own account his primary aesthetic ideal. Though all of what follows will draw on these hypotheses, I will close this section with an analysis of the opening of *La chienne* that offers a provisional illustration of how internal realism works in practice.

The story of *La chienne* concerns a married cashier's infatuation with a prostitute who strings him along to extract money as instructed by her pimp-lover; when the cashier discovers her duplicity and contempt for him he kills her, but circumstantial evidence results in the pimp being wrongly convicted and executed for the crime. Renoir precedes this bleak story with a prologue on the stage of a puppet theatre, where a succession of three puppet-narrators describe what the audience is about to see and hear. The first puppet announces: "Ladies and gentlemen, we have the honor of presenting you with a serious social drama proving that vice is always punished." As the first puppet continues to speak, a second puppet appears and offers instead "a comedy of manners with a moral." As the first and second puppets continue to declaim over each other, a third, Guignol, appears and chases the other two off the stage with his club. He then tells the audience: "Pay no attention to them: the play that follows is neither comedy nor drama, has no moral whatsoever and proves nothing at all—the characters are neither heroes nor villains but plain people like you and me. The three main ones are, as usual, *He*, *She*, and *the Other Guy*." As Guignol introduces each of these characters, vignettes of the actors playing the roles are superimposed over the puppet stage: "*He* is a nice timid chap, not that young, but much too naive; his culture and sensibility, so far above his milieu, make him look like a perfect fool" (Michel Simon's cashier, Maurice Legrand, stares warily and/or befuddled in the direction of the camera). "*She* is a creature with a special brand of charm and vulgarity all her own; she is always sincere and she lies all the time" (Janie Marèze's prostitute, Lulu, turns in profile and sighs, misty-eyed with romantic longing). "As for *the Other Guy*, he is just plain Dédé and nothing more" (the real-life street hustler Georges Flammand looks directly at the camera, smirks, and offers the audience a flippant salute).

What does this contradictory set of previews and introductions tell us about the film we are about to see? Putting the emphasis on the "realist" Guignol, who gets the last word, Alexander Sesonske describes this prologue as "a Renoir manifesto for the talkies" in which the director renounces "both the character-types and the stories [with] which filmmakers, including Renoir, had heretofore filled the screen—puppets, good and evil, manipulated to demonstrate the dubious clichés of conventional morality. Instead ordinary people—*comme moi, comme vous*—will work and love and die in the mixed genre that most resembles life. Surely, a program for most of the Renoir films from *La Chienne* to *La Règle du Jeu*."[72] As well intentioned as it is, this account offers a good example of how certain critical assumptions function to collapse the dialogical nature of Renoir's filmmaking. Sesonske's invocation of a manifesto implies an oppositional relation to popular culture, an effort on Renoir's part to reform and elevate the cinema in accordance with a high cultural imperative of realism, but this account of the prologue neglects the dialogical structure that its comic ironies articulate. To recover this we only need note how Guignol's reference to the familiar geometrical figure that links the three main characters functions to repudiate the realist program he has just announced, that is, as a gag in which he unwittingly endorses the melodrama and comedy he has just chased off the stage: realism inadvertently returns us to genre, and a dialogical conflict is again set in motion beneath the surface of realism's formal hegemony. While the descriptions of each character might seem at first to place him or her within one of three genres or idioms (Legrand's "tragic" elevation above his milieu; Lulu's "comic" contradictions; Dédé's "realistic" individuality) they also allow for the other possibilities, and the film will situate each of these types within a dialogical force field that gives each character moments of melodrama, comedy, and realism. Though this mixed genre may also "resemble life" by conforming to criteria of historical verisimilitude, its realism derives primarily from the way we are forced to engage with the characters; as Sesonske acknowledges, "Rather than merely designating character types, these introductions make complex claims which create questions we can only resolve by perceiving the characters for ourselves."[73]

The opening moments of the film proper offer a simple example of how the internal realism of Michel Simon's Legrand functions to launch the dialogical narrative structure outlined above. The first shot is taken from a dumbwaiter from which waiters take food to serve a long banquet table of jovial, well-dressed men. We cut to a medium close-up of an employee of Heriot et Cie, Lingerie Dealers, delivering a speech flattering his boss, after which the boss rises (in a long shot) to offer a bawdy toast ("As we say in the army, bottoms-up"), which provokes an excessive amount of raucous laughter, knowing looks, and asides to neighbors among the banqueters. The camera tracks slowly down the table in a close-up past several of these, fixing each in a distinctive attitude of inane mirth or good humor until it stops at Michel Simon's Legrand, whose dour or befuddled expression (downcast eyes, puffed-out cheeks, and pursed lips) immediately distinguishes him from the rest of the company. We cut to a long shot down the table with Legrand in the foreground as the laughter gradually subsides into silence. Legrand then leans forward and, turning in the direction of his boss (away from the camera) with a gleam in his eye and warmth in his phlegmatic voice, says, "That was a good one." Somebody says, "Good old Legrand, always up to date," and this provokes a new chorus of laughter, looks, and comments as Legrand calmly returns to his initial posture and expression. As the party breaks up, a wag organizes an excursion to a brothel, where he hopes Legrand will provide them with more amusement, but Legrand easily sees through the plot and, with a metallic glitter in his eyes, patiently lectures the wag on the ephemerality of such pleasures and the regrets that inevitably follow in their wake.

As a first illustration as to how internal realism works, let us assume that we, the spectators, initially interpret the first shot of Legrand in accordance with the previewed idea of his superior culture and sensibility isolating him from his milieu; in this context we read his silence and congested expression as measures of extreme boredom, of having had to endure this banquet and being far removed from the surrounding hilarity. Then he leans forward to deliver his "That was good one" comment, and the emotion in his voice and gleam of amusement in his eye forces us to change our interpretation of the previous shot; we now read his silence and expression as indexes of a retarded effort to comprehend the cause of the hilarity, as an example of the naïveté or obtuseness that was also mentioned in the preview. The quip at his expense confirms that this is how the rest of the company reads it, but as he settles back into place our reading of him changes again. Far from being embarrassed by the mockery, he seems to have noted it and be pondering, without any rancor, the distance between his own elevated reflections and the compulsive joking of his companions. We are now led to revise our reading of his "That was a good one" remark: rather than a retarded effort to catch up with his boss's wit, the emotion in his voice and gleam in his eye now appear to have been only a condescending concession, a Dandy's half-hearted and disdainful way of participating in society. We thus make a differential return to our original impression; he *is* slightly naive or obtuse but mainly in his own estimation and certainly not in the way that the others think he is (something that is confirmed by his deft escape from the brothel plot). Though the events I have described take only seconds of screen time, they serve to orient our attention on certain contradictions within Legrand (knowing and unknowing, witty and unwitting, offensive and defensive, out-of-sync because his refinement puts him ahead of others, out-of-sync because his naïveté puts him behind) and to inaugurate what will become a long process of engagement with the type.

When Bazin and other critics speak of Renoir's "love" for his characters, this does not refer to some soft-focus wash of sentiment he brings to their representation but points instead to his careful construction of contradictions within them that are capable of making us believe they exist. Their existence precedes and eludes, and continues to precede and elude, what we might feel or think about them; it is thus capable of provoking us to feel and think differently. If, as Simone Weil says, "belief in the existence of other human beings as such *is* love," then Renoir's love for his characters is nothing more than a set of aesthetic mechanisms designed to establish their existence, which in turn provides the motive for productive transformations of thought in the spectator.[74]

EXTERNAL REALISM: THE THEATRICAL MISE-EN-SCÈNE OF THE FRENCH RENOIR

RENOIR: I'm convinced that landscapes serve no purpose on the screen, landscapes don't count. What counts is that they help the actors and director to immerse themselves in a certain atmosphere.

DALIO: Yes, what you say is quite true because I know I got into theater not because of real châteaux, I got into it because of the backdrops, the painted châteaux, and I was really moved to see these painted châteaux on the stage in the old melodramas of my childhood.

RENOIR: We should add that a painted château can be much more real than a nonpainted château![75]

As our discussion of internal realism has already suggested and the remarks above serve to underline, Renoir does not consider "external realism" to be an aesthetic value in itself but a means to the greater end of focusing a certain quality of the spectator's attention on the performances of the actors. So far from appearing realistic in themselves, the stylistic strategies of "pictorial space" and "the dispassionate camera" that Renoir uses to create external realism can more usefully be characterized as "theatrical," though the diegetic worlds they create nonetheless ultimately cohere and impress us as "real."

Pictorial Space

I draw the concept of "pictorial space" from Erwin Panofsky's discussion of perspective in *Early Netherlandish Painting: Its Origins and Character*.[76] Panofsky distinguishes between two lineages in European painting, each with a distinctive approach to the representation of objects in space, and argues that each of these lineages mobilizes the techniques of Renaissance perspective in radically different ways:

> Perspective permits the artist to clarify the shape and relative location of corporeal things but also to shift the interest to phenomena contingent upon the presence of an extracorporeal medium: the way light behaves when reflected by surfaces of different colour and texture or passing through media of different volume and density. Since it makes the appearance of the world dependent on the freely determined position of the eye, perspective can produce symmetry as well as asymmetry and can keep the beholder at a respectful distance from the scene as well as admit him to the closest intimacy. Since it presupposes the concept of an infinite space, but operates within a limited frame, perspective can emphasize either the one or the other, either the relative completeness of what is actually presented or the absolute transcendence of what is merely implied.[77]

In the "plastic" tradition that culminates in the early Italian Renaissance, the focus is on the representation of solids in a three-dimensional space created by using single-point perspective and a uniform light that articulates a single coherent set of spatial relationships; the appearance of things in this type of painting is defined by their place in the spectator's "view through a window" co-extensive with the picture plane.[78] In the contrasting "pictorial" tradition that culminates in the Flemish Renaissance, the unity of the painting is created by "a homogeneous fabric of light and dark" within which both solids and voids, figures and grounds, "play an equally positive role." The appearance of things in this type of painting varies in relation to multiple perspective constructions (some of which entail spectatorial positions within the painting) and "localized" inflections of light; the singular use of light in Flemish painting allows it to integrate a microscopic attention to the details of small objects within a macroscopic representation of a cosmic landscape: space is thus defined by the spectator's shifting relations with things that themselves have no fixed spatial relations with each other.[79]

Panofsky illustrates these differences by contrasting two works taken as representative of Flemish and Italian uses of perspective, Jan van Eyck's famous portrait of the Arnolfini couple (1434) and Masolino da Panicale's *Death of St. Ambrose* (1430).[80] According to his account, in the van Eyck light is *qualitative* and used as a connective principle that acts on and modifies surfaces and solids, while in the Masolini light is *quantitative* and used to isolate and define the relative position of objects in space. In the former the luminous definition of figures and objects within the nuptial chamber causes the beholder to feel included within the room, a location that itself opens onto infinite distances bathed in light from beyond the frame; in the latter the death chamber is a complete and closed unit, one that places the viewer *before* rather than *within* the pictorial space.[81] If the plastic tradition valorizes the totality grasped by the subject's eye and tends to negate the infinity of space beyond the frame by accentuating the completeness of what is presented within it, then the pictorial tendency can be said to reverse this polarity by maintaining the integrity of the infinite distances that effects of light cause us to infer out of frame (and that are also typically represented in the background) while causing the position of the beholder to vary in relation to the figures he or she looks at. Infinite space thus measures and qualifies both the figures depicted and the potential totality of the spectator's gaze.

Panofsky goes on to discuss the philosophical positions that inform each tradition, noting that the pictorial tendency exhibits a reverence for the particular thing directly perceived by the senses that reflects the influence of the nominalist philosophy dominant in northern Europe, while the plastic can be said to render the world in accordance with a universal law to which all things conform and reflects the influence of Neoplatonism.[82] In opposition to the default assumption that the use of perspective always represents a modern technological worldview, a unidirectional totalizing gaze that locks the power relations between looker-as-subject and looked-at-as-object, Panofsky's observations allow one to recognize that pictorial perspective infuses the worlds it helps create with very different ideological values. To the extent that the many ways in which the pictorial tradition's reversed polarity forces the spectator to be mobile and responsive—the inference of an infinite out-of-frame space, the representation of spatial infinity within the frame, figures and details that correspond to multiple spectatorial positions—one might say that they can be said to qualify both his or her autonomous "subjectivity" and the "objectivity" of the particular things and people on-screen in favor of a more equivocal and reciprocal relationship.[83]

FIGURE 1.1.

Boeldieu and von Rauffenstein discuss history in *La grande illusion*.

Renoir uses a variety of compositional techniques to create a unique sense of space and place the spectator within the diegetic world of his films in a manner that is functionally analogous to Panofsky's concept of pictorial perspective. One such technique involves the creation of multiple planes within the audiovisual image that articulate a sense of qualitative discontinuity between the spaces each of the planes putatively represents. The memoirs of Eugene Lourie, Renoir's main art director from *Les bas-fonds* (1936) on, are filled with accounts of the efforts Renoir took to produce this effect. Here is a simple example from *La grande illusion*:

> The scene was the Fresnay-Stroheim conversation in front of the window. The backing for the window was a photographic blow-up of the castle walls at Haut Koenigsbourg. On this you could see a gallery running along the top of the crenellated wall. While rehearsing the scene, Renoir mentioned that

the castle walls looked quite real from the blow-up, but the illusion would be perfect if we could see a sentinel moving on the gallery. I hastily cut out the silhouette of a German soldier from a cardboard box. Hiding myself below the ridge of the photographic wall of the backing, I moved the silhouette by hand. The results were amazingly realistic.[84]

Despite the invocations of a perfect or seamless realism, this scene produces effects analogous to those produced by the use of multiple perspectives and localized effects of light in the pictorial tradition in painting. The actors inhabit a mise-en-scène that combines the three-dimensional space of a studio set with a two-dimensional photographic reproduction of three-dimensional space that is itself inhabited by a mobile two-dimensional figure. Though we are not conscious of the illusions involved in the representation of a finite space in this scene, the subtle disjunctions of surface and light between the three planes in question (interior studio set—photographic blow-up of castle—cardboard silhouette soldier) develop a sense of the indeterminate voids that separate them and function to create an effect of infinite space. This "infinity effect" is not represented in the manner that the plastic tradition might employ by, for example, offering the viewer a total view of parallel lines converging at the horizon; instead, it exerts a pressure on representation by asking the spectator to subliminally hold the scene in place and integrate its qualitative discontinuities, its phantom evocations of light and infinite space, into representation. The process of holding these incommensurable planes in place infuses the dialogue and action with significance derived from our subconscious awareness of an invisible cosmic setting; our infinitesimal movements in and out of the scene create a feeling of intimacy with the characters that has nothing to do with our physical proximity (that is, as in a close-up) but derives instead from our sense of their words and gestures being measured by infinite time and space; their discussion of broad historical processes resonates within a diegesis perfectly appropriate to a subject that we sense rather than directly see or hear.

This example combines two techniques—the use of apertures and disjunctions in visual and sound perspective—that Renoir often used separately to create the effect of pictorial space; because of the pervasiveness of these techniques in his films, it is worth taking a moment to briefly consider examples of how each works in isolation.

Renoir's use of apertures in built space is probably the most commented-upon aspect of his mise-en-scène in the critical literature, and it is only a slight overstatement to say that the diegetic worlds of his films are literally built around doors and windows. The first point to make about such apertures is that they typically serve to both reveal and occlude diegetic space and that it is the occlusive or masking function we need to focus on to understand how they create the effects of pictorial space.

I would identify two different ways in which such occlusion generally works. The first is when an aperture functions to make us conscious of the peripheral space it occludes. As an example, we might consider a shot in *Madame Bovary* (1934) facing toward Emma's bedroom door from the landing outside, a framing that is repeated several times throughout the film. The first time we are given this framing, Emma has ordered her nagging mother-in-law out of the house but has coldly relented after Bovary begs her to make up. As she starts up the stairs, we cut to a medium-close shot of her soft and luxurious bed that then tracks back to the position outside the door; Emma enters in the foreground, goes into the room, and slams the door in our face, and the scene fades to black. The next time we see this framing is shortly after Emma has been seduced by Rodolphe in the forest. Though it is on the same axis as the final position of the earlier shot, it is much farther back; with the dark hallway on either side, we look through a doorway that occupies less than one-fifth of the screen. The tiny figure of Emma sits immobile on the bed in the distant background while the maid plays with Berthe in front of her, rocking back and forth so that they are alternately in and out of view. Bovary emerges into the darkness of the foreground and moves slowly to the door, blocking the light in the scene as he passes into the room. He has come to discuss his disastrous operation on Hippolyte's clubfoot and the scandal that now threatens to destroy his reputation and life. He lumbers into the room, and we cut to a long shot inside the room at an indeterminate time later; Berthe and the maid are gone and Bovary is finishing up his assessment of his predicament to an unsympathetic but increasingly frightened-for-herself Emma. When he begs her for the comfort of an embrace, she pushes him away in disgust, runs out of the room, and rushes off to see her lover, Rodolphe.

The effect of the second shot through the door depends on the sense established in the first—that the bedroom is a space in which Emma defiantly retreats from the family she hates in order to indulge her romantic fantasies; we know her tiny immobile figure has now experienced the realization of those fantasies and feels trapped by the existence of the child in front of her who blocks the only aperture through which she can escape. Then Bovary blocks the door, enters, and, with the slow, commonsense manner that Emma finds odious, presents her with a scandal that promises to forever jeopardize her attempt to join high society: she can't take it any more and bolts from what has become a trap. The view through the doorway in these two shots functions to define and then redefine the space occluded. If in the first shot the passage from the bed to the closed door serves to define the room as an enclosed and voluptuous refuge for solitary fantasies, in the second the bed has become the last place where Emma can sit without having to touch the bodies that invade her space and block her access to happiness. This stark redefinition of the space has been made possible because in both cases Renoir used the aperture as a mask; we cannot see the space but are forced to imagine it from Emma's point of view. Though the space represented (that is, the one we eventually get to see) is the same in both cases, its affective charge has now been radically transformed; it has been given a history by having passed through Emma's consciousness. When we finally do enter the room, the opulent furniture, books, and romantic bric-a-brac, all the discarded props of a season now past, spring to our view like flotsam thrown up by the surf of Emma's frustration and panic; the mise-en-scène and temporal ellipsis work together to shape our reading of the dramatic action (that is, Bovary's obscene presence in the space and morose overview of his predicament—her mounting hysteria; his appeal for support—her flight). The doorway places the spectator within the diegesis by reproducing the masking effect of the cinema screen within the space; the occlusive mise-en-scène forces the viewer to engage with the internal realism of the character, thus making the room a unique centripetal location in the diegetic universe-as-labyrinth.

The second basic way apertures function in Renoir is to create a tension between what is visible through the aperture and the foreground area in front of it. A striking and much celebrated example of this is the shot from *A Day in the Country,* in which Rodolphe opens the window of the country inn and leans forward across the sill to appraise the distant figures of

FIGURE 1.2.

Rodolphe's desire mobilized through an aperture in *A Day in the Country*.

Henriette and Madame Dufour swinging in the sunlight. While on the most basic level of narrative event the opacity of the closed window gives way to the transparency of the open window, opacity nonetheless maintains its resistance through the smallness and flatness of the female figures, qualities that are accentuated by the pronounced three-dimensional recession of Rodolphe's body and the table in the foreground. The shot emphasizes qualitative differences of light and definition between the two planes to the point of discontinuity and serves to reproduce the window's function as mask set within the field of the visible; though the totalizing ambition of Rodolphe's male gaze is clearly represented, that representation is qualified by the spectator's experience of space as a distance that challenges and limits both his gaze and our own.

This qualification is then immediately confirmed by a cut to a medium-long shot of the family ordering lunch from the innkeeper Poulain. In contrast to the flatness, frontality, and relative immobility of the figures from Rodolphe's distant shotgun perspective, we are given a lateral view in which the alternating motions of the mother and daughter's swinging tends to place them on opposite sides of the frame and even, as Henriette swings ever higher, offscreen; from being center-stage and together in his view they now occupy either wing in rapid alternation. This shot cannot be located in relation to the view from the inn with any precision; we are now inside the space Rodolphe was looking at from the outside: the proximity, three-dimensional definition and mobility of the figures, and the narrative information conveyed by the addition of sound all serve to define this view as significantly discontinuous with his. Renoir thus uses the view through the window to stretch and thicken space along the axis leading into the screen and then anchors that distension with an edit that problematizes the cinematic spectator's natural feeling of being ubiquitous: it defines that space as a specific physical location and makes the spectator subtly aware of his or her bodily inertia. Though the sequence continues to develop the theme of the male gaze—alternating shots of Henriette's swinging with reverse angles of a leering Rodolphe, novice-priests who pause their walk to admire her, and a tableau of little boys watching over a wall—the editing of the sequence offers a series of deft mismatches, ellipses that problematize the spatial relations between the diegetic spectators and the figure they view; in particular, the unstable close-ups that move to follow Henriette's swinging through sunlight and shadow offer no purchase for a gaze seeking the intimate freeze-frame glimpse that promises possession (a fact made explicit in Rodolphe's complaint that Henriette is standing rather than sitting on the swing). The overall effect is of a space defined by a mobile figure's resistance to the erotic projects that would locate her as an object; our own efforts to take visual possession of the scene function to spin us around and disorient us, as the location gently reels around us.

What is crucial to take from these examples is that the indeterminate quasi-labyrinthine space they articulate is not a vast mechanism of entrapment or enclosure but an open continuum of unique locations that are always more than mere containers for the narrative action; Renoir's mise-en-scène and editing transform the abstract and homogeneous space created by standard continuity editing into a particularized, concrete space wherein the acts of the characters resonate with existential significance.

When Emma bolts from the bedroom, out of the house, and down village streets and country roads to her lover's house, the significance of this desperate act is defined by the distance between the warm, enclosed space of her room, fetid with her romantic fantasies, and the long shots of cold gray skies, echoing cobblestones, and bleak vistas of houses and trees that dwarf her tiny figure; her every step resonates with the distance between fantasy and reality that she is now crossing but will never understand. After Rodolphe opens the window and leans forward, the elliptical sequence of shots that follow—in which Henriette's body defines the space through shifting equations of gravity, weight, and momentum—articulates the resistance and liberty of a mobile figure in relation to the totalizing visual ambitions of his (or any) desire. Though the representational intention is completely different here—the teasing allure of natural stimuli and possibility on a summer's day rather than the fatal irreversibility of Emma's course of action—in either case the mise-en-scène gives the space a localized or centripetal intensity within which the actions of Renoir's types can resonate to their fullest.

In addition to his distinctive use of apertures, Renoir also employed subtle disjunctions in audiovisual perspective to create the effect of pictorial space. His frequent use of forced or diminishing perspective in the construction of settings was one way he produced such effects and also underlines the deliberate efforts he took to produce them. Lourie discusses how this technique was used to create the scene in *La bête humaine* (1938) in which Lantier and Séverine meet in the railroad yard on a rainy night and take refuge in a toolshed:

> On the largest stage at Billancourt, we built a set that combined live scale and diminishing perspective. The front part of the set was real: real ties and rails, adjoining brick walls, and a wooden toolshed. Toward the background, however, the rail lines started to run in diminishing perspective. The parked locomotives were the cutouts of photo enlargements, and farther back, the same photos were used but in smaller scale. The high pylons carrying railroad lights were miniaturized to scale, and some side buildings were also built in diminishing perspective. The set looked real and impressive. It fit with the other sequences shot in the actual railroad yard on location. The cutout locomotives emitted light steam; and under the somber lighting, the scene looked exactly as we imagined it.[85]

As in his discussion of the cardboard sentinel example from *La grande illusion*, Lourie emphasizes the fact that this type of construction does an effective job of creating a realistic illusion; in a general sense, the spectator is not conscious of the strategies that have gone into producing the space represented. This does not mean, however, that those strategies do not have important consequences for the spectator's experience of the space. Though the representational illusion is premised on the idea that the camera offers a unified view of the scene analogous to single-point perspective, the photographic image cannot but capture contingent details that highlight the seams in its construction: the myriad subtle disjunctions between the "real" three-dimensional foreground setting and the "toy" (that is, two-dimensional and/or miniaturized) buildings, pylons, and locomotives in the background, the different effects of light on the toy locomotives and the real steam they emit, our microscopic focus on the developing intimacy between the two characters and our macroscopic awareness of the somber fatality of distance evoked through diminishing perspective. Though the illusion of forced perspective is premised on a single, immobile shot, the scene actually involves several cuts and camera movements that cannot but function to subvert that illusion; each cut and camera move infuses the space with a sense of furtive movements as we subconsciously register backgrounds that seem to slide sideways around the characters. Where the mise-en-scène in the example from *La grande illusion* infused the finite space represented with a much wider sense of historical space and time appropriate to the dialogue of the characters, here the effect is close to being the opposite: the wider vista represented seems to be converging and collapsing inward toward the characters and thus resonates with the narrative action (which ends with the characters' physical/moral collapse on the floor of the toolshed in an adulterous embrace).

Lourie testifies to the fact that Renoir strove for such effects even when they verged on destroying the representational illusion. In a scene from *La bête humaine* shot inside a train workers' washroom, Lourie included a door opening onto a forced perspective representation of the depot that included cutout photographic enlargements of locomotives, escaping steam, and blinking lights:

> Using forced perspective meant that I had to calculate the perspective for a pre-determined camera position. The sequence was shot as calculated and the background worked fine. But Renoir, pleased with the effect of the background, decided to play another scene right in front of the open door, placing the camera much closer than the calculated angle and destroying, in my opinion, the methodically calculated perspective. I warned Renoir that it could appear all wrong. But Jean said: *"Mon vieux,* it looks all right to me. You would be amazed how flexibly our perception adapts to false perspective!" I learned once more that the rules of perspective can often be broken.[86]

What is important to extract from this anecdote is not merely Renoir's expedient use of certain representational illusions—that is, the idea the spectator would not notice the false perspective—but rather the deliberate efforts and risks he took to mobilize the spectator's processes of perceptual adaptation. Here, as in other domains, his style was designed to fully engage what he described as the "flexibility" of perception; the most significant effects of external realism are not derived from the representational illusion itself but from the activity such illusions can provoke in the spectator. Renoir's affirmation that "a painted château can be much more real than a nonpainted château" reflects his understanding that the unstable artifice of the former can more effectively mobilize and focus the spectator's attention and engagement with characters; like that of his cinematic idol Chaplin, Renoir's is an intensive, character-centered mise-en-scène, the logic of which cannot be reconstructed with reference to the external point of view of the spectator on a homogeneous diegetic space.[87]

In concluding our consideration of pictorial space, it is important to identify the way in which Renoir often used sound to reinforce or echo its disjunctive visual effects. This method stems from his habitual practice of synthesizing scenes from footage shot in the studio and on location. All things being equal, he always preferred to shoot interiors under the controlled conditions of a studio soundstage, but he also liked to include some interior shots through apertures that opened onto the sights and sounds of actual locations.[88] Renoir's most common approach to realizing these incompatible desires was to build interior walls with windows or doors on location and have a portion of the scene played in front of these; these shots were then integrated with studio footage to create a hybrid space.[89] Though the challenge of unifying the space represented frequently presented Lourie and other collaborators with a veritable "jigsaw puzzle" of continuity problems, Renoir clearly valued the particular effects such hybrid spaces were capable of producing.[90] His approach to sound in such scenes produced disjunctions analogous to the visual effects we have already considered; instead of trying to smooth out or minimize the perceptible differences between sounds produced in the studio and on location, Renoir typically gives the contingent aural qualities specific to each domain full play at different points within a scene. Thus in *La grande illusion*, scenes set in von Rauffenstein's castle-prison have a hybrid resonance that derives both from the wooden furniture and stone floors of the stage sets and the crisp winter air of the exterior location at Haut Koenigsbourg, while the scenes set in the Roubaud apartment in *La bête humaine* fuse the close, dry, and absorptive space of the studio set with the dampness and distant echoes of metallic noise that arise from the actual Le Havre rail yard. If occluded aspects of the actual location and climate come to figure in one's memories of such scenes (one can, I think, *hear* the presence of the Alps in the first example and the North Atlantic in the second), this is precisely because their aural presence has not been pervasive but has appeared only intermittently against the dominant resonance of the studio sets. Here again, we can posit a general rule that illuminates the relation between external and internal realism; though the dialogue in a given scene is most often delivered within the ambience of a studio set, our memories of location sounds nonetheless provide the ground against which we register certain qualities in the actors' voices: the significance of what they say and how they say it always resonates against our subconscious sense of where they are in the real world of the location.

The Dispassionate Camera

The aesthetic strategy I call "the dispassionate camera" can best be explored in terms of three aspects or stages. It appears first and most clearly as a principle that governs much of Renoir's editing and camera movements. Second, once the full implications of this mode of editing and camera movement are properly understood, it becomes evident that this principle implicitly informs the framing, camera distance, and length of *every* shot (to the extent that Renoir's style succeeds in determining our expectations). Finally, when treated as a comprehensive principle that determines all of the editing, camera movement, framing, camera distance, and shot length, the concept of the dispassionate camera illuminates the relations between Renoir's mise-en-scène, the cultural idioms he employs, and the dialogical structure of the films; because of these broader effects, it is an essential key to understanding how his films provoke reflection.

The principle in question comes to view most starkly in camera movements that have an ambiguous or out-of-sync relation to the immediate narrative action. Perhaps the single most pronounced example of such a camera movement in all of Renoir's work is the 360-degree tilt/pan around the courtyard in *The Crime of Monsieur Lange* (1936), which follows Lange from Batala's office, through the workroom of the publishing house, down the steps, and onto the stoop but then continues counterclockwise/left as Lange walks in the opposite direction/right and out of frame. Having manifestly abandoned the established focus of dramatic interest (that is, Lange), the pan continues around the entire empty courtyard until it arrives at the fountain where it picks up Lange, who is about to kill Batala. Bazin notes that most of the critics writing at the time of the film's initial release reproached Renoir for such "complicated and awkward camera work," that is, gratuitous displays of technique dissociated from any narrative motivation.[91] Though I do not wish to discuss all the aesthetic justifications for this particular shot here, I offer it as an unmistakable example of a camera movement that runs counter to conventional expectations that the film has itself established: what begins as a dramatically motivated following shot seems to lose itself temporarily in a meaningless formal digression.

Though the stark divergence of action and camera movement in this shot verges on producing an alienation effect that is not characteristic of Renoir's style, it nonetheless serves to illuminate a principle that is pervasive in his films of the 1930s. As a general rule, we can observe that Renoir's editing and camera movements are ambiguously motivated in relation to the narrative action and function to produce an ellipsis of space, time, and/or action; in contrast to the conventional system of using camera movements and/or continuity editing to produce a single, unambiguous interpretation of a given event, a style that is perfectly synchronized with the desired reading of events, Renoir often uses camera movements and editing that are manifestly out-of-sync with the expected trajectory of action and events. In terms of the overall effect, this approach creates a tension between attraction and distraction, engagement and disengagement, and makes the spectator aware of the equivocating "consciousness-at-work" in the framing, camera distance, and length of any shot.

As a first and defining example of this effect, I would like to examine a series of camera movements in the scene from *Les bas-fonds* where Louis Jouvet's Baron discovers Jean Gabin's thief, Pepel, in the process of attempting to rob his house. Having been caught embezzling state funds and with bailiffs coming to collect his possessions in the morning, the Baron has just returned from a casino where he made a last gamble to save himself and failed; from his behavior and comments to himself, we understand that he is planning to kill himself that night. After encouraging Pepel to take whatever he wants, the Baron offers him a drink, assures him that he is a "colleague" whom Pepel can trust, and asks if Pepel won't join him in the cold supper laid out on the table in front of them. They are now both in a tight medium shot. As Pepel politely demurs and the Baron asks him if he would feel more comfortable stealing it, the camera tracks back slowly, almost floating, to a medium-long shot that includes the table in front of them and a much larger portion of the room. Pepel gladly agrees to join the Baron on those professional terms, briskly takes his coat off and hangs it on a hook on the wall, and pulls out his chair and sits, while, during the same time, the Baron slowly and methodically sits down. In trying to follow the movements of *both* characters simultaneously, the camera moves with a pronounced uncertainty or ambivalence, at first tilting down to follow the Baron, then panning left to follow Pepel, then back to the Baron, then to Pepel as he moves to the table. This wavering motion then resolves into a slow floating track forward to a close-medium shot as both characters settle down to eat. A conventional shot-reverse shot sequence of close-ups begins as the characters continue to converse, with the Baron intently questioning Pepel about his way of life.

In analyzing the camera movements in this sequence, the first point to make is that only the last track forward can in any sense be understood to be motivated by a concern with the action. The action in this scene is in the dialogue, postures, and facial expressions of the characters. There is nothing in any of these that can be said to motivate the initial track back to a medium-long shot; though it enables us to keep the two characters in view when Pepel hangs up his coat, we could not have anticipated this action in advance and cannot but experience this movement when it occurs as a strange, inexplicable portent that seems to take us away from what we are most interested in. Then, once this backward movement comes to rest, the entire playing area of the two characters is clearly visible, and hence there is no justification for the anxious reframing movements that follow (that is, we would have seen everything they said and did just as well if the shot did not move). Though in both cases the camera moves in accordance with concerns that the spectator does not comprehend, the "consciousness-at-work" in each movement seems to be quite different, and each gains definition through the contrast between them; if the first movement seems to express (in retrospect) a confident *anticipation* of Pepel's hanging up his coat and joining the Baron for supper, the wavering reframings that follow express an inexplicable concern with *following*, somewhat ineptly or after-the-fact, the precise ways in which each character performs the simple act of sitting down. If the first movement is "ahead" of the action and seems to know something we do not, the second is "behind" the action and seems to express doubt and anxiety about issues that are also not clear to us. The mysterious expansion and contraction of time these movements articulate around the action generates a kind of attention surplus in the spectator that he or she then brings to bear on the action and the characters: our conception of both action and characters changes and becomes more three-dimensional. On another level, these two movements create the subtle feeling that the auteur's use of stylistic conventions slips slightly and becomes opaque; the first feels like a mistake in which the auteur lets his omniscience regarding future events show, while the second almost feels like a cover-up of that mistake in which he now pretends not to know what the characters are going to do. We are not fooled by Renoir's faux-documentary hesitations, but, precisely because we are not fooled, we come to scrutinize the image as if it were a documentary: we smugly walk out onto the trapdoor that Renoir has prepared for us. As with other aspects of his style we have looked at, Renoir deliberately flirts with our skepticism in order to trick us into believing in his characters.

The dispassionate camera is, in the first instance, a style of camera movement and editing that disjunctively departs from the conventional expectations that govern our understanding of the narrative action. In general terms, this style functions to reframe the action as a three-dimensional event wherein there is more going on than we were initially led to believe. As in our model of the narrative structure of the gag, and working in tandem with it, this style is designed to lead us from immediate perceptual disjunctions to uncertainties regarding the narrative action that can only be resolved by revising our understanding of the characters. In this particular example, Renoir uses these camera movements to produce a crucial shift in the way we view these two characters; to properly understand this particular effect we need to back up and briefly consider what has come before.

Up to this point, each of these two characters has been presented to us as completely enclosed within a particular milieu and fatalistic narrative trajectory. Gabin/Pepel inhabits the Naturalist chronotope of "the lower depths," a world where everyone but himself and the simpleton Natacha is in thrall to and degraded by a characteristic passion (alcohol, romantic love, resentment, greed, nostalgic regret); though he desperately longs to escape, he is unable to do so because his imagination is dominated by the feeling that, like his father, he is destined to a life of crime and imprisonment: his class position weighs on his spirit like an iron lid. Jouvet/the Baron can be said to have experienced the same gravitational force of society from the very different perspective of an attenuated romanticism. Born at the very top, his synoptic perspective made him unable to take any of the social conventions and roles proper to someone in his class position seriously. Though, like a nihilist Dandy out of Lermontov, he has engaged in romance, gambling, and embezzlement to alleviate his boredom, even these have become tiresome, and his heart is no longer in the game. In one sense, his entire life has been one long, slow free fall through a social world that he cannot bring himself to believe in; now that all the games seem to have run their course, he prepares, grimly but calmly, to commit suicide.

But though the contrast between the characters and the performance styles of the two actors seem as stark as one could imagine, there is also a crucial symmetry at work in the way each has been presented. Up until their meeting, each of these two characters has been presented to us as

FIGURE 1.3.

The Baron's nihilism liberates Pepel in *Les bas-fonds*.

absolutely isolated and alone within his respective chronotope; all their exchanges with other characters have served to emphasize the fact that nobody recognizes them for who they really are: the force field or gravity of social misrecognition that keeps Pepel down (despite his wish to rise) is exactly what has held the Baron up all his life (despite his utter contempt for it). This symmetry, what they have in common but have always experienced so differently, allows each to understand himself better by contemplating the other. Thus, when they "meet," the encounter inaugurates a strange transference wherein the gravity that has oppressed Pepel to the point of despair becomes, when recognized and contemplated by the Baron, something that gives him a concrete purchase on human existence and a reason to live, while the Baron's weightless nihilism becomes, when recognized and contemplated by Pepel, something that liberates his imagination and gives him hope.

FIGURE 1.4.

Pepel's despair liberates the Baron in *Les bas-fonds*.

The disjunctive camera movements just outlined play a crucial role both in initiating this process of transference and in expressing it. They deftly provoke us to bring a heightened quality of attention to their performances, and these performances in turn display hitherto unnoticed qualities that force us to revise our understanding of each of them. The Baron, who throughout the film so far has consistently projected a weary air of having seen it all before, now seems puzzled, curious, almost spellbound, by Pepel; this disjunctive reaction shot forces us to reconsider all the shots we have been given of Pepel and to now search for a cause in Gabin's ongoing performance. But as soon as we begin to do so, we discover that Pepel himself is no longer the character we have come to know; he has suddenly lost his characteristic bitterness and anger and become genial, serene, and reflective. The strangeness of the developing friendship forces us to reconsider our understanding of the characters that compose it, and the equivocating camera movements we experienced moments earlier come to make sense as an apt expression of the characters' developing responses to each other. The general rule we have posited in relation to other aspects of Renoir's style is again at work: a disjunctive failure or mistake with respect to default stylistic conventions (external realism) provokes a centripetal movement of inference into the consciousness of the characters (internal realism).

The ambiguous, out-of-sync quality that characterizes the dispassionate camera is also evident in Renoir's editing of the scenes from *Madame Bovary* and *A Day in the Country* that we examined earlier in this chapter. In the first scene from *Madame Bovary* that we considered, the cut to the bed after Emma leaves offscreen to climb the stairs forces us to wait in an empty and unfamiliar space for the action/actor to get there; in the second scene we examined, the cut from the hallway to the shot inside Emma's room effects a temporal ellipsis that forces us to imagine intervening events while following the action as it proceeds (that is, the remainder of Bovary's morose overview). As with the camera movements discussed above, Renoir's editing creates a subtle slippage in the synchronization between the spectator's attention and the action; in the first case the cut expresses a sort of premature eagerness, a curiosity that rushes ahead of the action, while in the second the ellipsis expresses an impatience that both expresses and heightens the effect Bovary's bad news is having on Emma. In both cases, the disjunction in continuity represents an attracted/distracted attention that is out of sync with the causal sequence of narrative events, as if the unstable or permeable consciousness at work is both bored/impatient with the narrative or curious/excited about something that is, at the moment, peripheral to the narrative. Similarly, the editing of the swing scene from *A Day in the Country* seems governed by a consciousness so attracted by Henriette's swinging that it cannot for the moment bother to establish the narrative action and the space in which it takes place; with one exception (the reverse-angle cut between the novice-priests and a point-of-view shot of Henriette and her mother), no cut in this sequence allows for an exact match between the shots it joins or any conjecture about what shot might follow the one we have in front of us. This style of editing is not categorically opposed to the concerns of the narrative, which are sufficiently supported by a very loose sense of continuity editing within scenes, but functions to give each scene an oblique, hesitant, indirect quality; there are narrative events that we do not see or hear, and we see or hear events that do not seem to be part of the narrative. This gives us the sense that any scene is inhabited by more than one narrative, that there is more going on than we are able to take in.

Having briefly characterized the explicit manifestation of the dispassionate camera in both camera movement and editing, we now need to consider the broader, implicit effect of this particular stylistic device on Renoir's mise-en-scène as a whole. One can quickly get a general sense of this effect by considering the feeling one has at the end of an unmotivated camera movement or cut such as we have examined. The camera has come to rest at a particular distance and framing, and the action now plays out for a certain amount of time, but we cannot but remain aware that the consciousness that determined the movement or cut is still present. The stasis of the shot is now infused with a sense of ambivalence since it is no longer a given that subsequent cuts or movements will now follow the logic of the narrative action; we are now aware of the living consciousness governing the camera and remember what it is capable of. Though critics have often commented on the fact that Renoir's staging of two or more pro-filmic actions within a shot demands an *extensive* scanning of the image, the coordinated role of his editing and camera movement in establishing an *intensive* form of attention has not been properly recognized. Though the camera movements or editing may fall into a loose and conventional pattern of matching on action or dialogue, we remain alert to the possibility of the action or dialogue taking unexpected turns.

Working in tandem, the aesthetic strategies of pictorial space and the dispassionate camera focus the spectator's attention on the internal contradictions visible and audible in the actor's performances. The uncanny sense one can get that the actors/characters are alive now, immediately present to us, is simply the result of the tremendous efforts Renoir takes to make them coherent and credible, and at the same time relatively unpredictable, vividly contingent, and fresh, regardless of how many times one has watched a given film. Having first imagined his characters at the level of the narrative, gags, and dialogue, often with the qualities of the actors already in mind, the Italian method of rehearsal further shapes the actors into their roles, and then, on set, the strategies of pictorial space and the dispassionate camera build a diegetic habitat specific to the characters and their story, one designed and carefully calibrated to foster our attentiveness to the possible relations between them, what can happen and might happen between them. The unique climate of possibility that the characters of a film inhabit, the world that shapes how they act and what we spectators can imagine for them, and from them, is what we have defined as a *chronotope*.

NOTES

1. Renoir also mentions Clarence Brown and Fred Niblo as American filmmakers who impressed him at the time. Renoir, *Renoir on Renoir*, 169.

2. Jean Renoir, "Memories," reprinted in Bazin, *Jean Renoir*, 150–51; Renoir, *Renoir on Renoir*, 40, 169–70; Renoir, *My Life and My Films*, 49.

3. Bazin, *Jean Renoir*, 150; Renoir, *My Life and My Films*, 40–43.

4. Renoir, *My Life and My Films*, 42–43.

5. Bazin, *Jean Renoir*, 151.

6. Ibid., 150–51.

7. Renoir, *My Life and My Films*, 45.

8. Ibid., 14.

9. Tom Gunning provides a comprehensive review of these scholarly debates in his entry on Early American Film in Hill and Gibson, *Oxford Guide to Film Studies*, 255–71.

10. Walter Benjamin, "The Work of Art in the Age of Mechanical Reproduction," in *Illuminations*, ed. Hannah Arendt, 217–51 (New York: Schocken Books, 1969); Hansen, "Benjamin, Cinema and Experience," 179–224; Gunning, "Whole Town's Gawking."

11. Benjamin, "Work of Art in the Age of Mechanical Reproduction," 227, 234, 250.

12. Ibid., 231, 241.

13. Renoir, *My Life and My Films*, 45.

14. Renoir, *Jean Renoir*, 174, 213, 303, 405, 446, 450; Renoir, *Écrits*, 104–9, 112–14. From a reading of the *Letters* alone one might come away with the impression Renoir was congenitally unhappy and/or paranoid.

15. This impression is accentuated by the almost total absence of positive references to contemporary French culture. Apart from reminiscences about his own collaborators, one would search Renoir's published writings, interviews, and letters in vain for a reference to a French film or filmmaker that he admired (with the qualified exceptions of Pagnol and his New Wave disciples). While this might be read as a typical manifestation of artistic egotism, his reverence for foreign filmmakers, certain of whom—Chaplin, Griffith, and von Stroheim—he acknowledges as direct and formative influences, suggests a more objective basis of discrimination. It is also interesting to note the extent to which Renoir's critical admiration for American cinema / antipathy toward French cinema was to be replicated, amplified, and polemicized in the *politique des auteurs* and diatribes against the French "tradition of quality."

16. Renoir, *My Life and My Films*, 44–45.

17. Thomas Elsaesser, "Tales of Sound and Fury: Observations on the Family Melodrama," in Landy, *Imitations of Life*, 44–79.

18. Brooks, *Melodramatic Imagination*; Peter Brooks, "The Melodramatic Imagination," in Landy, *Imitations of Life*, 61.

19. Representative examples of such criticism can be found in Christine Gledhill, ed., *Home Is Where the Heart Is* (London: British Film Institute, 1987); Bratton, Cook, and Gledhill, *Melodrama*; and Landy, *Imitations of Life*.

20. Rick Altman, "Dickens, Griffith, and Film Theory Today," in Gaines, *Classical Narrative Revisited*, 9–47.

21. Linda Williams, "Melodrama Revised," in Browne, *Refiguring American Film Genres*, 42–88; L. Williams, *Playing the Race Card*.

22. The theory underlying this model is expounded in L. Williams, "The American Melodramatic Mode," chap. 1 in *Playing the Race Card*.

23. Though the use of previews was a normal part of postproduction within the contexts in which he worked, it is worth noting that whenever possible Renoir restricted his previews to those who were *not* connected to the film industry (unpublished letter to Prince Fateh Singji of Limbdi dated September 18, 1950). In contrast to the common industry practice of getting adequate "coverage" of a scene—a range of master shots, shot-reverse shot sequences, cutaways, and the like—that allowed for considerable flexibility in adjusting the length of a scene in the editing, Renoir restricted his options by *not* getting coverage, shooting primarily in long takes, and discarding alternates as soon as possible to avoid possible interference from producers during the editing. The input of his preview audiences was in their response to whole scenes or particular combinations of scenes. In addition to his use of previews, Renoir's reminiscences are filled with anecdotes in which the experience of seeing his films with an audience precipitates a fundamental shift in his thinking. For some of these and accounts of how he used previews, see Renoir, *Renoir on Renoir*, 39, 237–39; and Renoir, *My Life and My Films*, 79–80, 84–85, 171–73.

24. Renoir, *My Life and My Films*, 133.

25. Renoir, *Renoir on Renoir*, 251.

26. Jean Renoir, unpublished letter to Radha Shri Ram, December 31, 1950.

27. Renoir, *Renoir on Renoir*, 171–72.

28. Bazin, *Jean Renoir*, 151–52.

29. Ibid., 152.

30. Charles Baudelaire, "The Painter of Modern Life," in *Selected Writings on Art and Literature*, 403, 408.

31. Ibid., 417, 416–33.

32. Renoir, *Interview*, 83; Renoir, *My Life and My Films*, 105, 159, 264; Renoir, *Renoir on Renoir*, 60, 215, 218.

33. Renoir, *My Life and My Films*, 105, 159, 264; Renoir, *Renoir on Renoir*, 60, 215, 218.

34. Though it appears in a variety of sources, this theatre-nature antinomy receives its most elaborate treatment in Braudy, *Jean Renoir*.

35. Renoir, *My Life and My Films*, 159; the same example is referenced in Renoir, *Interview*, 83–84.

36. Renoir, *My Life and My Films*, 133.

37. Renoir, *Renoir on Renoir*, 73, quoted in Sesonske, *Jean Renoir*, 87.

38. Renoir, *My Life and My Films*, 103, 105; Renoir, *Renoir on Renoir*, 77, 173.

39. Renoir, *Rules of the Game*, 13.

40. Baudelaire, "Painter of Modern Life," 422.

41. Ibid., 421.

42. Cavell, *World Viewed*, 33, 35, 36.
43. Bazin, *Jean Renoir*, 74–77.
44. Ibid., 78, 80.
45. Havel, "Anatomy of the Gag."
46. Ibid., 13.
47. Ibid., 17–18.
48. Ibid., 20.
49. Bazin's discussion of Chaplin as a mythical figure or type provides numerous examples that support Havel's model; one of his basic points is that the Tramp typically uses things without reference to the utilitarian purposes for which they were created. Bazin, *What Is Cinema?*, 1:145–48.
50. Bazin, *Jean Renoir*, 80.
51. Renoir, *My Life and My Films*, 74; Renoir, *Renoir on Renoir*, 43, 119.
52. Renoir, *Renoir on Renoir*, 119–20. In the documentary *La direction d'acteur pas Jean Renoir* (1968), Renoir illustrates the Italian method by directing Gisèle Braunberger's performance of a text taken from Rumer Godden's novel *Breakfast with Nicolaïdes*; the film testifies to both the painful labor involved in this method (Renoir's relentless patience in refusing all the actor's premature interpretations almost brings her to tears) and the quality of conviction that it produces when the actor finally discovers the role (Braunberger's brief speech to her character's mother conveys the complicated history of their relationship with tremendous precision and economy). Durgnat's discussion of Renoir's work on set includes many descriptions of this method from the recollections of actors and other of Renoir's collaborators. Durgnat, "Renoir at Work," chap. 4 in *Jean Renoir*, 12–17.
53. As discussed in the second section of this chapter, Renoir's preference for modern popular art was often articulated in opposition to middlebrow cultural forms, which he saw to be false and alienating; in this regard his most consistently expressed antipathy was for "psychological drama," which moved him to exclaim, "Oh, Freud, what crimes have been committed in thy name!" Renoir, *My Life and My Films*, 33.
54. Renoir, *Renoir on Renoir*, 152.
55. Marivaux, *Marivaux*, x.
56. Ibid., x, xiv.
57. Renoir himself was strongly aware of this connection: "You know you can't think of Marivaux without thinking of Italy. One mustn't forget that Marivaux started by writing for an Italian troupe, that his mistress was Italian, and that essentially, he took up the thread of the Italian theater." Renoir, *Renoir on Renoir*, 8.
58. Marivaux, *Marivaux*, xix.
59. Quoted without reference in ibid., xix.
60. Ibid.
61. Ibid., xx.
62. Ibid.
63. Ibid., 197–98.
64. Bazin discusses the commedia dell'arte lineage of slapstick comedy and develops general hypotheses that support this particular approach to type in "Theater and Cinema, Part Two" in *What Is Cinema?*, 1:120–21.
65. Renoir, *Renoir on Renoir*, 152.
66. O'Brien, *Cinema's Conversion to Sound*.

67. It was understood that "representational accuracy, in some cases, could prove problematic. With respect to sound for instance, attempts to capture reality sometimes undermined the story-world illusion, as when the physical presence of the actors, the recording environment, and/or the recording technology itself became overly emphatic." Ibid., 110; the entire argument regarding Hollywood's use of sound is made over pages 108–11.

68. Ibid., 111.
69. Ibid., 119.
70. Ibid., 117.
71. Ibid., 117–18.
72. Sesonske, *Jean Renoir,* 79.
73. Ibid.
74. Weil, *Gravity and Grace,* 56.
75. Renoir, *Renoir on Renoir,* 196.
76. Panofsky, *Early Netherlandish Painting.*
77. Ibid., 6–7.
78. Ibid., 4.
79. Ibid., 12.
80. Ibid., 3.
81. Ibid., 7.
82. Ibid., 8.

83. The conception of space attached to the plastic tendency is familiar enough that a quick review of some of the assumptions commonly associated with it should suffice to clarify what I mean by autonomy and modernity. This space is a theoretical construction derived not from actual perception but from a universal method for representing any solid figure by means of "a view through a window." Since the 1960s the analogous methods employed in photographic reproduction and cinematographic projection have kept this model current in discussions of film theory. Whether instigated by Marx's remarks on the camera obscura of ideology in *The German Ideology* or by psychoanalytic theories of the spectator-subject, theories of the apparatus have tended to focus on the effect of ersatz subjectivity or spectatorial mastery that the cinema can be said to manufacture for the spectator. A similar notion of autonomy, ersatz or otherwise, has generally been attached to Renaissance perspective because its *plastic* realization reproduces the beholder-figure relation as that between a subject and objects as these are conceived within the modern paradigm of scientific knowledge. While on the surface this connection implies nothing more than the shared indifference or neutrality of the "scientific" methods involved in both perspective construction and scientific experimentation, this neutrality has been reinterpreted, perhaps most famously by Heidegger, as the product of a prior stance of the will. In his view, modern natural science presupposes an attitude of *Ge-stell* or Enframing (a metaphor that is clearly congenial to Panofsky's observations), which challenges nature ("putting her to the test" in Francis Bacon's telling formulation) in order to produce the knowledge that gives human beings technological mastery. Thus what modern natural science itself considers to be merely the provisional bracketing-out of irrational value judgments becomes for Heidegger the dangerous blocking of the ethical claim or obligation that properly defines human destiny. Panofsky, *Early Netherlandish Painting,* 3; Mitchell, "The Rhetoric of Iconoclasm: Marxism, Ideology and Fetishism," in *Iconology,* 160–208; Heidegger, *Question Concerning Technology and Other Essays,* 14, 28.

84. Lourie, *My Work in Films*, 28.

85. Ibid., 51.

86. Ibid., 52.

87. In an essay on von Stroheim, Bazin recognizes the fundamental revolution in both acting and mise-en-scène represented by Chaplin: "After all, Chaplin—as much through his acting as through his narrative style—had taught us the value of ellipse and allusion. With him, screen artistry attained the sublime by what it did *not* show us." Bazin, *Cinema of Cruelty*, 7.

88. Lourie, *My Work in Films*, 12.

89. Ibid., 47–48.

90. Ibid., 26.

91. Bazin, *Jean Renoir*, 43.

2

Escaping from Flaubert;
or, Reflecting on Romanticism

THE FRENCH RENOIR AS A DIALOGUE OF CHRONOTOPES:
A PROVISIONAL ILLUSTRATION

In the preceding chapter we bracketed off any detailed consideration of narrative structure or cultural history so as to concentrate on the formal elements of Renoir's style, the coordinated complex of aesthetic devices whereby he intimately engages our skeptical belief in his characters. In this chapter we will focus on the generic paradigms those characters inhabit, adopting Mikhail Bakhtin's conception of the *chronotope* as a unique climate of human possibilities determined by a particular sense of time and space. In this section I present a reading of *A Day in the Country* as a provisional illustration of how Renoir uses elements of style and a dialogical narrative structure to stage a confrontation between chronotopes that provokes philosophical reflection in the spectator.

To set up this illustration it is useful to distinguish between two families of cultural idioms Renoir worked with during the 1930s, the romantic-naturalistic and the neoclassical. In speaking of a romantic-naturalistic group of idioms I mean to identify a broad and evolving cultural heritage, the origins of which can be traced back to philosophical assumptions first put forth by Jean-Jacques Rousseau. Though we can also recognize its persistence in the strains of romanticism and naturalism that informed French culture in the 1930s, the core of this dynamic meta-chronotope was established by the canonical tradition of nineteenth-century French literature (that is, Balzac, Flaubert, de Maupassant, and Zola) that Renoir frequently adapted. From a thematic point of view, these idioms draw on Rousseau's distinction between solitary and authentic natural Man and self-conscious social Man, focus on fatalistic relations between character and milieu, and assume that irrational, character-centered *passions* are always stronger than the *reasons* that society or the individual may try to oppose or govern them with. In examining the film culture of the 1930s within which Renoir worked, we can point to poetic realism as the most significant representative of this tradition. Though Dudley Andrew's extensive analysis of the cultural relations that formed poetic realism indicates that, strictly speaking, the romantic-naturalist is only one strain among many, we may nonetheless observe that the central "myth of poetic realism," with its particular inflections of social hope and private despair, can be seen as both a development of the Naturalist chronotope and a symptomatic return to certain founding assumptions: "That style, we have seen in case after case, turns inward to the solitary, orphaned self, to private morality based on private memory and experience, and to a solidarity among the downtrodden based on the intimacy of identification. When a response like this is appropriate to the key questions of the age, then, both through and beyond its style, a film finds itself appropriated by a culture."[1]

The neoclassical family of idioms gets its name from the theatrical tradition that provided Renoir with the sources for *The Rules of the Game*: Marivaux's *The Game of Love and Chance* (1730), Beaumarchais's *The Marriage of Figaro* (1784), and Musset's *The Caprices of Marianne* (1830). This essentially pre-revolutionary tradition can be said to begin with Corneille and Racine in the seventeenth century and to have survived within French culture after the Revolution through a series of compromises and accommodations with more modern generic idioms. From a thematic point of view, and in their pure form, these idioms fail to make any distinction between social and natural man and instead conceive of characters as social types with relatively fixed, and in that sense "natural," predilections. In contrast to the naturalist identification with those caught in the throes of passion, these older idioms turn the skeptical gaze of a worldly premodern rationality on their follies. In assessing the survival of this tradition in 1930s French cinema, Andrew argues that, in a general sense, it functioned to reinscribe the naturalness of social hierarchy; though the abrupt transition to sound in the 1930s allowed films based on theatrical models to dominate at the box office, the positive aesthetic possibilities of this tradition seemed to have been exhausted: "Contrived domestic (parlor) situations, abrupt changes in class, and witty dialogue link it [the contemporary French farce] to dramatic traditions that flourished in the eighteenth century, traditions that have always tended toward political and aesthetic conservatism."[2] The success of theatrically based films during the decade derived primarily from the institution of the star, an aspect of the French theatrical tradition that developed as the neoclassical theatre accommodated itself to a modern, bourgeois audience over the course of the nineteenth century.[3] In a general sense, the transfer from stage to screen of the "pact" between theatrical performers and French audiences can be assessed to have been regressive, both in terms of the rank cynicism of some of the most popular performers (for example, the comic actors Fernandel and Georges Milton) and insofar as films so often employed the star to evoke nostalgic memories of more intimate and socially cohesive entertainments, "an endless Belle Époque."[4]

Though we will later examine the cultural genealogies of these two traditions in greater detail, I would like to preview Renoir's engagement with them with the hypothesis that their role within French culture during the 1930s effected a dynamic of alienation wherein the leering complicity of address, relentless knowingness, and empty buoyancy that the neoclassical tradition had been reduced to (for example, Fernandel, Georges Milton) only exacerbated the extreme isolation and intense desire for oblivion expressed in poetic realism (for example, Jean Gabin in *Quai des brumes* or *Le jour se lève*) and related forms of popular culture (for example, the popular singers Damia and Edith Piaf). Each tradition radicalized the need for the other and thus served to articulate and reinforce an unacknowledged schizophrenia within the culture and the individual; by creating dialogical confrontations between generic idioms that French culture generally kept separate, Renoir attempted to force his society to reflect on its inherent contradictions.

To begin to understand how Renoir's style creates reflective engagements between generic idioms and chronotopes, we can observe that what André Bazin called Renoir's mistakes can also be understood as moments when a film shifts from one chronotope to another; as in Vaclav

Havel's model of the gag, we experience a rupture in the conventions of one chronotope because the conventions of another have been applied to the same event. As Bazin puts it, "The freedom of this construction, the contempt for dramatic and psychological verisimilitude, are the height of realism in the sense that Renoir—instead of taking the usual path from the idea to a simulated reality—*imposes the idea by departing from reality*. It is through Renoir's love, his sensibility, his intimacy with objects, animals and people, that his moral vision confronts us so strikingly" (my italics).[5] As confusing as the use of the term "realism" can get in Bazin, it is nonetheless possible to unpack the argument here and synchronize it with Renoir's own terminology. The "height of realism," what in the essay "The Ontology of the Photographic Image" he calls "true realism" and Renoir calls "internal truth," is defined by its dialectical relationship to—its "contempt for"—the unconscious ideological effect of verisimilitude that Bazin calls "pseudorealism" and Renoir calls "external realism": this is the reality that one "departs" from. The departure effects a striking confrontation with Renoir's moral vision and ideas because it forces us to reconfigure what we see and hear in terms of an entirely different set of philosophical assumptions. Renoir's "intimacy with objects, animals and people" brings to our attention contingent details that function to keep the contradictory claims of two or more chronotopes open in the back of the spectator's mind. The uncanniness one often experiences in watching Renoir's films, the dimly sensed undercurrents behind the scenes of the ostensible narrative, reflect the underlying fact that the chronotopes we will be examining are not discrete or self-enclosed in the manner of Kane's snow globe. Though we will need to isolate the dominant chronotope at work in each film as a necessary means to reconstruct the narrative logic of Renoir's filmmaking over a decade, we should never forget the dialogical chaos behind the scenes, the other chronotopes jostling in a mobile, porous, interpenetrated continuum, the leaky, unmoored cells of a beehive being jumbled and agitated like bumper cars by the kaleidoscope of Renoir's concerns.

As a striking illustration of Renoir's dialectical/dialogical style, both Andrew and Bazin point to the moment in *A Day in the Country* when Henriette (Sylvia Bataille) turns to face us in close-up after having responded to the amorous advances of Henri (Georges Darnoux).[6] In both accounts, this shot is described as an unexpected violation of the narrative and tonal unity of the film, a shift from which the film never recovers. Up to this point the film has systematically presented the characters to us as a variety of comic types whose responses to each other and the world are relatively predictable and based on social affiliation (class, locals versus Parisians, socially constructed clichés about the emotions proper to youth and age), and it seems to be moving directly toward a sequence of comic dénouements that will result in the relocation of each within their type. But when Henriette turns to face the camera, we (and she) are caught off guard by her sudden and self-aware carnality (Andrew) and/or revelation of Otherness and vulnerability (Bazin): "The scene opens in a light comic vein which one would logically expect to turn bawdy. We are ready to laugh, when suddenly the laugh catches in our throat. No sooner is the smile wiped from our faces than tears appear in our eyes. With Sylvia Bataille's incredible glance, the world begins to spin and love bursts forth like a long-stifled cry. I can think of no other director, except perhaps Chaplin, who is capable of evoking such a wrenching bit of truth from a face, an expression."[7] After this shot, a shot of Henri looking offscreen takes us to a sequence of shots of the natural environment around them, as Kosma's score indicates the advent of the impending storm (trees and bushes hushed and expectant and then buffeted by wind, the first few drops of rain on the river, and then a lengthy traveling shot from the back of a motorboat as the rain pours down). This storm carries us, as if solely on the strength of that one "wrenching" close-up, to the epilogue years later, where we discover that Henriette has married her boorish fiancé, Anatole, and a chance meeting between the former lovers informs us that she and Henri live only in their memories of that brief episode of romance: what began as a bawdy neoclassical comedy has somehow turned into a bittersweet romantic tragedy.

    How has this happened? Without denying the radicalness of the shift we have just outlined, it is important to recognize that, unexpected as it feels, we have in fact been carefully prepared for it. Were the new idiom to be absolutely unexpected, we would be disoriented rather than moved, and the paradoxical fact that we are shocked by the appropriateness or truth of the shift suggests that Renoir has somehow been engaging us with this particularly romantic variant of the naturalist idiom or chronotope all along. One way he has done this is by mobilizing our awareness of a sliding scale of acting styles, ranging from the gross theatricality of the Parents Dufour, Anatole, Rodolphe, and Renoir's innkeeper to the more restrained performances of Henri, Henriette, and marginal characters such as the maid. Our awareness of this continuum is sharpened by the pose of being sophisticated observers adopted by the two bohemians in relation to the spectacle presented by the bourgeois Parisian family; the scale of performativity running from pure social types to individualized characters with more solitary psyches opens us to the possibility of hidden depths beneath the theatrical surface.

Other strategies also serve to prepare the shift from one chronotope to another. In what seems at the time to be a throwaway anticlerical gag or in-joke, the seminarians (one of whom is played by Sylvia's husband, George Bataille) stop, stunned in their tracks, to watch Henriette on the swing; in retrospect, this moment can be seen to have subtly "punctured" (in the Barthesian sense) the comic *studium* of the film and prepared us for the shift to passion and tragedy that is to come.[8] Another important form of preparation results from the disjunction we feel between the dry, generic quality of the characters and the lush particularity of the scenery that surrounds them. This disjunction, which the dramatic logic of the film does not in any way foreground, nonetheless exerts a subconscious effect on the spectator.

In one sense it is clearly the repression of our peripheral awareness of nature in favor of the theatrical characters who have invaded it that makes the storm seem like a necessary form of rebalancing. In another, it is the fact that Henriette alone gives expression to this awareness of nature (especially through her swinging and discussion of nature with her mother) that makes her moment of truth so convincing for us. Despite the comic distanciation her theatrical qualities provoke in us, we have been nonetheless registering the nature in the film *through* her and so have been prepared to recognize the nature that is, as it were, *in* her. In retrospect, she was always traversed by both idioms, for her swinging and feelings for nature are at one and the same time the recognizably formulaic expressions of bourgeois maidenhood (as her mother more or less labels them) and the authentic expressions of her (and our) repressed desire for romantic communion with nature. Like Madame Bovary, her tragedy stems from

FIGURE 2.1.

Henriette equivocates in *A Day in the Country*.

an inherent equivocation between her social identity as a bourgeois and her individualized romantic identity (I am thinking here especially of the moment in the epilogue when Anatole awakens from his nap and starts yelling for her and she desperately searches Henri's face in vain for the clue that would allow her to escape from her typecast position as a *petit bourgeois* wife—a "wrenching" moment as powerful in its own way as the earlier one).

In retrospect we can recognize that this pattern of equivocation has governed the entire film from its outset and can see it as emerging from a process wherein Renoir's style functions to brush each idiom or chronotope against the grain of the other; the spectator's explicit or conscious engagement with the film's comedy is always haunted by our subconscious romantic attachment to the fleetingness, to the precious, never-to-return possibilities of a particular summer's day, a fleetingness that is eventually made explicit by the long "retrospective" traveling shot from the back of an anachronistically modern motorboat. Though on one level the comic narrative of clever and insistent seduction flows swiftly to its conclusion with no apparent casualties (when we last see her, Madame Dufour is clearly delighted by Rodolphe's satyr-like advances; Monsieur Dufour and Anatole will probably never know that they were betrayed and in any case do not have our sympathy), the close-up of Henriette explicitly testifies to the existence of a romantic countercurrent that has been flowing in the opposite direction throughout the film. This close-up constitutes a moment in which the gentle but pervasive friction between the two idioms/currents/chronotopes suddenly *grabs* and abruptly inverts the hierarchy of explicitness and implicitness that has hitherto governed their relationship. The comedic narrative of this fleeting day in the country is summarily dumped into the vast stream of time, and the romantic desire that has now come to the surface can only look back at the characters and events disappearing in its wake with affection and irreducible regret.

What makes this particular type of dialogical narrative structure *philosophical*? As outlined by the classics scholar Seth Benardete, philosophical narratives present us with an artificial experience from which we can learn something real; as with a Greek tragedy or a Platonic dialogue, we learn through *pathei mathos*, by suffering or undergoing an experience in which an understanding we initially take to be real and comprehensive is subsequently revealed to be imaginary and partial.[9] In the experience of a Greek tragedy or Platonic dialogue, we are first presented with a dominant narrative argument the poetic force of which persuades us to suppress or ignore certain troublesome details that do not cohere with that narrative argument; the philosophical work of art deliberately engages our "willfulness," our culpable eagerness to accept an all-too-simple and conventional interpretation of events, while simultaneously and stealthily planting evidence that can later be used to overturn that interpretation. At a certain point we reach what Benardete calls an "intentional flaw" or "trapdoor" in the apparent argument of the narrative that drops us beneath the surface to confront the details and issues which that argument had hitherto neglected.[10] The truth or reality that we now encounter thus is not an abstract proposition but is grounded in our own existential experience of error—the freshness and conviction it carries is not dependent on external verification but is already a matter of our own experience. The effect of philosophic truth is thus dependent on the real-time experience of reading or spectatorship. If traditional approaches to textual analysis generally interpret narratives from a synchronic or synoptic perspective—that is, as thematic wholes or arguments constituted of parts that cohere—a dialogical approach must recognize the ways in which the diachronic *incoherence* of a given sequence of narrative events can force the reader/spectator to revise his or her understanding of what is, in retrospect, a faulty argument or incomplete whole. Speaking of the Platonic dialogue, Benardete writes:

> Once argument and action are properly put together an entirely new argument emerges that could never have been expected from the argument on the written page. Something happens in a Platonic dialogue that in its revolutionary unexpectedness is the equivalent to the *periagoge*, as Socrates calls it, of philosophy itself. This turnaround has a peculiar structure. It has to be experienced and can never be formulated in such a way as to allow one anything more than an anticipation of an equivalent turnaround in another dialogue. There cannot be a method (*methodos*) of thought in the thoughtful going after (*metienai*) of thought.[11]

With these elements of Benardete's model in view, we can describe *A Day in the Country* as a philosophical work of art because its narrative structure provokes reflection on the arguments implicit in the two cultural idioms it engages with. It should also be clear how these macrolevel hypotheses concerning dialogical narrative structure and chronotopes line up with the microlevel explanations of internal and external realism in the preceding chapter. Whether one is looking at examples of the dispassionate camera and the gag or the narrative structure of a Renoir film as a whole, one can recognize the same principles at work. On whatever level one chooses to examine, the effects of realism and/or philosophic truth result from forcing spectators to confront contradictions in their own assumptions. Having said that the mise-en-scène of a Renoir film is built around windows and doors, we might now say that the dialogical narrative structure of a Renoir film is designed around trapdoors (and trapdoors-within-trapdoors-within-trapdoors), moments that drop us from what we think we know (and who we think we are) onto the terra firma of unacknowledged contradictions that we unwittingly live.

TYPES AND CHRONOTOPES IN THE FRENCH RENOIR

> The *Rules of the Game* also represented my desire to return to the classical spirit, my desire to escape from *The Human Beast*, from naturalism, even to escape from Flaubert.
>
> Jean Renoir, "Remarks," 1961, in Renoir on Renoir

In the preceding analyses we have concentrated on identifying certain of Renoir's formal devices in order to model his style and narrative structure as a complex aesthetic machine so that we can become sensitive to the effects of that machine. In this section we will begin replacing that machine in its historical contexts in order to flesh out those effects and give them philosophical content and significance. My approach to this task will be to jump to a much wider perspective that considers his work during the 1930s as a whole. The justification for this approach rests in my conviction that the philosophical significance of any individual film by an auteur best comes to light in the context of the broader conversations within which it is set. One axis of these conversations is the dialogue that Renoir had with himself during the period as displayed in the particular sequence of films he chose to make. Another axis concerns the relations between the chronotopes in the films and the contemporary political and popular culture within which they were situated. Only when these two axes are considered together and compared can we begin to recognize a third axis that articulates Renoir's reflection on the cultural philosophical issues at stake. In attempting to take a synoptic view of Renoir's evolution during the 1930s, I would distinguish between four distinct chronotopes, and we will examine each of these carefully before turning to consider the patterns they create when placed in chronological sequence.

The Flaubertian Chronotope

> Mealtime was the worst of all in that tiny room on the ground floor, with the smoking oven, the creaking door, the damp walls, and the moist flagstones; all the bitterness of her existence seemed to be served up to her on her plate, and the steam from the boiled beef brought up waves of nausea from the depths of her soul. It took Charles a long time to eat; she would nibble a few hazelnuts, or leaning on her elbow, would amuse herself by drawing lines on the oilcloth with the tip of her knife.
>
> Gustave Flaubert, Madame Bovary[12]

With Gustave Flaubert's novel *Madame Bovary* in mind as an ideal object of comparison, the first chronotope to appear historically I would label the *Flaubertian*. This chronotope manifests itself most explicitly in *La chienne* and Renoir's adaptation of *Madame Bovary*. This chronotope was where the French Renoir began but also represents, by his own account, a set of assumptions from which he was trying to escape. Erich Auerbach's account of Flaubert clarifies the author's historical relationship with the romantic tendencies in French literary culture that preceded him and offers a genealogy that illuminates the philosophical assumptions at stake in the Flaubertian chronotope and others we will examine.

In Auerbach's synoptic narrative of Western literature, Flaubert represents the end point of a specific tradition that began with Stendhal and includes Balzac and other writers in the lineage of naturalism. The crucial feature that distinguishes this tradition from the literature that preceded it is its treatment of time as fundamentally historical.[13] If prior to the French Revolution events could still be treated as instances of eternal patterns, as permutations and combinations the novelty of which nonetheless revealed their source in the regularities of human nature and an ordered cosmos, the tradition in question can be said to reflect and/or effect a fundamental critique of this faith-based worldview. In the work of Stendhal the Revolution constitutes the demonstration of a truth that the author is forced to reckon with despite his loyalty to the aristocratic values of the old regime.[14] This truth is that the patterns of human society and historical events can no longer be read in terms of an unchanging natural order, that is, eternity. "History" has emerged as the narrative that registers both society and the individual changing in fundamental ways, ways that are impossible to reconcile with traditional concepts of social order or human nature. Though the individual can strive to be equal to the dynamism of History (this is the characteristic goal of Stendhal's heroes), this romantic response carries with it the inevitability of boredom when the pace or nature of change falls short of awakened expectations.[15] In Auerbach's view the experience of enervating banality that the realistic novel of the nineteenth century (Balzac, Flaubert) can be said to begin with is an inevitable end point of romanticism; in David Depew's explicitly dialogical formulation we might say that Realism *is* disillusioned romanticism.[16] In any case, what is essential for this inquiry is the fact that Auerbach persuasively traces the root of this development back to Rousseau: "The Rousseauist movement and the great disillusionment it underwent was a prerequisite for the rise of the modern conception of reality. Rousseau, by passionately contrasting the natural condition of man with the existing reality of life determined by history, made the latter a practical problem; now for the first time the eighteenth-century style of historically unproblematic and unmoved presentation of life became valueless."[17]

Drained of their eternal meaning by the emerging sense of a universal and comprehensible history (the French Revolution, Napoleon) and then evacuated of that sense by a second, socially fragmenting wave of historicism, everyday phenomena become subject to the possibility of seeming absurd for perhaps the first time. With this experience of disillusionment providing the impetus, Balzac's project of mapping the multifarious complexity of post-revolutionary French society can be seen as an effort to discern the original Rousseauian nature of his characters through the corruption of this nature effected by the variegated social milieux in which we find them. According to Auerbach, every character in Balzac is enveloped in a pervasive atmosphere, at once "organic" and "demonic," that impregnates and shapes his or her physical environment.[18] The fate of his characters within these social milieux reflect the playing out of a prior "Animality" that "floods over into Humanity by an immense current of life."[19] In Auerbach's view this potentially awkward conflation or synthesis of the biological and the historical is aesthetically successful because Balzac imagines both processes as driven by the impulses of irrational instinct; they intertwine to produce a fatalistic narrative logic at an occult or melodramatic level.[20] In Balzac we see the origin of a set of generic effects that continue to operate in the cinematic idiom of poetic realism that dominated French cinema during the 1930s:

> The atmosphere that dominates poetic realist films is less interesting for its meaning or tone than for its function as a medium blending characters with the worlds they inhabit. Atmosphere as an effect of cinematic texture, as a pervasive overtone emanating variously from cinematography, set design, sound, music, script, and acting, is also a figure. It speaks of sublimation (mists of feeling rising from a plot), of envelopment (where the spectator is suffused in the same light and sound as the character), and of figuration itself (where the visual and aural milieu embodies the character's way of being, *becomes* that being).[21]

Despite the vividness of its effects, for Auerbach Balzac's realism is, as it were, suspended between two stools. Because his characters' fates are determined by their specific locations in a multifarious and ever-changing society, they fail to achieve the universal applicability proper to the tragic; though Balzac calls Goriot *ce Christ de la paternité*, this character's fate carries no ennobling sense of divine necessity and in fact often verges on the comic, especially as manifest in his ludicrous and unrequited acts of parental self-sacrifice.[22] At the same time, Balzac's melodramatic insistence on the hidden, occult significance of his characters' fates prevents him from achieving the lucidity, the "objective seriousness," that was to characterize the next development in this tradition.

This next stage, represented for Auerbach by Flaubert, can be understood as a reaction to the melodramatic romanticism in Balzac and at the same time a reaffirmation of certain Rousseauian assumptions. Flaubert typically describes a scene with reference to the emotional state of one of the characters within it, illuminating the affective logic behind details of phenomena and perception that bind the character within a limited worldview. No hidden or occult forces animate the Flaubertian milieux, which are presented as neutral and lacking in inherent motion. But the Flaubertian character is unable to see either this milieu or his or her fellow characters with any degree of objectivity. Each individual's defining desire or passion has made subjectivity itself into a type of fate, though the shapes of that fate will vary in accordance with the limited, historically conditioned idiom the character uses to interpret the world (that is, a form of romanticism for Emma Bovary, a complacent bourgeois ideology for Charles): "What is true of these two, applies to almost all the other characters in the novel; each of the many mediocre people who act in it has his own world of mediocre and silly stupidity, a world of illusions, habits, instincts, and slogans; each is alone, none can understand another, or help another to insight."[23] While the lucid, objective, judgmental gaze of the author/reader in Flaubert is clearly a reaction against the melodramatic and sentimental excesses of a Balzac, Flaubert nonetheless retains a sense of fatality comparable to Balzac's: there is an implicit connection between the blind and irrational history of human culture and the shortsighted stupidity of Flaubert's characters. Unlike their omniscient author, Flaubert's characters are incapable of seeing through or beyond the various ideologies that shape the solipsistic worlds they inhabit; they are trapped and isolated by the fundamental appropriateness of the fit between false historical ideologies and their mediocre desires. Like Rousseau, Stendhal, and Balzac before him, Flaubert presents a vision of human nature corrupted by society and history. But unlike his predecessors, he neither romanticizes his characters' desires nor the movement of history but judges both against the perfection of his art, against the dispassionate objectivity of his disembodied and synoptic gaze.

Renoir's *La chienne* and *Madame Bovary* are perfect illustrations of Auerbach's account of the Flaubertian chronotope. Both films present us with a variety of human types that, like Flaubert's characters, are completely isolated from each other by their mediocrity and stupidity, their inability to see beyond what their characteristic passions and ideologies allow them to see. Every scene of interaction between the main characters in *La chienne* demonstrates that the characters do not really recognize each other and illustrates the extent to which the intertwined narratives of deception (Lulu and Dédé deceive Legrand; Dédé deceives Lulu; Legrand deceives Adèle; Legrand deceives Godard) depend on the prior self-deception, the solipsistic self-envelopment and isolation, of each character. Just as Lulu is isolated between her deception of Legrand and her deception by Dédé, Emma in *Madame Bovary* is systematically presented as both a deceiver in relation to her husband and deceived in relation to her succession of lovers. Though the main characters in these films all imagine they alone see the true or common world that certain others do not, Renoir's ruthlessly impartial and synoptic perspective shows us that none of them is capable of breaking free from the ideological reflexes or automatisms that determine their perceptions and assessments.

Renoir's mise-en-scène in these films maintains a dispassionate distance from the characters analogous to Flaubert's style in *Madame Bovary* or the clinical, still-life tone of Edouard Manet's paintings. Though the passion-driven narratives would certainly allow for a treatment that involved the spectator in those passions as a popular melodrama might choose to do, Renoir rigorously avoids close-ups or any other technique that might allow for such involvement. Instead, this chronotope employs long takes, long shots, and occlusive framings to emphasize a pervasive

FIGURE 2.2.

Occlusive framing of the love triangle in *La chienne*.

feeling of chilly detachment. Even the inherently melodramatic scenes in which deceptions are revealed to the deceived are treated with a cold and lucid irony that brings out the feelings of abjection, humiliation, and cruelty that a von Stroheim or Fassbinder might draw from them. The scenes in Emma Bovary's bedroom that were discussed in chapter 1 offer a case in point, as does the scene in *La chienne* in which Legrand discovers Dédé and Lulu in bed. Having deftly arranged a reunion between his wife and her long-lost first husband, Alexis Godard, Legrand eagerly climbs the stairs to his love nest with his suitcase in hand and—he imagines—complete happiness imminent. From the time he gets to the top of the landing, fiddles with the lock, opens the door, and finds the two lovers sitting up in bed, we hear Dédé and Lulu hastily discussing a ridiculous cover story (that Dédé is her sick brother) that they drop the moment the door swings wide open. Renoir holds this occlusive shot—our view of the lovers is from the hallway, through the outer door, past the figure of Legrand, and through the bedroom door—as we take in their hapless responses: Lulu stares at Legrand coldly and with a hint of amusement while the normally irrepressible monologist Dédé now stares woodenly at the floor. We then cut to a shot from outside the building through the bedroom window that first centers the lovers but then tracks laterally left and tilts right to give us our first distant reaction-shot view of Legrand. But if we imagine that all this distance represents some sort of sympathetic discretion on Renoir's part we are immediately disabused of this by the shot that follows, a jump cut to a medium-close shot of Lulu (with Dédé still staring at the floor in the background) from inside the room in which she is in the middle of a harsh harangue affirming her relationship with Dédé and mocking Legrand for imagining she could ever love a repulsive specimen such as himself. We then cut to a long shot from the back corner of the room that allows us a brief glimpse of the devastated Legrand's face before he picks up his bag, and we get a series of shots following him out the door, down the stairs, out of the building, and down the street (none of which allow us to get a good view of his face, though we register his abjection through his posture and pace). After Legrand walks down the street and out of frame, we cut back to a long shot inside the bedroom; after having "played dead" the entire scene, Dédé suddenly springs up and races to the door to make sure Legrand is really gone and then swings into his usual hyperanimation, pacing, getting dressed, blaming Lulu for forcing him to go to bed and thus ruining their cozy set-up, and slapping her a few times before rushing out: if Legrand is in bad shape, this clinical view of the lovers reminds us that their relationship is based solely on the coincidence of his finding her a useful prop in his petty schemes and her boundless masochistic willingness to be used.

Taken as a whole, Renoir's Flaubertian chronotope offers us a vision of its characters taken from the outside—whether they are magnificent spectacles of instinctive venality like Dédé or well-meaning and thoughtful like Legrand and Charles Bovary, the narrative and mise-en-scène make such fine points of melodramatic morality secondary to the fact that they are all equal in their culpable blindness to the truth about others and themselves, the truth that Renoir and the spectator recognize so easily: as

FIGURE 2.3.

Lulu looks at Legrand in *La chienne*.

far as Renoir's question of "meeting" goes, it is clear the characters neither meet each other nor achieve self-understanding (meet themselves).

A specific index of this issue of meeting that we will track throughout our examination of all four chronotopes is the quantity and quality of eye contact between characters. The Flaubertian chronotope is characterized by the fact that eye contact between characters is extremely scarce; there is an almost total absence of shot-reverse shot sequences, and instead we are typically given conversations in which there is no eye contact or where characters "look at" each other, that is, a character looks at another who is engaged elsewhere. Even where there is mutual eye contact, this quality of *looking-at* is maintained insofar as the characters' performances and the dialogue serve to underline the fact that their intentions are at cross-purposes; the facial expression and dialogue of one character objectify (deceive or express contempt, frustration, or an ironic, knowing amusement toward) another whose expression and dialogue show that he or she is unaware of the attitude or objectives of the first (consider Legrand's interactions with Adele, Dédé's with Lulu, or Emma's with Charles). Both in its relative scarcity and consistently nonreciprocal nature, eye contact in the Flaubertian chronotope articulates the solipsistic isolation of the characters. Renoir gives us a cold, brutally realistic view of a world of types enclosed within stupid reflexes and unrealistic fantasies, a world in which any genuine meeting between the characters is completely out of the question.

The Cytherean Chronotope

The Flaubertian perspective on human life was not, thankfully, Renoir's final word on the subject. With the painting of Antoine Watteau in mind as an ideal object of comparison, I would label the second distinct chronotope to appear historically during the 1930s the *Cytherean* in honor of Cythera, the mythical island of ineffable pleasures that was a key reference point in several of Watteau's paintings.[24] Though it was to receive even more elaborate treatment in later films (*The River*, 1951; *The Golden Coach*, 1953; *Elena et les hommes*, 1956; *Le déjeuner sur l'herbe*, 1959), during the 1930s this chronotope is clearly articulated in *Boudu sauvé des eaux* (1932) and *Une partie de campagne*. To clarify the relevance of Watteau's art to these films I would like to begin by identifying some of its characteristic figures, aesthetic effects, and, by way of a considerable digression, philosophical themes that will be of importance for the project as a whole.

Watteau's signature genre was the *fête galante,* a scene taking place in a verdant park or country setting and depicting two types of figures and activities. In one subgenre he painted groups of actors and musicians who seem to be relaxing and enjoying each other's company, performing, playing lutes, or simply standing around, "hanging out." The most prominent theatrical tradition featured in this subgenre was the Italian commedia dell'arte, with certain of its stock types (Gilles, Harlequin, Mezzetino) recurring again and again. In a second subgenre he painted men and women in elegant clothes who seem to have become enchanted by the sensual stimuli of the natural environment and are engaged in a variety of erotic

FIGURE 2.4.

Henri seduces Henriette in *A Day in the Country*.

games: flirting and seduction conducted via intense private conversation, dancing, making music, amateur theatricals, or gentle horseplay. As art historian Pierre Schneider emphasizes, what distinguishes Watteau's art from that of lesser artists working in the same genre is the fact that it hardly ever depicts erotic acts such as kissing or embracing directly but focuses instead on pauses or distractions from the action of *la chasse*: "the scent of love floats the more effectively over Watteau's pictures for the fact of its not being flaunted."[25] Schneider echoes Bazin on Renoir in noting that the painter's apparent indifference to the action was often assessed by his contemporaries to be a "mistake": "This strange indifference of Watteau's personages to the action in which they are supposedly engaged puzzled and irritated even his supporters. 'His compositions are lacking in one of the most fetching parts of painting: I mean action,' Watteau's friend, the Comte de Caylus, writes petulantly."[26] As a representative example of Watteau's pauses, I would offer the image of a male figure intent on a female companion and in some sense active (bent over her and whispering something or pulling her up from the ground to take a little walk away from the group) and the female figure being in some sense passively resistant (looking off at another couple, looking abstractedly at the ground, adjusting her costume).

To begin to appreciate the particular aesthetic effects that Watteau produces from such repeated visual formulae, one can start, somewhat paradoxically, with the issue of sound, for the explicit representation of certain sounds creates a peculiar feeling of distance that has very specific consequences. Because we are provided only with the representation of a pause or break in an otherwise sketchy narrative action (a seduction, a musical performance, the course of a summer's afternoon), we feel uncertain as to what point we are at in that action: are we at the beginning or end of a seduction, the beginning or end of a song, the start of the afternoon or its close? The common image of a man bending close to murmur in a woman's ear epitomizes the kind of effect Watteau's visual representations of sound have on the spectator, for it both promises and withholds the answer to all such questions—the visual representation of an inaudible sound produces a paradoxical effect of both distance and proximity. As Schneider puts it: "The sounds in Watteau's paintings are at once mysterious and dainty, like the confidential murmur one hears in a sea shell, the tinkle of two wineglasses, a lute tuning up, a guitar strumming with subdued vehemence, the bubbling of a fountain, the rustle of foliage, the whisperings of shy, young lovers."[27] Schneider's evocation of the seashell (which happens to be the defining symbol of the cultural style of the age in which Watteau lived, the rococo) suggests an apt phenomenological analogy for this "sound effect" that can, I think, be elaborated to illuminate a particular structure of time at work in both Watteau's paintings and Renoir's films.[28]

Holding a seashell in one's hand and looking at it, it is only a small and silent object, but as one brings it into proximity with one's ear and out of one's field of vision, one starts to hear the gentle roar of the ocean, at first faint but increasingly louder until it conjures up an indistinct aural picture of our vast and watery planet: the child in us is amazed at the paradox that an infinity of space is contained within this small, finite object. One moves the shell away from one's ear and back into one's field of vision, and the soft roar fades back to silence. The experience of looking at a Watteau painting is defined by the feeling that one can *almost hear* the sounds of the fete represented visually—that is, it is defined by something analogous to the moment of transition between the vast, aural-but-invisible ocean and the small, visible-but-inaudible shell: one's inability to hear the sounds represented in the painting carries a feeling of poignance and loss comparable to the feeling children have when they realize that they can never actually perceive the shell and the ocean at the same time, can never really *share* this experience, even with themselves. What we might call the radical fleetingness of this experience derives from the sharp contrast between the forms of intentionality in each of its two component moments. In holding the shell in one's hand and looking at it, one controls the time and space of the experience, one bears down on a present and object the possession of which seems increasingly meaningless or absurd. In listening to the ocean, on the other hand, the imaginative act of measuring this vast indistinct space inevitably splits the present time of intentionality. Standing on a beach in one's mind's eye and imagining the passage to a distant shore, one cannot place the self who reaches that shore and the self who remains on the beach within the same moment: one part of the self remains in the present while another inhabits either the future or the past. The sublime quality of the ocean's spatial magnitude, which was radicalized and made explicit in the work of romantic poets and German idealist philosophers, overwhelms any intention we might have of being equal to it through the imaginative representation of a single synoptic view or moment in time. Rather than measure the ocean in *our* time (that is, the only time we possess, the immediate present), we find ourselves measured—divided and reduced to nothing—by a sense of cosmic space and time: we are happily dispossessed of the burden of being ourselves.

This sublime seashell effect is re-created in Watteau's fêtes galante partly by virtue of the fact that the fetes are typically presented to us in a long shot; at this distance we can *see* certain sounds represented (murmured sweet nothings, music being played on instruments) but cannot reasonably imagine *hearing* the details that would allow us to properly constitute the fetes as narrative events: we cannot properly possess them within the present time (or single view) of spectatorship. As in the moment of looking at the seashell, we are made to feel the absurdity and relative powerlessness of our visual intentions, and as a consequence the spatial distance comes to be felt or translated into an irreducible distance in time. On the other hand, and as a direct consequence, we can well imagine hearing (and also feeling through the sense of touch) what covers or muffles the sounds of the fete, what we would hear and feel if we were really viewing the scene from a long shot: the cooling breeze in the trees, birds chirping, the noise of insects, and the warmth of the midafternoon sun, all the ambient sounds and sensations of a landscape that extends beyond the spatiotemporal frame of the fete itself. When we contemplate such a painting, the landscape thus functions as the ocean does in our seashell analogy, as if the scene we are looking at is always in the process of dissolving to an identical framing at an indeterminate time *later* (later in the same day, the next day, many years later) wherein the fleeting characters and events of the fete are all long gone and/or elsewhere: the image of the fete we see is thus ghosted by the image of an empty landscape we hear. To translate this effect into terms we have used to characterize the style of Renoir's films, we might say that the theatrical human-centric centripetal space and time represented by the characters and events of the fete (within the frame of the picture; on-screen) are always in the process of imaginatively dissolving into the cinematic cosmos-centric centrifugal space and time represented by the landscape (beyond the frame of the picture; offscreen).

This effect is also articulated and reinforced by the performances or attitudes displayed by certain figures in the fetes, figures whose distraction is highlighted by contrast with the passionate intensity of their companions. This distraction serves to produce the effect we are concerned with insofar as it represents a centrifugal trajectory of thought leading out of the centripetal events of the fete, as if the sensual stimuli of the environment are causing these figures to "forget themselves" or "be elsewhere":

> Conversation, dance, song are magically suspended. A strange golden silence holds everything and everyone under its spell. And this silence leads us to reconsider more attentively the heroes and heroines of Watteau's parties.
> They are not as happy as we thought they were, but to say they are sad would

> be going too far. They appear not to believe in their happiness. They seem curiously uninvolved, as if listening less to a sweetheart than to an invisible, pressing interlocutor, a voice from within. In the message of that voice lies the secret of Watteau.... What we took for unconcern on the part of Watteau's personages is really intense concentration. Somewhere around them or inside them a grace note is being sounded which they must catch if their love—and if the picture—is to attain perfection.[29]

What Schneider calls a grace note is, in the terms of our seashell analogy, the sound of the ocean landscape, a sublime quality of sound that situates the fleeting sensual beauty of the moment within the vastness of cosmic time and space. Though love provides the ostensible subject matter of Watteau's painting, time and mortality are what its aesthetic structures actually force us to contemplate: the abstracted female figures in the fetes are mirror images of the spectator.

Before we turn to examine how these effects are manifest in Renoir's films, it is worth pausing to consider this theme of fleeting time, for the reflections of Schneider and John Berger on *why* the theme emerged as th central preoccupation of Watteau's art also serve to introduce and illuminate the philosophical significance of Renoir's mobilizations of the chronotope:

> Watteau could have introduced his esthetic revolution at no other moment in history. For the incipient 18th Century really discovered time. Historical consciousness, the sense of relativity, the belief in progress—all these signs of the awareness of time and of its passing have their roots in the early years of this century. Time is born out of the disintegration of eternity; it was thus natural that an intense feeling for time should spring up in the shambles of a regime which men—or at least Frenchmen—had become convinced was immortal: the absolute monarchy of Louis XIV, the Sun King.[30]

Schneider identifies various reasons for this new consciousness of "flux, change and restlessness," from the disorienting social impacts of an incipient capitalism—"a valet on Monday became, through speculation, a financier on Wednesday"—to the middle-class preoccupation with "news" and the nobility's obsession with what Casanova called the new "divinities" of novelty and fashion.[31] He also isolates the essential feature that distinguished this particular experience of historical change from both earlier and later experiences:

> Up to then changes had always been followed by long periods of stability, and although they often caused violent uproar and protests, the ensuing calm gave everyone ample time to assimilate novelties. In the end people forgot that these changes had only been expressions of relative tastes, and worshiped them as if they were absolute laws. The new thing, therefore, was the acceleration of change. The wind of time began to turn the pages of history's book with such speed that people no longer had the leisure to learn its contents by heart.[32]

With this disorienting two-level movement in view (the sheer velocity of change and its acceleration), the period in question can be understood as an unstable moment of transition between two coherent conceptions of time, each governed by laws or regularities that reference a philosophical ground of cosmic order. If the order of the past was still largely grounded in the religious conception of time-as-eternity, human life *given* meaning by striving to conform to ethical ideals, the sensed-but-as-yet-indiscernible order of the future was to be grounded in the modern conception of time-as-history, a dynamic narrative wherein meaning is *created* through active participation in historical events such as the French Revolution. In a general sense, both before the eighteenth century and after the French Revolution, people could imaginatively live within the phases of historical change, could situate changes in terms of a master narrative (either religious or secular-progressive), but in the eighteenth century itself they were forced to live through those phases, to live through the experience of historicity, with what we might call insufficient ideological clothing. This metaphorical sense of vulnerability or exposure to historical change informs the representation of fleetingness and mortality in Watteau's painting. John Berger notes that the dominant view of Watteau's art tends to read its concern with mortality as simply a nostalgic reaffirmation of an ahistorical and premodern (classical or Christian) framework: "'The content of Watteau's art, if we may state it in a word, is mortality—that fatal sense of life's transience about which his every picture whispers but never speaks openly,' as Mr. Gordon Washburn has put it."[33] But without denying this retrospective affiliation, Berger emphasizes an equally significant prospective orientation:

> He remained (and was born) outside the social order he painted, but the ambivalence of the mood of his work was a perfect expression of the nature and

destiny of that order. It was to be said later, "Under Louis XIV no one dared open his mouth, under Louis XV everyone whispered, now everyone speaks out loud in a free and easy way." The whispering in Watteau's paintings (which both quotations refer to) is partly a nostalgia for a past order, partly a premonition of the instability of the present, partly an unknown hope for the future. The courtiers assemble for the embarkation for Cythera but the poignancy of the occasion is due to the implication that when they get there it will not be the legendary place they expect—the guillotines will be falling.[34]

As Berger's brutal gag makes clear, the philosophical importance of Watteau's art lies in its Janus-faced ambivalence with regard to the cross-faded disintegration of time-as-eternity and advent of time-as-history. In a sense, Watteau creates images that allow us to feel and contemplate the transition between eternity and history; in a sense the two main attractions of the painting (that is, the "historical" actions of visible human bodies and the "eternal" rhythms of the invisible body of nature) split our desire and identify what is at stake in the transition, our fleeting possession of human bodies open to both religious and modern interpretations of the cosmos. When we fully engage with it and come to understand all that it implies, Watteau's art converts our bodies into sensitive instruments that register our thoughts about modernity.

This extended digression through several nested analogies for Renoir's Cytherean chronotope was designed to inaugurate one of the most important of these thoughts, to begin a process of systematic disorientation that the argument of this book will depend on. Each of the effects we have looked at (the seashell analogy, Watteau's painting, that painting as a symptom of its own historical moment) is manifestly produced by the particular structure of time that frames or organizes it; though the basic experience of Cythera—for example, being conscious of the freshness and sweetness of fleeting sensual stimuli—may well appear to be primary or natural, the successive thought experiments in the digression were designed to show that it is in fact a secondary effect, an epiphenomenon produced within and by a particular historical context, the unfinished, and perhaps unfinishable, event of modernity. The importance of this distinction comes to light when one appreciates just how much of modern culture and philosophy is built on interpretations of this experience as primary, natural, or prehistoric.

Without a doubt the most influential of these interpretations is Rousseau's description of the state of nature in the *Second Discourse* ("Discourse on the Origin and Foundations of Inequality among Men"), which became the wellspring of broadly diffused romantic cultural tendencies and of a philosophical lineage that includes Kant, Hegel, Nietzsche, Freud, and Heidegger. Though we will consider the specific consequences of this influence later in this study, at this point I simply want to present the hypothesis that the historical influence of Rousseau's account of the state of nature is dependent on the aesthetic/ideological conviction it receives unacknowledged from the specifically *modern* experience of Cythera.

By treating "modern Man," characterized as an anxious, self-alienated, social-role-playing bourgeois hypocrite, as an artifact of what human nature had *become*, Rousseau covertly jettisoned the eternal sense of fleetingness as an awareness of mortality in favor of an interpretation that was strictly historical. The experience of abundant time, freedom, and ineffable sensual experience lost was now interpreted to be the distant *memory* of an original human nature violated by the events of humanity's historical evolution; the lived experience of a particular elite segment of eighteenth-century French society was thus given a radical new interpretation, enlarged, and projected back onto human history as a whole.

In contrast to all preceding accounts, Rousseau envisions our original human nature as being so underdetermined by either internal desires and needs (only the moderate and easily satisfied needs for food, sex, shelter, and sleep) or external necessities and obligations (since nature itself easily satisfies the individual's basic needs, there are no family or social responsibilities, nor any natural causes for human conflict) that the capacity to reason and the existence of other human beings was almost superfluous: "Let us conclude that wandering in the forests, without industry, without speech, without domicile, without war and without liaisons, with no need of his fellowmen, likewise with no desire to harm them, perhaps never even recognizing anyone individually, savage man, subject to few passions and self-sufficient, had only the sentiments and intellect suited to that state; he felt only his true needs, saw only what he believed he had an interest to see; and his intelligence made no more progress than his vanity."[35] For our purposes, Rousseau's portrait is significant not for the many bizarre or counterintuitive details required to support an image of natural man as fundamentally solitary, pre-rational, and pre-ethical (for example, the fact that, unlike all other species of mammal, savage human beings are presumed not to recognize their own children) but for the fact that the strangeness of those details was "suppressed" because they served to redefine Cythera as a *historical* memory of surplus time and radical human autonomy, that is, as an ideal that the "willfulness" of eighteenth-century France (and modern human beings of later times and other places) found irresistibly compelling.[36] If, as I have tried to argue, the experience of Cythera is only an effect of certain living contradictions—a by-product of the unfinished transition between religious and modern worldviews—then Rousseau can be said to have appropriated that effect (and turned it into a problem) in order to project a contradiction-free image of its opposite (the solution to the problem). Rousseau deftly drew on the anxieties and feelings of loss engendered by early modernity to establish a number of fundamental oppositions (between human nature and human history, the individual and society, human desire and reason, and so on) that did not previously exist; whether we consider the carefree, undetermined "wandering" of the savage human being or his or her frictionless amorality ("Do what is good for you with the least possible harm to others"), in either case we are presented with an unprecedented utopia of individual autonomy or freedom—a prehistoric moment that allows one to measure one's discontent with the present and thereby project future goals achievable through human action.[37] It was in order to concretely imagine both the loss of that primordial utopia and those future goals that modern practices of historical representation, and the commonsense notion of "history" we now take for granted, dramatically emerged as the dominant mode of organizing time.[38]

The work of cultural historian Stephen Bann illuminates this hidden connection between romanticism and the emergence of the modern conception of historical time:

> "History" is the relentless appropriation by text, figure or scenographic representation, of what is already irretrievably lost. It is an effect of camouflage, or perhaps, in Freud's sense, a work of mourning, which achieves the displacement of one type of dispossession (the loss of the centrality of "man") onto another (the loss, or absence, of the past).... One of the most potent causes,

and one of the most widespread effects, of Romanticism was a remarkable enhancement of the consciousness of history. From being a literary genre whose borders were open to other forms of literature, history became over half a century or so the paradigmatic form of knowledge to which all others aspired.[39]

With Rousseau's image of a past utopia in view we can begin to appreciate the tremendous dynamism of his influence, for what was understood to have been lost in historical time must, in principle, be regainable through various forms of historical action, whether through individual attempts to return to the past via romantic self-fashioning, communion with nature and artistic self-expression, collective projects of rediscovering and restoring the "natural" integrity of national cultures (*culture* in the modern, quasi-organic sense being a concept that the German philosophers Hamann, Herder, Kant, and Hegel all derived from Rousseau's critique of the Enlightenment ideal of *civilization* as unnatural, alienating, and so on), programs of revolutionary action put forward by the ideologues of the French Revolution and further developed by Hegel and Marx (all motivated by *The Social Contract*'s vision of a prospective utopia based in the "general will"), or the project of representing and in some sense recovering the lost origins of a unique individual self developed by Nietzsche and Freud, Proust and Lacan. Though on one level all these tendencies appear to be distinct and have often been defined by their conflict with each other (that is, the conservative or right-wing concern with restoring national culture versus the progressive or left-wing concern with achieving social justice through revolution), they can nonetheless be said to compose a single movement insofar as they spring from a common set of assumptions first made explicit by Rousseau. As Bann argues, their manifest diversity and antagonistic relationships have served to conceal the concept of time-as-history they share and the common root in romanticism that is exposed whenever the master-narratives of History give way to the counternarratives of historicism:

> Much has been written about the collapse, over the last few decades, of the ideology of modernism, which like Romanticism before it was a pervasive cultural movement involving every aspect of social, political, and intellectual life. This is not the place to comment on the various attempts to formulate a compelling definition of "Postmodernism," which would effectively describe the eclectic and diverse tendencies of the present day. But one point is

obvious. To the extent that Modernism has receded as a cultural paradigm, it has inevitably brought back into view the lineaments of Romanticism, which now appear uncomfortably plain to us once again. The progressive and internationalist ideology of modernism can hardly survive an epoch that, in Europe at any rate, makes us witnesses to the gradual disintegration of cultural identity into its component parts. We seem to be living through once again (though in vastly changed circumstances) the shock of new nationhood emerging from the supranational groupings that marked the experience of contemporaries of the French Revolution and the Napoleonic invasions. In other words, we can grasp the Romantic experience in a way that was inconceivable when the modern paradigm was still in place.[40]

Though the specific reference here is to the demise of the Cold War masternarrative (interpreted by some to be the "end of History") and the resurgent nationalism manifest in the disintegration of the former Yugoslavia in the early 1990s, one can see this pattern continuing to reproduce itself in various domains of global culture.[41] Anyone browsing a bookstore should be able to recognize or sense the connection between the not-so-quiet desperation of global society—the unacknowledged dispossessions of the contemporary cultural moment and our post-9/11 sense of endless war— and the "effect of camouflage" performed by the exuberant proliferation of nonfiction (led by short histories of everything from time and Islam to codfish and the smile), the comforting undergrowth of the past in which we hide from the bewildering chaos of the present.[42]

Rousseau's radical reinterpretation of the experience of Cythera represents a major turning point in the development of modernity because it set romanticism in motion and made the lived experience of the present comprehensible as a moment of passage between two historical moments of utopia, the retrospective utopia of the state of nature and various prospective utopias in which that natural state is imagined to be recovered. Within the ideological penumbra of romanticism, the lived experience of the present was understood to be less real or authentic than the utopias against which it was judged, and as a consequence the suffering and dissatisfactions of human life increasingly came to be seen as historically created problems that romantic abstractions in the form of historically realizable utopias could solve. This movement from a pervasive and ambiguous experience (Cythera) to a radical reinterpretation of that experience (Rousseau's account of the state of nature) whose historical consequences (romantic thought and projects of action) then obscure their starting point is the moment of thought we are concerned with: if Rousseau's interpretative hijacking of the experience of Cythera is a pivotal moment in the history of modernity, then Renoir's return to the Janus-faced Cytherean chronotope manifest in Watteau's painting can start to be appreciated as an act of critical reflection on everything that followed from Rousseau's interpretation, that is, modernity itself.

Having sketched the big picture of what is at stake, we need to return to the films and begin to examine how Renoir creates the effect of Cythera in *Boudu sauvé des eaux* and *Une partie de campagne*, and with our earlier consideration of the second film in mind, several connections with what we have said about Watteau should already be obvious. The film clearly represents a modern-dress *petit bourgeois fête galante* and gives us an explicit acknowledgment of this lineage in Rodolphe's play-acting the role of a neoclassical satyr. The relevance of the seashell effect to what we called the dialectic of idioms in the film should, I hope, also be manifest. While on one level we are engaged in a comedic narrative of seduction analogous to the "action" in Watteau's fetes, on another level both we and certain of the characters are "distracted" by the "grace notes" of the natural setting; an image perfectly comparable to one of Watteau's "pauses" would be the shot of Henri and Henriette in the boat discussing whether they should turn back and rejoin the group, he in the back, rowing and leaning forward to apply insistent pressure through quiet questions and suggestions, she in the front and facing away from him, her head tilted to the side and down, hesitant (until her mother and Rodolphe catch up and pass them, with her mother shouting that they are, as the popular euphemism has it, "going all the way"). The storm sequence and epilogue that follows the celebrated close-up of Henriette allows the film to actually represent something that Watteau's painting can only suggest, deftly framing the events of the day within a romantic interpretation of the cosmic time and space of nature. Renoir's narrative thus renders Watteau's invisible dissolve or ghosting effect visible, but to fully understand how he achieves this effect we need to consider how the character types of this chronotope interact within the matrix of Renoir's style.

Like those in the Flaubertian, the types in the Cytherean chronotope are defined by the ideological attitudes proper to their respective places in society (that is, Lestingois the Parisian bourgeois, the Dufours as Parisian *petit bourgeois*, Poulain the provincial *petit bourgeois*, Boudu the homeless nomad), but they are not, like the Flaubertian, completely enclosed within those attitudes. In contrast to the blinding and compulsive passions that drive the Flaubertian types and ultimately determine the narrative outcomes of their films, the social reflexes of the Cytherean types simply keep them—loosely, and most of the time—within the bounds of their humdrum routines. In contrast to the desperate strategies concocted and enacted by Emma Bovary and Maurice Legrand to escape their ennui-ridden life-traps, we have the bookseller Lestingois and his maid, Anne-Marie, getting through the droning hours of the day by fantasizing about their nightly metamorphosis into "Daphnis" and "Chloe," or the tramp Boudu wandering the streets and parks of Paris and gleaning his daily bread (other people's leftovers) almost by accident/chance: if the narratives of the Cytherean films depended solely on the routine passions of their characters, they would be entirely episodic. The films are not in fact episodic because the characters always become animated by an external force that attracts them to one another, a sort of spring fever that ambiguously blends carnal desire, curiosity, and amusement but seems to be governed by a more general sense of simply wondering about the otherness or difference of the Other. When Lestingois first catches sight of Boudu in his telescope, his admiration for the "perfect specimen" of a tramp is only a product of his amateur Balzacianism, that is, based on what he wrongly takes to be the exact correspondence between Boudu and the idea of a tramp given in his literary culture. In contrast, his attraction to Boudu after he saves him from drowning is driven by the amusing pleasure of realizing what he *does not* know, by the fact that everything Boudu says and does is contrary to his bourgeois expectations. Boudu himself is at first simply a fish out of water who just wants to get back in the water, but he soon finds himself in the grips of what is for him an unfamiliar carnal attraction to both Anne-Marie and Madame Lestingois, an attraction that motivates him to spruce himself up in order to gain their favors. Madame Lestingois, who for most of the film seems to be the only member of the household impervious to Boudu's charms, is, close to the end, quickly seduced by him; in retrospect we are led to reinterpret the recurrent tropes of her character—her protests at his presence, her complaints of exhaustion and ennui, her constant sighing and displays of indolence and abstraction (almost always wearing her dressing gown, lying down in bed, or flopping over comfortable chairs)—as being the unmistakable signs of a disavowed attraction. It is important to recognize, however, that the external force in question cannot simply be reduced to sexual desire; as both Lestingois and Anne-Marie soon come to realize, a practical consequence of the former's attraction to Boudu is that they are prevented from fulfilling their desire for each other. The force in question affects the characters like the grace notes of the landscape in Watteau; with the fine, soft frenzy of a nonviolent Dionysius it gently dislodges them from their routines and identities. It is desire without a clear goal or orientation, a boat that happily yields and allows itself to be carried by the current toward an unknown and unimaginable destination. When Boudu and Madame Lestingois rise into the frame after the ellipsis in which they have sex, there is no sense of any provisional narrative closure (for example, "repressed desire consummated," "the bourgeois hypocrite unmasked," "the wild man tamed"); though she is giddy with delight and he is wide-eyed with the novel intensity of the experience, they cannot be said to have arrived at Cythera because, though they are no longer who they were, it is unclear (both to themselves and to us) exactly who they have become: they are still only "embarking."

This external force of attraction between the characters in the Cytherean chronotope also produces human figures analogous to the abstracted women in Watteau's fetes. Like the types in the Flaubertian chronotope, there is little direct eye contact between those in the Cytherean. Any dialogue between characters who have a familiar or routine relationship (such as that between Lestingois and his wife or the members of the Dufour family) is typically presented in medium shots that include both parties, neither of which looks directly at the other. This recurrent composition expresses the fact that each character's familiarity with the other renders any effort of undivided attention unnecessary; whether they are bored, annoyed, or simply comfortable with the other's predictability, they can in any case interact while part of their attention is manifestly elsewhere. As a representative example of how such figures operate, I would point to a medium two-shot in the Lestingois residence just prior to Boudu's return from the barber and seduction of Madame Lestingois. Madame Lestingois has just discovered two different messes Boudu has made (leaving the water running in the kitchen and using her underwear to polish his shoes), and, in a moment, Lestingois is about to discover what for him will be "the last straw," the fact that Boudu, in a gag of exquisite depth, spat in a first edition of Balzac's *The Physiology of Marriage*. As the two characters sit and come to agree on the fact that Boudu has to go, they both face in the same direction, occasionally turning in each other's direction but never making eye contact. While on one level their dialogue expresses a familiar opposition in their attitudes to Boudu (Lestingois's now-attenuated feeling of responsibility for "the poor wretch," his wife's consistent aversion to "the brute"), the abstracted quality of their respective gazes reveals other issues that each is feeling and thinking about. In Lestingois's gaze we recognize the extent to which his affection for Boudu has been ground down by the embargo that the tramp's presence has inadvertently placed on his affair with Anne-Marie; we can see him re-weighing that affection against the prospect of ongoing sexual starvation and more outrages against propriety from Boudu. In Madame Lestingois's gaze we can start to discern what her imminent seduction will soon make clear, that she has all along been "protesting too much" and has been privately enjoying the frissons produced by her proximity to Boudu. Her consistent refusal to look directly at Boudu, which we might have read as only an expression of her disdain, now appears to have been the measure of her disavowed desires; when her husband suddenly agrees to get rid of the tramp, the unexpectedness of this event forces her to acknowledge those desires, and she now seems to be stalling for time, nodding and softly huffing, until she arrives at a comically expedient, Chaplinesque means of resolving the contradiction between her professed stance and her real feelings: after her husband discovers the crime against Balzac and the institution of marriage, she tells him that *she* will be the one to tell Boudu he has to leave, thus creating the opportunity for her seduction. The performances of both characters here articulate complex trajectories of thought that lead out from the action their dialogue represents, trajectories that testify to the impact of the spring fever that Boudu introduced to their lives.

If the performances in the Cytherean films reproduce Watteau's abstracted figures, their mise-en-scène is designed to articulate a sharp contrast between two spatiotemporal worlds analogous to those in our seashell example. In *Boudu sauvé des eaux* we are, on the one hand, presented with the world of the Lestingois bookshop and residence, a dry, close, sound-absorptive studio space in which the silence and the relentless immobility of objects, furniture, and dust reign supreme; the drone of the empty hours in this setting is underlined by the many scenes in which characters idly fiddle with a book or other object, cast about for something to do, or simply sigh and shrug to themselves. On the other hand we are presented with the open location space of Paris and beyond, a world of diverse and unceasing human activities, the movement of fresh and polluted air, sunlight, dappling shadows, flowing water, and a dense, ever-changing mix of ambient sounds—traffic noises, crowds, children's cries, street musicians, wind in trees, the buzz of insects, birds chirping—that are reflected and absorbed in rapid alternation. If the first world is defined by the feeling of an unrelenting homogeneity (characters listlessly pass from one room to another but the silence and sense of life suspended does not change), each of the exterior locations we encounter is defined by a unique audiovisual texture, from the echoing, shadow-dappled, cathedral-like gloom of the Bois de Boulogne where Boudu searches for his dog, Black; to the hot, sunlit, sound-absorbing pathways of the park, where he has a series of episodic encounters; to the vast, open, noise-filled portion of the Seine, where his attempted suicide and rescue take place. Taken as a whole, the heterogeneity of this world contrasts strongly with the first, a contrast that Renoir take pains to underline by boosting the sound of the location space every time a door or window between the two is opened or shut. The mise-en-scène of the film forces us to feel and subconsciously reflect on the starkly different possibilities of experience that obtain within the centripetal space-time of the Lestingois establishment and the centrifugal space-time of Paris and the wider world offscreen.

As we have already seen in the case of *Une partie de campagne*, the ending of *Boudu sauvé des eaux* demonstrates the ontological primacy of the ocean landscape of the location space through a process analogous to Watteau's invisible dissolves. But whereas the fact of such a dissolve transition in *Une partie* was made explicit through the representation of a temporal ellipsis separating the events of the fete from the epilogue (the dissolve that starts somewhere in the middle of the backwards tracking shot from the boat clearly ends in the titles that announce the epilogue), in *Boudu* the dissolve is truly invisible insofar as it cannot be located in representational terms; here, as so often throughout this study, I am forced to defer to the incomparable precision and flow of Bazin's account, which I must quote at length:

> Boudu, newly wed, throws himself into the water. Dramatic or psychological logic would demand that such an act have a precise meaning. Is it despair, suicide? Probably not, but it is at least an attempt at escape. Boudu is fleeing the chains of a bourgeois marriage. This interpretation, although more ambiguous, would still lend a certain meaning to the shot. Boudu's fall would remain an *act*. But Renoir, like his character, quickly forgets the act in favor of the *fact*, and the true object of the scene ceases gradually to be Boudu's intentions and becomes rather the spectacle of his pleasure and, by extension, the enjoyment that Renoir derives from the antics of his hero. The water is no longer "water" but more specifically the water of the Marne in August, yellow and glaucous. Michel Simon floats on it, turns over, sprays like a seal; and as he plays we begin to perceive the depth, the quality, even the tepid warmth of that water. When he comes up on the bank, an extraordinary slow 360-degree pan shows us the countryside he sees before him. But this effect, by nature banally descriptive, which could indicate space and liberty regained, is of unequalled poetry precisely because what moves us is *not* the fact that this countryside is once again Boudu's domain, but that the banks of the Marne, in all the richness of their detail, are intrinsically beautiful. At the end of the pan, the camera picks up a bit of grass where, in close-up, one can see distinctly the white dust that the heat and the wind have lifted from the path. One can almost feel it between one's fingers. Boudu is going to stir it up with his foot. If I were deprived of the pleasure of seeing *Boudu* for the rest of my days, I would never forget that grass, that dust, and their relationship to the liberty of a tramp.[43]

By the end of the sequence Bazin describes we have decisively yet mysteriously passed between two incommensurable worlds; the "water," "countryside," "grass," and "dust" represented in the theatrical narrative have undergone a process of transubstantiation and are now real, irreducibly contingent water, countryside, grass, and dust. This feeling of contingency is articulated by the shift in what Bazin is describing as he passes from Boudu to Michel Simon and from the actor's body to the imagined sensations of color and touch that it allows him to infer (the tepid, glaucous quality of the yellow water, the movement of dry hot air, white dust against one's fingers and Boudu's foot); though Boudu is still present before us, his

FIGURE 2.5.

Grass, dust, and the liberty of a tramp in *Boudu sauvé des eaux*.

body is now only a fact in the material infinity of cosmic time and space, one contingent detail in what has effectively become an empty landscape devoid of figures or action. The dissolve is truly invisible because Renoir and the spectator literally forget the world of representation (and cannot specify exactly when or where we forgot it).

It is this chronotopic transmutation that produces the concept of liberty that Bazin derives from the scene and not, as he takes pains to point out, some banal theatrical representation of "Boudu's liberty regained"; far from being Rousseauian abstractions, the pleasures and freedom of nature are simply the result of paying attention to the sensual qualities and true dimensions of what is present in front of us. It is significant that over the course of the passage Bazin shifts from describing the general effects of the film image on an abstract spectator to describing the specific effects of individual referents on himself. Bazin's affirmation of an intrinsic connection between the grass and dust and liberty is not mere poetic hyperbole; contingent details one cannot forget are connected with the experience of liberty insofar as they liberate us from our own willful habits of thought and perception and, in a paradoxical sense, allow art to transcend its own mediation. Roland Barthes offers an example that is strikingly similar to Bazin's to make this very point:

> There is a photograph by Kertész (1921) which shows a blind gypsy violinist being led by a boy; now what I see, by means of this "thinking eye" which makes me add something to the photograph, is the dirt road; its texture gives me the certainty of being in central Europe; I perceive the referent (here, the photograph really transcends itself: is this not the sole proof of its art? To annihilate itself as a medium, to be no longer a sign but the thing itself?), I recognize, with my whole body, the straggling villages I passed through on my long-ago travels in Hungary and Rumania.[44]

Just as the dust on the grass in *Boudu* provides Bazin with an inalienable sense of liberty, so does the texture of the dirt road in the Kertész photograph allow Barthes to recover his long-ago experiences in central Europe with certainty; what is important to note in each case is the existential dimension of the experience ("recognizing with one's whole body") and that it happens independently of any willful intention. We do not need to remember or imagine what we cannot forget, nor, even if we wished to, could we: it only can arrive as a gift from an anonymous friend.

In Renoir's Cytherean films the contingency of nature is used to express a sense of possibility and openness, the common and ordinary utopia of the present, the new world that can appear whenever the faculty of loving attention causes our willfulness to give way. As in many of the landscape paintings of the impressionists (especially those of Renoir *père*, Monet, and Sisley), Renoir's mobilization of the Cytherean chronotope offers an explicit representation of cosmic space and time as a utopian site of possibility somewhere in between the ideological regimes of eternity and history, and like Watteau's paintings, it stands as an implicit critique of cultural modes that totalize time-as-history (in the case of the impressionists, David and the *genre historique* that dominated academic painting during the early nineteenth century). In Renoir's version this ground of Cythera is something that over the course of the film either appears (*Boudu*) or disappears (*Une partie*). In either case, the finite events represented in the centripetal space-time of the film's narrative ("the shell") are contrasted with the infinite possibilities of the centrifugal space-time of the cosmos ("the ocean"); though the first film sets the narrative comically within the infinite ground of these possibilities and the second tragically contains the possibilities within a moment of the romantic narrative (for the rest of their days Henri and Henriette believe that what happened or might have happened on that day in the country is *more* than they will ever experience), in either case nature-as-Cythera is invoked as a utopian place where things can be radically different, where anything can happen, where you can simply and efficiently forget yourself.

The experience of Cythera is like falling asleep somewhere unusual (in a public park, on the couch in someone else's home, in the back of a car, or in various university settings) and then waking up and wondering for a moment where and who you are. It is a brief moment when the old world based in one's sedimented disposition of conscious and unconscious allegiances to eternity and history has yet to click back in place, when one recalls the experience of waking up as a child and almost feels one might be somebody else; though a second later we usually remember with a sad jolt exactly where and who we are, the memory of Cythera nonetheless remains as a small yet intractable object of hope and/or regret. However dim or fleeting such experiences may be, their memory remains in us because it is rooted in the profound trust in our parents and the infinite world behind them, the overflowing sense of giftedness and hope, the oceanic feeling, that most of us experienced as children; though life may have eroded most of that feeling, our memory of it nonetheless continues to play a crucial, if confused and submerged, role in shaping our expectations and actions as adults: though we consciously organize the narratives of our adult lives in terms of historical time, the utopias we unconsciously seek are rooted in our memories of the eternity we experienced as children.

At this juncture it is necessary to state as a blunt hypothesis what the reader will be able to reasonably accept only after this book's attempt at a demonstration is complete: that Renoir believed that what we have called Cythera is the permanent ground of human experience, reality, and that the skeptical agenda of his philosophical critique of modernity was based in this conviction. Though it would probably be impossible to reconstruct the process of reasoning that led Renoir to hold such a belief, positing it now will help orient our attempt to develop the concept of Cythera and allow us to start to make sense of Renoir's frequent but often ambiguous references to "reality": "When you drive around at night on the roads outside Paris, you're in a fairyland. In the end, reality is always fairylike. In order to avoid making reality seem fairylike, certain writers go to a great deal of trouble to present it in a truly strange light. But if we leave it as it is, it's fairylike."[45] With the faith that reality-as-Cythera is the natural ground and object of human desire, the single issue of cultural politics that Renoir addresses most consistently in interviews is the romantic reinterpretation, hijacking and/or misdirection of that desire:

> I love reality, and I'm happy to love it because it brings me infinite joy. But it happens that many people hate it, and most human beings, whether or not they make films, whether they're workers, store owners, or dramatists, create a kind of veil between reality and themselves. And in order to create this veil more easily, they use elements provided by society: the people around them, conversations in the street, newspapers, theatrical productions. This veil is extremely monotonous, because it becomes the same for everybody. And so when someone pierces through it and shows the reality behind it, people say, "Oh, no! That's not true! That's not the way it really is!" But it is the truth.
>
> After all, the reality is in being enchanted. It demands great patience, work and good faith to find it. I'm convinced, in any case, that it isn't a question of talent or gifts, just of good faith. If you want to find reality, you'll find it. You just have to eliminate whatever seems to you to have been created by the habits of your times, to eliminate these habits first, but to take back later the ones that seem to conform with reality. The reality of daily events, of romantic adventures, is absolutely twisted, deformed, as if they were seen in a funhouse mirror. I even think the reality of romantic adventures is the one that is the most deformed, even more than that of films, novels, or newspapers. It's insane how lovers who fight can suddenly see facts and the world through a distorted glass and lose all sense of reality. It's the romantic tradition. We have to deal with a hundred and fifty years of romantic tradition concerning love, women, the way to approach women, what we call emotions. Despite its lace covering, the reality of love seems much truer to me in Marivaux, and up until the end of the eighteenth century, even in the revolutionary works. It must have changed during the Empire. It might have been Germany's influence.
>
> Anyway, because romantic adventures are often used as the basis for literature and because these romantic adventures are very distorted, we wind up with a literature and films that are rather distorted.[46]

This passage serves to make several key points of Renoir's philosophical project explicit. The first is that he identifies romanticism as the root of a broad spectrum of ideological tendencies that veil or obscure reality. In Renoir's view the influence of romanticism stretches from our intimate understandings of our own emotions and relationships through the culture we consume to the public events we read about in newspapers; for him fundamental reflection entails recognizing the effects of such tendencies and discarding the assumptions that estrange one from reality. The second point worth noting is that understanding the problem of romanticism entails reflection on the large-scale narrative of cultural history that has brought it into being; Renoir's remarks show that he takes the necessity of such reflection for granted, and they echo both Auerbach and Bann in identifying the French Revolution and the Napoleonic period as key moments in that narrative. A third and crucial point is that Renoir reverses the romantic understanding of reality as the experience of disillusionment, wherein the reality of the present is always experienced as *less* or *worse* than we thought; for Renoir the enchantment of Cythera is the permanent or primary cause and our experiences of disenchantment with the present are the distorted effects of conditional or secondary causes such as romantic ideologies. The fourth and final element worth noting is the archaic virtue of good faith or sincerity that Renoir resurrects as the only prerequisite for arriving at the truths of Cythera. A moment's reflection on how insipid and disparaging the adjectives "sincere" and "earnest" have become in postmodernity should be sufficient to illuminate the provocative anachronism of Renoir's use of the expression "good faith." As our examination proceeds, this archaic virtue will emerge as an important element in his rethinking of modernity, and, in a more general sense, the conceptions of Cythera and romanticism we have developed in this section will be crucial to understanding the next two chronotopes we need to examine.

The Naturalist Chronotope

Toni (1935) and *La bête humaine* are the purest examples of the third main chronotope to appear in the historical sequence of the French Renoir, and I label this *Naturalist Melodrama* in view of the fact that the narratives of the films represent the deterministic relations between protagonists and milieux found in the tradition running from Balzac and Zola (author of *La bête humaine*) to Gorky (author of *The Lower Depths*), von Stroheim, and poetic realism. As outlined by Auerbach, this chronotope presents us with characters whose fates are ultimately seen to be determined by a complex of environmental and/or hereditary factors. In contrast to the Flaubertian chronotope, where the original cause that envelops each character in a solipsistic bubble is located deep within the type (for example, the mythical moments of determination in a distant, unrepresented past that made Emma Bovary and Maurice Legrand romantics, Charles Bovary a bourgeois, Dédé a pimp), in naturalism the causes that determine the fate of the characters are seen to act on them from the outside. This allows for the representation of tensions within the characters as they struggle with their situations; they *can* struggle with their situations in a way the Flaubertian types cannot. In both films, the main protagonists, Toni and Lantier, are in the grip of a semiconscious dissatisfaction with their lots in life, the hard present and empty future of being, respectively, a migrant laborer and a locomotive driver. Though they both know they do not like where they are, their exhausted imaginations cannot see beyond the implacable ruts of their lives; they cannot imagine a real alternative and can only act—or rather *react*—in a more-or-less unconscious fashion. In this context, each finds an escape from his dissatisfaction in the form of a woman who will, in the end, be the death of him.

This narrative trajectory from physical and mental imprisonment in a milieu to the doomed attempt to escape through romantic union with an object of desire is what Renoir takes from the tradition of naturalism, but what distinguishes his mobilization of the chronotope from the canonical examples of the tradition is that he does not represent his protagonists' fates as necessary or inevitable, as the inescapable result of the milieu galvanizing their natural impulses. Gilles Deleuze argues that in the classic naturalism of, for example, Zola or von Stroheim, the human characters and milieux represented always "communicate" with unrepresented "originary worlds" where the characters are animals ("the fashionable gentleman a bird of prey, the lover a goat, the poor man a hyena"), the milieux constitute "an immense rubbish-dump or swamp," and all human impulses converge in a single "great death-impulse": "The originary world is therefore both radical beginning and absolute end; and finally it links the one to the other, puts one into the other, according to a law which is that of *the steepest slope*. It is thus the world of a very special kind of violence (in certain aspects, it is the radical evil); but it has the merit of causing an originary image of time to rise, with the beginning, the end, and the slope, all the cruelty of Chronos."[47] As in Auerbach's account of the organic-occult dimension in Balzac, Deleuze recognizes in naturalism a more primary "Animality" that "floods over into Humanity by an immense current of life" and leads us to feel that the actions of the characters are "prior to all differentiation between the human and the animal."[48] With this quasi-Darwinian deterministic metaphysics in view, we can describe the typical narrative of a naturalist text as enacting a fatalistic variant of an invisible dissolve, wherein the gravitational pull along the "steepest slope" drags the purportedly social and rational human world back to its true beginning and ultimate end in irrational impulses; the narrative action becomes transparent to a cosmos-as-primordial-swamp where, in effect, dinosaurs still rule the earth. Though it subtracts the sense of individual autonomy from Rousseau's portrait of the state of nature (and thus turns the amoral "innocence" of nature into the "radical evil" of a Hobbes), canonical naturalism nonetheless depends on the concept of time-as-history that Rousseau first put into play; the civilized human world of social relations and rationality is represented as being only one big historical accident or fluke, an ephemeral bubble that is always in the process of bursting on both the microlevel of the individual psyche and the macrolevel of historical events. Deleuze correctly points out that while Renoir adopted elements of naturalism in many of his films, his versions of the chronotope always failed to take it to its logical conclusion in this historical conception of time. Though Deleuze does not speculate as to the reasons for this "failure," our preceding discussions allow us to suggest an obvious one: Renoir could not bring himself to believe in the steepness of the naturalist slope because his fundamental belief in Cytherean reality would not let him.[49] In Renoir's modified version of naturalism, the relations between characters, and between the characters and their milieux, always have a Cytherean quality, a lucid openness of possibility and purchase, which indicate that "the steepest slope" could, in principle, have been climbed.

Unlike that found in poetic realist films like *Quai des brumes* or *Le jour se lève*, Renoir's mise-en-scène in these films does not isolate the protagonists within the enclosure of a pervasive "atmosphere."⁵⁰ The effect of the milieux on the protagonists is neither occult nor organic but is better understood in a Marxist sense; their jobs imprison Toni and Lantier within a relentless, exhausting routine of physical labor and social humiliation. Rather than allow himself to be ground down and negated by that routine, each protagonist asserts himself through what he believes to be a free act of romantic rebellion in which he commits himself to a woman he thinks he loves. Over the course of each film we come to realize that these acts are not meaningful because they are based in defective recognitions of their objects of desire. However charming they may be, both Josepha and Séverine are opportunistic schemers who hide truths about themselves from their lovers while using the romantic passions they incite to accomplish their own pragmatic goals. In retrospect, both Toni's and Lantier's acts of rebellion are free only in the sense of being irrational and gratuitous responses to their situations; because they are unconscious of the fact they are being used, their fate is, in the final analysis, determined by their own culpable romantic blindness. Renoir takes pains to define this blindness as culpable by showing that it is underdetermined, that it is the result of a choice, and demonstrates this definition through three figures in which the gaze of characters enables the spectator to reflect on their paradoxical decision to be blind.

The first figure is one in which a friend and coworker of the protagonist notices a certain abstraction and rigidity in the latter's behavior, considers him with a worried and attentive gaze, and sometimes offers comments that attempt to break the spell. This figure is most frequently enacted by Toni's fellow-laborer Fernand and Lantier's fireman Pecqueux. Because these characters share the hard life of the milieu in common with the protagonists, their reflections on the cause of their comrades' behavior often seem to involve a moment of self-reflection in which they try to imagine making such a romantic commitment themselves but cannot find any grounds to do so: their deliberations consequently resolve into a facial and/or verbal expression of concern for a friend who seems to be acting irrationally. The protagonist himself generally registers this gaze and/or comments with a sort of peripheral vision that indicates a

FIGURE 2.6.

Pecqueux contemplates Lantier in *La bête humaine*.

brief but inconsequential pause of thought; he listens but cannot hear anything, or what he hears seems insubstantial, and he soon returns to the energizing comfort of his romantic abstraction: the lucid gaze and commonsense reasoning of his comrade is only so much insipid white noise that is quickly drowned out by the deeper music of his passion. Though one may recall many scenes in which this figure is enacted, the final sequence of *La bête humaine* pushes it to the bitterest of ends: in the midst of their run to Paris, Lantier (Jean Gabin) tells Pecqueux (Julien Carette) that he has killed Séverine. After advising Lantier to turn himself in and explain everything that happened ("they'll understand—I do"), Pecqueux numbly considers both his comrade's present behavior and his own useless foresight until the moment Lantier leaps from the locomotive to his death. Carette's limpid attentiveness to Gabin during this sequence dramatically expresses what is implicit in every example

FIGURE 2.7.

Lantier blinded by desire in *La bête humaine*.

of the figure, the sense that the person being looked at is in some sense insane.

The second figure that articulates the romantic blindness of the protagonists is one in which it is recognized by characters who are for some reason opposed to their union with the desired woman. This figure reproduces the hostile and knowing quality of the gaze, the sense of looking-at or objectifying that we saw to be definitive of the Flaubertian chronotope. Toni's rivals for Josepha's affection, Albert and Gaby, often display this quality of looking-at in expressions of ironic amusement at the rigid earnestness of his passion for a woman both consider only a convenient plaything. We can also discern this knowing quality of gaze in the jealous watchfulness of Toni's lover Marie and in Séverine's husband, Roubaud, after Lantier has cuckolded him. Roubaud clearly recognizes a new assertiveness in Lantier and the current of complicity flowing between the driver and his wife, but at this point in the narrative (he has committed a murder and believes Lantier knows about it) he lacks the courage to pursue his reflections much further. In both films this second figure further articulates the blindness of the protagonist's passion through its reflection in the cold gaze of characters who lucidly consider it as an objective fact.

The third and most important figure that serves to define romantic blindness as culpable is one in which the protagonist either is in direct eye contact with the object of his desire (when the desire is actively reciprocated) or deliberately avoids direct eye contact with her (when the desire is not actively reciprocated). In both variants of this figure the gaze of the protagonist reveals a process of inner transformation in which he assents to being blindly dominated by his desire. In the case of Lantier, this process begins in the scene in which he first meets Séverine in the corridor of the train on which she and Roubaud have just killed her godfather and former lover, Grandmorin. As Dudley Andrew notes, Lantier makes "a pact with her eyes" that is then reaffirmed by an exchange of glances at the inquiry into the murder where he says he saw nothing; he explains this to her later by saying, "You asked me with your eyes."[51] In both these instances and in other moments throughout the course of their affair, the process of "answering" the questioning submissiveness of Séverine's gaze is manifest in a three-stage movement that begins with a hard and objectifying attentiveness, proceeds through an inward turn or softening in which Lantier registers the numbing and gratifying effect of her submissiveness on his will and body, and then returns to a new projection of a hard and attentive gaze that is now shot through and fixed in place by his own decision to submit to a love he does not care to understand: Lantier never wonders *why* Séverine gives herself to him—*that* she does so is sufficient. The reciprocated looks between Lantier and Séverine represent a mutual knowingness or complicity predicated on a deliberate obliviousness to certain aspects of oneself and the other. Andrew's evocative descriptions of this process rightly emphasize both the representation of causal circuits flowing between instinct and milieu (characteristic of canonical naturalism) and a culpable, narcissistic blindness:

Desire turns eyes prehensile and follows a biological instinct of looking. Earlier this instinct was directed at Flore by the local men and then by Lantier until Flore drove him mad by looking back. In his awful frenzy his eyes had dropped first to her neck, then rolled up into some inner haze that literally made him blind to his actions. Passion can short-circuit vision and arc lethally behind his eyes. Now Lantier finds in the murderous Séverine the one woman with whom he can exchange looks. Deprived of social affection—the one for reasons of genetics, the other from a trauma of upbringing—they find in the mirror of each other's eyes a self-love that degradation cannot corrode.[52]

The determinism of the naturalist idiom represented in this figure does not have the last word because we have already seen Lantier prove himself capable of resisting his irrational impulses in the case of his innocent sweetheart, Flore; though he almost strangles her in a fit of passion he manages to stop himself, and his ethical recognition of her existence makes him commit to never seeing her again. His relationship with Séverine, on the other hand, is an unlawful love based in a leveling complicity in adultery, crime, and self-deception, a romantic oneness in which a culpable blindness to the Otherness of the other is also an efficient means to avoid the truth about oneself: "They pursue this love to its apotheosis outside the toolshed, as they gaze together at the moon. Here subject and object, image and reflection, are joined on the great mirror of the screen for us to contemplate."[53] Though Lantier is fully absorbed in this lunatic fusion on one level, on another he still knows and appreciates the difference between his true love for Flore and his narcissistic passion for Séverine. His decision to be blind and insane is therefore a culpable one.

His submerged awareness of his own blindness is given its most chilling expression in a shot just after he has stabbed Séverine to death in the Roubaud apartment. He stands in front of a mirror with his back to the camera and is looking down and examining the knife in his hand. A popular love song being sung at the train workers' ball wafts through the window, making us aware of the soft night air caressing the body of the earth and reminding us that Lantier's pal Pecqueux is waiting for and worrying about him at the ball: the brutal gratuitousness of Séverine's murder is accentuated by evoking a world of Cytherean possibilities which that act has now foreclosed. He looks up from the knife and notices his reflection but quickly, almost instinctively, looks down again. But a split

FIGURE 2.8.

Lantier looks in the mirror of self-negation in *La bête humaine*.

second later he looks at himself again, and what we see in this gaze is remarkable, for he is clearly looking at *someone else* whom he considers with a mixture of curiosity, anger, and pity; he seems to remember the face, but since he cannot recall where or when he last saw this person, he simply lets it drop. He no longer recognizes the self he negated, and with his passion for Séverine fully discharged in the act of murder he has become an empty man contemplating his emptiness. He leaves the apartment and spends the night walking the railroad tracks, stumbling and staggering over the ties in a catatonic stupor. A passage in a story by Bennett Sims offers a remarkably apt phenomenological analysis of Lantier's mirror of self-negation, the process of looking-at-oneself that we will return to at various points later in the book; with that larger purpose in mind, and as a kind of not-so-subtle foreshadowing, I believe it is worth briefly digressing to quote from it at length:

You focus on your eyes. You look into them until they begin to look back at you, and your face grows estranged in this way. In no time at all, you cease to recognize your reflection. It looks like a stranger's face: the sunken eyes, the sharp cheekbones. Deep down you know that it is your face. But the more intently you stare at it, the less yourself it seems, for it keeps staring intently back at you. In the muscles of your face—in the sensation of the skin on your cheeks and forehead—you feel your expression to be one of focused concentration and scrutiny. Except this is not the expression that the stranger has on its face. Seeing your so-called concentration and scrutiny reflected on its face, you would swear that it is an expression of tranquil hatred. The face in the mirror regards you with quiet, simmering intensity, the sunken eyes murderous above the sharp cheekbones. It looks as if it wants to kill you. It looks as if it is fantasizing about it right now. And the more frightened that this makes you—the more fearful you feel your own face becoming—the more hateful grows the expression on its face. Its hatred seems to grow in direct proportion to your fear. You even feel a paradoxical fear of becoming any more afraid, a panicked need to stop being afraid *this instant*: not only because your fear is irrational—the face is merely a reflection—but also because you want to staunch the strengthening hatred of its face. Yet you cannot help growing afraid: your fear only mounts, and with it, the hatred, and with it, more fear. When you feel the blood draining from your own face, the reflection's face grows pale, as with rage. And when this makes you short of breath, the reflection's face tightens, as with rage. And when at this your own eyes dry and widen, the look in the reflection's eyes is like a nightmare you are having.[54]

Turning to consider the articulation of the figure of romantic self-deception in *Toni*, we find that it is quite different from that enacted by Lantier, in part because Toni's narrative trajectory moves in the opposite direction from Lantier's: Toni's story begins in a modern relationship with Marie, comparable in certain respects to that of Lantier and Séverine, but throughout the film he pursues the archaic ideal of a pure and noble relationship with Josepha similar to the one between Lantier and Flore. The film opens with a prologue in which Toni arrives in the Midi on the train from Italy and takes a room in Marie's boardinghouse. Then there is an indeterminate ellipsis, and we next find the two of them in a bedroom, with Marie prodding him to wake up, complaining about the lack of ardor in his good-morning kiss, reminding him that things used to be different ("When you came here a foreigner I didn't have to ask you—you held me in your arms, wanted to kiss me all day"), and denigrating other women she thinks might be the cause of his listlessness ("Maybe Josepha? She arrived not long ago and couldn't speak a word of French, and already she's chasing all the men in the neighborhood"). We are led to infer a season past when Toni and Marie found solace from their hard and degrading lives in a love based on mutual recognition; their relationship was not an active leveling based in a complicity in crime but grounded instead in the passive acknowledgment of a common experience of deprival; Marie's comments indicate that though she still thinks they "were made for each other," she now recognizes that he has become tired of her. Here and in later scenes it is made clear that Marie believes Toni's dissatisfaction is the product of his misrecognizing Josepha to be a paragon of sweetness and innocence; for her own reasons she hopes that once Toni sees Josepha for "the cat" she really is he will fall back into his proper place in her arms. Though Marie is largely right about Josepha, she is dead wrong in underestimating the capacity for misrecognition in Toni's brand of romanticism.

Toni's fixed idea of Josepha derives from a much earlier moment in the genealogy of romanticism than the naturalist one that determines Lantier's passion for Séverine. If Lantier is involved in a quasi-Hegelian process of negation in which he and Séverine unite in a base pact to annihilate their own nobility, Toni's love for Josepha derives from a vernacular survival of the chivalric tradition in which the lover commits himself to the height or nobility of the beloved as a means to annihilate his own baseness. We can recognize this lineage in Toni's proposal to Josepha's uncle and guardian, Sebastian, wherein he ardently confesses that he is "afraid to hold her hand"; to Toni, his abject reverence for Josepha's purity and innocence is the measure of true love and should be sufficient reason for Sebastian to "give" Josepha to him in marriage. Sebastian's deadpan reaction to this strange blast from an archaic past articulates the function of the chivalric tradition within peasant culture ("it's alright with him," that is, Toni is a "good sort" who won't fool around on Josepha and endanger the integrity of his family's lineage) and more pragmatic concerns (Toni would be a useful worker on his farm, but he has to "see what Josepha thinks about it," that is, he hasn't kept track of all her ongoing flirtations). Though Sebastian values Toni's anachronistic brand of romantic love (he demonstrates this later by insisting that Toni be godfather to Albert and

Josepha's child), his reaction also expresses an awareness of how inappropriate Josepha is as its object.

Toni himself enacts the figure of his "decision to be blind" most dramatically in the scenes in which he is brutally confronted by the fact of Josepha's relationships with other men. We can see it in the scene where he first discovers her relationship with Albert and the scene much later when he learns of her long-term affair with her cousin Gaby. In each scene the discovery forces Toni to pause his relentless fight to serve her and reflect, and in each case this process of reflection is depicted in a shot in which he turns his gaze away from the other characters. What is striking about the actor Charles Blavette's expression in these shots is how suddenly far away he seems from the dramatic events that have just happened; we experience the turn of his head as an abrupt ellipsis in time that carries us not to the angry or horrified beginning of reflection on what he has just learned (that is, as the causal logic of the situation would lead us to expect) but to what appears to be a calm and familiar locus of earlier reflections: his instinctive reaction to being confronted with a harsh truth about Josepha is to turn away and *return* to some distant romantic comfort zone. His actions and comments when he returns from that zone allow us to infer what happens there; because he always returns to fight on Josepha's behalf we understand that he has somehow managed to believe in her purity by reinterpreting every damning situation she is involved in as one in which her innocence was (yet once again?!) taken advantage of: the romantic commitment that grounds his identity comes to increasingly depend on the counterfactual conviction that Josepha is an innocent child.

These moments in which Toni turns away from the melodramatic action in front of him only push to an extreme a more general quality of his gaze and body language wherein he shrinks from making direct eye contact with Josepha or any other character who might trouble his romantic convictions; though he likes being close to her, doing physical tasks for her, and fighting on her behalf (that is, *serving* her as a knight serves his lady), his gaze instinctively turns inward and becomes occluded by a mist of tenderness at any prospect of any contact that might put those convictions to the test. Though by the end of the film Josepha and several other characters have all noticed this abstraction and have either explicitly called Toni a child or made comments implying he is one, it seems that nothing they might say or do can break the spell. Since he is not in fact a child, we can only assess this pattern of turning away from what is in front of him, this regressive blindness, to be a deliberate and irresponsible act. Though Toni may believe himself to be engaged in a clear-sighted and noble endeavor, he is, like Lantier, deep in the grip of a solipsistic masochism.

My purpose in connecting *Toni* and *La bête humaine* along the axis of these figures is not to deny the many differences between the two films but rather to pull those differences into sharp focus and illuminate the dialogical tensions within the Naturalist chronotope. Although the contrasts between the mise-en-scène, location, and representation of society in the two films could not be greater, the similar narrative trajectories of their protagonists allow us to reflect on these contrasts; reconstructing a common axis of internal realism enables us to recognize the significance of their respective treatments of external realism.

The representation of working-class society in *Toni* is connected to an awareness of the warm and sensual body of the planet. With the signal exception of the northern overseer Albert, who rides a noisy motorcycle that drowns out the sounds of nature, all the working-class characters are shown traversing the lush, hilly landscape of the Midi in ways that make us aware of both the pull of gravity on their bodies and the Cytherean qualities of the environment: jaunty newcomers walk down from the train station while singing and playing guitars like strolling players from the commedia dell'arte; weary veterans trudge in small groups to and from the quarry where they work; characters stop to chat with friends; they ride or walk bicycles, give each other lifts on bicycles, and borrow/lend bicycles; they help each other to pull carts or carry things; they take desperate shortcuts across wild, pathless portions of the landscape. The practical decisions in which characters select from the available routes, means, styles, and rates of locomotion articulate their mediation of the physical demands of the location, their routines, and the possibilities of communion provided by acts of comradeship. The distinctive ways they move, pause, and/or resume moving reveal who they have chosen to be within a larger context that was not their choice; though their routines are determined by the boss's clock, they build their identities through the liberty of their responses to the chance encounters that each day offers, encounters that typically occur in a Cytherean space-time in between the main phases (work and rest) and locations (the quarry and boardinghouse) of that routine. They constantly "pause" somewhere in the middle of the landscape and through the community built of such pauses mitigate the depressing narratives of their lives. Renoir's mise-en-scène articulates the connection between this camaraderie and the landscape in many shots in which characters occupy different spots on a hillside and the camera pans and tilts to follow shouted greetings from one to another and in following shots of small groups walking that flow over and caress the landscape.

The camaraderie and comfortable inhabitation of the landscape expressed in these mobile figures and shots contrast with the stiff, repetitive figures of romantic blindness enacted by Toni and with sequences in which a series of static long shots depict the struggle of lone individuals up and/or down inclines. The apotheosis of this kind of sequence is the extended series of shots that follow Toni's absurdly noble decision to take responsibility for Josepha's murder of Albert. The last desperate acts of Toni's life—his frantic efforts to hide the body in the wilderness and represent the death as a suicide, his discovery while doing so and confession to the murder, his escape and run along the railroad bridge before defying his captors and being shot—are all presented in dispassionate long shots that accentuate the tragicomic vehemence with which he carries his romantic commitment to an unnecessary end.

Toni's isolation and fate are defined as absurd precisely through the contrast with the possibilities of meeting and belonging that surround him. Though the social world of *Toni* is made up of displaced peasants who tend to keep their own counsel and mind their own affairs, these characters are also curious about each other and capable of being frank, affectionate, and generous with those they consider their "mates." Their camaraderie is the result of paying close attention to one another and recognizing the subtle difference of each person's response to common situations. This mutual recognition is articulated in a common figure in which two or three characters conduct a conversation while simultaneously engaged in a practical task that connects them to the landscape; though their task typically forces them to face in the same direction, their conversation is punctuated by moments when they turn to look at each other. Whereas in the Cytherean chronotope this disposition of characters was expressed in their distraction and lack of attention to each other, here it fuses practical concerns and peasant reserve with the self-restraint involved in really *listening* to someone else: the characters' expressions as they perform a task also reveal the respect and attention they are giving to each other's words. Their occasional turns toward each other also have a different value than those in the Cytherean version of the figure; in contrast to the unconscious automatism that governs the latter, in *Toni* the turn to look at one's comrade is an act of showing that one has reflected on what he or she has said, an act that is itself often recognized by the speaker turning to meet the listener's gaze and hear his or her response. This periodic meeting of looks is a moment in which each character appears to "check" the sincerity of what the other is saying by looking in his or her eyes, while at the same time implicitly offering his or her own eyes for "checking." The usual result of these look-meetings is that a light of recognizing something new comes into the eyes and expression of one or both of the characters: the Cytherean possibilities of their comradeship are forged by a dialectic of skepticism and trust that takes place within an ongoing physical engagement with the environment.

We can recognize the articulation of this figure in the sequence that begins with Toni and Fernand laying a charge of explosives high up on the wall of the quarry. We first see them in a medium shot looking up the wall from below as they pack the explosives and lay out the fuse. The framing of this shot emphasizes the steepness of the slope and produces a feeling of vertigo in the spectator, which contrasts with the deft movements of the characters and the conversation in which Fernand is telling Toni about Albert being unfaithful to Josepha; the spectator's disorientation serves to accentuate the characters' comfort in the landscape and ability to carry on several activities simultaneously. They light the fuse and walk off, and we cut to an extreme long shot of the floor of the quarry where the unnamed black worker, who also lives at Marie's boardinghouse, walks into the center of the frame and blows a horn that signals the impending blast: the antlike workers scattered throughout the location immediately begin to move away from the quarry wall. Here the deft ellipsis of a causal link (that is, the fact that we do not hear or see Toni or Fernand call or signal the black worker) suggests a sort of telepathy, an invisible communicative economy premised on the workers' constant peripheral awareness of each other. We cut back to another medium shot of Fernand and Toni continuing to talk about Josepha's situation while they are on a ledge, arranging the rope they will use to climb down from it. This shot is from above looking down to the distant floor of the quarry, and our sense of vertigo is even more pronounced than in the first shot of the sequence, while the dangers of the space are now also accentuated by our awareness of the time constraints imposed by the burning fuse. In this "charged" context the discussion of long-term issues—Sebastian's ill health and impending death, the farm having to be sold to pay Albert's debts, and so on—makes us aware of how at one the characters are with each other and the environment; their unconcerned slowness in leaving the ledge and ability to focus on these issues register as a measure of the speed with which they have already thought through their relationship with the situation. This communal process of precise and habitual reflection is made explicit in the next shot in which the black worker and another one are pushing a cart along a track; the other worker remarks that they are far enough away, but the black worker observes that they could still get stray stones at that distance.

The dialogue in the shot that follows illuminates the way the characters use their shared relationship with their job and environment as a means to discover things about others and themselves. We cut to Toni scrambling up to join Fernand sitting under a tree, a vantage point that offers a view of the entire quarry; Toni continues to worry out loud about what will happen to Josepha, while Fernand wonders why the fuse is taking so long. The black worker joins them, and Fernand turns to him and asks if he would go down to get 100,000 francs if they were lying on the quarry floor; the black worker says yes, the fuse won't go off just yet. Fernand turns to Toni and says, "Oh, he's a cocky one, isn't he?" to which Toni replies, "You would end up in a thousand pieces." The black worker looks hurt for a moment, but then his expression changes and he says, with both wonder and conviction, "What wouldn't we do for 100,000 francs?" Fernand's question and the black worker's philosophic inversion of it express their shared understanding that personal values are defined by one's consciousness of concrete situations and dependencies. A moment later the charge goes off, the quarry wall dissolves into a wave of rock and dust, and the scene ends with both Fernand and the black worker nodding their heads in the direction of the explosion. This strange behavior makes sense as a sort of ritual affirmation of their relation to the environment, which at the same time comically references their differing assessments of the hypothetical situation (that is, we infer that the black worker nods because he takes the timing of the event to prove one could have got the money unharmed, while Fernand nods because he takes it to prove that one could not have). Considered as a whole, the dialogue and behavior of Fernand and the black worker in this shot serve to identify a sort of vernacular existentialism at the base of their comradeship; even as they disagree they are in sync with each other because they are in sync with their common situation, while Toni's immobility in between the two nodding figures articulates the abstraction that isolates him from them. Toni's romantic-obsession-unto-death seems absurd when set against his comrades' groundedness in the present, their lucid contemplation of the landscape and each other.

The starkly different representation of a working-class society and its milieu in *La bête humaine* can and should be taken to measure the attenuation of Renoir's hopes during the three years since he made *Toni*. The differences between the two films are all the more striking because *La bête humaine* begins by evoking the workers' efforts to create a community of comrades similar to that in the earlier film. Like that of the quarry workers in *Toni*, the camaraderie of the train workers is rooted in the unique communicative economy that allows them to do their jobs. The opening sequence of the film places us on Lantier's locomotive as it hurtles toward Le Havre and provides us with many shots from his optical point of view, leaning out to the side and looking forward, his head grazed by bridges and tunnels with only inches of clearance. In this dangerous environment of constantly changing landscapes, relentless speed, and deafening noise, Lantier and Pecqueux communicate with whistles, gestures, and meaningful looks that cut through the jostling and noise with razor-like precision. Even more than the quarry workers, their lives clearly depend on the immediate efficacy of every act of communication, and by the time the sequence is over we have come to appreciate the existential dimension of their comradeship. Like the foreign migrants of *Toni*, the train workers of *La bête humaine* are also shown to be dislocated from their homes and families and to have forged pragmatic networks of camaraderie to compensate for this. Thus Pecqueux has a girlfriend at Le Havre and other stations where he has to stop over; when Lantier and Pecqueux are delayed in Le Havre with repairs, the latter easily finds someone to pass the news to his wife (who is a lavatory attendant at a station in Paris); and when the Roubauds need to go to Paris they arrange to stay at Pecqueux's wife's apartment. The easy grace with which the stationmaster Roubaud asks for and receives this favor from the fireman Pecqueux deftly evokes a society of dignified professionals wherein social hierarchies of position (that is, management-labor) are moderated by the mutual and leveling recognition of each individual's indispensable function within the common enterprise.

But even as he sketches the solidarity of this emphatically modern, rootless, working-class domain, Renoir starts to identify the fissures running through it. When Lantier informs the mechanics office at Le Havre about his locomotive's overheated axle box, the manager there clearly follows an unwritten company policy by blaming Lantier for the breakdown and telling him he will have to pay for the repairs himself; Lantier says, "We'll see about that" and later grumbles about the encounter to Pecqueux, saying that the mechanics in Paris are much better than those in Le Havre. Though Renoir does not track the consequences of this incident any further, it serves to illuminate the way in which the capitalist priorities of the railroad bosses infiltrate the community of train workers and divide them against each other.

The fragility of the community of workers, its inherent vulnerability to the capricious actions of external forces, is also illuminated by the causal sequence of events in the film's main narrative, which begins with a chance encounter between Roubaud and *un gros* that will in effect determine all the major events in the film. On the platform at Le Havre, a woman complains to Roubaud that another passenger is carrying a dog on the train in defiance of regulations; when Roubaud instructs this passenger about the regulations the latter becomes angry, asks for Roubaud's name, and tells him he will be hearing from him. An onlooker to the dispute warns Roubaud that this passenger is the famous sugar tycoon "le Grand Turlot" and that he has more than enough clout to destroy Roubaud's career if he wants to. Roubaud's tiny bump against a powerful capitalist then sets in motion the chain of events that leads to the four untimely deaths in the film (the murder of Grandmorin, the arrest and impending execution of Cabuche for that murder, the murder of Séverine, and the suicide of Lantier): it forces Roubaud to protect himself by making Séverine visit her rich and influential godfather, Grandmorin, who can fix things with Turlot; that visit results in Roubaud learning about her affair with Grandmorin and deciding to murder him; the Roubauds' need to cover up the murder of Grandmorin leads to Lantier's affair with Séverine; that affair leads Lantier to offer false testimony that helps to condemn Cabuche and eventually results in his own murder of Séverine; murdering Séverine leads Lantier to commit suicide.

Without denying the responsibility of Roubaud, Séverine, and Lantier in bringing about all these events, it is crucial to recognize the extent to which their actions are represented as *reactions* to the power of *les gros* to humiliate and destroy *les petites gens* at will. Though we never get a good look at Grandmorin himself, Séverine's behavior and a photograph of him with the young Séverine lead us to infer that their affair began with him sexually abusing her as a child, an inference that is later supported by Cabuche's self-incriminating litany to the police of the old man's many crimes against innocent young girls. The capriciousness with which Turlot squashes anyone who rubs him the wrong way and with which Grandmorin preys on young girls articulates the survival of *les droits de seigneur*, the absolute power and impunity of those at the top of contemporary capitalist society.

La bête humaine demonstrates that the external effects of this power on *les petites gens* are accentuated by the fact that they are already dominated internally by their unceasing fear of it. After his run-in with Turlot, Roubaud believes he can protect himself by temporarily abasing himself before Grandmorin, but in the process of doing so he discovers that he has in effect abased himself permanently by marrying the old man's discarded mistress. The tormented fury he displays toward Séverine and his decision to murder Grandmorin are driven less by a betrayal that happened long before he ever met his wife than by the way this discovery catalyzes the *ressentiment* of a lifetime of defending himself from social humiliation. The Roubaud we see before this discovery is a man who believes that he has finally made it according to the terms of his *petit bourgeois* ideology: his professionalism and careful negotiation of capitalist society have resulted in a respectable position and a lovely wife with whom to enjoy it. As he walks back to his apartment after the encounter with Turlot, all his

FIGURE 2.9.

Roubaud's puppy-dog grin at the catlike Séverine in *La bête humaine*.

passing comments to the people he runs into are transparently designed to remind them that he has a young and beautiful wife, as if Séverine is a trophy that should elevate him in their estimation. The impression of a pathetic dependence on the recognition of others is then developed when Roubaud arrives home and finds Séverine standing by a window stroking a cat. We get an extreme close-up of his rather grotesque puppy-dog grin that Séverine only bothers to answer with a catlike glance of wariness, annoyance, and ironic amusement: we immediately register her boredom with being the prized possession of a man too blind and stupid to recognize that boredom or any other feeling she might have. In retrospect, the cool wariness in her glance also reflects the awareness that her status as trophy is precarious: she knows she is only a fluctuating currency in the volatile economy of male recognition and that she could easily become an emblem of disgrace. When Roubaud runs from Turlot only to learn that he has already been ripped off by Grandmorin, his decision to kill the old man underlines the inevitability of revenge in a society thoroughly corrupted by the capricious power and ideological values of the rich.

One can also recognize the function of social resentment in Lantier's attraction to Séverine and in the motivation of Séverine herself. Though this does not play a direct role in Lantier's two attempts to kill Roubaud (in both cases he is reluctant and acts only under pressure from Séverine), the adultery itself is in part a way of luxuriating in the power his knowledge of Grandmorin's murder gives him over a high-class lady and her husband. Séverine herself turns out to be the very model of a murderous *ressentiment* that has bided its time from the moment Grandmorin first laid hands on her. As soon as Lantier fails in his first attempt to kill Roubaud she immediately starts to flirt with a handsome young man named Dauvergne; when Lantier questions her about this she sweetly explains that she has to take up with Dauvergne because Lantier's inability to kill Roubaud leaves her "with nothing left to hope for." She rejects Lantier's suggestion that that they simply run away to live elsewhere by saying she believes Roubaud would eventually find and kill her: "only death can break the ties" that bind her to Roubaud. Simone Simon's condescending tone as she gently explains all this to the impassive and uncomprehending Gabin almost feels like a lecture by Hegel in which she tries to make him aware of the dialectical implications of their love (that is, that one can't get off the train of negation until the last stop); it becomes clear that the only freedom and happiness she can imagine is based on successively eliminating every man she becomes entangled with and that this unending process of serial negation would inevitably claim Lantier himself in due time.

By the time *La bête humaine* draws to its close, we have come to recognize the ways and extents to which Roubaud, Séverine, and Lantier are all corrupted and blinded by the resentment that a brutal capitalist society has reproduced within them. The film's narrative demonstrates that it takes only one accidental bump against a big shot to activate that resentment and set lethal circuits of causality in motion. Though it also offers examples of Cytherean possibilities (Flore) and clear-sighted stoicism and camaraderie (Pecqueux) that Lantier might have paid more attention to, *La bête humaine* nonetheless constitutes the strongest example in the French Renoir of a Rousseauian vision of individuals corrupted and destroyed by the ideological power of bourgeois society.

The chronotopic continuum that links *La bête humaine* to *Toni* allows one to recognize the difference of their respective treatments of the tragic effects of romanticism on individuals in modern society, and contrasting the very similar endings of the two films—both Lantier and Toni die on an embankment surrounded by comrades just after crossing a railroad bridge—illuminates the range of Renoir's reflection on those effects.

The dislocated peasants of *Toni* squat on the margins of an already globalized capitalist society and stoically contemplate their situation. They know they are not going anywhere, so they remember where they have come from and pay close attention to where they are and who they are with; within the narrow domain allotted to them they move and act at their own deliberate pace. In this context the lateral tracking shot that follows Toni's run across the bridge reads this act as a defiant assertion of his own anachronistic difference in the face of modern life; the dull echoing thud of his footsteps makes us aware of both the sheer drop beneath him and the infinite vista behind him and produces a queasiness that accentuates the feeling of pathos his determined movements provoke. During the time he runs along the bridge we also feel his dangerous exposure to the train that might pass over it; both the run and the subsequent refusal to surrender that leads to his death fall into place as only the last two in the series of rebellious dismissals of reality that have carried him away from his comrades. The film ends with the arrival of a train filled with yet another batch of hopeful newcomers, and this figure of technology depositing groups of premodern people on the shores of modernity in unceasing historical waves both frames and accentuates Toni's solitary movement in the opposite direction. Toni's narrative is that of a boat beating upstream against the current of modernity, and his fate illustrates the futility of opposing that current.

In contrast to *Toni*'s fable from the border between capitalist modernity and the premodern world of peasant life, the melodrama of *La bête humaine* takes place deep in the belly of the beast. The train workers are fixed in unceasing forward movement by their function as cogs in the machinery of technological modernity; unlike the laborers of *Toni* they have no liberty to pause and reflect on where they have come from or to vary their

FIGURE 2.10.

Lantier cracks up in *La bête humaine*.

routes, styles, and rates of locomotion. Lantier's job is to drive *Lison* as fast as she will safely go while keeping his gaze rigidly fixed on the empty tracks ahead. The extended forward-facing shots from Lantier's point of view in the train sequences remind us that his main function is simply to make sure the tracks *are empty* every second of every minute of every hour, day after day, year after year: his job literally dictates that he spend most of his life staring hard at the emptiness of his own future. This figure of a man whose immediate practical relationship to his situation affords him no time to remember the past or imagine the future also resonates with the film's portrait of characters like Roubaud and Séverine, both of whom anxiously "watch the tracks" of a society driven by the unpredictable caprices of the rich and seething with the resentment of everyone else. The exhaustion and despair that inevitably result from this constant anxiety is brilliantly condensed in the final shot from Lantier's point of view in which the train traverses a bridge. The blinding white light that flashes like a strobe through the shutters created by our movement through the pylons and wires works in tandem with the deeper, slower resonance of noise on the soundtrack to produce a horrific impression of frozen immobility. This subliminal impression is immediately confirmed by the reaction shot we get of Lantier; his eyes glazed, he blinks and shakes his head in a last desperate effort to return to the real world of minutes and hours that might add up to something. He cannot do it: he backs away from the window with his whole body quaking with the horror of what he has seen, turns to Pecqueux, and yells that he can't go on. Pecqueux attempts to restrain him, but Lantier knocks Pecqueux down, climbs up on a platform, takes a last look around *Lison*, and jumps to his death.

Reconstructing the chronotopic continuum that links *Toni* and *La bête humaine* allows us to recognize the genealogical extent of Renoir's critique of romanticism as an ideology that veils reality and prevents one from meeting either others or oneself. If Toni's fate illustrates the futility of running away from modernity by committing oneself to a premodern romantic ideal, Lantier's fate illustrates the equal futility of attempting to escape one's situation by masochistically submitting oneself to modernity's mastery. The deaths of Toni and Lantier are defined as unnecessary and absurd because we have been made aware of possibilities of comradeship they chose to ignore; though these are everywhere in the first film and starkly attenuated in the second, in both cases they serve as the ground against which we register the culpable and fatal blindness of these protagonists.

The Revolutionary Chronotope

Le crime de Monsieur Lange and *La Marseillaise* (1938) are the films that define the fourth and final chronotope we will examine in this chapter. Each film approaches the interplay between popular culture and political revolution from an angle that can, for a variety of reasons, be described as an exact reverse angle of the other; examining the films together allows one to recognize a consistent view of the subject that might otherwise go unnoticed. In characterizing this chronotope I will begin by identifying aspects of the films that illuminate this differential symmetry before discussing the character types and defining figures of internal realism they share.

Le crime de Monsieur Lange is an important artifact of the cultural and political revolution of the Popular Front (1936); it is probably the single most famous of such artifacts and is widely treated as a representative articulation of the challenges and hopes of its historical moment.[55] The film explores the revolutionary effects of popular culture on politics within the microcosmic milieu of a building in Paris that contains flats, a laundry, and a publishing house. The main story of the film is framed as a flashback narrated by Valentine (Florelle), the lover of a murderer named Lange (René Lefèvre), to the people at a hotel on the border who want to turn Lange in to the authorities. She begins by outlining the isolation of the characters who inhabit this milieu and their economic and sexual exploitation by the entrepreneur Batala, who owns the publishing house; the characters we meet are enclosed either by a defining passion or ideology (Batala's assistant, Lange, is lost in daydreams about the Western stories he writes each night; the racist, authority-worshipping concierge, Besnard, is lost in his memories of military grandeur in Indochina) or by a class-specific naïveté that makes them vulnerable to exploitation (the workers in the publishing house cannot see that Batala's flagrant mismanagement is gambling away their wages; Batala's secretary, Edith, and the laundress Estelle are seduced by the tawdry grandeur of his words and gestures; Besnard's son, Charles, suffers by having the window to his room covered by a billboard advertising one of Batala's magazines). Though certain characters are attracted to certain others—the laundry manager, Valentine, loves Lange and Charles loves Estelle—their love is initially unrequited, and these figures of unrequited love articulate the sense of a community indefinitely suspended at its own moment of possibility. This sense of suspended animation is highlighted by the frantic animation of Jules Berry's Batala, who seems to be incessantly surprised and delighted by his ability to dupe the slow-witted stooges who surround him; he revels in his power by grabbing, pushing, poking, or patting everyone he encounters with his splayed, froglike hands. With the exception of Valentine, whose past seduction by Batala has made her wise to him (and the world), none of the other characters are capable of returning the sadistic objectivity of Batala's gaze or defending themselves from his manipulations. He clearly regards them as a personal fief of toys to play with, and as his perfidies mount, both in number and magnitude, we become impatient for these toys to wake up and open their eyes to him and each other.

Like the historical events that determined the formation of the Popular Front itself, the events that break the incipient community's state of suspended animation can best be described as a series of fortunate coincidences. Though Batala has hitherto been indifferent to Lange's literary ambitions, when he is confronted by a capitalist he has swindled named Baigneur, Batala deflects this threat by introducing him to the "genius" Lange and offering Baigneur an option on the proceeds of his soon-to-be-famous work; though Batala tricks Lange into signing away the rights to his own work and cynically inserts product placements in them without the latter's consent, Lange's Arizona Jim stories in any case get published and will soon become a wildly successful pop-culture phenomenon that all the inhabitants and workers of the building will get to contribute to. But this success and the community that results from it are also shown to depend on a series of four additional coincidences. Lange's first appearance in print happens to coincide with the arrival of an inspector from the Sureté Nationale looking for Batala; though we later learn that this person is only an indigent cousin of Batala's, an *ex*-inspector who is looking for a job, Batala mistakenly believes he is about to be arrested and decides to leave town on the first train. This train is then wrecked, and it is incorrectly reported that Batala is killed. When the publishing house workers and Batala's creditors meet to sort through the financial mess he left behind, the workers' proposal to reform the enterprise as a cooperative is rejected by the creditors until the happy-go-lucky son of the principal creditor, Meunier, shows up (because his father is sick), declares that he loves cooperatives (though he later confesses he doesn't know what they are), and thus puts the Arizona Jim revolution into motion: in the space of a single morning the courtyard's collection of alienated individuals is transformed into a vibrant and cohesive community.

Though the communal enthusiasm and activity that is released by this sequence of events is palpably real and effective, the community is shown to be fragile to the extent that its existence really depends on a series of mistakes and coincidences and not on the conscious efforts of its members. When Batala returns and threatens to destroy the community by asserting his legal rights of ownership, Lange is forced to act deliberately and take—on behalf of the community—what had hitherto been a gift of chance; the act of killing Batala is an explicit negation of an evil man that also functions as an implicit negation of the social institutions that secured that man's privileges. When the people at the hotel finish listening to Valentine's story, they collectively affirm the justice of Lange's act of murder in defense of a microcosmic community, and the film ends with their seeing the two fugitives off across the border.

If *Lange* examines the effects of culture on politics, *La Marseillaise* examines the effects of politics on culture; in contrast to *Lange*'s study of the microcosmic political effects of a nationwide pop-cultural phenomenon, *La Marseillaise* examines the title song's gradual emergence from the microcosmic obscurity of its origins (at once local and foreign—we are told the Rhine army song was brought to Provence by a Jewish peddler) to become a cultural medium that binds people isolated by age, gender, occupation, class, and region into a coherent and dynamic nation. In contrast to *Lange*'s opening evocation of an enclosed society blind to its own oppression, the first two sequences of *La Marseillaise* present us with an entire country of characters already in the process of opening their eyes to each other and the radical possibilities of the French Revolution.

The opening sequence takes place at Versailles on July 14, 1789, and introduces us to Louis XVI (Pierre Renoir) blithely eating a breakfast in bed that is more like a three-course dinner. When his adviser La Rochefoucauld arrives, the king immediately starts blabbing on about the previous day's hunt and forces his adviser to interrupt him with the news about the Bastille. Still not grasping the gravity of the situation, the king matter-of-factly asks if it is a revolt, to which La Rochefoucauld replies, "No sire: it's a revolution." The king's response to this distinction—which deftly marks the shift from the eternal cycles of revolt to the irreversible linear movement of historical time—is to look up and open his eyes wide as the scene fades to black. At this moment and in many others throughout the film, Pierre Renoir's face expresses both alarm and a genuine inability to comprehend the significance of the events overtaking him; he would really like to understand what is going on, but his swaddled isolation at the very center of French society has left him with no real reference points with which to do so.

After the prologue at Versailles the location shifts to a village in Provence, where a peasant named Cabri is arrested for poaching a pigeon; when the noble in charge of the case proposes sending him to the galleys as an example for others, his fellow peasants help him escape, and he takes refuge in the hills. On a mountaintop he meets and joins up with three other proto-revolutionaries-in-hiding, the mason Bomier, the intellectual clerk Arnaud, and the priest Paget. After quickly identifying what they have in common—they all attest that they are not criminals but patriots with legitimate grievances against the status quo—the sequence develops their camaraderie by interspersing the recounting of those grievances with the practical challenges of camping that require the skills and cooperation of all: Bomier knows how to build a hearth but only Cabri knows which way the wind is going to blow; Cabri can kill birds but needs Bomier's belt for a sling; Cabri advises Bomier on how to roast a rabbit; the priest's unquestionable status and mobility give them access to food and information; the calm authority and synoptic perspective of Arnaud are required to organize all their activities. When Paget informs them the Revolution has begun and they are needed in the world below, their vantage point allows them to identify the various chateaux burning in the valleys below and to discuss the significance of these events. Their existential situation on the mountaintop and the panoramic view it affords allow them to see each other and their world differently; the social divisions that separated them back in town are dissolved by recognizing the immediate practical value of each individual and their common domination by larger power structures. But we also feel that their temporary abstraction from society gives their vision a clarity that will prove difficult to maintain when they descend to participate in history. The heroic music that comes up as they descend from the mountain in single file, lost in their own reflections, enhances our sense that it will be difficult to reproduce their microcosmic experience of Liberty, Equality, and Fraternity in the world below.

If the opening of *Lange* lays out the difficulty of recognizing a microcosmic revolutionary situation in the first place, the mountaintop utopia in *La Marseillaise* presages the difficulty of maintaining a clear revolutionary vision after one enters the macrocosmic ocean of historical events. In contrast to the frame story in *Lange*, Valentine's public justification of a conscious act of murder in defense of a revolutionary community that arose through a series of coincidences, the narrative of *La Marseillaise* presents us with a series of episodes in which the acts of the revolutionaries from Marseilles unconsciously coincide with larger events to result in a regicide that none of them seems to want, expect, or understand. As Dudley Andrew and Steven Ungar describe it, "In 1792 the people succumb to a historical moment they sense in the making; in a decision that is both active and passive, they join up so as to be carried along by it. Those participating had little sense of the outcome. They marched to protect the king from false advisors. They wound up executing him and making way for the deeper revolution."[56] If Lange's murder of Batala is a clear-sighted act justified by the manifest evil of the murdered man and the manifest good of the community he threatens, *La Marseillaise* explicitly represents the execution of Louis XVI as an almost meaningless coincidence; far from being a villain in need of punishment, he is simply in the wrong place at the wrong time as a historical process that is blind to individuals inexorably negates the social order he represents. As the film draws to its close and the Hegelian logic of historical events tightens around the palace, Renoir highlights the inappropriateness of Louis's impending death by reminding us that he has never really acted responsibly *as* a king. The act of putting forward the provocative Brunswick Manifesto that leads to his death is shown to be motivated less by a lucid assessment of the political situation than by an immediate desire to placate the willful Marie-Antoinette; even as the palace is on the verge of being attacked, Louis is more interested in sampling the new cuisine (tomatoes) that the revolutionaries from Marseilles have made popular in Paris than in exercising his power to save himself; even as he and his family are being led across a courtyard to their deaths, his children's enchantment with a pile of fallen leaves causes him to pause, look up at the trees, and reflect on the cycles of nature: "So many leaves. They have fallen early this year."[57] The congenital inability to take politics and his place in history seriously that we have seen from the film's outset renders Louis's execution less necessary and tragic than absurd, and the film's deliberate emphasis on the absurdity of his death produces a sour note that troubles the harmonious processes of mutual recognition that we have seen bind the revolutionary characters into a community.

Though the participation of the film's main protagonists in the Revolution is based on conscious political judgments that emerge from the warm and sincere dialogue between them, the film never suggests that any of them, even the intellectual Arnaud, can see where the events they participate in are leading; the film represents history as a cold, impersonal movement, a "deeper revolution" that always outflanks any picture of it that its individual actors are capable of framing. This outflanking movement is condensed in the nighttime episode in which two disenchanted volunteers (played by Gaston Modot and Julien Carette) sit over a fire in the woods while the movement of troops deserting to the enemy can be heard in the darkness behind them. Their discussion of the betrayal by their officers and the lives they abandoned at home is intermittently punctuated by Carette turning to shout futile insults in the direction of the deserters. The camping elements this scene shares with the earlier ones on the mountaintop in Provence lead us to contemplate the difference between the theory and practice of history: in the silent panorama of theory we imagine we know where we are going, but in the darkness and noise of actual events we realize we never do. Though *La Marseillaise* was intended to remind its audience of the debt of humility it owed to the anonymous individuals who brought France and the modern world into being, the film does not shrink from exposing the gulf between what those individuals imagined they were doing and what they actually accomplished, the tension between the warm desire for communion animating the revolutionaries and the cold logic of history that harnesses and uses that desire for its own inscrutable ends. As Alexander Sesonske observes, "The action that dominates the final section of the film overshadows the characters who engage in it; it is the revolution that triumphs, not the chorus of Marseillaise."[58]

Though *Le crime de Monsieur Lange* and *La Marseillaise* consider the revolutionary process from different angles, their treatments of that process are, in the final analysis, complementary. The first film examines a microcosmic revolution that is cut to the exact measure of its protagonists' desires and situation; the fact that the film's case for revolution is based on specific processes of recognition that take place within a "centripetal" milieu sets implicit limits on its extension. Though the sympathetic tribunal of the framing story might seem incendiary in encouraging spectators to draw analogies between the fictional narrative and their own situations (that is, if you have a boss like Batala you are justified in killing him), Valentine's defense of Lange nonetheless hinges on a villain (Jules Berry's inimitable *salaud*) and situation (the series of coincidences that create and threaten to destroy the community) that are sui generis. The film's justification of murder is based on the fact that we are given a clear and intimate view, a *complete* view, that allows us to judge both the community and the threat to it, but if we accept this premise we also accept the isolation of this community in relation to the wider society around it. This sense of isolation is why *Lange* feels more like a self-enclosed *fable* akin to one of Lange's Western stories than an episode in an open and expanding revolutionary event taking place in the historical world of 1930s France; even the decision of the tribunal not to turn Lange in fabulizes the historical response the film anticipates from its audience and in that sense incorporates the audience within the fable. Though the film was clearly intended to be an event in an actual revolution, a historical act in support of the newborn Popular Front, it does not in fact treat the revolution it represents as taking place in historical time: *Le crime de Monsieur Lange* is a fable of social possibilities understood to have taken place at a strange indeterminate time *before* the historical moment the film's original audience reentered when they left the theatres in 1936.

Though *La Marseillaise* was, like *Lange*, also intended to be an episode in a real-life revolution, a historical act in defense of the withering Popular Front, it looks back at the French Revolution from a time *after* history. The film's perspective is post-historical in two senses: it is *after* the events it depicts have passed into the master-narrative of the French Revolution, and, more important, it is *after* the cohesive ideological power of that master-narrative has disintegrated. Looking back at the Revolution from the disenchanted perspective of France in 1938, riddled with internal divisions and encircled by fascism, Renoir looks beneath the contested wreckage of history (that is, major figures and events) to focus on one of the anonymous microcosmic communities that preceded and created it. With a deliberate emphasis on historiographic or counterhistorical details that Renoir gleaned firsthand from a variety of sources, the film examines the consequences of trying to realize *Lange*'s utopian vision of social possibilities in historical time: it contemplates the relation between "history from below" and "history from above."[59]

In contrast to the chance coincidences that create the community in the first film, the events that collect the proto-revolutionaries on the mountaintop and then take them to Paris are meant to exemplify a process of world-historical necessity (that is, the recognition of new social possibilities and negation of the old society they entail) that is taking place throughout the country and will soon be extended into the world beyond; far from being the product of mere chance coincidences, the community that forms on the mountaintop is a scientific demonstration of a Hegelian truth that we presume is being replicated on other mountaintops throughout the country (and, soon enough, in principle, the entire world). But after they descend from the mountain the film highlights the revolutionaries' limited understanding of the events in which they participate by showing the extent to which it is governed by the centripetal priorities of their immediate situations and the mediated representation of those events in popular culture. After we have been shown that the king's decision to publish the Brunswick Manifesto was determined by a strictly personal problem (that is, Marie-Antoinette's threatening a tantrum), two of the Marseilles revolutionaries attend a shadow-puppet play where they take advantage of the darkness to make out with their Parisian girlfriends. The play presents an allegory in which Marianne/the Nation rejects the King's attempt to embrace her across a destroyed bridge that represents the effect of the Brunswick Manifesto; after this rebuff a few ducks swim into the stream beneath the bridge quacking and we hear the audience laugh. In this carnivalesque laughter charged with erotic arousal we can hear the unconscious process of desacralizing the king that will allow for his execution. This scene suggests that the revolutionaries' impending negation of the king is less a deliberate act than an unintended consequence of a process in which their attraction to each other has simply carried them away from a world in which his existence has any meaning: recognizing each other entails misrecognizing or simply forgetting the king and the symbolic order he represents. Renoir represents Louis XVI's death as a result of the arbitrary or blind play of Dionysian forces within a revolutionary context: the public event of the regicide is shown to be the product of crisscrossing ripples (that is, coincidences) that flow out from a vast, unimaginable archipelago of unrelated private events (for example, Marie-Antoinette's tantrum and the lovemaking of the revolutionaries). The act of murder shown to be conscious and justifiable in the centripetal and fabulous world of *Lange* is thus represented as unconscious and absurd in the centrifugal and historical world of *La Marseillaise*. Our admiration for Louis in his final moments comes from the fact that he is the only character who seems to be aware of this absurdity, from his lucid contemplation of the fact that he and his family are only the fallen leaves of a season in which individuals do not matter.

Despite their very different angles on the revolutionary process, *Le crime de Monsieur Lange* and *La Marseillaise* are bound by a single figure that combines, develops, and transforms certain figures we have already examined in other chronotopes. In it the unconscious force of attraction that we identified in the Cytherean chronotope becomes self-conscious and results in a knowing objectivity of the gaze superficially similar to that in the Flaubertian chronotope; the characters who perform this figure have, as it were, become conscious of the spring fever animating them and now explicitly recognize its source in certain other characters whom they look at with a lucid and affectionate skepticism. If looking-at in the Flaubertian chronotope represents the characters' fundamental inability to be surprised by each other, the reciprocal isolation that results from their "cold knowledge" of each other's predictable sameness, here a knowing gaze represents the characters' confidence in both the ability of others to surprise and delight them and their own capacity to surprise and delight others: the "warm knowingness" in their gaze articulates the pleasure they derive from an ongoing discovery of differences. If the Flaubertian characters' misrecognition of each other's sameness charges the space between them with a feeling of fixed and irreducible distance, the revolutionary characters' recognition of each other's differences can be seen to charge the space between them with a feeling of fluid, eroticized proximity.

The subplot that traces Valentine's patient seduction of Lange offers the most systematic exposition of this figure in either of the two films. In the first scenes in which they meet she looks at him with a frank and affectionate skepticism and makes flirtatious comments that are transparently designed to get him to pay attention to her. But Lange is oblivious to her,

FIGURE 2.11.

Valentine fingers Lange in *Le crime de Monsieur Lange*.

lost in languid daydreams about the fictional Arizona Jim or his fictionalized version of the laundress Estelle. After Lange's first date with Estelle ends in disaster (she wrongly thinks he is interested only in sex and runs away), he accepts the invitation of a friendly prostitute and has what we can presume to be his first sexual experience. His demeanor after this intimate and pleasant encounter with reality immediately changes. He stands straighter and looks around at his environment and other characters with a heightened attentiveness and vigor; when he next meets Valentine and she informs him about Batala's insertion of the product placements in his stories, his angry reaction displays a vehemence of the will that we have never seen before. Lange's comically abrupt transformation from blind and flaccid to alert and rampant introduces a bawdy analogy that will subtly infuse all the communal activity in which he plays a leading role with a cohesive erotic friction.

The static cling of the new Lange is clearly evident in his next meeting with Valentine. As they pass in the courtyard and exchange greetings, he at first behaves like the old Lange by incorrectly addressing her as "Madame" Cardet; her exasperated response to this mistaken formality is to pointedly inform him, as she has tried to do several times before, that her name is *Va-len-tine* ("Think about what my name means, you fool!"). This time her message finally gets through and Lange stops, turns, and orients himself directly in front of her, smiling. He daftly repeats her name, she repeats it again herself to confirm the message, and then asks him his first name. When he tells her it's "Amédée" she cracks up laughing but then suppresses her laughter in order to ask him to supper; as Lange considers this proposal (and, as if for the first time, her), Valentine moves in close to him and starts to stroke his chest, her fingers plucking at and penetrating inside his shirt. Only when he finally agrees to come to supper does she relent and pull herself away, and they jokingly use their new names to bid each other farewell until the evening.

When we next see the couple it is after supper in her apartment, and Valentine is in the process of singing a popular song to an entranced Lange. After the song finishes she moves closer to Lange, and they obliquely discuss the love of others (Estelle and Charles) until Valentine questions him about the real-life model for the recurring heroine of his stories, *la belle Mexicane*. Valentine's question reveals to us that her love for Lange is partly based on the fact that she has recognized herself in *la belle Mexicane*; we understand that Valentine assumes there must be a real-life model because Lange's passion for the character has made her feel more real, more alive: we understand that she loves him in part because his romantic vision has allowed her to recognize aspects of herself repressed by her own disillusioned brand of realism. At this point we know that Lange had in fact based this character on his romanticized image of Estelle (during their date he told her that she looks Mexican) but that the botched date and his encounter with the prostitute has made him aware of the gap between this image and who Estelle really is; in searching for a response to Valentine's question we see a brief flicker of thought in which he recalls his date with Estelle and then says the character is just "a woman," that is, an ideal woman he has yet to meet in reality. Valentine aggressively, almost growling, says "une *femme*, une *femme*," and moving closer tilts her chin up in a

FIGURE 2.12.

Valentine and Lange negate Batala in *Le crime de Monsieur Lange.*

gesture that challenges him to recognize *la belle Mexicane* in her eyes and body. Lange stares at her for a moment and then suddenly gets it and kisses her; just as the realist Valentine has blossomed by recognizing herself in a character created by the romantic Lange, so Lange now begins his own transformation by recognizing the object of his previously misdirected romantic desires in the warm flesh and blood of this beautiful woman.

The next scene in which we see the couple recapitulates the transformation we have witnessed while at the same time sketching out the brutal implications of their love. As they lay in her bed in postcoital contentment they hear the news about Batala's death from a radio in another apartment, and the old Lange immediately sits up to express shock and dismay: "But he was alive just this morning." Valentine dismisses this comment as insincere and meaningless ("People always say that") and, moving closer to Lange, repeats the challenging gesture from the previous scene, which now functions as a request that he confirm the value of the body he has

FIGURE 2.13.

Lange and Louis share a joke in *Le crime de Monsieur Lange.*

just enjoyed; she defiantly purrs, "Am I alive?" Lange again stares at her for a moment before answering, "Yes, more alive than anyone" and, turning off the light, embraces her. The deliberate oblivion of their renewed lovemaking is at once a deeper recognition of each other and a negation of the man who exploited them both: they brutally and actively forget Batala ever existed.

The Lange we see the next morning is a completely changed man with no trace of the old daydreamer left in him. As the printshop workers and other characters gather in the courtyard to discuss the news, he stands at the center of the group directing the conversation with a confidence, an energy, and a direct, incisive gaze that we infer to have been infused into him by the night making love with Valentine. When someone observes that Batala was "alive just yesterday morning," the new Lange coldly repeats Valentine's comment: "People always say that." When Batala's cousin admits that he lost his job as an inspector for certain "minor transgressions," Lange turns briefly to look back at Louis, the shop foreman, with a knowing amusement in his eyes and the slightest of smiles playing around the corners of his mouth; the speed and compression of the implied joke (that is, "Here's a dumber version of the Batala species") reveals a man with his eyes wide open and his mind in rapid motion. As the group moves upstairs to the printshop where the stakeholders in the enterprise debate its future, it is Lange's pronounced attentiveness to what is going on that seems to keep things moving in the right direction; though he is rarely the one talking, he directs the debate by standing in the middle of the group and quickly turning his body and attention to support the positions of speakers saying productive things and quickly turning away from those whose positions are unproductive. His timely interjections of approval or disapproval deftly orient the debate in a progressive direction and force the other characters to recognize the community that is taking shape before their very eyes. The cooperative seems to become real because Lange desires it to be real; if the old Lange closed his eyes to the people around him and spilled his seed nightly writing escapist fiction, the new Lange looks at the characters around him with the serene authority and love of a man in the process of engendering them. René Lefèvre's expression in this sequence is analogous to the one we might imagine on Renoir's face as he watches a scene being shot; though he seems to anticipate every detail of the events that unfold before him, he is nonetheless anxious about the outcome and surprised and delighted by the way everything comes together with a perfection he could not have predicted. This figure of a knowingness that takes an erotic pleasure in anticipating and recognizing the *difference* of others has an effect that is the exact opposite of the one produced by Balata's Flaubertian anticipation of their gullible *sameness*; if Batala's selfishness coated the community in a stupefying contraceptive foam, Lange's attentiveness to the people around him functions like an aphrodisiac ointment that makes the members of that community aware of and attracted to each other.

By recognizing each other, Valentine and Lange have channeled the power of Cythera into society and thereby inaugurated a revolution; to recall the terms of Renoir's governing question, the sense of belonging that allows the community to cohere is clearly shown to be the result of a prior meeting between these two individuals. The disruptive centrifugal force of attraction we saw to be definitive of the Cytherean chronotope has through a conscious and reciprocal act of recognition now been given a centripetal orientation, and this reorientation immediately germinates a microcosmic community whose activity will in turn have a disruptive centrifugal effect (that is, the rapidly expanding Arizona Jim phenomenon) on the infertile status quo of the larger society: the external force of Cytherean attraction has, by being consciously internalized, been transformed into a revolutionary force within society.

The evolution of Valentine and Lange's relationship traces a narrative of the Revolutionary type that allows us to recognize elements of that type in other characters. The relationship between Bomier and Arnaud in *La Marseillaise* picks up the trajectory of the type at the exact point where *Lange* leaves it on the doorstep of history. When we first meet these two characters on the mountaintop, the warm and affectionate skepticism with which they treat each other leads us to infer that they have passed through the initial stages of the evolutionary narrative and are now in the process of following their friendship wherever it might lead them. The erotic differential of the Valentine-Lange relationship whereby she led or seduced him into recognizing her (and himself) is rearticulated here by the way in which the serious facial expressions and sharp political judgments of the masculinized realist Arnaud lead Bomier into making a revolutionary commitment, while the bubbling contradictions and enthusiasms of the feminized romantic Bomier seduce Arnaud by providing him with a congenial condensation of the nation he wants to help bring into being.

Like the love between Valentine and Lange, the ongoing process of recognition that defines the Arnaud-Bomier friendship involves a transference of qualities and ideas that Renoir often highlights to comic effect; the various episodes through which they pass typically end on moments that foreground either the romantic credulity of the realist Arnaud or the skeptical incredulity of the romantic Bomier (that is, the contradictions that their friendship has produced within them). The most explicit demonstration of this transference occurs in a scene in which Arnaud watches Bomier boast to another revolutionary about his prophetic recognition that "La Marseillaise" was a song capable of uniting all Frenchmen. As Arnaud listens to Bomier's boasting he stares at him in disbelief, clearly remembering an earlier scene in which the two of them discussed the song while fishing; at the time, Arnaud romantically confessed the song overwhelmed him and seemed to echo his thoughts while Bomier skeptically dismissed it as only a passing craze. When Arnaud finally interrupts Bomier to ask if he remembers the last time they went fishing and what they said about the song then, Bomier immediately replies yes, he remembers very well: "I said it was the echo of my thoughts." Arnaud is rendered speechless by this appropriation of his words and identity while Bomier smugly interprets his friend's silence to mean that he has won the argument; he grins and on a deeper level we understand that he is right to do so because in fact he has won the argument on the terms established by their friendship: the ongoing dialectical imbrication of their identities produces a wake that rolls into and erases, or at least transmutes, the facts of the past.

The couples Valentine-Lange and Arnaud-Bomier articulate the most complete and definitive figure of the Revolutionary type, a figure distinguished by the lucid and mutual recognition of the characters that enact it. As in the Arnaud-Bomier example discussed above, this figure is typically presented in a two or three shot in which one character looks at another with an affectionate skepticism, while the character being looked does not look directly at the other but is nonetheless aware of the other's gaze and attention; in one sense this second character is performing for the other, and we can infer his or her peripheral awareness of this audience from both a self-conscious gleam in the character's eyes and the alacrity with which he or she responds to the actions and comments of his or her friend/lover. This figure clearly suggests that the words and actions of the characters are preceded and created by the erotic and dialogical relationship between them; the public words and actions that effectively realize the historical revolutions in which they participate are, at the same time and in the first instance, private words and actions that occur in the intimate context of their ongoing reflection on each other's otherness or difference.

This central figure of the Revolutionary type is flanked by two subordinate versions, each of which highlights certain of its aspects while omitting others. The first of these subordinate figures reproduces the stoic camaraderie that we identified in the Naturalist chronotope. The minor characters in *La Marseillaise* who enact this figure are individuals whose solitary contemplation of their situations has led them to commit themselves to the revolutionary cause, but their words and actions display none of the erotic fervor and dynamism of the central figure. Like the wary peasants of *Toni*, their inherent skepticism and self-respect keeps them at a certain distance from those around them; though they listen attentively to what others say and freely offer their own opinions, the dead weight of their Old World common sense functions like ballast that keeps the ship of Revolution steady. The representative enactment of this figure synthesizes and refunctions elements of figures we considered in the Naturalist and the Cytherean chronotopes; it is typically presented in two shots in which the characters argue while facing in the same direction and occasionally turn to look at each other. Though they pay attention to each other's words (as in the Naturalist chronotope), the non-coincidence of their looks (characteristic of the Cytherean) and inconclusive endings of their arguments (which are usually interrupted and terminated by other characters) articulate a sort of reflective distance or skeptical inertia within the community of comrades that can be felt to exert a moderating influence on the dynamism of the historical events in which they participate.

The second subfigure highlights exactly those qualities of the central figure that are omitted from the first. The minor characters in *Le crime de Monsieur Lange* who participate in the cooperative are shown to do so because they have become infected by the external force of collective enthusiasm, not because they have taken the time to consciously reflect on their situations. The representative enactment of this figure blends the skeptical and affectionate gaze of the central figure with the sense of an unconscious disorientation we examined in the Cytherean chronotope. The party to celebrate the young Meunier's idea for an Arizona Jim movie constitutes a strong and explicit exposition of this figure. The members of the community sit crammed around a table and look around at each other, their eyes glazed with inebriated mirth and a diffuse erotic desire. Unlike the reflective revolutionaries who perform the first subfigure, these characters do not quite know how they got here but do know that they are enjoying the wine and stimulating contact with the people around them. The cohesiveness of the group is defined by the erotic postures and activities (hands around shoulders and waists, or ostensibly "resting" out of sight in laps) of the couples we recognize (Valentine-Lange, Estelle-Charles) and others we can see in the process of forming and by the fact that the booze has artificially leveled the differences between them. Meunier and Lange make brief speeches that are greeted with affectionate mockery (groans, laughter, quips). Then the concierge Besnard gets up to sing a sentimental song about a poor orphan at Christmastime, and the others greet this ridiculous offering from a man who embodies an anachronistic right-wing politics with the same affectionate mockery as everything else. On one level we are ourselves drunk on the warmth and eroticism of the moment and are moved by the comedy of Besnard's bizarre way of including himself in the group and the group's touching, inclusive response to his offering. But on another level we are still lucid enough to imagine that most of the characters will be suffering from hangovers tomorrow and will have difficulty remembering what happened the night before. Viewing the scene from this more sober and reflective perspective, we cannot but be skeptical about the reality (that is, permanence or depth) of Besnard's inclusion, and our sense of the leveling superficiality of this event subtly informs our understanding of the community that performs it. Though they may want to recognize and include each other, they have not yet done the hard work of reflection required to make such recognition real and lasting; though they have allowed themselves to be carried away by a collective intoxication, they have not yet taken the time to meet each other in a full and conscious contemplation of their differences. If the skeptical reflection of the self-possessed characters in the first subfigure provides the ballast that keeps the ship of Revolution steady, here we see the blind, eros-inspired oblivion of self and others that puts the wild winds of enthusiasm in its sails.

In concluding our consideration of this chronotope, it is crucial to recognize that its complex figure of Revolution-as-Cythera-in-historical-motion is fundamentally Janus-faced; though it always begins in and is driven by the warm and lucid affirmation of differences within a centripetal context, the centrifugal motion it dialectically entails is shown to enmesh it in broader processes of historical negation that always exceed the intentions and imaginations of its protagonists: if Valentine and Lange's lovemaking is a conscious act of forgetting a man they know and rightfully detest, the lovemaking of the revolutionaries at the shadow-puppet play enmeshes them in an unconscious process of negating people whom they do not know and will never meet. Though the centripetal Cytherean face of the process/figure is identical in both instances, the wider, post-historical perspective that *La Marseillaise* takes on the subject makes us aware of the romanticism that animates its centrifugal face; the clear-sighted pursuit of otherness within a centripetal context seems to entail a blindness to and negation of the Otherness of the world as a whole. Revolution is for Renoir a profoundly ambivalent process that spirals simultaneously into two distinct dimensions of time and experience; as in Deleuze's concept of the crystal image, events seem to take place in both an "actual" or historical dimension that proceeds into and creates the future and a "virtual" or reflective dimension that preserves and contemplates the past. As Deleuze observes, and as our examples of transference serve to illustrate, these dimensions often seem impossible to distinguish from the other, or seem to become the other.[60] If, for example, we take the reflections and acts of the characters to be fully conscious and real, then we can only regard the historical effects they inadvertently cause with the ironic gaze of a Flaubert. If, on the other hand, we privilege the reality and logic of larger historical events, we are forced to turn that ironic gaze on the characters, whose reflections and acts now appear to be only the unconscious by-products of a Hegelian dialectic that alone knows where it is going (that is, we understand history to be a "book whose characters do not yet know they are being read").[61] Either what happens in the centripetal world is actual and history is virtual, or history is actual and events in the centripetal world are virtual; in either case we are asked to contemplate and accept the absurdity or meaninglessness of human existence, and it is our reluctance to do so that causes us to equivocate between microcosmic and macrocosmic perspectives: it is this movement of reflective equivocation that renders the two views "indistinguishable."

There are, I think, two ways to interpret the absurd picture of human existence manifest in the Revolutionary chronotope. It would seem that for Deleuze the split in time made visible in the crystal-image is a fundamental model of the human condition: time-as-history (reality as Becoming) throws up a stream of irreducibly singular or novel events (the "actual"), and the only legitimate function of reflection (the "virtual") is to respond by recognizing and affirming these events, along the lines of a Stoic-Nietzschean *amor fati*—"love of one's fate." In this view Renoir's articulation of the crystal-image represents a visionary affirmation of the ever-changing Dionysian "Life" of the cosmos: "We see in the crystal the perpetual foundation of time, non-chronological time, Chronos and not Chronos. This is the powerful, non-organic Life that grips the world. The visionary, the seer, is the one who sees in the crystal, and what he sees is gushing of time as dividing in two, as splitting."[62] Though none of the characters in the Revolutionary films are privy to this cosmic vision, and though Renoir deliberately highlights the non-coincidence of their reflections and events, Deleuze nonetheless reads Renoir's deployment of the crystal-image as a brutal affirmation of the primacy of cosmic-time-as-history over any individual's ability to be equal to it. The revolutionary characters' reflections on each other and the world around them are, at best, noble attempts that necessarily fall short, and their falling short measures the infinite height or nobility of the cosmos, articulates another version of the romantic sublime.

Though I am ready to admit that Renoir considered the Nietzschean vision that Deleuze ascribes to him, I do not think that he affirmed it as the fundamental or final truth of human existence; it was, instead, something that brought certain philosophical issues he was concerned with to a pitch of explicitness. The other possible way of interpreting the articulation of the crystal-image in these films is to posit that the split or non-coincidence of the characters' reflections and reality is a logically necessary consequence of the contradictory modern assumptions that underlie those reflections. On this view, which I would ascribe to Renoir, there is something defective about the Revolutionary characters' way of recognizing each other that creates the split between reality and their understanding of it. Though they appear to suffer historical events "from the outside" (something that finds its most poignant expression in Louis XVI's last bewildered attempt to return a gaze coming from somewhere "behind" the bleak gray sky above him), we can nonetheless posit a hidden causality that links the elements of romanticism informing their thoughts with the events that overwhelm them.

This causal connection is perhaps easier to recognize if we consider a simpler example. If we can understand how the "actual" storm and backward tracking shot on the river in *A Day in the Country* became for Henri and Henriette a "virtual" image of the sublime suddenness with which the irreversible stream of time carried them away from each other, then we recognize the ways in which Henri and Henriette organize the actuality of their lives in terms of certain fatalistic romantic assumptions. Though they may feel that their brief encounter and tragic separation is something that happened *to* them, we can nonetheless recognize the extent to which they are themselves the authors of their own misery. Things happened in a certain way, and will continue to happen in a certain way, in part because they want them to happen in a certain way: the Cytherean possibilities of their lives are thrown out of focus and obscured by the romantic narratives that they never cease to tell themselves. In the same way, we can recognize the extent to which the blind enthusiasm of the revolutionaries of *Le crime de Monsieur Lange* and *La Marseillaise* leads them to commit acts that unconsciously mesh with those of others to produce historical effects that they then experience as happening *to* them; they are, like the lovers of *A Day in the Country*, the unconscious authors of their own fates. Far from being Nietzschean affirmations of cosmic chaos, in these films one can recognize Renoir struggling to identify and untie the knots of romantic contradiction that bind time-as-reflection to time-as-history. To understand *why* Renoir might have come to feel the bad thinking of romanticism to be a real philosophical problem, a burning or existential issue, we turn in the next chapter to examine the real world context of France and Europe in the 1930s.

NOTES

1. Andrew, *Mists of Regret*, 332.
2. Ibid., 122.
3. Ibid., 119.
4. Ibid., 121.
5. Bazin, *Jean Renoir*, 107.
6. Andrew, *Mists of Regret*, 301.
7. Bazin, *Jean Renoir*, 78–79.
8. The distinction between studium and punctum is made in Barthes, *Camera Lucida*.
9. Benardete, *Argument of the Action*, ix.
10. Ibid., x–xi.
11. Ibid., 409.
12. Flaubert, *Madame Bovary*, 81–82.
13. Auerbach, *Mimesis*, 458–59.
14. Ibid., 465.
15. Ibid., 462.

16. David Depew, private conference, December 2000.
17. Auerbach, *Mimesis*, 467.
18. Ibid., 478.
19. Ibid., 476.
20. Ibid., 482.
21. Andrew, *Mists of Regret*, 270–71.
22. Auerbach, *Mimesis*, 482.
23. Ibid., 489.
24. Though I intend to give it a much wider application than he does, I should acknowledge that, like so much else, I got the idea of this connection from Bazin, who uses this adjective in passing in his manuscript notes on *Tire au Flac* in Bazin, *Jean Renoir*, 218.
25. Schneider, *World of Watteau*, 79.
26. Ibid., 80.
27. Ibid., 54.
28. "The word itself derives from the French word *rocaille*, meaning an ornament made of rocks and shells." Ibid., 55.
29. Ibid., 80–81.
30. Ibid., 82.
31. Ibid., 82–83.
32. Ibid., 83.
33. Berger, "Watteau as the Painter of His Time," in *Selected Essays*, 53.
34. Ibid.
35. Rousseau, *First and Second Discourses*, 137.
36. Ibid. The fact that Rousseau gave up each of his five children to the foundling hospital (and later came to bitterly regret this) is itself a telling commentary on this aspect of his thought.
37. Ibid., 133.
38. Ibid.
39. Bann, *Romanticism and the Rise of History*, 3–4, 10.
40. Ibid., 4.
41. Fukuyama, *End of History and the Last Man*.
42. I am indebted to discussions with Michael Meneghetti for this understanding of the turn to history within film studies; the ideological collapse of political modernism is recounted in Rodowick, *Crisis of Political Modernism*. The "short history" genre seems to have been set in motion by Stephen Hawking, *A Brief History of Time* (New York: Bantam, 1998)—a book that is itself symptomatic of the loss of any conception of time other than the historical. Karen Armstrong, *Islam: A Short History* (New York: Modern Library, 2002); Mark Kurlansky, *Cod: A Short History of the Fish That Changed the World* (Toronto: Vintage Canada, 1998); Angus Trumble, *A Brief History of the Smile* (Toronto: Harper-Collins Canada, 2005).
43. Bazin, *Jean Renoir*, 85–86.
44. Barthes, *Camera Lucida*, 45. The photograph that Barthes describes is reproduced on page 48 of the book.
45. Renoir, *Renoir on Renoir*, 77.
46. Ibid., 77–79.
47. Deleuze, *Cinema 1*, 123, 124.
48. Auerbach, *Mimesis*, 476; Deleuze, *Cinema 1*, 124.

49. "Everything which inspires Renoir turns him away from the naturalism which, nonetheless, continued to torment him." Deleuze, *Cinema 1*, 133.

50. Andrew, *Mists of Regret*, 270–71.

51. Ibid., 312.

52. Ibid.

53. Ibid.

54. Sims, "House-Sitting," 108–9.

55. The film's status as the definitive cultural artifact of the Popular Front is evident in its extended treatment in Faulkner's *Social Cinema of Jean Renoir*, Andrew's *Mists of Regret*, Rearick's *French in Love and War*, and Andrew and Ungar's *Popular Front Paris*.

56. Andrew and Ungar, *Popular Front Paris*, 164–65.

57. Sesonske quotes Renoir's claim that these comments are taken from the historical record and his assessment of what they tell us about Louis's character: "These words, which I did not invent, seem to me rather poignant. And they tend to confirm that aspect of a knowing victim which I believe I found in Louis XVI." Sesonske, *Jean Renoir*, 343.

58. Ibid., 342.

59. Renoir's historical research for the film is outlined in Andrew and Ungar, *Popular Front Paris*, 166–74.

60. Though Deleuze's philosophy is in the final analysis based on assumptions that are different from my own, his account of the crystal-image can nonetheless be seen to make a basic distinction between time-as-history (the "actual," the causality of events) and the time of contemplation (the "virtual," reflection on the causality of events) that I will be focusing on in the next chapter:

> What constitutes the crystal-image is the most fundamental operation of time: since the past is constituted not after the present that it was but at the same time, time has to split itself in two at each moment as present and past, which differ from each other in nature, or, what amounts to the same thing, it has to split the present in two heterogeneous directions, one of which is launched toward the future while the other falls into the past.... In fact the crystal constantly exchanges the two distinct images which constitute it, the actual image of the present which passes and the virtual image of the past which is preserved: distinct and yet indiscernible, and all the more indiscernible because distinct, because we do not know which is one and which is the other. This is unequal exchange, or the point of indiscernibility, the mutual image. The crystal always lives at the limit, is itself the vanishing limit between the immediate past which is no longer and the immediate future which is not yet ... mobile mirror which endlessly reflects perception in recollection. (Deleuze, *Cinema 2*, 81)

A brief reconsideration of an example we have already discussed can, I hope, illuminate the relevance of this difficult metaphor-concept to the *chronotope* as a whole. Which character first said *La Marseillaise* echoed his thoughts, Arnaud or Bomier? If we answer Arnaud we might imagine that we are correctly distinguishing "the actual" (i.e., the dialogue that we heard and saw take place in the fishing scene) from "the virtual" (i.e., the false revisionist account of the scene preserved in Bomier's memory), but we can also be described as doing the opposite; if one of the effects of Arnaud's speech was to have transformed Bomier's self-understanding and memory, then in denying the "actuality" of this effect we are rendering that speech "virtual" by subtracting it from the causality of historical time. If, on the other hand, we answer Bomier—privileging the "creative powers" of his memory and defining actuality retrospectively in terms of its historical effects—we are nonetheless contradicting ourselves by denying the equally actual effect Bomier's disclosure of that memory has on Arnaud (i.e., it causes him to return to and reflect on the past): though Bomier's memory may seem to have erased it or rendered it virtual, Arnaud's original speech remains the end-point of the chain of causality that it set in motion.

61. Jameson, *Geopolitical Aesthetic*, 114.
62. Deleuze, *Cinema 2*, 81.

Loving the Distance; or, Historical Experience and the Fruits of Reflection

My father was terrified at the thought that I might be taught silly prejudices, but he also knew that a good teacher must of necessity be prejudiced. As a result of these views, I was not sent to school until time came for my secondary education. Instead, I was entrusted to two private tutors: one was the priest of the village where I was raised, and the other was the local communist. These two actually preached the very same gospel: try not to shit on other people unless you have no choice. Of course, I had to grow into maturity to realize the paradox, and the realization explained something which had puzzled me when I was fifteen and sixteen: how could my father seem equally fond of people who were left-wingers and of others who were right-wingers. I used to wonder whether he was addled or two-faced. The truth, as I realized later, was that these oppositions were of less importance to him than the nature of each proponent.

Alain Renoir, letter to the author, 2003

It should come as no surprise that so little has been written on the history of the couple "right and left," paired terms firmly ensconced in the intellectual and symbolic workings of contemporary societies. Thinkers are never keen to reflect on that which enables them to think.

Marcel Gauchet, "Right and Left," 1992

VICIOUS CIRCLES: THE CHRONOTOPIC EVOLUTION OF THE FRENCH RENOIR

Having spent considerable time inside the fictional worlds of Renoir's imagination, it is time to resituate those worlds within the historical contexts from which they emerged. We are now in a position to examine the historical sequence in which the four chronotopes were manifest, consider the relationship of this pattern to the culture and events around it, and use that consideration to bring to light certain issues of political philosophy. To create a provisional backdrop for our reexamination of the films, I would like to begin with a brief review of the common knowledge regarding Renoir's political engagement and, by way of context for this, a brief sketch of France during the 1930s.

The explicitness of Renoir's commitment to the cause of the French Left during the 1930s—together with the absence of any such commitment after that period—has made the question of Renoir's politics a recurring topic of debate ever since. In addition to the general attention to social and economic relations that informs all his films of the period, Renoir's engagement is made explicit in the Frontist fable *Le crime de Monsieur Lange*, the Parti Communiste Français–commissioned propaganda of *La vie est à nous* (1936), the utopian financing scheme for *La Marseillaise* (a public subscription sponsored by the Confédération Générale du Travail, one of the largest federations of labor unions), and the strident antifascism of the polemical journalism he wrote from 1936 to 1938; for all these reasons Renoir was often described as the "leading film-maker of the Left," and Jonathan Buchsbaum aptly observes that "no other film-maker of the period compared even remotely in the public visibility of his stance as supporter of the Popular Front."[1] As the topics of his journalism make clear, and as Renoir frequently noted after the fact, the main impetus for his engagement derived from an awareness of the pathological effects that the radical polarization of European politics was having on French society.[2] In political terms France appeared to be the last open question amid a group of nations that had either decided in favor of communism (the Soviet Union) or fascism (Italy, Germany, Portugal, Yugoslavia, Greece, and Bulgaria) or were in the process of being decided through civil war

(Spain) and/or invasion (Austria, Czechoslovakia, Finland, Poland); given the enframing motion of events taking place in the countries around them, it is, I think, easy to draw an analogy between the French people of the 1930s and the rabbits and birds in the hunt sequence of *La règle du jeu*—they hear the sound of the beaters' sticks echo through the crisp November air and hunch down or run for ideological cover but are incapable of imagining, let alone defending themselves from, the implacable technological mechanism flushing them into the open field to be shot and killed.

Set within this broader context of encroaching dangers, historical narratives of France during the period typically focus on three defining moments. At the front end, we have the riots and political restructuring prompted by "the Stavisky affair" (January–February 1934), violent events that pulled the contradictions of the nation into sharp focus and radicalized the divisions between Left and Right. In the middle we have the rise and fall of the Popular Front, a much-celebrated achievement of solidarity and consensus that was in fact quite shaky and brief (the Radical Party did not complete the Front until January 1936 and brought down the first Blum government in June 1937, while the second Blum government formed and disintegrated in the spring of 1938); though certain "Cytherean" aspects of this moment have passed into left-wing legend (the strikes and carnivalesque occupation of workplaces during the spring and summer of 1936; the law granting three weeks of paid summer vacation that came into effect in August 1936; the efflorescence within popular culture that produced artifacts like *Lange*), the fragility of the achievement was retrospectively demonstrated by the series of events that immediately followed.[3] The final episode of the story traces the process of France's collapse and generally emphasizes the cowardice, self-deception, and hypocrisy of both the major political players and the public. Though this process can be seen to begin during the Popular Front itself (for example, the Blum government's refusal to come to the defense of the Spanish Republic in 1936), the main events that mark it are the Munich Agreement of September 1938 (in which France colluded in forcing the Czech government to hand over the Sudeten provinces to Germany); the Hitler-Stalin Pact of August 1939 and subsequent invasion of Poland in September 1939; the relatively meaningless stand against further appeasement that led to the empty bravado of the *drôle de guerre* or "phony war" (October 1939 to May 1940); and the invasion of France, complete in little more than a month and experienced as an "utter humiliation, almost too deep for any Frenchman to comprehend."[4] After this series of events, the establishment of a puppet-regime at Vichy led by the hastily disinterred "hero of Verdun" Pétain could not fail to remind the French people of two things: that they had in some sense been living a lie during the 1930s (whether wittingly or unwittingly) and that they were now forced to start living a new set of lies in a degrading and futile attempt to forget the first set.

This long shot of France during the 1930s—this poignant spectacle of a proud nation caught up in historical events that laid bare its all-too-human contradictions and carried it unwillingly toward an unimaginable degradation—has exerted a powerful fascination on historians ever since. Where did things go wrong? Who was responsible? What might have been done to make things go better? All professional alibis aside, I believe our fascination with this kind of narrative derives from the way it raises the ethical dimension of questions that we prefer to consider in a more disengaged and piecemeal fashion: the nature and extent of political responsibility, free will, and determinism and the relation of thought and action. Set within this larger context, the much-debated story of Renoir's engagement and disengagement also focuses our attention on these issues. To what extent did Renoir really believe in the utopian goals of the political cause to which he committed himself? Is it possible to reconstruct the relations between his public stance and his films? Did he decide to become engaged only because, as his retrospective account above suggests, a specific moment of crisis put "his back against the wall," or was a genuine commitment to a leftist vision simply beaten out of him by the course of events? Though I doubt anyone would support either of these extreme hypotheses in isolation—total free will or total determinism—the question nonetheless helps to focus our attention on the relationship between his films and their historical context; if recent scholarship on Renoir has often tended to privilege the determinist hypothesis, the account that follows will attempt to test the limits of the first by reading Renoir's filmmaking as a process of reflection that was undoubtedly shaped by historical events but nonetheless, in an important sense, free.

I will present my reconstruction of Renoir's process of reflection in three stages. In the first stage I will identify and discuss the significance of certain patterns in Renoir's filmmaking over the course of the decade, and in the second I will attempt to show how those patterns can be read as a response to the context sketched above. In the third I will examine *Les bas-fonds* and *La grande illusion*, two films based on philosophical assumptions that are quite different from those manifest in the French films and culture of the time, two films that realize Cytherean possibilities that remained only latent in the films we examined in the last chapter. My decision to neglect these two films in the preceding chapter and to defer discussion of them until later in this chapter derives from the philosophical design of this inquiry; in my narrative they represent the fruits of Renoir's reflections, films whose thought-provoking difference will make sense, have the required "trapdoor" effect, only after we have examined the dialectic of historical experience and reflection that led to them.[5]

The list below lays out the historical sequence in which the chronotopes discussed in chapter 2 appeared:

La chienne (1931), Flaubertian I
La nuit du carrefour (1932), Flaubertian II
Boudu sauvé des eaux (1932), Cytherean I
Chotard et cie (1933), Cytherean II
Madame Bovary (1934), Flaubertian III
Toni (1935), Naturalist Melodrama I
Le crime de Monsieur Lange (1936), Revolutionary I
La vie est à nous (1936), Revolutionary II
Une partie de campagne (1936), Cytherean III
Les bas-fonds (1936)
La grande illusion (1937)
La Marseillaise (1938), Revolutionary III
La bête humaine (1938), Naturalist Melodrama II
La règle du jeu (1939)

A first reading of this long shot registers a simple pattern of alternation between the four chronotopes, one that we can imagine to have been determined both by box office trends and other industrial circumstances and/or by the auteur's autonomous and capricious (that is, random) selection from a preferred palette of dialogically related genres (as in Howard Hawks's career-long alternation between comedies and adventure dramas).[6] But to treat the story of the French Renoir in this way would be to arbitrarily discard the possibility that it can be reconstructed to reveal a coherent dialogical relationship with its context, and it is precisely this possibility that we are concerned with. Our having accepted Renoir's testimony that the question of "meeting" or "belonging" governed the development of his filmmaking allows us to register the chronotopic evolution of the French Renoir as a pattern of provisional affirmations, radical breaks, and surprising, differential returns. A careful examination of this pattern reveals a single figure that, fractal-like, reproduces itself at various scales of analysis (within individual films, within each chronotope, and within the chronological sequence of the French Renoir as a whole over the course of the 1930s). When recognized and replaced in its historical context, I believe this figure articulates a coherent process of reflection on those contexts.

The first large figure we need to take note of is articulated by the sequence in which each of the four chronotopes first appeared: Flaubertian (*La chienne*), Cytherean (*Boudu sauvé des eaux*), Naturalist Melodrama (*Toni*), and Revolutionary (*Le crime de Monsieur Lange*). How does this sequence make sense as a figure of reflection in which what happens within each chronotope logically motivates the shift to the next?

Renoir first posed the question of "how to meet" by using a modernist idiom in which the distance between the characters, and between the characters and the author/spectator, is represented to be absolute and irreducible. As in Flaubert's *Madame Bovary*, the lucid objectivity with which we view the characters is implicitly premised on a sublimation/negation of our own desire; if we are given what we understand to be a total, God's-eye, mental X-ray view of each character, this is only because we have been allowed our own desire to be reduced to and satisfied by the godlike feeling of power we get by looking-at and judging them from an abstracted position outside the world in which they live. The figure of looking-at that dominates this chronotope from the author/spectator on down can be seen as a synthesis of the attitudes of modern science (that is, the cold patience of a scientist observing an experiment) and modern historicism (that is, the satisfied smirk with which one "places" others by recognizing causes of their behavior that they themselves could never recognize). In a genealogical sense, the sense of judgment specific to this perspective derives from the basic modern reaction to the experience of historicity or human difference; one does not judge the characters individually by measuring them against positive ideals of human nature or morality, as "bad" or "good" relative to transcendent models of the virtues, but one judges them all equally "bad" for being equally enclosed within limited cultural perspectives—what Nietzsche called "horizons"—determined by their location within a historical world: in the final analysis, we judge them for simply existing, for being actual, from what is, for modernist authors (for example, Flaubert, Joyce, and Nabokov) and modern philosophers (for example, Nietzsche and Heidegger), the more exalted position of pure possibility.[7]

The Flaubertian chronotope offered Renoir a very ambiguous and problematic answer to the question he was concerned with. Though it pulled the contradictions in his characters into sharp focus and allowed him to meet the audience in a knowing complicity, a shared assumption of being superior to the characters, he also recognized that this meeting was premised on an abstraction from one's own desires and dependencies that could legitimately be described as a form of self-deception or bad faith, a solipsism as total as that which it presumes to judge. Since looking-at reduces one's desire for the other to the measure of what one already knows about the other, desire becomes little more than idle curiosity in search of occasions to flatter itself, a form of narcissism; even worse, it becomes impossible to distinguish from the active inversion of desire in hate and resentment. With this limited and limiting attitude in view, we can appreciate why Renoir might have found the Flaubertian approach to his driving question unsatisfactory; his decision to break with this chronotope can be said to stem from the understanding that the narcissistic and/or resentment-driven form of recognition it entails could never result in the quality of meeting or belonging he desired.

Renoir's shift to the Cytherean chronotope represents an explicit affirmation of a model of human desire the phenomenology of which is the exact opposite of Flaubert's. Love is not possessing others within a synoptic view, it is an external force that disturbs our complacency and makes us aware that we already belong to others; we do not select what to love from an abstracted position of pure possibility but are ourselves chosen by what we love in what seems to be a gift of chance; we do not love what we already know, we respond to the prior love of something we don't know; the whole is not measured and defined by the self, the self allows itself to be measured and defined by the whole. Each of the Cytherean films we examined in chapter 2 begins by evoking a Flaubertian world in a state of dormancy or boredom that leaves it open and vulnerable to the transformative effects of love-as-spring-fever. We then observe a process in which certain characters become affected by this external force and embark on a voyage of discovery. It is worth quickly reminding ourselves of everything that is condensed in the lovely figure of embarking that Renoir can be said to have adapted from Watteau. Strictly speaking, the voyage the characters are embarking on cannot be represented or imagined; we see *that* they are going somewhere but cannot see or imagine *where* they are going. We can only infer the attraction they are experiencing from the evidence of their distraction; like them, through them, we feel the erotic pull of the ocean landscape, but we cannot represent that sublime infinity to ourselves. This figure of Cythera as the vanishing point of representation is consistent with the model of human desire outlined above; if love proposes to enact a complete transformation of the self, this completeness is manifest in a radical self-forgetting that, as it were, covers its tracks. The characters can get to where they are going only by forgetting where and who they are, and in doing do they seem to be vanishing before our eyes: they offer no purchase for a Flaubertian gaze seeking to "place" them.

This figure of embarking enacts the invisible dissolve that we discussed in relation to Watteau's painting, and, in a general sense, this dissolve happens "somewhere" in the middle of each of the Cytherean films. But by the end of each film we are back where we started from as if this dissolve has been reversed. The misery on Boudu's face just before he overturns the boat containing the wedding party already tells us that something is not quite right about the happy ending his patron has arranged. Though Boudu's marriage to Anne-Marie seemed to be a stroke of genius that would allow the characters to continue to embark, to pursue the countercultural utopia of their *ménage-à-quatre* under the cover of bourgeois respectability, Dionysius can tolerate no such compromise; he immediately repossesses the gift of Boudu and leaves the other characters high and dry—stripped of their wet clothes and covered with the local equivalents of fig leaves—on the river bank. Madame Lestingois reverts to her old self and calls Boudu a "savage," Lestingois reverts to speaking in metaphors (Boudu has been reclaimed by the "currents of destiny"), and we swiftly understand that these characters are now fallen from the Eden that enveloped them only moments before. In a similar manner, the real storm and backward tracking shot in *A Day in the Country* dissolves back into a romantic metaphor through which Henri and Henriette nostalgically mis-remember their Cytherean encounter; the penultimate shot in which Henriette searches Henri's face in a desperate attempt to regain some purchase on that encounter measures the distance that separates the reality of Cythera from its romantic misrepresentation. When viewed as a whole, each film traces the process whereby Dionysius/Cythera suddenly appears within a Flaubertian milieu, creates a disturbance, and then just as suddenly disappears, leaving only a residue of romantic regret. But though we might now be tempted to "re-place" the characters in accordance with a Flaubertian perspective and interpret the disturbance as being only a collective hallucination brought on by their romanticism, there is something mysterious and irreducible about what happened that prevents us from doing so with a good conscience: though we could never say how, Renoir's invocation of Cythera has found roots in our historical experience, in our own "forgotten memories," and it is these memories that offer stubborn resistance to any easy restoration of the Flaubertian status quo.

Unlike the Flaubertian, the Cytherean chronotope allowed Renoir to develop his inquiry into the fundamental questions of meeting and belonging he was concerned with. The figure of embarking for Cythera articulates a transformative meeting between characters that promises to bring the fullness or height of their otherness into being; precisely because it never announces or represents the fact, *Boudu* is a film that articulates a tremendous sense of expectation or hope, and it thus represents a radical break with the inherent despair of the chronotope that preceded it. But there is a fundamental problem with the Cytherean proposal that the film also articulates: the force that moves the characters is "external" (that is, unconscious) and unstable, and as soon as they make the slightest effort to become conscious of it, secure it, or possess it, it dies. Cythera is a gift that they do not know how to handle, and so they eventually fall back into the solipsistic mire of ideology and conditioned reflexes from which it briefly raised them. The Cytherean formula for meeting and belonging now seems to depend on *knowing how* to let go and forget oneself, knowledge the characters in the film lack.

Like the work of Plato, the Cytherean chronotope suggests that erotic knowledge or wisdom (the only wisdom that Plato's Socrates ever claims to possess) is the key to all knowledge or wisdom; *Boudu* can be said to have reoriented the question of meeting and belonging by making it depend on erotic wisdom.[8] Recognizing this reorientation allows us to make better sense of the passage from Renoir's 1957 interview with Rivette and Truffaut quoted in chapter 2: "After all, the reality is in being enchanted. It demands great patience, work and good faith to find it. I'm convinced, in any case, that it isn't a question of talent or gifts, just of good faith. If you want to find reality, you'll find it. You just have to eliminate whatever seems to you to have been created by the habits of your times, to eliminate these habits first, but to take back later the ones that seem to conform with reality."[9] In the first instance, "the reality is in being enchanted," having let go and allowed oneself to become enchanted. This formulation implies a conception of both love and reality as gifts that precede the recipient/subject/self; if *wanting* to find reality (loving it in "good faith") is the only prerequisite for *finding* it (acquiring knowledge of it), this implies that our desire somehow remembers something that we ourselves do not, that it orients our search for something we were given in the past but have now lost or forgotten: though strictly speaking we do not know what we are looking for or where to look, our desire as it were assures us that "we'll know it when we see it." But according to Renoir, "finding reality" is no easy matter; arriving at an understanding of reality "demands great patience, work and good faith," a rigorous application of methodical reflection (patience, work) and an ethical purification of the self (good faith). "Eliminating the habits of your times—first" clearly indicates the radical skepticism of a Socratic self-questioning; only after thoroughly reflecting on the ideologies that enclose the self can one recognize what to "take back," the truths worth retaining.

The shift from the Cytherean chronotope to that of Naturalist Melodrama represents an effort to examine the bad habits of romanticism in a way that is more sincere, self-reflexive, and dialogical than the Flaubertian approach. If the perspective of the author/spectator in the Flaubertian chronotope can be said to totalize the figure of looking-at enacted by the characters, Renoir's version of Naturalist Melodrama can be described as totalizing the sympathetic perspective of the romantic protagonists' closest comrades, the friends who contemplate them over the course of each film and who sincerely mourn their deaths (Fernand in *Toni*, Pecqueux in *La bête humaine*). Despite everything I said about the culpable blindness of the protagonists, their comrades never judge them for this, for they also recognize something noble in their friends' actions that they themselves lack: a sincere, if misguided, effort to realize the height or infinity of their desire. Both Fernand and Pecqueux know that the clear-sighted stoicism of their own response to the life situations they share with the protagonists is a compromise wherein they have given up wanting something they believe life won't give them. Their concern for their comrades, the thing that makes them study the protagonists with such care and attention, derives from the fact that the protagonists have not given up: though they could never do what their friends do, contemplating Toni and Lantier gives Fernand and Pecqueux hope. In this sense Naturalist Melodrama constitutes an ambiguous synthesis of the "knowing" of the Flaubertian chronotope and the "wondering" of the Cytherean: from the perspective of the sympathetic comrades, which we share, the protagonists seem to be motivated both by women whose limitations are clearly displayed (the knowing part) and by a height or infinity beyond representation (the wondering part). The ending of each film makes us conscious of a contradiction that we infer the bereft comrades are also reflecting upon, that the protagonists' deaths are both unnecessary (when measured against the worth of the particular woman in question) and necessary (insofar as they accurately measure the height or infinity of human desire, something the loss of their friends makes them feel most acutely). Naturalist Melodrama ends with a tragic figure of unrequited love: a sympathetic friend contemplates a romantic commitment the nobility of which he recognizes but which he nonetheless cannot fully understand or accept as good, as a rationally desirable end or ideal.

The ending of Naturalist Melodrama highlights an issue of not-meeting or alienation in a way that can be seen to motivate the shift to the Revolutionary chronotope. The deaths of the protagonists impress their friends with the truth that there is something inadequate about both their positions (that is, a clear-sighted stoicism that affirms the world but negates its own desire, a blind romanticism that negates the world but affirms its own desire), and arriving at this truth can be said to have prompted Renoir to imagine what a synthesis of those positions might look like. It is, I hope, relatively easy to see how the figure of mutual recognition at the center of the Revolutionary chronotope synthesizes the figures of the chronotope that preceded it: the clear-sighted stoic Valentine allows herself to be carried away by her love for the blind romantic Lange, and he in turn finally opens his eyes to her and the world. The meeting between these two characters is shown to be the result of a synthesis within each of them of the human qualities and positions that are kept separate in Naturalist Melodrama. Unlike Fernand and Pecqueux, Valentine lets go and allows herself to be transformed by the passion and hope she sees in Lange; unlike Toni and Lantier, Lange opens his eyes both to her own Cytherean reality and to the realism of her perspective on the world. The meeting between this couple and between the couple Arnaud-Bomier in *La Marseillaise* inaugurates a revolutionary process that proposes to realize the height or infinity of their desires through historical action. This process has both immediate effects on the people around them (that is, creating microcosmic communities in the courtyard and on the mountaintop) and broader effects on the country as a whole (that is, the national communities that cohere as a result of Lange's Arizona Jim stories and "La Marseillaise"), and the couples might well imagine that, in accordance with Hegel's progressive conception of history, every form of human difference will eventually be recognized and find a home within their revolution.

What *Lange* suggests, through the fragility of its happy coincidences, and what *La Marseillaise* demonstrates, through the fatality of its unhappy ones, is that this utopian hope is, in the end, unjustified; in the final analysis, the view each film takes on the revolution it examines remains that of a sympathetic comrade who appreciates the nobility and benefits of the enterprise but who also cannot help recognizing its inherent blindness and divisiveness. Just as the romanticism of the protagonists in Naturalist Melodrama blinded them to the truth about their love objects and the Cytherean possibilities of world around them, here too we can recognize how a revolution seems to focus the attention of its participants on those within the community but renders them blind to the Otherness of those outside it. Revolution is a form of collective romanticism that turns individuals as different as Jules Berry's Batala and Pierre Renoir's Louis XVI into shadow-puppets of equal value; like one of Lange's stories, the revolutionary narrative of history-as-melodrama magnifies and distorts the difference between individuals within the community (all "working-class heroes") and those outside it (all "bourgeois villains") while simultaneously leveling or negating the differences between individuals within each domain (who all are "equally" heroes or villains). Though the Revolutionary chronotope begins in a Cytherean moment in which two individuals open their eyes and affirm each other's difference in a genuine dialogue, it is shown to end in a blind love for those within the community (a collective monologue governed by unconscious narcissism or masochism) and an equally blind hate for those outside it (a collective monologue governed by unconscious sadism or resentment). In the final analysis, revolution is a fundamentally Janus-faced and divisive phenomenon; its centripetal face reproduces the figures of blind love enacted by the protagonists of Naturalist Melodrama, while its centrifugal face reproduces the figures of looking-at that characterize the Flaubertian chronotope. The inadvertent process of reflection whereby Renoir explored each of the four chronotopes in turn carried him back to the point he started from, to a Flaubertian position from which he could not escape.

This narrative interpretation of the sequence in which each of the four chronotopes first appeared traces a figure that reproduces the two invisible dissolves of the Cytherean chronotope, both the embarking and the returning, on a much larger scale; the evolution of the French Renoir as a whole can thus be seen to enact a reflective reexamination of what happens within the Cytherean chronotope, an extended close-up on the habits of romanticism which that chronotope itself offers only a brief and suggestive long shot of. Renoir's shift from the Flaubertian to the Cytherean chronotope reproduces the first invisible dissolve within that chronotope (the disorientation of a Flaubertian world by the external force of Cytherean attraction), and each of the two shifts that follow represent attempts to examine the processes whereby the romanticism of the characters enacts the second invisible dissolve (the collapse of Cythera and return to the Flaubertian status quo); Naturalist Melodrama contemplates these processes at the level of the individual, while the Revolutionary chronotope considers how they work at the level of the collectivity. Like the Cytherean chronotope, both Naturalist Melodrama and the Revolutionary chronotope can be said to end in a return to a Flaubertian perspective on the characters, but in each case that return is now informed by a more self-aware genealogical understanding of that perspective and a more sympathetic identification with the characters. Far from being the measure of a self-sufficient complacency, looking-at now takes a reflective measure of our own isolation and erotic dependency, our own unrequited love. We have examined the ways in which the "habits of our time" alienate us but have not yet discovered anything worth "taking back," that is, erotic knowledge or wisdom that would help to address our predicament. When considered as a whole, the sequence in which each of the four chronotopes first appeared poses the question Renoir is concerned with in all its existential explicitness but does not disclose an answer to that question.

The Cytherean figures reproduced in the chronotopic evolution of the French Renoir as a whole can also be discerned in the historical development of each chronotope, that is, in the tonal differences manifest between earlier and later films outlined in the list below:

Flaubertian: *La chienne* (1931)–*Madame Bovary* (1934)
Cytherean: *Boudu sauvé des eaux* (1932)–*Une partie de campagne* (1936)
Naturalist Melodrama: *Toni* (1935)–*La bête humaine* (1938)
Revolutionary: *Le crime de Monsieur Lange* (1936)–*La Marseillaise* (1938)

If we reexamine these pairs in light of what was said about the films in chapter 2, we find that in each case the first film evokes Cytherean possibilities that are absent in the second.[10] In each case, the milieu of the earlier film is more open than that of the later film, as if the ocean landscape, the prehistoric, eternal cosmos, is waiting, patiently and hopefully, for the characters to open their eyes to its infinity; in the second film of each pair the power of romanticism to enclose the characters is totalized and effectively remakes the Cytherean cosmos into an image of its own despair. In each case the first film articulates a palpable sense of hope in the possibility of meeting that is starkly attenuated in the second film; whatever note the first films end on, we can nonetheless still imagine that things might have gone otherwise, whereas the endings of the second films impress with a sense of inescapable necessity. If the evocation of Cytherean possibilities in the earlier films raises the issue of romanticism, the later films can be said to decide that issue, however unhappily and reluctantly, according to terms dictated by romanticism. The evolution of each chronotope over the course of the decade thus retraces the second invisible dissolve of the Cytherean chronotope—the return to the solipsistic Flaubertian enclosure—and in doing so it makes that movement visible, necessary, and inescapable, the image of an ideological fatality that encloses both the individual and the collectivity.

If the preceding account of the logic of reflection shaping the narrative of Renoir's filmmaking during the 1930s has been successful—that is, if the phenomenological analyses of Cythera and romanticism cohere—the reader should be able to understand why I have named this book after the poem by Eugenio Montale below, which also encapsulates everything I might wish to say about boats and rivers in Renoir's films. Published in 1939 in his second collection, *The Occasions*, "Boats on the Marne" articulates a structure of time that is analogous to that of Cythera as we have described it while at the same time foreshadowing the more brutal experiences of history and modernity, what Renoir described as the "absolutely uncontrolled reshaping of the world," which we are about to explore next; in addition to the image of cork in the river, Renoir's famous metaphor for the artist's relationship to the world around him, the poem offers an aptly impressionist rendering of the Belle Époque of Cythera that Renoir grew up in, the optimistic phase of modernity that was shattered by World War I.[11]

Boats on the Marne

Bliss of cork bark abandoned
to the current
that melts around bridges upside down,

and the full moon pale in sunlight:
boats on the river, nimble, in summer
and a lazy murmur of city.
You row along the field where the butterfly
catcher comes with his net,
the thicket across the wall where the dragon's
blood repeats itself in cinnabar.

Voices from the river, cries from the banks,
or the rhythmic stroking of canoes
in the twilight filtering through
the walnut leaves, but where
is the slow parade of the seasons
which was a dawn that never ended, with no roads,
where is the long expectation, and what is the name
of the void that invades us?

The dream is this: a vast
unending day, almost motionless,
that suffuses its splendor between the banks
and at every bend the good works of man,
the veiled tomorrow that holds no horror.
And the dream was more, more, but its reflection
stilled on the racing water, under
the oriole's nest, airy, out of reach,
was one high silence in the noontime's
rhyming cry, the great turmoil
great repose.
      Here ... the color that endures
is the gray of the mouse that leapt
through the rushes or the starling, a spurt
of poison metal disappearing
in mists along the bank.
      Another day,
you were saying—what were you saying? And where
does it take us, this river mouth gathering in a single
rush?
      This is the evening. Now we can descend
downstream where the Great Bear is shining.

(Boats on the Marne, on a Sunday outing
on your birthday, floating.)[12]

THE VICIOUS CIRCLES OF A SCHIZOPHRENIC
SOCIETY: THE FRENCH RENOIR IN CONTEXT

Having seen in some detail how the films of the French Renoir addressed the problem of romanticism, we turn to the question as to why—why living through the 1930s in Europe would lead Renoir to be concerned with the problem of romanticism. According to the common historical understanding, romanticism was a high-cultural movement that reached its apex in the early nineteenth century and survived in attenuated forms such as Victorian sentimental literature until it was decisively buried by the experience of World War I; on the basis of this understanding, Renoir's concern with romanticism might seem to be anachronistic and misguided, for it does not appear to be a high-stakes issue, an immediate and pressing "danger." To understand why it was such an issue for him we have to recognize the connections between the historical events of his time and philosophic assumptions that romanticism first made explicit; in other words, we have to recognize the influence of romanticism long after the high-culture movement itself disappeared and the persistence of certain philosophic contradictions that we are living with today.

According to an anecdotal legend, one of Renoir's younger contemporaries, the philosopher Denis de Rougemont, was dismayed to recognize those contradictions within himself when he attended a Hitler rally in Nuremburg in September 1938. Though he attended the rally only out of professional curiosity, he found himself swept up by the frenzy and genuinely tempted to become part of the masses professing their allegiance to the Führer; though he managed to resist this temptation he was left with a terrifying sense of his own vulnerability to the irrational force of a collective passion.[13] How had all his intellectual and political principles given way to that passion? Which of his own assumptions had left him open to it? The horrifying and ironic paradox of the experience was that he had set out the answers to those very questions a few months before while writing his most famous book, *L'amour et l'Occident* (translated as *Love in the Western World*). In that book Rougemont traced a genealogy of romantic ideology from the Tristan myth and Christian mysticism through the mainstream of Western literature (medieval romances, Dante, Petrarch, Shakespeare, Racine, Rousseau, Stendhal) to its first "transplanting" into the modes of modern warfare (the "revolutionary war" of the French Revolution and Napoleonic period; the "national war" of the later nineteenth century; the "total war" of 1914–18) and its "second transplanting" into the mass politics and ideological conflicts of the 1930s (which were "simply an extension of total war by other means").[14] Though positing a link between troubadour poetry and Nazism may seem ridiculous and improbable, Rougemont's analysis demonstrates that, as different as they may be, both depend on the same set of assumptions about human nature; in all the examples he examines there is a shared conception of human desire as a blind and irrational instinct that causes one to seek fusion with others and the corollary recognition that one's self-sacrifice and death were the only measures of the purity and integrity of the self/desire. Given these assumptions, the transplanting of romantic passion from the personal into the public domain was, he argues, an inevitable result of the liberalization of modern societies; insofar as the romantically conceived self requires "absolute obstructions" in order to intensify its passion and provide opportunities to demonstrate its purity through self-sacrifice, the lack of such obstructions in socially mobile modern societies left individuals who depended on romantic assumptions with an identity crisis that war and ideological conflict provided a way of addressing.[15] Though Rougemont had arrived at his diagnosis of romanticism months before he attended the Nazi rally, his experience there revealed the extent to which his own imagination was still unconsciously held by it, and the anecdote suggests that he had not himself discovered a set of alternative assumptions that he could completely believe in. For our purposes, it constitutes one example as to why Renoir might have felt that romanticism was in fact the issue of political philosophy that the historical experience of his time most made urgent.

We can begin our reexamination of French politics in the 1930s by returning to the synchronic long shot we took earlier of Europe as a whole. If we said that France was essentially the last open or undecided question in a map of nations that had already decided in favor of one of two extreme political programs (that is, fascism or communism), it is now important to remember—cutting back along the diachronic axis to a moment 150 years earlier—that it was France itself that gave birth to the possibility of those radical extremes. As François Furet reminds us, neither of the two revolutions that preceded the French Revolution (the English Revolution of the mid-seventeenth century or the American Revolution of the late eighteenth century) conceived of its enterprise as a complete break with all existing forms of social organization, and neither imagined it could found a new social order with no reference to religious systems of meaning.[16] The French Revolution's reduction of the past to an "ancien régime" was an unprecedented leveling equalization of every preceding form of social organization and philosophy, a project of forgetting so radical that its utopian proposals inevitably replicated the absolutism of the systems of political and religious domination that it proposed to negate:[17] "The Revolution sought to reinstitute society in the manner of Rousseau, that is, to regenerate man through a veritable social contract. This universal ambition was akin in its abstraction to a religious message but different in its content, since regeneration was now without a transcendent foundation of any kind, and indeed claimed to take the place of transcendence."[18] As Furet points out, the intellectual origins of the Revolution can be traced to an earlier moment in which modern philosophy rejected its dialogical heritage and began to model itself on the experimental method of modern natural science, a method that neglected the role of chance, contingency and individual particularities in order to produce the technological understanding that allowed one to master human and non-human nature:

> The most spectacular aspect of the event, that which its contemporaries found most striking, was indeed the ambition to rise above the details of how the Revolution had come to pass, to abstract from the particularities of the moment in order to attain the universal. The men of 1789 wanted to emancipate not the French but man in general. In their attempt there was something akin to Descartes's rejection of everything that had been thought before him: a negation of what had preceded them in the history of France, all of which was branded irrational and particular. The idea that society was to be made over from top to bottom, literally reconstructed, was in any case so intimately intertwined with French philosophic rationalism that it predated the Revolution.[19]

The French Revolution was conceived quite explicitly as a scientific experiment based on the hypotheses put forth in Rousseau's *The Social Contract*. Since Rousseau believed it was already too late for human beings to attempt to preserve their original nature on an individual basis, the only solution to their current degradation was to remake themselves by becoming the citizens of a collective body governed by the "general will." Insofar as human beings recognize themselves to be part of such a body, insofar as they negate themselves in order to identify with it, "the common good reveals itself plainly so that nobody with a little good sense can possibly fail to see it."[20] The citizens then make laws that foster this common good and submit themselves to the sovereign authority of those laws. Rousseau argues that this state of freely willed obedience offers the closest possible approximation of the freedom we experienced in the state of nature; through the free act in which we negate our individual wills in favor of the general will, we achieve a "harmony of obedience and liberty" that promises to recoup all our individual losses with collective benefits.[21]

There are three aspects of Rousseau's proposal in the *Social Contract* that Renoir's concern with the problem of romanticism would lead us to highlight. The first is simply that it entails the deliberate violation of what Rousseau claims to have been our original nature in the *Second Discourse*; the naturally amoral, antisocial, individualistic human being is asked in the name of morality to destroy his or her own individuality and merge into society. Though there may be complicated ways to explain it, the *Social Contract* appears to contradict Rousseau's account of human nature in the earlier text.

The second aspect we need to address is that the *Social Contract* proposes that we apply the technological assumptions of modern natural science to the realm of human affairs; the truth of its hypotheses cannot be discerned in advance by individual reflection but can be demonstrated only by the performative results of collectively putting those hypotheses into practice. As Rousseau conceives it, the concept of the common good has no transcendent content that one might access via an individual act of reflection but is an inherently new, unprecedented historical event that emerges to view only after a multitude of individual acts of self-negation have (as it were) unconsciously registered their vote. Only after we have "blindly" identified ourselves with the body politic, totalizing the two-become-one fusion model of the romantic tradition, do the elements of the common good become apparent; our freedom does not consist in acting consciously on the basis of a rational assessment of a given situation but in deciding to be unconscious in order to let the collectivity do our thinking for us. After the collectivity has rather mysteriously arrived at its formulation of the common good, our only choice is to simply "obey" the result of the vote, for anything less, the slightest hesitation, would imply a disavowal of our original act of identification with the collectivity: the required conditions of the experiment would retrospectively be revealed to have been destroyed at the outset. At no point in the process is there a moment in which we are expected or allowed to reflect on a given formulation of the common good and affirm that it makes sense to us as individuals; though we understand that such reflection does play a role in the actual practice of political debate, our already contracted absolute obedience to the final result of any debate changes the orientation and content of that reflection: in place of a graduated criterion of *sincerity* ("To what extent does what I'm thinking, saying, and doing accurately and honestly reflect the truth of my own experience?"), our reflection is now governed by an absolute and inflexible concern with the *authenticity* of our self-negation ("How does what I'm thinking, saying, and doing reflect my total identification with the group?").

The third aspect of this proposal we need to highlight is the model of human desire it presupposes. As Rousseau provocatively announces in the first paragraph of the *Social Contract*, he does not propose to do away with bondage but proposes to solve the bondage problem by making it legitimate through an agreement or contract.[22] As Rousseau sees it, masters and slaves are equally in unlawful bondage because their relationship is largely the product of chance, of the blind play of historical forces and circumstances in the past, rather than something that they themselves have willed into being; they are both alienated because they have not understood that "social order is a right—a sacred right, which serves as the basis for all other rights."[23] Acting on one's sacred right essentially means contracting a relationship wherein we all become equally masters and slaves of each other, a relationship that depends on a paradoxical fusion of the attitudes of sadism and masochism. As Elizabeth Rose Wingrove argues in her book *Rousseau's Republican Romance*, the "consensual nonconsensuality" that the *Social Contract* entails derives from a primal erotic fantasy that can be discerned throughout Rousseau's writings.[24] She quotes a passage from *Emile* that offers a condensed genealogy of this fantasy: "It is an invariable law of nature which gives woman more facility to excite the desires than man to satisfy them. This causes the latter, whether he like it or not, to depend on the former's wish and constrains him to seek to please her in turn, so that she will consent to let him be the stronger. Then what is sweetest for man in his victory is the doubt whether it is his weakness which yields to strength or the will that surrenders."[25] In addition to the question as to whether the situation truly represents an "invariable law of nature," this passage offers an account of human desire that contrasts starkly with the self-sufficient autonomy of natural man presented in the *Second Discourse*. Here human desire begins in a natural imbalance of bodily forces that, if left to their own devices, would become even more unbalanced and irreconcilable: simply put, and as far as I can make out, the man's tendency towards premature satisfaction (the result of the greater "force" of the woman's body) would generate a dissatisfaction in the woman greater than he could ever hope to address. To avoid this dreary outcome, the man and woman behave in accordance with an implicit contract. The man submits himself masochistically to the woman's will by developing his stamina and patience in order to be allowed to dominate her; his apparent domination is in fact the measure of a deeper submission, and her apparent submission is in fact the measure of her prior, deeper dominance. For Rousseau, human desire achieves its greatest height and most exquisite sweetness not in the certainty of an ethical commitment to the infinity or height of another human being but in the fundamental ambiguity, the irresolvable doubt or confusion, that is generated by an implicit sadomasochistic contract. As Wingrove explains: "The expression of will takes place in a physical exchange whose 'sweetness' derives precisely from the confusion of coercion and consent: desire intensifies in the interplay between force and will. For this reason a woman's sexual submission, like the citizen's obedience to the general will, is consistent with consent because her desire, like his interest, materializes only through relations with another whom she has 'let' be stronger. A show of force is necessary to the expression of will, and consent is always consent to the terms of one's own domination."[26] Recovering this primal fantasy allows us to recognize that the *Social Contract*'s solution to the political problem of liberty versus domination is to put every individual in a romantic relationship with the collectivity that makes him or her incapable of telling the difference between the two states. The *Social Contract* proposes to solve the political problem of liberty versus domination by rendering us incapable of recognizing it as a problem.

It is worth noting that Rousseau's solution depends on a radical substitution of concepts that few people noticed at the time of the Revolution but that will prove to be of paramount importance for understanding Renoir's critique of modernity. By deftly replacing the religious concept of transcendent ethical *obligations* (what we owe to others) with a comparably "sacred" concept of historically contracted *rights* (what others owe to us), the *Social Contract* allows us to forget the existence of any ethical obligations we have not contracted; though it may seem to propose an inclusive recognition of all human difference or otherness in the general will, it actually reduces our ethical obligations to the measure of our narcissistic desires: in principle and in practice, we recognize the rights of others only so that "they will consent to let us be the stronger."[27]

How can we summarize the results of Rousseau's proposal in a way that will usefully characterize France in the 1930s? Strange as it may seem, contemporary scholarship on the history of France since the Revolution generally agrees on what happened in trying to realize Rousseau's bedroom utopia in the political realm. Every entry in Pierre Nora's monumental three-volume compendium *Realms of Memory: Rethinking the French Past* testifies to the fact of a basic binary division in the framing categories it uses ("Catholics and Seculars," "Gaullists and Communists," "Right and Left") or by showing how the totems of French identity (such as Joan of Arc and "La Marseillaise") and certain events (the Dreyfus affair) become the object of intense ideological conflict governed by those binary categories. Pierre Birnbaum's *The Idea of France* offers an illuminating overview of the process whereby the utopia proposed by the Revolution immediately generated a counterutopian vision of Catholic France that was to remain as compelling to its own adherents as the former was to the people attempting to realize it. By the time of the Revolution, Rousseau's German followers had developed his contrast between modern man and natural man into the opposition between an unnatural *civilization* (exemplified by the French Enlightenment) and a romantic ideal of national *cultures* wherein individuals existed in a natural and harmonious accord with their fellows, a collective reinterpretation of Rousseau's original state of nature, and the political reaction to the Revolution seized upon this as the basis of its own program. Birnbaum's analysis of political rhetoric from the Revolution until World War II shows how ideologues on both sides of the divide adopted Rousseau's idea of the nation as collective body and consistently resorted to organicist metaphors of degeneration and regeneration in order to make their case.[28] For both sides, the body of the nation becomes an absent object of romantic identification; instead of uniting the nation around a single vision of the common good, the Revolution produced two incommensurable visions of an absent good and two corresponding visions of the present evil that had to be overcome; for each side, the existing state of affairs presented the horrifying spectacle of a sick, decaying, or monstrous body that the other was responsible for.[29] Birnbaum's analysis demonstrates that, far from resolving the issue of liberty and domination, the Revolution's attempt to realize the proposals of the *Social Contract* made that issue a divisive national obsession, with each side masochistically imagining itself to be victim of an unlawful domination while at the same time looking-at its opponents with a cold, sarcastic hatred. As philosophers as different as Isaiah Berlin and Simone Weil have observed, the virulence of post-revolutionary political debates articulates the persistence of a contradiction not just between two groups within France but one that can also be said to exist unconsciously within each of the individuals engaged in those debates; the sweet irresolvable doubt that Rousseau imagined would satisfy us once and for all became instead the engine of an irreconcilable conflict that was to reach its highest pitch of explicitness in the 1930s.[30]

As a younger contemporary of Renoir, equally engaged in the political and social predicament of France during the period and driven to reflect on the philosophical roots of the crisis, Simone Weil offers a diagnosis that can, I believe, help us better understand the concerns Renoir addressed in his journalism of the time. Commissioned in 1942 by General de Gaulle to draw up proposals for a reconstructed France, Weil chose to begin her analysis with a brusque critique of the modern concept of rights upon which the Revolution was based:

> The notion of obligations comes before that of rights, which is subordinate and relative to the former. A right is not effectual by itself, but only in relation to the obligation to which it corresponds, the effective exercise of a right

springing not from the individual who possesses it, but from other men who consider themselves to be under a certain obligation toward him. Recognition of an obligation makes it effectual. An obligation that goes unrecognized by anyone loses none of the full force of its existence. A right which goes unrecognized by anybody is not worth very much.

Rights are always found to be related to certain conditions. Obligations alone remain independent of conditions. They belong to a realm situated above all conditions, because it is situated above this world. The men of 1789 did not recognize the existence of such a realm. All they recognized was the one on the human plane. That is why they started off with the idea of rights. But at the same time they wanted to posit absolute principles. This contradiction caused them to tumble into a confusion of language and ideas which is largely responsible for the present political and social confusion.[31]

We can trace the philosophical origins of the conflicts that European society lived through so painfully during the 1930s and World War II back to the Revolution's rejection of all transcendent ethical obligations. Weil's analysis implies that the ability to conceive of a given right as a specific historical objective depends on being able to measure that right in relation to the ethical obligation to which it corresponds. The infinity of an ethical obligation is precisely what allows us to measure the finite value of a given right within a given situation; it is what allows us to perceive the relations between our concepts and reality.

> In every sphere we seem to have lost the very elements of intelligence: the ideas of limit, measure, degree, proportion, relation, comparison, contingency, interdependence, interrelation of means and ends. To keep it to the social level, our political universe is peopled exclusively by myths and monsters; all it contains is absolutes and abstract entities. This is illustrated by all the words of our political and social vocabulary: nation, security, capitalism, communism, fascism, order, authority, property, democracy. We never use them in phrases such as: There is democracy *to the extent that*... or: There is capitalism *in so far as*... The use of such expressions is beyond our intellectual capacity.[32]

Weil describes the politics of Europe in the 1930s as entirely dominated by romantic abstractions, dangerous words that both register and effect the blindness of the individuals who use them to the real conditions of their existence, and she singles out the distinction between Left and Right as one of the most meaningless and dangerous abstractions:

The fact that this opposition constitutes today the double threat of civil war and world war is perhaps the gravest of all our symptoms of intellectual atrophy, because one has only to examine the present-day meaning of the two words to discover almost identical political and social conceptions. In each of them the State seizes control of almost every department of individual and social life; in each there is the same frenzied militarization, and the same artificial unanimity, obtained by coercion, in favour of a single party which identifies itself with the State and derives its character from this false identification, and finally there is the same serfdom imposed upon the working masses in place of the ordinary wage system. No two nations are more similar in structure than Germany and Russia, each threatening an international crusade against the other and each pretending to see the other as the Beast of the Apocalypse. Therefore one can safely assert that the opposition between fascism and communism is strictly meaningless.[33]

Insofar as we allow ourselves to recognize the truth of Weil's concise equation of these two ideological positions, we might well ask ourselves how and why the historical proponents of each position did not recognize it at the time. Her answer is that they did recognize it, and that it was precisely because they did that the ideological struggles of the time were so virulent and irreconcilable: "In Berlin, in the summer of 1932, it was common to see a little group of people gathered around two workmen or two petty *bourgeois*, one a communist and the other a Nazi, who were arguing. After a time it always became clear to both disputants that they were defending exactly the same programme; and this made their heads swim, but it only exacerbated in each of them his hatred for an opponent separated from him by such a gulf as to remain an enemy even when expressing the same ideas."[34] Weil's anecdote allows us to recognize how the sweet doubt of Rousseau's bedroom utopia functioned to generate and sustain the political conflicts of the 1930s. On one level the two disputants recognize the identity of their positions, that they are actually pursuing a common set of goals, they don't have to fight, they could perhaps be friends: they catch a glimpse of a liberty that would free them both from the domination each attributes to the other. But on another level the cognitive act of recognizing all these things registers as a horrifying betrayal of the collective body they have freely chosen to identify with, as something that threatens to destroy the very roots of their personal identity. They are briefly suspended in a Cytherean moment in which they could, in principle, choose to abandon that identity in favor of something else, but to do so would require both tremendous courage and something analogous to religious faith. Insofar as they lack these things, they are left with the feeling of self-hatred generated by their betrayal; to escape from that feeling they quickly redefine that betrayal as a weakness of the will, which they can erase only by demonstrating a more resolute hatred of their enemy.

Simone Weil's overview of the situation of Europe in the 1930s—which presents the spectacle of an ideological domination so intimate that it short-circuits all capacity of rational thought—also serves to identify the pressing causes of Renoir's concern with the problem of romanticism. An examination of his journalism from the period reveals that he was concerned with the same complex of intertwined issues—self-deception and hypocrisy, the abstraction of political discourse, ideological conflict and war—as she was. More important, it reveals that he, like she, recognized that the only solution to the general problem rested in diagnoses that exposed social contradictions to ridicule and in realistic proposals that used language in a precise and relative manner; rather than being a display of his blind engagement with one term of an ideological binary, such as the French Left, Renoir's journalism can be seen as an attempt to take the capital letters off the murderous abstractions of the time. In one column he rejects as "arbitrary stupidity" a proposal to "nationalize" French film distribution and instead proposes a tax that would establish a parity between French and foreign films, and in another he offers a set of pragmatic reasons why the practice of shooting French films abroad is detrimental to the industries of either country.[35] In one article he reminds his readers that there are two sides to German culture, the authoritarian Germany of Bismarck and Hitler and a more basic spirit of anarchic irony (he assures his readers that the good German people laugh at those comical figures as much as they do), while in another ("Integral Masochism") he chides his French readers for their secret admiration of Hitler.[36] In an article titled "Racism" he proposes that simply ridiculing the category of race offers an elegant solution to the global crisis and proceeds to trace the historical intermingling of peoples beneath the presumed racial homogeneity of modern European nations.[37] Taken in isolation, each article represents an attempt to show how the abstractions that governed the political discourse of his time needed to be qualified and deconstructed with reference to specific contexts, and he consistently tries to make his readers recognize their inescapable connections to others across the ideological divides of the time. Taken as a whole, the comprehensiveness and consistency of their critique testifies to an understanding of human identity and community that was radically different from that of his contemporaries. We turn now to examine the positive articulations of that understanding in *Les bas-fonds* and *La grande illusion*.

THE EVER-PRESENT UTOPIA OF HUMAN CIVILIZATION: THE FIFTH CHRONOTOPE

> People thought that, in writing *Rules of the Game*, I was criticizing society, but not at all. I wish I could live in such a society—that would be wonderful.
>
> Jean Renoir, "Celebrity Lecture" at the London Film Festival, 1967

A positive articulation of Renoir's philosophical understanding is evident in the two important films we neglected to examine in the preceding chapter, *Les bas-fonds* and *La grande illusion*. These two films represent the Fifth chronotope of the French Renoir, and examining and reflecting upon the meetings between the main characters in these films will allow us to recover assumptions regarding human identity, desire, reason, and time that are very different from the ones that have dominated modern philosophy since Rousseau.

Considered as a whole, *Les bas-fonds* is a film that in effect *reverses* the second invisible dissolve of the Cytherean chronotope, the phenomenological movement we characterized as a fatalistic return and reinscription within the solipsistic bubble of one's Flaubertian limitations (class and gender ideology, defining passions, and so on). As we briefly discussed in chapter 1, the film begins by showing us the extent to which each of the two main characters, Pepel (Jean Gabin) and the Baron (Louis Jouvet), is enclosed both within a specific milieu (the lower depths of a flophouse; the highest heights of high society) and within his fatalistic view of his own life. Pepel believes that, like his father, he is fated to a life of crime and punishment, while the Baron believes that, with all of life's possibilities of diversion exhausted, his only option is to kill himself. The film begins exactly where the Cytherean chronotope ends, with the two characters trapped by the accidental conjunction of circumstances and their own romantic attitudes. Then they meet, and that meeting changes everything; the intensity of Pepel's desire for another life is something the Baron has never encountered before, and it forces him to reconsider his own nihilism, while the Baron's ironic detachment is something that Pepel has never encountered before, and it forces him to reconsider his own fatalism. Their chance meeting inaugurates a friendship that continues for the rest of the film and, one presumes, ever after; moving from romantic enclosure to Cytherean openness, the trajectory of that friendship articulates a reversal of the second dissolve of the Cytherean chronotope that we understand to be lasting and permanent.

The ending of the film highlights what is so distinctive about this friendship, what distinguishes the Fifth chronotope's version of meeting from those in the preceding four: Pepel and Natacha leave the flophouse to start a new life; the Baron will stay there. There has never been a moment in the entire film in which either of the two friends has suggested they need to stay together, nor has there been a moment in which either expresses needing anything from the other; though they often ask each other for favors, the excessive courtesy with which they do so always articulates a conscious and mutual respect for the difference or otherness of the other. There is equality between them because each wishes to preserve both his own freedom and that of the other; each one seems to know that were either of them to show the slightest emotional dependence on the other, their relationship would lose its unique, mutually liberating character. If Simone Weil was able to help us to come to terms with the problem of romanticism, it is no accident that her work illuminates the principles of this conception of friendship, that is, the elements of a solution to that problem:

> When a human being is in any degree necessary to us, we cannot desire his good unless we cease to desire our own. Where there is necessity there is constraint and domination. We are in the power of that of which we stand in need, unless we possess it. The central good of every man is the free disposal of himself. Either we renounce it, which is a crime of idolatry, since it can only be renounced in favour of God, or we desire that the being we stand in need of should be deprived of this free disposal of himself.[38]

Weil argues that true friendship—the reciprocal recognition of difference and autonomy—requires that we deliberately sublimate our instinctive desire to be one through self-negation (masochism) or negation of the other (sadism):

> A friendship is tarnished as soon as necessity triumphs, if only for a moment, over the desire to preserve the faculty of free consent on both sides. All friendship is impure if even a trace of the wish to please or the contrary wish to dominate is found in it. In a perfect friendship these two desires are completely absent. The two friends have fully consented to be two and not one, they respect the distance which the fact of being two distinct creatures places between them. Friendship is a miracle by which a person consents to view from a certain distance, and without coming any closer, the very being who is necessary to him as food.[39]

When carefully examined, every detail of Pepel and the Baron's behavior testifies to the fact that their relationship lines up with Weil's Platonic model of eros as friendship. At the end of the film, the physical distance that will most likely separate them for the rest of their lives registers both as a beautiful testimony to the miracle of their friendship and as a liberating effect of it; their friendship has opened the Naturalist milieu of the flophouse onto the infinity of the cosmos and allowed Pepel and Natacha to escape. The liberty to act in the world is represented to be the product of a reciprocal realization of a transcendent ethical obligation.

In certain superficial respects, the central figure that defines this chronotope resembles the central figure of the Revolutionary chronotope; it is typically articulated in a two-shot in which one friend speaks while the other looks at him or her from the side and listens. But in this case, the performances display nothing of the competitive enthusiasm that animates the revolutionary figure; there is no erotic differential or implicit contract between the two characters and hence neither a "wish to please" nor a "wish to dominate." Unlike those in the revolutionary figure, the conversations between Pepel and the Baron never take the form of a debate or argument in which they each put forward opposing positions; though Pepel typically speaks in monologues accompanied by broad gestures or listens with a smile on his face and the Baron generally maintains a restrained expression of bewildered irony whether speaking or listening, these differences have to do with their characters and the acting styles of Gabin and Jouvet and do not express a direct emotional response to what the other is saying or doing. Instead, whether speaking or listening, their attitudes articulate something similar to the Cytherean chronotope's figure of abstraction; they seem to be listening to "an invisible, pressing interlocutor, a voice from within." The behavior of both speaker and listener expresses a profoundly attentive response to the content of what is being said, as if the two of them are listening to a third whom the speaker happens to be channeling.

This figure is given its clearest, most memorable articulation in the famous "snail scene" set in the very Cytherean location of a patch of waste ground next to the river Marne (littered with tumbledown shacks, dozing bodies, stray dogs, and wandering toddlers). After Pepel and the Baron wake up from their nap on the grass, their conversation develops from a discussion of what Pepel just dreamed (that he was fishing), to a monologue in which he expresses being fed up with all the people in the flophouse, and then to a speech in which the Baron claims that all he can remember about his life is the succession of different costumes he wore (school clothes, wedding suit, government uniform, and so on)—it is all just an absurd dream to him now. As he delivers this speech, both he and Pepel focus their attention on a snail climbing up his hand; the Baron briefly picks it up with his other hand, then puts it back. Pepel asks him if he has ever been in prison, and the conversation segues to a speech by Pepel in which he expresses his belief that like his father he is fated to die in prison; the only thing that could release him from that fate would be if Natacha agreed to run away with him. Then he genially asks the Baron, "What about you?" The Baron says he'll stay where he is. Though he didn't really believe it when Pepel said it was pleasant to sleep on the grass, now he knows it's true. They both laugh at this, the Baron tosses the snail into the grass, and they lie down to take another nap.

The first thing that is essential to recognize about this scene is the detachment with which its dialogue is delivered. Even as Pepel angrily itemizes the lies, stupidity, and obsessions of the various flophouse residents, he seems to be laughing at his own anger, as if the fact that the Baron is listening makes him aware of the contradiction of being obsessed with the obsessions of others. Both the Baron's autobiographical narrative and Pepel's projected narrative of his fate are delivered in a way that makes

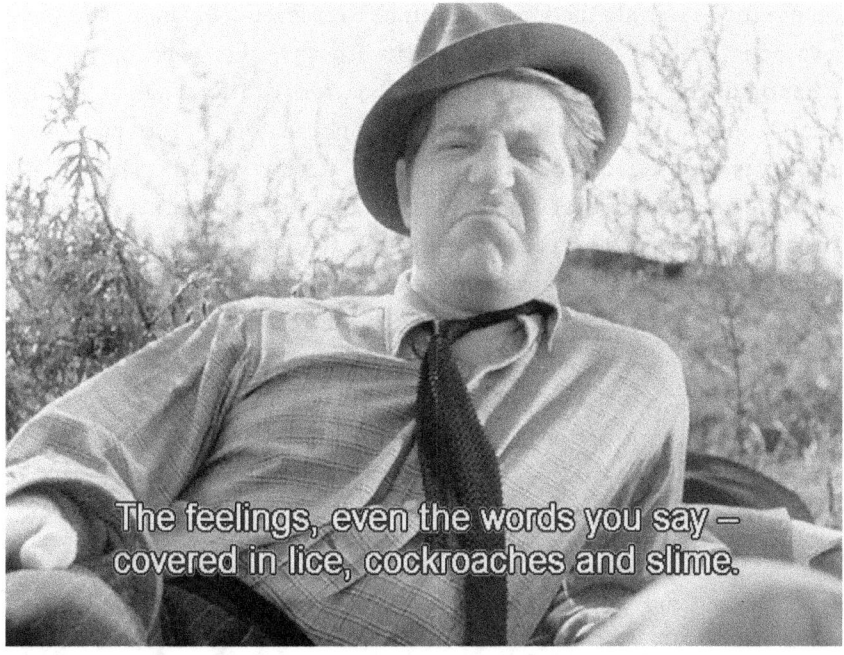

FIGURE 3.1.

Pepel describes the squalid life in the flophouse in *Les bas-fonds*.

us aware the speaker is simply essaying a formulation, not asserting an absolute or final truth; if either of them completely believed in what he was saying, his detached way of saying it would make no sense. Though each recognizes that his own understanding of his life is as limited as the snail's understanding of the man upon which it crawls, there is a relaxed modesty about the way they speak that indicates a powerful sense of trust in their friendship to deliver them from the prisons of their own imaginations; this trust is not in each other but in the friendship itself, a "third person" that their sublimated attraction to each other has generated: the contrast in scale between their heads and the tiny head of the snail turning this way and that subtly articulates their detachment from their own autobiographical narratives. The third person's perspective allows them to understand their past lives and envision their futures with greater clarity; they can now recognize differences in themselves and others where before they saw only the same old thing. Their friendship has made them aware that the autobiographical narratives they tell themselves are partial; it has made them aware that all historical narratives are partial: in the final analysis, it makes them aware that time is not history, not because every history is opposed to a counterhistory in which it is locked in an agonistic struggle but because every history is surrounded by an infinity of alternative histories. By setting their conversation against the bewildered movements of the snail and framing it between two experiences of dreaming (Pepel's fishing dream and the dreams they are about to have), this scene tenderly reminds us that we will never know the historical causes that determine our fate, that our thoughts and actions take place within an infinite number of spatial frames and dimensions of time; it articulates a skeptical response to the experience of historicity analogous to that of Michel de Montaigne, who wrote,

> Now, if we can see the influence of the stars makes an art or opinion to flourish; and if a particular age produces a particular trait of nature and inclines the human race towards some particular trait of character (their spirits producing good crops then lean crops, as fields do): what happens to all those special privileges which we pride ourselves upon? A wise man can be mistaken; a hundred men can; indeed, according to us, the whole human race has gone wrong for centuries about this or that: so how can we be sure that human nature ever stops getting things wrong, and that she is not wrong now, in our own period?[40]

Yet at the same time the scene also articulates the quality of faith that corresponds to this skeptical attitude, faith in the ability of sincere, ethics-inspired reflection to see things differently; human nature being wrong means the world is always better than we are capable of imagining. By patiently recognizing the differences between our views and those of others, by contemplating the distance between us, we can achieve a clearer, more detached, liberating perspective, the third person's perspective, on the contradictions that had unconsciously separated us. This lucid and mutual recognition of shared limitations becomes the basis for actions that are of necessity more free because they are based on an enlarged awareness of the possibilities of human experience; though it articulates their awareness of their own limitations, the contrast in scale between the snail and the faces of the two characters looking at it measures the cosmic infinity of possibilities they now sense around them.

FIGURE 3.2.

The Baron describes his life of changing costumes in *Les bas-fonds*.

With this ideal of friendship Renoir had arrived at the erotic wisdom he was looking for, wisdom grounded in assumptions regarding human desire, will, reason, and time that are fundamentally different from those put forth in Rousseau and disseminated through romanticism to become the defining ideology of modernity. In mobilizing these assumptions in his films, Renoir can be understood as affirming Platonic principles that were restated in an early modern context by Montaigne and have been carried forward into contemporary philosophy by thinkers such as Emmanuel Levinas, Jean-Luc Marion, and Simone Weil. I will draw on work in this tradition to outline a few key concepts before turning to consider their articulation in Renoir's films.

We can begin by noting that Weil's idea of the ethics-inspired distance that constitutes true friendship derives from the famous myth of the charioteer outlined in Plato's *Phaedrus*.[41] In that myth, the human soul is represented in the form of a chariot pulled by two horses, one motivated by carnal appetite and possessiveness and the other motivated by an awareness of ethical obligations to oneself and the other; if left to their own devices, the bad horse always wants to get too close to the beloved and the good horse always wants to stay too far away, and there is disorder and conflict within the soul. The function of human reason, represented by the charioteer, is to govern the actions of the two horses so as to place the soul at the exact distance from the beloved where he or she allows the soul to recollect the Form of Beauty itself; when both lover and beloved arrive at this point of balance they no longer consider themselves to be "lovers" but to be "friends" devoted, "with the consent of their whole mind," to a common pursuit of wisdom: the love between the two friends generates a third, whose thoughts they now follow.[42]

This conception of human desire wherein two become three is also put forward in Diotima's myth of love-as-pregnancy in the *Symposium*, where it is opposed to Aristophanes's proto-romantic conception wherein two lovers recover their lost wholeness by reunifying into the one creature they once were.[43] As Louis Ruprecht argues in *Symposia: Plato, the Erotic and Moral Value*, Diotima's generative conception of human desire can be discerned throughout Plato's work and underlies his decision to present his philosophy in the form of dialogues:

> There are, finally, three terms in a dialogue, not two: the self, the other, and truth which both conversation-partners are ideally pursuing. No one possesses it; it is not a commodity in that way, not a singular possession.... Truth is an *event*, a horizon that comes gradually into view when two come together—or more specifically, when two persons come together in the interest of giving birth to a third.[44]

Ruprecht unpacks the central metaphor of pregnancy in Diotima's speech in such a way as to highlight both the ethical obligation it springs from and the singular complex of radical and liberating differences that comprise the ultimate result of acting in accordance with that obligation:

> What is pregnancy, if it is not the miraculous moment in which two beings create a third, in love? It is a bloody and bodily experience, none more so, the moment in which excruciating physical pain brings new life into being. As such, it is one of the most "spiritual" moments in a life. Self and other give birth to that which is both self and other, together, and yet neither of these

selves at all—all of this in the same singular moment. Parenting must rank as another of the most radically vulnerable moments in a properly constituted human life. Just as we do not come to knowledge or to *eros*, so we do not come to our children. They also come to us. We *receive* them, if we are so fortunate. We do not *choose* them. We do not know exactly where they come from. We can only open up our home to them, accept them, nurture them. We cannot even teach them, finally, only help them to learn, accompanying them on the vast journey. The two become three—in a manner that is completely out of our own limited control. A more fitting image for the risk, the vulnerability, the mutuality, and the spiritual ecstasy of an erotic bond is scarcely imaginable.[45]

With these two Platonic models of love in view, we are now in a position to develop and clarify the content of the formula of "great patience, work and good faith" that Renoir claimed is necessary to secure the experience of Cythera, enchantment, or reality. To relate this positive formula to Renoir's critique of romanticism we can contrast it at each point with Rousseau's response to the same experience, and this should serve as a concise summary of the entire inadvertent argument we have been tracing to this point.

Both Rousseau and Renoir can be said to begin with a very basic or common experience of doubt or disorientation, the sense that one is somehow "not oneself." We can understand this in terms of specific experiences that produce it, feeling alienated from or being in conflict with others, or in more general terms as an experience of historicity, realizing the symbolic narratives that secure one's identity are relative and in a certain sense fictional. But though they can be said to share a common point of departure, Renoir and Rousseau differ in the way they experience and process this moment of disorientation and vulnerability.

For Rousseau this moment is always an experience of *disenchantment*; any contact with the irreducible difference of others—any encounter with the brutal fact of historicity—is painful and provokes anxiety. It causes one to "remember" (that is, to imagine one remembers) and develop a narcissistic attachment to the natural self that has been violated by the series of accidental events that has constituted the historical development of human civilization. Since they are always experienced as painful, the chance encounters that bring one into contact with otherness or difference are understood to be instances of bad luck, and their aggregation in human history is the collective narrative of an unhappy fate. As it is already too late to reverse the collective fall from freedom into bondage, the only option left for humanity is make bondage legitimate through a collective act of will (the *Social Contract*'s proposed confusion of sadism and masochism) that deliberately forgets (is blind to) the legacies produced by chance and history (the existing diversity of cultures and individuals). We forget the legacies of the past evident in the present in order to arrive at a collective wholeness that is the only possible approximation of our original happiness as solitary narcissistic individuals. Both the uniqueness of individuals and the diversity of cultures must perforce dissolve into the universal homogeneous soup of the General Will. For Rousseau this is the only political solution to the problem of disenchantment.

For Renoir, "the reality is in being enchanted": the meeting or chance encounter with the irreducible difference of another human being or culture can and should be an experience of Cytherean enchantment.[46] Though it destabilizes one's identity and may involve a certain amount of anxiety, doubt, vulnerability, and risk, this encounter is not inherently painful or repulsive but has, if one is capable of being open to it, the potential to be pleasant and attractive. Instead of reinforcing melodramatic narratives of victimization by positing the primal violation of natural man as their metanarrative, Renoir assumes that a genuine encounter with another will enable one to forget those fatalistic narratives, relativize them, and become detached from them. The chance encounter with the fact of historicity or human difference is thus experienced as an instance of good luck, as a gift that, if handled properly, can deliver one from the prison of one's self-obsessed and self-defeating imagination. The formula of patience, work, and good faith refers to the effort of restraint, lucid attention, and ethical regard for oneself and the other outlined in Simone Weil's model of true friendship. The experience of Cythera, which begins in an unconscious attraction to the difference of the Other, continues and becomes fruitful only through a conscious renunciation of the desire to possess (sadism) or be possessed (masochism), through the act of loving the distance between oneself and the other.

Ruprecht's description of parental love—the dominant analogy for God's love in the Jewish and Christian traditions—vividly illuminates the affective structure of this renunciation. To the extent that they love them, the existence of children establishes a permanent anxiety in their parents; they are aware of unique and hence precious human beings that they cannot completely protect, for to do so would stunt the development of the faculty of free consent that is the children's central good. This anxiety on the part of the parents provides us with a concrete example of the paradoxical combination of courage and sensitivity involved in finding the right distance in Plato's myth of the charioteer. Parents want their children to be happy and safe but also know that they have to give them the liberty to find their own happiness and safety; their policy on any given issue (for example, at what age a child can walk to school alone; how late and with whom a teenager can stay out) is always a product of the tension between these two impulses. If, as Ruprecht puts it, parents receive their children as a mysterious gift, the attitude of graciousness proper to receiving a gift, one that implies humble stewardship rather than proud ownership, governs the parents' behavior for their entire lives; just as they first brought the children into being physically, the parents continue to bring them into being both physically and spiritually by maintaining the delicate balance between hands-on and hands-off love that allows the children to grow into adulthood. Parental love entails living with uncertainty forever, but it is precisely this acceptance of uncertainty—this faith in the face of doubt and anxiety—that allows children to come into being as unique and precious constellations of human difference. The ever-renewed renunciation involved in loving the distance between themselves and their children is the clearest measure of the parents' unselfish and unrequitable love.

Ruprecht's model of parental love illuminates the attitude adopted by any two people engaged in what Weil calls a true friendship, the attitude upon which Renoir's positive vision of all social relations is based. Though the two friends in Weil's model may want to "make the other happy" or be "made happy" by the other, though they may long for the certainty of a romantically conceived fusion, their respect for the liberty of the other and themselves prevents them from pursuing this. They renounce or sublimate their desire to possess or be possessed in order to maintain the productive differences between them; contemplating those differences from a chaste distance allows the liberating event of truth, the third person's perspective, to come into view. As Weil puts it, "It is an act of cowardice to seek from (or wish to give) the people we love any other consolation than that which works of art give us. These help us through the mere fact that they exist. To love and to be loved only serves mutually to render this existence more concrete, more constantly present to the mind. *But it should be present as the source of our thoughts, not as their object*" (my italics).[47] As for Weil, for Renoir the intertwined possibilities of philosophical insight and of human community in general have their roots in the model of friendship we have sketched out. Relations with others analogous to friendship are the precondition for any original thought, any escape from the enclosure of our limited, ideology-determined imaginations. Any real improvement in one's understanding of the world can be seen as dependent on the invisible network of one's productive ethical commitments; the liberty to think and the value of thought itself depend on the explicit or implicit dialogues that one has established with others whom one treats as friends.

Michel de Montaigne reaffirmed the basic elements of this Platonic model of philosophy and human relations in an early modern context, and a brief reconsideration of his work and its context can assist us in the task of recognizing the articulations of this model in Renoir's films. The age in which Montaigne lived and thought was, as Zachary Sayre Schiffman puts it, "on the threshold of modernity" for a variety of reasons.[48] On a theoretical level, the Renaissance revival of interest in antiquity had made the conflicting accounts of pagan and Christian philosophies a smoldering source of ideological instability within high culture. The technological-social revolution that resulted from the invention of the printing press also fed into what was becoming a pressing concern with the problem of relativism. Long before Walter Benjamin took up the theme, there was a widespread consensus among Renaissance intellectuals that mechanical reproduction wrenched words from the contexts that gave them meaning and thus rendered them unstable, ambiguous, and equivocal; though there were a variety of attempts to solve this problem by positing and applying technical rules of interpretation, these projects inevitably foundered on the fact of their own historicity.[49] As the problem of relativism emerged on a theoretical level, the historical events of the age gave it a broader relevance and urgency. The voyages of exploration and discovery of the New World caused a profound decentering and disorientation of European identity; the awareness of New World cultures and expansion of trade with Asia worked in tandem with the heightened awareness of pagan antiquity to make the Christian civilization of Europe increasingly self-conscious about its own historicity. Last, and more direct and painful, the ideological divisions and military conflicts engendered by the collective passions of the Reformation and Counter-Reformation made the problem of cultural diversity the burning issue of political philosophy for the age.[50]

In *Michel de Montaigne: Accidental Philosopher*, Ann Hartle claims that Montaigne recognized in its earliest stirrings what would become the dominant modern response to the problem of historicity or cultural relativism. The mainstream of modern European philosophy would deal with this problem by adopting the technological maxim of "rising above the details," ignoring the stated, historically conditioned "reasons" of cultures and individuals in favor of the authority of autonomous Reason (Descartes to Kant) and subsuming the "histories" of cultures and individuals into a master narrative of History (Rousseau to Hegel).[51] Hartle argues that though Montaigne clearly recognized these emerging tendencies, he deliberately rejected both their assumptions and their methods; while he experienced the problem of historicity or relativism as profoundly as any of his contemporaries, his philosophical response to it was unique, distinguishing him from most of the ancient philosophers and medieval theologians who preceded him and almost all of the modern philosophers who came after him.[52]

Hartle defines Montaigne's "accidental philosophy" by contrasting it with what she calls "deliberate philosophy" (which she sees as the dominant form of both ancient and modern philosophy).[53] Deliberate philosophy is based on the premise that human reason is in principle identical with the divine ruling principle that governs the universe and as such can have a synoptic view of the laws governing the universe. Since Aristotle this mode of philosophy's primary concern has been with causation, with distinguishing the causes at work in any event and separating these into the ones that spring from nature and those that originate in custom or historical difference.[54] The role played by chance, contingency, or alterity in any event and the contingent imperfections of the human body that shape our experience of any event are not significant to the deliberate philosopher, whose method is primarily deductive and who proceeds by grouping particulars within various general categories.[55]

Montaigne's accidental philosophy is, by contrast, skeptical and inductive and is driven by the sense of wonder produced by the experience of chance, contingency, and alterity. It takes the form of a circular dialectic in which thought moves from the common and familiar (oneself) to the rare and strange (the other) and then returns to find the rare in the common and the strange in the familiar (the otherness of oneself); it reaffirms Montaigne's maxim that "there is as much difference between us and ourselves as between us and others."[56] The acknowledged role of contingency in inaugurating this dialectic precludes any presumption to distinguish between natural and historical causes, because the strangeness of the "accidental particular" that unites those causes is precisely what leads one to think a different truth about the world and to become different oneself. To the extent that a specific effect of chance (that is, something that eludes the laws of causality) is itself recognized to be the cause of a beneficial transformation, one can infer the workings of the supernatural (luck or grace) without necessarily having a theory of the supernatural (metaphysics). The most radical skepticism can thus at the same time be an expression of humility and faith: Montaigne's faith allows him to believe that what he does not know is better—more real, true, and good—than what he does know, and hence he is as unrelenting and ardent as Plato's Socrates in his pursuit of this unknown truth.

In contrast to the pride of possessing knowledge implicit in the activity of the deliberate philosopher (expressed, for example, in Aristotle's contention that "the great-souled man is necessarily proud"), Montaigne's accidental philosophy implies another type of philosopher, "the great-souled man without pride," who combines the courage needed to live with uncertainty with the sensitivity needed to be receptive and open to the experience of contingencies.[57] Erich Auerbach notes that though Montaigne had, among all his contemporaries, the clearest conception of the modern problem of self-orientation, the "task of making oneself at home in existence without fixed points of support," he rejected what would become the default modern way of framing this problem; the great-souled man's lack of pride represents an implicit rejection of the romantic recuperation of the classical conception of the tragic as "the highly personal tragedy of the individual."[58] The courageous stance taken by this type of philosopher suggests that his or her experience of self-transformation has already given him or her the hope necessary to resist the temptation to interpret experience in romantic or melodramatic terms.[59]

As Hartle points out, the radical transformation of both self and worldview in this model of philosophy entails conceptions of ontology and metaphysics quite different from those that have dominated the history of Western philosophy from Aristotle to Heidegger:

> Circular dialectic ends in wonder at the most familiar. This implies an absolutely contingent, created world, a world created out of nothing and, at the same time, a world in which the divine is somehow present. Contingency is the fundamental condition for being and for thought. Montaigne's reconciliation to nothingness shows itself especially in the way he embraces our temporal condition. Creation out of nothing implies the ontological primacy of contingency and possibility. Therefore, being must be such as to allow for the most radical transformation.[60]

Like Plato's dialogues and Renoir's films, the often meandering essays in which Montaigne expressed himself are designed to allow the reader to experience the existential, real-time astonishment of discovering truth for oneself. In contrast to the treatise form of deliberate philosophy, wherein the writer knows exactly where he or she is going and organizes his or her argument to compel the reader's assent to a preordained end, Plato, Montaigne, and Renoir all make the defamiliarizing experience of contingency the moment in which, the Cytherean place where, their dialogical equality with the reader-spectator is made manifest. Just as Plato's dialogues and Renoir's films are both structured around trapdoors (in the conception of characters, the design of the narrative and the mise-en-scène) that as if by accident drop the spectator from a common and familiar understanding of an issue onto the terra firma of hitherto-unrecognized contradictions (the rare and strange in the common and familiar), Montaigne's essays are built around examples and anecdotes any one of which might, by chance, provoke a defamiliarizing insight in his reader, an insight that, by his own admission, he himself does not necessarily see.[61] Like Plato and Renoir, Montaigne explicitly doubts himself and the value of his own knowledge but nonetheless believes in the power of dialogue to generate philosophical insight: all three gamble on the possibility that the reader or spectator might turn out to be a friend. The theme of friendship as an ideal paradigm for all social relations in the work of these three artist-philosophers is thus connected to the digressive, hesitant, and unfinished qualities of their work, qualities that those with a taste for deliberate art and philosophy can find maddening. But properly understood, these same qualities are an indication of the courtesy and respect that the artist-philosophers feel toward their unknown interlocutors and constitute a tacit admission that they need our help to finish their thoughts.

If the preceding analysis of Renoir's philosophical affinity with Plato and Montaigne is cogent, the structuring of human desire into friendship seems to constitute a necessary prerequisite for both philosophic insight and human communion: it represents the first answer to the two-part question that has guided our explorations, "how to meet, how to belong." Having arrived at an answer to the first part of that question in *Les bas-fonds*, Renoir would turn in his very next film to the larger and more complicated question of how friendship might become the sustaining basis of a larger community in which everyone "belongs."

To set up our examination of how *La grande illusion* poses this question, I would like to outline a model of community as *civilization* that our preceding analysis of friendship would support by way of a contrast with the model of community as *culture* that developed out of Rousseau's philosophy.[62] The concept of culture is rooted in the premise of an original quasi-organic identity, a sameness, that all members of the culture share, something that once united them in a primordial unity analogous to an American family having Thanksgiving dinner, all differences between its members erased by the stupefying satisfaction of Mom's turkey and stuffing. As with Rousseau's hypothesis of natural man, this retrospective utopian image of culture emerges as an inference from one's present experience of disenchantment, from the feeling that one has somehow lost that identity and/or become separated from one's family. Since the model of culture imagines any larger community in terms of the one-and-the-same-ness of its conception of the family, it is typically forced to define that community in terms of the quasi-natural categories, rituals, and symbols found in nationalist discourses (the homogeneity of the French race, red wine and pot-au-feu, the Eiffel tower), discourses of sameness that depend on inane tautologies (red wine is French because French people drink it; French people are French because they drink red wine). One's identity as a member of the French nation derives from one's romantic attachment to such things and from not being attracted to or associated with anything foreign (for example, Chinese people, Chinese food, Chinese philosophy). Starting from the melodramatic premise that the integrity of the national culture-as-family has in some sense been lost or contaminated, nationalist discourses orient their narratives around the goal of restoring that lost integrity or sameness through political actions and cultural policies that will purify the nation and result in what is effectively a family reunion.

In contrast to the model of community as culture, *civilization* is the term I would propose for a society of friends and potential friends open to the possibilities of dialogue, a society that aspires to acknowledge and include any and all forms of individual and cultural difference. As Ruprecht's elaboration of Plato has indicated, one can see how the principles of friendship such as "loving-the-distance" already operate at the level of the family through parental love and how the very concept of family can thus be quite different from the one put forth in the culture model. Rather than being premised on the recognition of a common sameness, the bonds between the parents and between parents and children are based in the reciprocal acknowledgment of difference and autonomy. The strength of a family does not derive from the extent to which its members believe they are all one and the same or are certain of possessing and being possessed by each other; instead, a good family is one where each member can both "be who they are" (different from each other) and grow to "become who they are meant to be" (different from themselves). Though the children in such a family do appreciate Mom's turkey and stuffing, this appreciation does not prevent any of them from falling in love with someone from China and developing an equal or greater appreciation of Chinese cuisine. If one of them happens to do so, this is understood to be something that allows the individual member and the family itself to grow by becoming different. Though the family may experience some growing pains or awkwardness as each of its members becomes who he or she is meant to be, and though its members might sometimes feel nostalgic for the comfort food and simplicity of the family's past configurations, their love for each other and for those outside the family establishes a centrifugal dynamic that enlarges it (through, for example, the addition of Chinese in-laws) and changes its material and intellectual culture (through, for example, the addition of hot and sour soup and discussions of Confucianism to Thanksgiving dinner). The status-quo culture of the family is thus constantly being transformed from within and without by the effects of civilization, the process in which individuals and their cultures meet and through that meeting become different.

Unlike the concept of a national culture, civilization cannot be defined in terms of its geographic location because its function is to link two or more individuals, locations, and cultures in an ongoing dialogue that maintains the distance and differences between them; putting this in positive terms, we might say that its function is precisely to produce a Cytherean dislocation of individuals, locations, and cultures: it enlarges both self and world by recognizing and articulating the fullest possibilities of the self and the world. Though our Thanksgiving dinner may take place in Toledo, Ohio, USA, in 1977, the contingent facts of the occasion (the presence of the Chinese in-laws, the hot and sour soup, and the discussion of Confucianism in American politics) allow those participating to forget the clichéd reflexes that might normally determine the way the occasion is experienced. Instead of falling into the familiar ruts of status-quo culture (the same old compliments for Mom's cooking, the same old jokes from Dad, the same old arguments between siblings) that would relocate the family in Toledo, Ohio, USA, in 1977, the family's civilized response to the Cytherean possibilities of the occasion allows everyone present to embark, to be somewhere else. If the conversation between Dad and Mr. Wang provides each man with a new and surprising insight into the thought and political life of the country in which he lives (the "Confucianism" of American society, the "Americanness" of Chinese philosophy) and subtly dislocates their previous culture-based understandings of what it meant to be American ("not-Chinese") or Chinese ("not-American"), their children and wives are astonished to discover that the two rather predictable men are even capable of such a conversation; in one way or another, everyone present discovers something new and different both about the others and themselves.

With this rudimentary example in view, we can see that civilization can be distinguished both from the individual's spontaneous experience of Cytherean enchantment and from the friendship between two people. Civilization is the product of a conscious attitude that governs the relations between three or more people. Treated in isolation, the conversation between Dad and Mr. Wang is only an example of friendship, but the context of their families listening in on the "third person's perspective" they are channeling turns it into an epicenter of civilization. If civilization as a historical phenomenon is the achievement of an open and diverse society of friends, it has as its precondition a collective climate of expectation or faith, a heightened attentiveness to whatever happens to be going on.

La grande illusion examines the death of one historical form of civilization and the possibility of another form being born. As the last melancholy discussions between Boeldieu and von Rauffenstein make quite explicit, their relationship is a vestige of a pan-European aristocratic civilization that is, as it were, in the process of contracting back into isolated nodes of friendship; both men agree that the end of the war will also be, in von Rauffenstein's words, "the end of the Rauffensteins and the Boeldieus"—the names themselves may carry on, but their meaning and function within a living civilization will have disappeared. From the very beginning of the film this contraction or decline is already evident in the fact that each of these two characters is in his own way a perfect embodiment of Baudelaire's conception of the Dandy, someone who recognizes the inevitable decline of aristocratic values but who nonetheless chooses to maintain those values in personal rituals of costume and manner; the fastidiousness of Boeldieu and von Rauffenstein with regard to their military uniforms and white gloves, the measured precision with which they deliver their dialogue, and the chilly formality of their bearing when dealing with the nonaristocratic characters all express the combination of "cold exterior" and "latent fire" of which Baudelaire speaks.[63] Boeldieu's status as a Dandy is also manifest in his final act of self-sacrifice, the flute-playing diversion that allows Maréchal and Rosenthal to escape; because it articulates in action what his pride would never allow him to say to them—that he believes in the possibilities of a new civilization they embody—it also registers as an aristocrat's symbolic gesture of defiance in the face of a historical fate he recognizes to be inescapable.

Two complementary moments in the conversations between Boeldieu and von Rauffenstein raise the issue as to whether the transition from an aristocratic civilization to something else is a good or bad thing. In a brief conversation in the French prisoners' room in the fortress, von Rauffenstein asks Boeldieu to give his word that there is nothing in the room against regulations. Boeldieu does so but then asks why take his word and not that of his comrades. Von Rauffenstein glances over at the others and asks with an ironic smile, "The word of a Rosenthal and a Maréchal?" to which Boeldieu (having come to appreciate his French comrades in a way he could never directly acknowledge to them) firmly asserts: "It's as good as ours!" Von Rauffenstein ponders this for a moment and then says, "Perhaps"; the two men salute each other and von Rauffenstein walks off. Later, during a conversation in von Rauffenstein's room, Boeldieu responds to von Rauffenstein's assertion that the war's end will also mean the end of the Boeldieus and von Rauffensteins by saying, with a glib smile, "We're no longer needed." Von Rauffenstein counters Boeldieu's ironic attitude by saying, "Don't you think that's a pity?," which makes Boeldieu ponder and say, "Perhaps." The first "perhaps" indicates that their friendship has made von Rauffenstein contemplate the possibility that commoners and Jews might be capable of embodying the noble values implied in the act of giving one's word, while the second indicates that it has made Boeldieu contemplate the possibility that something uniquely valuable might be lost in the demise of their aristocratic civilization. Their friendship leaves them both suspended between Boeldieu's hope for a new civilization he could never imagine joining and von Rauffenstein's nostalgia for the old one they belong to; though they both feel it is too late for either of them to change—the transformative effects of their friendship are limited by their shared romantic attachment to their vanishing way of life—that friendship nonetheless allows them to contemplate the value of the changes taking place around them, allows them a third person's perspective on a world neither will ever inhabit.

The dislocating and democratizing aspects of modern warfare—mass conscription, the obsolescence of aristocratic skills like horsemanship in the context of trenches, machine guns, and poison gas, the very things that Boeldieu and von Rauffenstein feel have rendered their existence useless—are at the same time what allow for the possibility of friendships that might be the beginning of a new form of civilization. The artificial situation of the prisoner-of-war camp, which collects in one room a diversity of men who would have little occasion to really "meet" during peacetime (actor, teacher, aristocrat, Jewish businessman, blue-collar worker, small tradesman), creates the possibility of friendships that transcend the vertical and horizontal stratifications of class, race, and profession that govern French society. Though the conversations between the roommates do not have the transformative intensity of true friendship, the common predicament, the collective task of digging the tunnel, and Rosenthal's generosity in sharing his parcels of food and drink all function to produce a camaraderie that allows each of them to speak frankly about his life back home and point of view on various topics; though the culture-based differences between them are not erased by this camaraderie—the actor, Maréchal, and Boeldieu briefly unite to mock Rosenthal's Jewishness—their very diversity is nonetheless the basis for a fundamental equality, for no two of them have any real basis to join together and form a subculture distinct from the others.

From this starting point the relationship between the Jewish businessman, Rosenthal, and the mechanic, Maréchal, develops into a liberating friendship that contrasts sharply with the arrested development of any such relationship between Maréchal and Boeldieu. Throughout the first half of the film both Maréchal and Rosenthal remain somewhat self-conscious about their class or racial background. Their gratitude for his generosity notwithstanding, the other prisoners never forget Rosenthal's difference as a rich Jew; he is not really able to forget it himself until he and Maréchal plan their escape together and it is clear that Maréchal accepts him as a friend. For his part Maréchal is grateful for the fact that Rosenthal is someone he *can* accept as a friend, someone who wants such a relationship. The working-class dignity that Maréchal displays from the beginning of the film is often tinged with a self-consciousness and resentment aggravated by the cool formality of Boeldieu's behavior toward him; though Maréchal and Boeldieu have been together from the beginning of the film, Boeldieu has never let Maréchal forget the class differences that continue to separate them. As Maréchal explains to Rosenthal before their escape, he has never felt at ease with Boeldieu; if Maréchal and Rosenthal were broke they would just be two bums (that is, the leveling contingency would remind them of their fundamental equality as human beings), whereas if Boeldieu was in the same situation, he would still be

"Monsieur de Boeldieu" (that is, an intransigent Dandy whom no contingency could ever change).

By the time he and Rosenthal are ready to escape from the fortress, Maréchal has lost the tinge of class-based self-consciousness, the combination of pride and resentment, the touchiness that he displays during the first half of the film; in his own way he has developed into a "great-souled man without pride," someone who has achieved the combination of courage and sensitivity to engage others with dignity and ease. His courage and sensitivity are evident in the scene in which he tries to engage Boeldieu before he and Rosenthal make their escape. As Boeldieu washes the white gloves he will wear for what will be his final gesture, Maréchal tries to have an exchange that will acknowledge all they have been through together, but each time he begins to speak, Boeldieu interrupts him with a pointed rebuff. When Maréchal starts to say, "I want you to know that whatever happens . . . ," Boeldieu cuts him off by saying, "I'm not doing it for you personally, so we needn't get mawkish"; when Maréchal attempts to continue by saying, "But there are moments in life, *mon vieux* . . . ," Boeldieu again cuts him off by saying, "Let's avoid them, shall we?" Despite these rebuffs, Maréchal continues to pursue Boeldieu around the room, observing that though they have been together eighteen months, Boeldieu still stands on ceremony, but Boeldieu responds by proudly boasting that he uses "*vous*" with both his mother and his wife. With a gleam of amusement in his eyes at the absurdity of Boeldieu applying his prophylactic code to conjugal relations, Maréchal says, "*Alors* . . ." and gives up trying to connect; the expression of sad wonder that settles on his face articulates his recognition that Boeldieu's rigid narcissistic code had already eliminated any possibility of friendship from the outset.

As a striking contrast to this failed attempt at a farewell, the liberating nature of the friendship between Maréchal and Rosenthal is vividly articulated in the way they say good-bye before crossing into Switzerland. Standing at the margins of a forest with an expanse of snow-covered mountains and fields in front of them, they pause to discuss the immediate challenge of getting across the border and the prospects beyond (returning to fight in the war, Maréchal returning to marry Elsa after the war, putting an end to "unnatural" borders and "whorish" wars). Having recognized that they may have to split up if they run into a patrol,

Rosenthal says they had better say good-bye and "see you soon"; the glistening in his eyes and smile on his face registers his hope and delight in the hard-won prospect of a reunion with Maréchal back in Paris, of a friendship that will dislocate him from his place as a rich Jew and allow him to belong to French society in a way he could never have previously imagined. Maréchal confirms his own delight at this prospect by warmly turning to embrace him and saying "Good-bye, dirty Jew." The ironic use of this racial epithet alludes to and acknowledges the moment after their escape when, in his frustration with Rosenthal's inability to keep up with him, Maréchal was reduced to telling him that he could never stomach Jews. Repeated here, it condenses both an apology and the fact that their friendship has placed them beyond the need for apologies; it measures the distance their friendship has achieved from such debilitating categories, the distance they have achieved from their old selves. Rosenthal responds in kind by saying "Good-bye, old dog," they kiss each other, and they then turn to proceed down the mountainside. Our final long shot of the two friends struggling across a snow-covered field is freighted with the question of whether their friendship will survive reentry into the ideological force fields of French society.

Beyond the survival of the friendship itself, our picture of the two friends at the end of the film is also freighted with their responsibility for the microcosm of a new civilization created in Elsa's farmhouse, something we can characterize by looking at a few representative figures. Once set in motion by Elsa's decision to forget the fact that they are enemy combatants (inviting them into her house, not turning them in to the German soldiers who stop to ask for directions), the formation of a family that transcends the divisions of class, nation, race, and religion proceeds at a strange pace, at once fast and leisurely, that indicates an instance of Cytherean enchantment. After the night the Frenchmen arrive, the next scene opens with Elsa telling Rosenthal that her husband and brothers all died in the war, ironically in battles that were considered Germany's greatest victories; her comments indicate her detachment from the nationalist rhetoric behind the war and help explain her decision to shelter the escapees. Maréchal is in the barn feeding and talking to Elsa's cow, noting that she smells the same as his grandfather's cows and that their different nationalities don't stop them from getting along. His first comment

FIGURE 3.3.

Rosenthal translates for Maréchal and Elsa in *La grande illusion*.

to the cow ("Don't worry, it's just me") and the fact that he is wearing Elsa's husband's clothes and seems well-fed and rested suggests that more than just a night has passed since they arrived, that the momentum of their escape has to some degree been slowed. He enters the house, where Rosenthal is having a playful chat with Lotte while Elsa scrubs the floor. He stares at her with frank and ardent admiration, and Elsa, somewhat flustered, responds by standing up and asking Maréchal to get her some water. As Rosenthal translates what she says and Maréchal says he already understands her better than the German guards he knew for eighteen months, we cut to a medium shot of Elsa in which Maréchal moves forward to face her, both of them in profile, while Rosenthal and Lotte are centered between them in the background. In a halting mixture of French and German Maréchal says he'll go look for water, and both he and Elsa smile happily. Maréchal walks off and Lotte jumps up from Rosenthal's lap and hops to her mother as the scene fades out.

The shot compositions and narrative elements of this scene articulate a figure that represents a translation of the triangular figure of friendship (that is, two people listening to a third) into the terms of a larger community (a family, a possible civilization). On the most obvious level the scene establishes the basic division of labor and roles in this family: Lotte adopts the role of being "niece" to Rosenthal, Rosenthal adopts the role of being "uncle" to Lotte and translator for Maréchal and Elsa, and Maréchal adopts the clothes and household functions of Elsa's "husband." By taking on the role of uncle, Rosenthal relieves Maréchal and Elsa of the premature burden of being "mother" and "father" and buys them the time they need to become "wife" and "husband" first. But the necessity of his function in this role is deliberately contrasted with the redundancy of his function as a translator. Though he continues to function as a "third person" to whom they both listen, their expressions and Maréchal's comments make clear that they have already understood each other without his translation, as if the old cosmopolitan civilization represented in Rosenthal's ability to translate for them is already being surpassed by the new civilization the couple is in the process of creating. Though the familial tenderness and effortless communication between Rosenthal and Lotte give us an image of the goal toward which Maréchal and Elsa are heading, it is, in another sense, already a redundant placeholder, as if one triangular figure in the shot (Elsa-Rosenthal-Maréchal) were dissolving into another (Elsa-Lotte-Maréchal) that renders Rosenthal and the cosmopolitan civilization he represents more or less unnecessary.

The completion of this invisible dissolve is articulated in a very precise and moving way in the Christmas scene that immediately follows this one. We begin with a close-up of the Nativity tableau the adults have made for Lotte that highlights its various characters (Jesus, Joseph, Mary, donkey, ox). Rosenthal makes a quip about Jesus being one of his ancestors, a remark that reflects both his desire to belong here and his sense that he might not. As Maréchal and Elsa move toward Lotte's bedroom and, in the process, briefly hold hands, Rosenthal goes to light the candles on the Christmas tree and start the gramophone. Maréchal turns off the lights and stands at the door as Elsa goes into Lotte's bedroom, tells her that baby Jesus has come, and leads her out into the kitchen in a medium close-up. There is a brief cutaway to an excited Rosenthal saying, "Lotte, come!" as we track back to follow Elsa leading her to the tableau. Maréchal crouches down next to Lotte, his face beaming affection, while Rosenthal, grinning but with another, suppressed, emotion, fiddles with straw on the stable roof. Lotte says she wants to eat baby Jesus and the adults all laugh at this, Maréchal picking her up and saying the only German phrase he learned in captivity ("strictly forbidden"). Lotte then says she wants to take Joseph to bed with her, a phrase that Rosenthal repeats ironically and as if it has something to do with him. As Maréchal carries Lotte back to her bedroom door with Elsa, Rosenthal follows the incipient family, telling Lotte she's a good little girl and playfully poking her with a piece of straw. Maréchal asks Rosenthal how to say "Lotte has blue eyes" in German, Rosenthal tells him, and Maréchal says the phrase with butchered pronunciation, which Elsa corrects, staring directly at him. Maréchal turns to meet her gaze, holds it, and slowly and meaningfully repeats the portion of the phrase she corrected ("*blaue augen*"). She nods to indicate that it's okay for a start and turns to lead the way into the bedroom. Maréchal follows, puts Lotte in her crib, and kisses her on the forehead while Rosenthal stands at the doorway peering in and twisting his piece of straw. Maréchal emerges from the bedroom, and he and Rosenthal then walk back toward the table with the tree and Nativity tableau. Elsa emerges and thanks Rosenthal for everything they have done; he demurs and says it is they who owe her so much. She says good night, and Rosenthal says good night and then turns to Maréchal with a sharp and knowing look that he then turns back toward Elsa, a look that signals his appreciation of the impending consummation of the relationship between the two. As Rosenthal moves toward his bedroom, he turns and says good night a second time, as if ironically giving his blessings on the union between his friend and Elsa. After he and Maréchal retire to their rooms and bid each other good night, Maréchal catches sight of Elsa continuing to stand, waiting for him, in front of the tableau; he slowly walks up to her, they embrace, and the scene fades out.

 Every detail of Rosenthal's behavior in this scene articulates his mixed feelings, his joy in having helped create this family and his sadness at having become redundant to it. Being a member of a cosmopolitan, multilingual civilization allowed him to translate for the couple and be a surrogate parent to Lotte, but he now realizes that his successful performance of these roles has rendered his existence superfluous. Like Boeldieu and

FIGURE 3.4.

Rosenthal has mixed feelings in *La grande illusion*.

von Rauffenstein, he recognizes that he is no longer needed and yields his place in the family graciously but with a measure of sadness and reluctance that derives from his quasi-parental bond with Lotte. In addition to all the adults' manifest delight in staging the spectacle for Lotte, the feeling of tenderness that suffuses the scene derives from Rosenthal's renunciation of his temporary relationship with Lotte, their "two-ness," in favor of the "three-ness" of the family that relationship allowed to generate; in this instance, the invisible dissolve in which one provisional form of family gives way to another is shown to depend on a surrogate parent's consent to loving the distance that will henceforth separate him from his child.

Treated as a whole and in terms of its narrative causality, *La grande illusion* articulates the way in which the possibility of a transnational civilization emerges from nodes such as this new family; to the extent that the formation of the Maréchal-Elsa-Lotte family is shown to be the direct result of successive acts of renunciation undertaken by representatives of two older forms of civilization (Boeldieu and Rosenthal), one might suggest that faith in an as-yet-unmanifest form of civilization and acts of renunciation undertaken on its behalf are in a sense its necessary preconditions. Though the artificial and dislocating context of the prisoner-of-war camp allows the men there to contemplate each other's differences in a way that would not have been possible in French society, it is also evident that only some of the men (Boeldieu, Maréchal, and Rosenthal) take advantage of this opportunity. Boeldieu is incapable of the reciprocity and radical self-transformation of true friendship, but his contemplation of Maréchal and Rosenthal nonetheless changes his understanding of their worth, and it is this new understanding that motivates his final act of self-sacrifice, effectively a gallant gift from a dying civilization to another in the process of being born. This act of self-sacrifice allows the transclass and transracial friendship of Maréchal and Rosenthal to continue, and this friendship in turn motivates Rosenthal's nurturing of the transnational family formed by Maréchal, Elsa, and Lotte. In both Boeldieu's and Rosenthal's acts we can see a civilized recognition of possibilities of connection between others that they can bring into being only by renouncing their own claims on those others; they act precisely because they feel obliged to do so, because their feeling of obligation toward others renders their own rights relative and secondary.

Though Cytherean enchantment begins in a spontaneous attraction to the difference of others, it develops and grows into friendship and then civilization only when individuals deliberately renounce their desire to possess or be possessed; reversing the causality, we might say that one's attraction to others develops into true friendship only after one has adopted a civilized, nonpossessive attitude toward them. One can belong to a civilization only by resisting the temptation to belong to an exclusive friendship or self-identical group presented by the culture model of human community. Being civilized means never taking the existing forms of civilization too seriously; it means that one's faith in the possibilities of civilization—in a different understanding of the past, present, and future—is stronger than one's attachment to existing forms of civilization, attachment that always reduces a civilization to a culture. The steps Boeldieu and Rosenthal take to engender the possibility of civilizations neither will belong to underlines the fact that in principle, civilization always reproduces itself in a different form. Though any existing form of civilization is liable to romanticize its own past and thus become the self-identical and closed form of culture embodied in the two dandies Boeldieu and von Rauffenstein, civilization as a theoretical ideal or aspiration always involves the recognition of new forms of human difference and connection and the willingness to renounce its own earlier forms. Civilization can thus be defined as a collective project that constitutes the fullest and most self-conscious development of the experience of Cytherean enchantment, of treating the dispossessing and dislocating experience of contingency as a gift and allowing oneself to be transformed by it, even when, as in the case of both Boeldieu and Rosenthal, that transformation takes the form of an obligatory renunciation.

In the Fifth chronotope to appear in his films of the 1930s, Renoir gave himself the freedom to explore a set of human possibilities that were strikingly different from those he examined in the other four chronotopes. The major characters in *Les bas-fonds* and *La grande illusion*—Pepel, the Baron, Boeldieu, von Rauffenstein, Maréchal, Rosenthal, and Elsa—all forge modes of meeting and belonging that represent a distinct alternative to the romantic models of human relations and community that govern both the nine films that preceded them and the two films that followed them. As we saw in chapter 2 and in the first section of this chapter, the films of the first four chronotopes explored how the ideological habits of romanticism function on various scales of magnitude to enclose, blind, and/or carry characters away from Cytherean possibilities that Renoir believes to be the deeper permanent strata of human existence. In contrast to the critical, self-conscious fatalism of those films, *Les bas-fonds* and *La grande illusion* offer a utopian vision of characters whose erotic wisdom makes them capable of responding to the Cytherean experience of contingency in such a way as to make it the basis of human relation and community; *Les bas-fonds* demonstrates how the exercise of friendship between two individuals delivers both of them from the imprisonment of their romantic self-understandings, while *La grande illusion* demonstrates how the civilized attitudes of its principal characters result in friendships, families, and other bonds of connection that transcend divisions of class, nation, race, and gender. In the films of the Fifth chronotope, Renoir imagined and presented his audience with a philosophical alternative to the romantic models of human nature, community, and history that dominated, debilitated, and divided the society and culture of the time. He had discovered a positive way of understanding the world that he would pit against the much stronger forces of romanticism in *La règle du jeu*, after having taken the full measure of those forces in *La Marseillaise* and *La bête humaine*.

NOTES

1. Buchsbaum notes that though many critics described Renoir this way, perhaps the earliest to do so was Roget Leenhardt in *Esprit* (February 1937): "Unknown yesterday, everyone knows today that Renoir is the director of genius of the left." Jonathan Buchsbaum, *Cinema Engagé*, 161, 183.

2. This journalism is collected in Renoir, *Écrits 1926–1971*, 79–182. I will be discussing the content of these articles later in this chapter.

3. Major political events from the Popular Front period to the invasion of France are outlined in chap. 31, "Crisis and Collapse: 1936–1940," in Wright's *France in Modern Times*, 386–405; chaps. 7 and 8 ("Bonhomie and Militancy" and "Struggle and Vacation") of Rearick's *French in Love and War* discuss the cultural implications of the Stavisky affair, workplace occupations, and law granting paid vacations.

4. Wright, *France in Modern Times*, 405.

5. I should note here that my neglect of *La nuit du carrefour*, *Chotard et cie*, and *La vie est à nous* in chapter 2 was driven by simple expediency; as their labels in the chronological list indicate, I believe these films can be treated as minor variants of chronotopes that were articulated more fully in the films I chose to examine.

6. Wollen, "Auteur Theory."

7. The process through which the Possible came to be exalted over the Actual in modern philosophy is outlined in chap. 4, "Historicity and Political Nihilism," in Rosen, *Nihilism*, and is summarized in his account of Heidegger on pgs. 97–98.

8. Ruprecht, *Symposia*, 30.

9. Renoir, *Renoir on Renoir*, 77–78.

10. The disappearance of Cythera within each chronotope should already be evident from what was said in chapter 2. The only chronotope in which this may not yet be evident might be the Flaubertian. Where are the Cytherean possibilities in *La chienne*? Despite the bleakness and chilly detachment that pervades the film, by the end of it we are given to understand that the experience of killing Lulu and seeing Dédé tried and executed for the murder has opened Legrand's eyes to the tragicomic absurdity of human existence; though his new view of the world may amount to a form of nihilism, it in any case constitutes a liberation from and an improvement over the romanticism that enclosed him. In the last shot we get of him he jokes about life's absurdity with Alexis Godard (his fellow bum and fellow ex-husband of Adele), and we understand their fall to the bottom of society has at least had the benefit of freeing them from its ideological power; as many critics have observed, we might well imagine that Legrand's brutal experience of life has turned him into Boudu.

11. Renoir, *Renoir on Renoir*, 21.

12. Montale, *Occasions*, 115–17. "Boats on the Marne." Copyright © 1957 by Arnoldo Mondadori Editore, Milano. Translation copyright © 1987 by William Arrowsmith, from COLLECTED POEMS OF EUGENIO MONTALE 1925–1977 by Eugenio Montale, edited by Rosanna Warren, translated by William Arrowsmith. Used by permission of W. W. Norton & Company, Inc.

13. This anecdote was recounted by Eugène Ionesco in the preface to his *Rhinoceros* and is discussed in Andrew and Ungar, *Popular Front Paris*, 109.

14. Rougemont, *Love in the Western World*, 268.

15. Ibid., 267.

16. François Furet, "The Ancien Régime and the Revolution," chap. 2 of Nora, *Realms of Memory*, 79–84.

17. Ibid., 79, 85.

18. Ibid., 79.

19. Ibid., 84.

20. Rousseau, *Social Contract*, 13, 119.

21. Wingrove, *Rousseau's Republican Romance*, 3.

22. Rousseau, *Social Contract*, 2.

23. Ibid.

24. Though almost everything I have read on Rousseau takes time to ponder this paradox, Wingrove's *Rousseau's Republican Romance* shows it to be at work in every text Rousseau ever wrote. She introduces the term "consensual nonconsensuality" on p. 5.

25. Rousseau's *Emile* quoted in ibid., 3.

26. Ibid., 3–4.

27. Simone Weil offers a definition of ethical obligation consistent with our formulation of Cytherean desire:

> There exists an obligation toward every human being for the sole reason that he or she *is* a human being, without any other condition requiring to be fulfilled, and even without any recognition of such obligation on the part of the individual concerned. This obligation is not based upon any *de facto* situation, nor upon jurisprudence, customs, social structure, relative state of forces, historical heritage, or presumed historical orientation; for no *de facto* situation is able to create an obligation.... This obligation is an unconditional one. If it is founded on something, that something, whatever it is, does not form a part of our world. (Weil, *Need for Roots*, 4–5)

28. Birnbaum, chap. 2, "The Body of the Nation," in *Idea of France*, 56.

29. Ibid.

30. Writing of the reactionary ideologue Joseph de Maistre, Berlin observes: "Temperamentally Maistre resembled his enemies, the Jacobins; like them he was a total believer, a violent hater, a *jusqu'au boutiste* in all things.... He attacked eighteenth-century rationalism with the intolerance and the passion, the power and the gusto, of the great revolutionaries themselves. He understood them better than the moderates, and he had some fellow-feeling for their qualities; but what was to them a beatific vision was to him a nightmare." Quoted in Birnbaum, *Idea of France*, 72. We will consider Simone Weil's thoughts on French politics later in this chapter, but here is her more general statement of this psychological paradox: "Why is the determination to fight against a prejudice a sure sign that one is full of it? Such a determination necessarily arises from an obsession. It constitutes an utterly sterile effort to get rid of it. All the Freudian system is impregnated

with the prejudice which it makes its mission to fight—the prejudice that everything sexual is vile." Weil, *Gravity and Grace*, 49.

31. Weil, *Need For Roots*, 3–4.
32. Weil, "The Power of Words," in *Simone Weil Reader*, 271.
33. Ibid., 273–74.
34. Ibid., 274.
35. Renoir, *Écrits 1926–1971*, 82–86, 93–95.
36. Ibid., 98–99.
37. Ibid., 107–8.
38. Weil, *Waiting for God*, 202.
39. Ibid., 205.
40. Michel de Montaigne, *An Apology for Raymond Sebond* (New York: Penguin Books, 1987), 156.
41. Plato, *Phaedrus and Letters VII and VIII*, 61–66.
42. Ibid., 64.
43. Ruprecht, *Symposia*, 76.
44. Ibid., 90.
45. Ibid., 92.
46. Renoir, *Renoir on Renoir*, 77.
47. Weil, *Gravity and Grace*, 58.
48. Schiffman, *On the Threshold of Modernity*, 5.
49. Ibid., 6.
50. Ibid., 5.
51. Hartle, *Michel de Montaigne*, 1.
52. "The interpretation I present here is based on the moment of self-discovery that occurs in 'The Apology for Raymond Sebond.' Montaigne is 'a new figure: an unpremeditated and accidental philosopher!' I take him at his word: what he is doing in the Essays has never been done before." Ibid., 1.
53. Ibid., 3.
54. Ibid., 4.
55. Ibid., 3.
56. Ibid.; Montaigne's maxim is quoted in Schiffman, *On the Threshold of Modernity*, 53.
57. Hartle, *Michel de Montaigne*, 7.
58. Auerbach, *Mimesis*, 311.
59. Hartle, *Michel de Montaigne*, 171.
60. Ibid., 6–7.
61. Hartle contrasts the structure of the essay with the forms favored by deliberate philosophy:

> The syllogism, the disputation, and the treatise all constrain thought within the limits of a rigid method that requires precise definitions of one's terms, that assumes the truth of one's premises, and that aims at a pre-determined conclusion. The essay, on the contrary, embraces the full range and depth of meaning of its terms and thus allows a deeper meaning, a "second sense," to emerge. The essay begins in opinion but does not treat that opinion as a premise—that is, opinion is taken as revealing truth but only after it is examined as if it were untrue. In Oakshott's words, we begin

with something known but, at the same time we assume it not to be known. The essay does not aim at a predetermined conclusion. It is rather a way of discovery that allows the accidental "some authority." (Hartle, *Michel de Montaigne*, 86, 87)

62. It is worth noting that, as I will attempt to define them, the concepts of civilization and culture are not in all respects analogous to the German terms *Gesellschaft* (society) and *Gemeinschaft* (community) as used by, for example, the sociologist Max Weber; the genealogy of the concepts I will present is somewhat idiosyncratic insofar as I have tailored it to its expression in Renoir's films.

63. Charles Baudelaire, "The Painter of Modern Life," in *Selected Writings on Art and Literature*, 422.

4

La règle du jeu; *or, Putting Modernity in Question*

THE DIALECTIC OF CIVILIZATION AND CULTURE: RENOIR'S RADICAL ANACHRONISM

I had no intention of making a controversial film, believe me. I had no intention of startling conventional people. I simply wanted to make a film, I even wanted to make a good film, but one that, at the same time, would criticize a society that I considered to be rotten and that I continue to consider to be absolutely rotten, because this society is still the same. It's still rotten, it hasn't finished drawing us into some very pretty little catastrophes.

Jean Renoir, 1961, in Renoir on Renoir

What may be interesting about this film is the time I filmed it. I shot it between Munich and the war, and I shot it at a time when I was very affected, very upset by the state of mind of a part of French society, of a part of English society, of a part of world society.

Jean Renoir, 1966, in Renoir on Renoir

All these people are sentimental, as are all these types of societies, as are all the people who give in to their instincts and close their eyes to the world.

Jean Renoir, 1966, in Renoir on Renoir

TO BEGIN TO UNDERSTAND the powerful but mysterious effect that *La règle du jeu* has on us, and as a necessary preparation for the close reading of the film in the final section of this chapter, we need to clearly identify the most pervasive and profoundly unconscious assumption that the film provokes us to reconsider, that is, the very idea of history. Our unexamined belief in time-as-history is the subject of what we might call the big gag or shock of the film, and to appreciate the effect of this gag it may be useful to imagine, via a brief thought experiment, the all-encompassing perspective on human history of a typical modern philosopher such as Hegel.

Suspended out in space, Hegel sees civilizations rise and fall as spirit works toward the realization of a universal homogeneous state in which the basic human desire for liberty, knowledge, and recognition achieves its final and lasting satisfaction. In each age, humans become conscious of the historical totality of their world and change it through the slow, painful labor of negation: slaves and masters reflect on their relationship to the world and progressively transform the archaic world of faith into the modern world of culture, the world they were given into the world they freely create. In this narrative, the French Revolution represents the point at which Spirit becomes finally conscious of itself, and the drive to realize freedom through historical action becomes increasingly dynamic. In this context, the agonized dynamism of events during the 1930s—the Depression, the struggle of Left and Right, of nation against nation—is for Hegel simply a messy but unavoidable passage in the realization of modernity and progress. Hegel looks confidently ahead to the new order of the postwar world—the Cold War, the collapse of communism, the contemporary battle between jihad and McWorld—and he smiles, for he believes this is all necessary and inescapable and, in the end, the best of all possible worlds.

Now imagine that out of some sort of perverse curiosity or doubt Hegel decides to rewind the tape of his master plan and go in for a closer look at France in 1938 and that what he looks at is the world of *La règle du jeu*. How does he react to what he sees? He can't believe his eyes, he shakes his head, he blinks, he's flabbergasted, he's disgusted: as far as he can tell, not a single part of his master plan seems to be working, everything seems wildly out of sync. At first he thinks he likes the opening, the plane landing to the triumphant roar of a crowd, the spectacle of humanity asserting its technological mastery over nature, the collectivity recognizing itself in the world-historical achievement of an exemplary individual; in this last regard it reminds him of the morning of October 13, 1806, when Napoleon and his troops entered Jena after a night of furious bombardment and he wrote to his friend Niethammer, "I saw the Emperor—that World Soul—riding out to reconnoitre the city; it is truly a wonderful sensation to see such an individual, concentrated here on a single point, astride a single horse, yet reaching across the world and ruling it."[1] But then he remembers that he's already seen the exact same scene some ten years before with Lindbergh, and it dawns on him that it doesn't represent something new but is actually some sort of romantic fixation, a degrading and compulsive repetition. He catches the allusion to the French prime minister Daladier's recent return flight from the appeasement in Munich and winces at the broad slapstick of treating an act of cowardice as if it were heroism. Then comes André Jurieu's revelation of his absurdly chivalrous motivation for the flight, something directly out of the Middle Ages—he did it for a woman who, because she is not there, has let him down. The airplane and the radio, those magnificent instruments capable of welding humanity into a unified global culture, are being put to the service of the silliest and most anachronistic forms of escapism, of a headlong flight from historical reality. What initially seemed part of the master plan now seems to be completely regressive, a calculated mockery of the plan. Hegel realizes he has been set up, that he has been made the subject of a gag.

Then it gets worse. He follows André Jurieu's revelation as it ricochets through the airwaves into an entire world of people who have managed to successfully opt out of the plan, who have passed through the transformations of the last two centuries without being transformed in the slightest. In stark contrast to the linear motion of the flight and the impetuous revelation of the pilot, we enter a world governed by the circular motion of various games: card-playing, wind-up toys, the daily transit from wife to mistress and back again, the weekly and yearly round of social engagements. Far from trying to negate the anachronism of their existence—the fact that they are "late as usual"—some of these masters embody prerevolutionary ideals with conviction. The Marquis's decision to invite André into his home reflects his willingness to pit his civilized ideals of friendship and openness against the romanticism of the latter, and Hegel watches helplessly as the film stages an encounter between two sets of values that are, from his standpoint, equally anachronistic. Where are the slaves, who by becoming conscious of their condition are the real agents of progress and culture? In their place, we get the blood-and-soil fantasies of the Alsatian Schumacher, the anti-Semitic nastiness of the chauffeur, the servile loyalty of Corneille and the chef, the deft game-playing of Lisette, the pathetic uniform fetish of Marceau—in short, nothing capable of cohering into a meaningful or positive image of historical change. The film provides us with characters who embody subtle gradations of Enlightenment and romantic attitudes and uses comic juxtapositions to force us to think those attitudes through. But where can such thinking lead us? What kind of future does it point to? This is what infuriates Hegel, that he can't find a way to situate the film within a coherent historical narrative. Instead, this rich complex world of activity, this monstrous testimonial to anachronism, stares back at him like uncontradicted evidence and makes him feel negated: the film is going nowhere fast and taking him with it.

I have permitted myself this caricature of Hegel as a crude but hopefully expedient introduction to the comic mechanism whereby the film's philosophical critique engages with the experience and beliefs of its audience. While I doubt that any of us believe in the totality of Hegel's master plan, I would venture that most of us still interpret our experiences according to certain of its basic assumptions; as properly disenchanted postmodernians, we no longer believe in Progress with a capital *P*, Modernity with a capital *M*, or Culture with a capital *C*, but we probably consider ourselves progressive, modern, and sensitive to cultural differences. Whether or not we explicitly believe in historicism or the doctrines of modern philosophers, we all believe in technology and therefore assume that time is, in its most fundamental significance, history, a meaningful narrative of technology-enabled human action. Despite its theoretical "end" over twenty years ago, it is all too obvious that history is still being made by human beings seeking to overcome their material and ideological alienation and that the hierarchical structure of social relations within and between nations and the irreducibility of certain cultural differences have led to the new normal of a globalized war without end, daily suicide bombings, and the secular ritual of taking off our shoes in airports. Though this is probably not what Hegel had in mind, the underlying assumptions at work are those he carried forward to us from Rousseau.

The dangerous effects of these ideas and tendencies on Europe in the 1930s are the context for the intervention of *La règle du jeu*, for the haunting evocation of Civilization it can be said to produce. In a striking contrast to the Rousseauian model of the state of nature as antisocial, amoral, and irrational will, the Marquis's ideal of civilization presumes that human desire is inherently social, ethical, and rational and that each of these aspects of human nature depends on the others to function effectively. In a similar fashion, the Platonic model of friendship and the Rousseauian model of collective self-negation differ so greatly that it can be hard to understand them as comparable figures of thought, dialogically engaged with the same issues. With this potential difficulty in mind, I believe that it would again be expedient, as a kind of warm-up to the sequential analysis of the film's narrative, to consider two scenes in the film that articulate these incommensurable models of "meeting."

The first is the scene in which the Marquis and Octave sit down to discuss the geometry problems that each is respectively concerned with (Christine-Marquis-Geneviève; André-Christine-Marquis). From their earlier exchanges in the hall and in Christine's bedroom, we have only a vague picture of familiarity and mutual indifference, with perhaps a trace of restrained hostility on Octave's part. Then they sit down at either end of the couch, and we immediately sense a whole history, the three years of sizing each other up, of measuring the wealth and connections of the rich husband against the memories and affection of the poor childhood friend; their frank words and restrained postures testify with incredible compression to the many accommodations they have reached in defending their respective stakes in Christine. Though they are far from being friends, their common concern for Christine nonetheless forces them into a position analogous to friendship; it places them at a distance where they can measure the sincerity of their own motives against the ethical obligation they both feel toward her, as if she is a third-person-as-child who has put them into a quasi-parental relationship. Then the Marquis asks Octave if he needs money, and this kind gesture, which reminds him of everything he owes the Marquis, throws the delicate balance of

FIGURE 4.1.

Octave and the Marquis discuss geometry problems.

Octave's calculations out of whack. He broaches the question of inviting André to La Colinière but immediately seems to be questioning his own motives for doing so: is he doing it to make Christine happy or to make André happy? And what exactly does he, Octave, get out if it? Is he doing it because the union of André and Christine would somehow satisfy his own unconscious desires by proxy? This horrifying prospect on the ambiguity of his own motives—together with the fact that the Marquis now proclaims his love for Christine with the same vehement words and gestures that André used the day before—leads directly to Octave's celebrated speech on the "awful" fact that "everyone has their reasons." We seem to have reached a Hamlet-esque moment when the action of the narrative might grind to a halt because of Octave's moral paralysis, but then the Marquis picks up the thread of Octave's reflections somewhat differently, saying, "Of course they do—and I'm all for their free expression." He goes on to affirm his faith in the ideals of an open civilization he tries his best to represent and says that he will, on the basis of those principles, invite André to La Colinière.

What is crucial to recognize about this scene is that their dialogue has taught each of the characters something new about the other and that the final outcome of the dialogue is something neither could have imagined ahead of time. They began their conversation by being clearly opposed— Octave thinks inviting André is a good thing; the Marquis has grave doubts and fears—but by the end of scene the positions are completely reversed: the Marquis seems genuinely happy to have accepted Octave's proposal, but Octave himself seems disconsolate. If we consider the logic of their reflections, we realize that the Marquis's decision stems from a kind of happy accident; while Octave plumbed the awful depths of human motivation, the Marquis reinterprets his comments to be a reminder that Christine is entitled to her reasons, awful or not, and that it was up to her, a matter of her own free consent, whether to remain with him or to be with André: realizing this turns him from a jealous, worried man into a wise and generous one. The surprising reversal of their positions is a "happy gag" that enlarges them both and keeps them both thinking, a fact that is deftly underlined a few moments later when the Marquis returns to the room, grinning, to tell Octave (now happily flirting with Lisette), "You know?—you're no idiot—you're a poet—a *dangerous* poet." That said, this delayed and uncanny echo of Octave's earlier comment to Christine in a mix of German (first) and then French ("You are an angel—a *dangerous* angel—but an angel all the same") also registers as a bit of a non sequitur and, because of the uncanniness of the echo, possibly too much of a good thing, a project with too much momentum, out of control.

The figure of friendship and reflection in this scene offers a stark contrast to the one in which Marceau and Schumacher collaborate to kill Octave but end up killing André instead. They stand with their bodies glommed together outside the greenhouse and squint uselessly into the darkness; when Marceau suggests they separate so that Marceau can keep watch and Schumacher can get his gun, Schumacher says, "No—from now on we stay together." After the entire film has shown us exactly how different they are, after watching Schumacher spend the second half of

FIGURE 4.2.

Schumacher and Marceau sticking together.

the film trying to kill Marceau, they are now suddenly united only by their shared resentment of the master who fired them and of another who appears to be stealing the woman they both think they own. Their degrading union, ironic and amusing as it may be, neutralizes anything unique, different, or productive in either of them and will result only in the accidental death of a man neither has anything against. Their fascistic fusion is a "sad gag" that evacuates and collapses them as distinctive individuals.

In conjunction with my Hegel thought experiment, the analysis of these two scenes should suggest that the philosophical battle between Civilization and Culture is not something that is worked out in the film's narrative but is instead a kind of afterimage that its gags develop over time in the back of the spectator's mind; as the well-coordinated mechanism of the film's comic devices penetrate and defamiliarize the Rousseauian assumptions that structure our experience, they produce a utopian afterimage of the Civilization those assumptions repress, which one might perhaps imagine in the form of a vast baroque coral reef, teeming with life. Renoir uses aesthetic strategies such as the gag because the philosophical danger he is concerned with is not something that can be represented in a historical narrative, as something that human action can avoid, overcome, or succumb to; this danger is in fact omnipresent, happening all the time, constantly at work repressing possibilities that are right there in front of us, relationships that never grow because we are incapable of imagining them. Civilization is not something in the historical past that Renoir wants us to return to, nor is it a project of the human will to be realized historically in the future: it is a dimension of contemporary experience, the Cytherean face of the present that modern assumptions render us incapable of recognizing.

From this perspective, my argument entails a fundamental reinterpretation of the myth of the film's premiere, a myth that despite subsequent revision continues to shape its critical reception. According to the legend, members of the original theatrical audience for the film recognized themselves in its portrait of French society and found the portrait unflattering: the film was a mirror reflecting their hypocrisy, their adultery, their frivolous passions, and their parasitical and anachronistic existence; they didn't like what they saw and revolted. I would argue instead that the deep provocation of the film, for its original audience and also for us, hinges on the fact that we *cannot* recognize ourselves in the film, *cannot* see ourselves in the characters. We come to know them intimately but are at the same time separated from them by what seems to be the infinite distance between "their time" and "our time"; thus, as far as I can recall, my reaction to the death of the last rabbit in the hunt scene was not that it died before my eyes in 1938/1983 but that the rabbit and all the other characters were still somehow very much alive in "another time and place," a time and place that is manifest every time I watch the film. If I—and perhaps others?—have experienced the ontological effects of the film in this strange way, we are now in a position to identify the real reasons why, for the distance we are talking about is not the historical period of time from 1938 to the present but the thought-time of modernity itself, a distance that can be crossed only via a Cytherean process of embarking, the hard labor of

FIGURE 4.3.

Christine sees an event from a time when she didn't exist.

forgetting modern assumptions, a kind of philosophical rapture the comfortable inhabitants of Plato's Cave will always find preposterous. I believe the deep provocation of the film, for those open to it, is that it retrieves and gathers our precious real-life memories of Cythera and strands them in a world beyond our philosophical reach.

The last hypothesis I would like to put forward as a frame for the analysis that follows is that the emotional-cognitive impact of the film derives from the way in which the narrative creates a palpable evocation of Civilization in the first half and then brutally destroys it in the second half. The decisive moment of transition between the two halves is a brilliant crystallization of the theme of anachronism that illuminates the structure of the whole. The narrative of the first half of the film is driven by André's public declaration at the airport and the effects of this within the world of aristocrats and *grande bourgeoisie* (*les gros* from *La bête humaine,* now viewed from a very different angle). That declaration prompts the Marquis to be worthy of his wife and give up Geneviève, it causes Octave to sponsor André's entry into that world, and it leads to Christine's speech about friendship that effectively repairs the damage caused by André's declaration. By the time we get to the hunt, the internal balance of the Marquis's world is on the verge of being completely restored. Both André and Geneviève are reconciled to giving up their love-objects, and the for-old-time's-sake kiss that Geneviève asks for can be felt to be bringing the entire first movement of the film to a close. But then Christine looks through the telescope and everything changes. What exactly does she see? The image that strikes her eye crosses not only the space of the swampy landscape but three whole years of time: it does not reflect the actual state of her husband's relationship with Geneviève but rather the moment three years earlier when—in Geneviève's words—Christine did not exist. The image is in fact an anachronistic fiction, a historical reconstruction of the past, but she understandably takes it to be the reality of the present—it is an image that negates her and that furthermore evokes an entire offscreen world of characters who have all been "in on it," tacitly or deliberately complicit in negating her. She immediately understands that her romantic worldview is anachronistic, worse than meaningless—absurd—and becomes determined to negate it herself; after her bold "woman-to-woman" exchange of confidences with Geneviève confirms her worst fears, she removes herself from her role as symbolic linchpin of the microcosm of Civilization and releases the mayhem of negation and self-negation that dominates the second half of the film. She inaugurates a mindless chaos that comes to rest only through a fascist restoration of order.

With this big picture of the story and other critical hypotheses in view, we are now in a position to track in and consider the sequence of four overlapping movements, four successive invisible dissolves, through which the film articulates the philosophical conflict between Civilization and Culture. This consideration should allow us to register the aesthetic powers of the film with greater understanding and hopefully confirm it to be the crowning achievement of a decade of profound cinephilosophical reflection.

FIGURE 4.4.

Christine as the mysterious object of desire.

LA RÈGLE DU JEU; OR, HOW CIVILIZATION DISINTEGRATES

First Movement: The Contest for Christine, the Dangerous Angel

The Greeks and Trojans massacred each other for ten years on account of Helen. Not one of them except the dilettante warrior Paris cared two straws about her; all of them agreed in wishing she had never been born. The person of Helen was so obviously out of scale with this gigantic struggle that in the eyes of all she was no more than a symbol of what was really at stake; but the real issue was never defined by anyone, nor could it be, because it did not exist. For the same reason it could not be calculated. Its importance was simply imagined as corresponding to the deaths incurred and the further massacres expected; and this implied an importance beyond all reckoning.

Simone Weil, "The Power of Words"

The opening movement of *La règle du jeu* presents us with a sharp contrast between two distinct worlds in flight from their own contradictions. The mob at the airport presents us with the spectacle of a mass society that has seized on André's flight as a means to forget both the dangers that surround it and the ideologies that divide it; by identifying themselves with the national hero, André, the members of this mob can briefly escape the intolerable reality of their situations. Then he delivers his petulant speech about some woman who let him down—who is "disloyal"—and this confuses the mob; it thought André was making the flight for the sake of the nation, for its sake, but now it realizes that it was wrong; like André, it also feels let down and now starts to feel jealous and angry toward this mysterious rival for his affections. Who the hell is she? Frustrated, the mob goes home to bed, eager to hear what the media will have to tell it tomorrow morning.

The film abandons the mob of the wider society at the airport and never returns to it, but the reorientation of the mob's attention on Christine immediately makes the inhabitants of the world of the *haute bourgeoisie* feel self-conscious and vulnerable; they have in effect been hiding from this mob ever since the Revolution and are well aware of what it is capable of when roused in anger. With the exception of Christine herself, who is concerned only with understanding how she got into a personal predicament and how to get out of it, one can recognize an anxious awareness of public opinion in the expressions and dialogue of all the other characters we see listening to the radio report: Lisette feels protective toward her mistress, the Marquis quickly calculates the best way to spin the story, and the characters hanging out in Geneviève's apartment (Geneviève, Dick, and St. Aubin) debate whether the sudden chill of exposure they feel is caused by André's specific act of "exhibitionism" or is a more general effect of "Progress," a technology-enabled society of the spectacle in which the mass media increasingly expose the most intimate details of private lives to public scrutiny. Our final shot of the confused mob of mass society demanding to know who André Jurieu is in love with is followed by a series of reverse shots in which the people who know the answer keep their heads down (literally) and refuse to meet the gaze of the mob (figuratively).

The narrative of the film follows André's revelation over the airwaves directly to the woman whom that revelation has made an object of intense public curiosity and swiftly provides us with a set of facts that would, on the surface, satisfy that curiosity. She is Christine, the Austrian wife of an aristocrat named Robert de La Chesnaye, who because of her naïveté and lack of familiarity with Parisian manners has inadvertently led André Jurieu to imagine that her friendship was something more. Christine's dialogue and expression in the first two scenes with Lisette and the Marquis, together with St. Aubin's comments about her cultural dislocation, convince us that André must have misunderstood her good intentions, and nothing in the rest of the film ever suggests that she feels anything toward him stronger than mild affection. The absolute transparency of Christine's intentions regarding this issue introduces us to an aspect of her character that remains constant throughout the entire film; with the partial exception of her confidential woman-to-woman chat with Geneviève, every time she speaks or acts we immediately understand what her intentions are, and subsequent events never cause us to revise those understandings. Even when, in the second half of the film, she tries and fails to convince both herself and a succession of men (St. Aubin, André, Octave) that she loves them, we can easily see that these efforts are feeble experiments in which she tries to generate desires inside herself that she does not feel, desperate attempts to negate who she is in order to take revenge on La Chesnaye and escape the humiliation of her situation; though the men involved may not recognize her motives, or her lack of them, we always do.

If there is a mysterious aspect to Christine's character, this does not derive from any uncertainty about her desires but from the fact that, apart from a stated and credible longing to have children, she does not appear to have any strong desires; in a world in which every character seems to have more romantic, passion-derived "reasons" than either they or we can keep track of, her serene self-possession and transparent sincerity make her stand out sharply from all the people around her. In an interview with Jacques Rivette, Renoir responded to the suggestion that Christine is the character about whom the spectator wonders the most by saying, "Of course, because her logic is so clear. What she says is so simple, so direct, so clear and transparent, it winds up seeming mysterious. But I think that all absolutely simple and direct beings are like that, they seem mysterious. You say to yourself, 'My God, he said, "It's raining." That must mean something!' Not at all, it means that it's raining."[2] Recognizing this underdetermination or deficit of desire in Christine's character is one of the two keys to understanding her central place in the symbolic economy of the film. The second key is that, as both audiences and critics felt at the time and have never ceased to remark on since, Nora Gregor's Christine also seems to suffer from a deficit of desirability; she has a strange, almost anamorphic quality that separates her out from the other characters and makes the motives of those pursuing her seem obscure or implausible. Over the twenty years that I have been discussing the film with students, film scholars, and a variety of educated laypeople, the near-universal condemnation of Gregor's performance has never ceased to amaze me; even as people acknowledge the perfection of the film, they feel compelled to identify the casting of Christine as being an undeniable mistake. When asked to specify what is wrong with her performance, people invariably pause and hesitate, as if they don't really know why she bothers them, and when I've pressed the issue, they never address the fit between actress and role as one might reasonably expect but instead point to the actress's physical characteristics (her matronly body, the sound of her voice, her accent, the stiffness of her diction and mannerisms) or to her "unbelievable" naïveté, the very elements that Renoir claims to have had in mind when casting her in the role.[3] Reflecting on the paradox of Renoir placing a mistake at the center of what is considered to be his masterpiece, I have come to the conclusion that the repulsion effects in question are actually a crucial part of the film's design. It is not that there is anything inherently undesirable about the actor or defective about her performance but that her all-too-perfect embodiment of an anachronistic model of feminine sincerity, her physical and psychological difference from everyone around her, makes it difficult to imagine an erotic attraction between her and the men who profess to love her.

It is important to recognize that this imaginative blockage derives as much from the behavior of the men who claim to love her as from the behavior of Christine herself. The narrative of the first movement of the film is built around the process in which Octave arranges a contest between the Marquis and André for Christine's love, but from the outset the motives of the two contestants are called into question by their actual interactions with Christine. From our first shot of Christine looking thoughtfully at the radio, we start to sense that André's outburst was based on his misunderstanding their relationship, and this understanding is subsequently confirmed by her conversations with Lisette, her husband, and Octave in which she suggests she tried only to be friends with him. Though we never learn what was said during the chats that preceded his flight, the contrast between the disinterest Christine displays toward André through most of the film and his vehement avowals of love lead us to wonder what his feelings are really based on. Not once in the entire film does he ever reference a specific detail or quality that attracts him to her; instead, his professions of love are filled with the litany of things he hates about La Chesnaye. André and Christine make eye contact only twice in the entire film, when he first arrives at the chateau and in the late scene in which she declares her love for him, but in both cases this contact is sustained for only a second. In the second scene, as soon as she proposes that they leave the chateau right away, his eyes become occluded with a mist of tenderness, and he launches into a prepared speech in which he says he knows how to make her happy and then lays down the rules he intends to follow in doing so. Neither here nor at any other point in the film does he show the slightest sign of reflecting on a word she says or of registering the expression on her face; as far as one can tell, so far from loving her, he does not even perceive her. Like Toni's love for Josepha, André's love for Christine is really a romantic fixation on certain abstractions, the symbolic values of purity and innocence that he ascribes to her. As Renoir once described him, he is himself pure in contrast to the impure society of *haute bourgeoisie*; his flight is an exhibition of his own purity, a feat of bravery that is meant to demonstrate the sincerity of his motives.[4] He recognizes that Christine is being deceived by her husband and does not belong to the game-playing world of Parisian high society, and therefore he wants, like a knight-errant, to rescue her from what he sees to be a degrading predicament. But if he is more or less right about the injustice of Christine's position, he is also, as Octave describes him, a "modern hero," a romantic with "his head in the clouds," someone who is blind to other human beings and life on the ground of human society. His motives may be pure, but they are also empty of any positive content: he knows what he hates, but he does not in any sense know the woman he says he loves.

Despite the fact that the Marquis has, as Octave tells André, "his feet on the ground," the motives underlying his professed love for Christine are just as obscure as those of his rival. We are never given any information regarding the events of their courtship and marriage, and the coolness of the relationship established in their first two scenes together—the formality of their dialogue, their separate bedroom suites, the constant mediation of servants who open and close doors for them—together with the absence of children and the reality of the Marquis's continued relationship with Geneviève make the motives behind their alliance somewhat obscure. As the film proceeds we are led to infer two possible motives on La Chesnaye's part. The many comments made throughout the film regarding Christine's naïveté and foreignness as an Austrian brought up in a rarefied and sheltered artistic milieu lead one to imagine that the Marquis's proposal might well have been an impulsive gesture of protection and social inclusion that he then had to live with; the plot presents us with two examples of such impulsive noble generosity (inviting André to La Colinière and hiring Marceau as a servant), and it is easy to imagine his proposal as being motivated by his sympathy for her plight as a vulnerable displaced person.[5] A somewhat less noble and subordinate motive one might also infer is that her status as the daughter of a great composer makes her a sort of high-culture trophy for him; though she is not really analogous to the mechanical toys he collects (only her object-like passivity, anachronistic appearance, and stiff demeanor support the analogy), his proposal of marriage may well have originated in a similar impulse to acquire and possess the totems that reflect his civilized values. In either case, we can surmise that the Marquis's proposal of marriage was based more on what she represents than on an attraction to the flesh-and-blood specifics of who she is as a woman; like that of André, the Marquis's love for Christine is really a fixation on certain symbolic values he takes her to embody.

In support of this claim it is important to recognize that his decision to break off with Geneviève is not based on discovering something specific in Christine that he finds attractive; it arises very abruptly, and at first somewhat obscurely, from Christine's statement that she has complete confidence in him. She says this in the hall in response to his question as to whether she thinks he's a liar and just after the scene in which he presents his explanation for Jurieu's radio outburst that generously lets Christine off the hook. His rather suspicious and comical response to her avowal of trust is to abruptly hand his gloves and valise back to the valet, ask her to excuse him for a moment, and bolt back into his study to call Geneviève. The next day in Geneviève's apartment he explains that he needs to break off with her because he suddenly decided to be worthy of his wife. Geneviève mockingly outlines what is meant to be an absurd picture of domestic life ("knitting, slippers, pot-au-feu, and plenty of kids"), and Robert says that's exactly what he's ready for, that he feels he's had enough of a good time. Geneviève then asks him to specify what in his present relationship with Christine would change (improve) as a result of breaking off with her; dumbfounded, Robert sputters, "Why, everything! . . . Everything!!" Geneviève harshly counters that nothing would change; Christine has remained "too Austrian" (that is, innocent and old-fashioned for him), and unlike a Parisian woman Christine would never forgive him for having lied to her. Geneviève goes on to say that, whether from love or force of habit, she would herself be very unhappy if Robert left her; Robert seems surprised and moved by this, says he didn't want to hurt her, and offers her his hand in a gesture that indicates he will rethink his decision. She takes his hand, he kisses hers, and she observes that it's a good thing he is a weak man.

This brief sequence of events, from the phone call to set up a breakup meeting with Geneviève to the end of that meeting where he yields to her desire to continue, incisively exposes the abstract nature of the Marquis's desire to be worthy of his wife. In the first place, it is difficult to imagine how Christine's declaration of trust in her husband would suddenly make him desire her or that it would lead him to suddenly develop a taste for the cozy trappings—knitting, slippers, pot-au-feu, kids—that might follow from a decision to take his marriage seriously. Though there is nothing in particular that he wants to change about his life, Christine's declaration nonetheless acts like a bullet hitting a sore spot he did not know he had. We are forced to infer that he suddenly feels bored with Geneviève and his complicated, duplicitous life as a whole and has seized upon the possibility of a revolutionary transformation in which "everything changes," suddenly becomes pure, innocent, and fresh; he does not know where the project of being worthy of Christine will take him, but he decides to experiment with the sincerity she represents as a means of escaping the ennui of his existence. But though he is shown to be sincere in this intention, his ability to realize it is limited because he is a weak and sentimental man, someone who cannot bear any evidence of suffering in others or himself; he is always liable to be swayed or distracted by the circumstances of the moment and is therefore unable to live by the hard and permanent decisions that the project of sincerity entails. This sequence of events sketches out the possibility of a microcosmic Civilization built around the sincere and mutual love of a monogamous marriage—a true friendship—and projects this as the goal of the private revolution that the Marquis will attempt to realize for most of the film. But it also gives us a first example of how the Marquis's sentimentality causes his project to collapse back into the circular ruts of routine that govern his life. In this instance and throughout the film, we are led to infer that such collapses happen because of the abstract nature of his desire to be worthy of Christine; he does not have the kind of relationship with her that would give his project the imaginative purchase and generative pull of living Cytherean desire.

We become aware of this deficit of desire because the interactions between Robert and Christine demonstrate that their intentions are always at cross-purposes, that there is no genuine understanding or contact between them. Like André, the Marquis never references a single quality or detail that he finds attractive about Christine, nor does he ever look at her with anything resembling carnal desire, attention, or tenderness; despite the steps he takes to be worthy of her by divesting himself of his relationship with Geneviève, despite his frantic search for Christine during the fete, whenever he actually comes into proximity with her his posture, gestures, and gaze testify to the existence of an instinctive aversion. This lack of chemistry is highlighted by a series of exchanges in which the abstraction and formality of Robert's behavior toward her leaves Christine increasingly puzzled, sexually frustrated, weary, and bored. All these emotions are evident in the scene in which he comes to the door of her room to say good night after the public relations exercise in which she "confessed" her friendship with André to the assembled guests. He begins by thanking her. Surprised, she asks why; he says for not making him look foolish and goes on to note that the situation was very delicate and that Jurieu handled it well too. As she listens impatiently to her husband's postgame commentary, Christine gently tilts her head from side to side, trying to find the angle that will allow her to connect with him, but the

FIGURE 4.5.

Christine tries in vain to connect with the Marquis.

Marquis drops his gaze from her face to her body, abstracted in trying to imagine a fitting gesture of gratitude; he shows not the slightest interest in getting her own perspective on the exercise. He grabs one of her hands, kisses it, and continues to hold it with both his hands; when she wearily responds to his relentless formality by saying good night, he shakes her hand with excessive, un-erotic vigor and, with a grave expression meant to underscore his admiration, says good night, turns, and brusquely walks off down the hall.

Throughout this brief dialogue, Christine's facial expression and posture show that she feels confused and almost affronted by her husband's unconscious condescension, by the distance implied in his act of thanking her; at one point her posture and gestures clearly indicate that she wants to erase this feeling by hugging him—an act that, if reciprocated in the manner she desires, would lead to something more—but the unceasing flow of Robert's remarks forces her to stop, and she finally gives up trying to connect. As she turns back into the room lost in thought, she dismisses Lisette for the evening but then calls her back; she bites her lip and swallows, as if she is troubled about something. She then asks Lisette if she doesn't want children; Lisette replies she does but that then you have to look after them. Christine says that's exactly the beauty of it—they become your sole preoccupation. Uninterested in following this train of her mistress's thoughts, Lisette changes the topic to the new servant, Marceau. Christine's dialogue and expression during this exchange, coming right after the one with Robert, reveal the depths of her boredom and dissatisfaction with her marriage and way of life. Surrounded by admirers and friends, she is lonely, unhappy, and sexually unfulfilled; though they all want to serve her and be worthy of her, neither her husband, nor André, nor Lisette, nor Octave (for whom she will always be "the little girl from Salzburg") is interested in recognizing what she really wants or who she really is.

By highlighting the fact that none of the other characters care to understand what Christine wants or who she is, the first movement of the film establishes her as the purely symbolic stake in a struggle between two men who embody and represent different paradigms of philosophical values. André is a "modern hero," a man who represents an anachronistic and comical synthesis of modern technology and the chivalric values (courage, fidelity, purity) that constitute his particular strain of romanticism. The image of the transatlantic night flight that precedes the opening of the film deftly sketches the Rousseauian dimensions of his character (solitary communion with nature; the blind, linear trajectory of irrational instinct) and establishes him as a representative of a modern Culture based in the value of authenticity. In pointed contrast to the sentimental weakness of his rival the Marquis, André is represented as strong in two different senses: like Lantier, his character is informed by an association with the strength of modern transportation technology (being an aviator, driving his car too fast and crashing), and he is also strong because, like Toni, he is single-minded and unswerving in his quest for the woman he loves (his dialogue and behavior never suggest that he thinks of anything else). The zigzag trajectory traced by his series of linear movements articulates the unceasing orientation of his attention on Christine: he flies the Atlantic

FIGURE 4.6.

André trying to find Christine during the fete.

with her in mind, he drives and crashes his car with her in mind, he convinces Octave to help him see her again, he frantically searches for her during the fete, and he dies running to see her. Whenever he is forced to stop his movement to get close to her, he displays his frustration to Octave (after the crash, in their bedroom at the chateau, during the hunt) and thus reminds us of the "unswerving" orientation of his desire (despite all the zigzagging). But each stage of his trajectory also expresses the blindness of his desire: we imagine him in the plane staring into blackness or enveloped in cloud, he crashes the car because he cannot see what is in front of him, he looks for Christine during the fete but cannot find her, and when he does find her he doesn't really look at her or listen to what she says. His unswerving orientation is in fact a function of his blindness: he won't look at or listen to anyone or anything that stands in the way of his movement toward a purely imaginary goal. The fact that he never specifies what the achievement of that goal might look like—we hear only about a transition period during which he proposes that Christine live with his mother, something that can be read as an unconscious strategy to delay and avoid actual contact with her—suggests that his goal is an abstraction with no positive content, a utopia of romantic fusion that the absence of substantive contact between the two characters on-screen makes impossible to imagine.

The personal qualities and activities of the Marquis represent philosophical values that are the antitheses of those represented by André. They represent a formal allegiance to—a sincere but weak aspiration toward—the paradigm of Civilization presented in the last chapter, more specifically, toward a proto-modern version of that paradigm developed by the cosmopolitan thinkers of the European Enlightenment. In contrast to the linear movements that articulate André's single-minded and solitary pursuit of Christine, the figures of circular movement associated with the Marquis—the daily, weekly, and yearly rounds of his social engagements; the gamelike and theatrical nature of those engagements; the sweeping gestures of inclusion that open the circle of his world to add new members as players (Christine, André, Marceau); and the totem-objects of such circular movements, his antique windup toys—can all be understood as expressions of the pre-revolutionary paradigm of *sociabilité* he aspires to embody. As this model of Civilization has important differences that distinguish it from the Montaignean model, a consideration of some key features will be the most efficient means of explaining the philosophical significance of the Marquis's commitment to it.

Daniel Gordon's *Citizens without Sovereignty: Equality and Sociability in French Thought, 1670–1789* presents an account of how the political conditions of eighteenth-century France (an absolute monarchy governed by a bureaucratic police-state) led members of the nobility and middle classes to derive the countercultural paradigm of *sociabilité* from the dialogues between certain philosophers of the European Enlightenment (Pufendorf, Holbach, Diderot, Montesquieu, Hume).[6] While these thinkers appear to have tacitly accepted the Hobbesian position that the natural unsociability of human passions made a sovereign necessary to political order, they focused their attention on the possibility that the "latent sociability" of human beings could be cultivated in such a way as to tame

FIGURE 4.7.

The Marquis's ideal of *sociabilité* in action.

those passions, and their speculations gave rise to the ideal of an open and cosmopolitan domain, *le grand monde,* where human virtues and excellences would flourish in way not possible within the closed, anxiety-driven world of the royal court.[7] The premise that the exercise of reason led to sociability and that the exercise of sociability in turn produced ethical virtues was a reaffirmation of Montaigne's assumptions that at the same time radically altered these by making the realization of virtue conceivable as the historical product of human activity. If Montaigne followed Plato in treating ethical obligations as the eternal or transcendent preconditions of a perfected humanity, as the invisible Forms or models that guided human beings into dialogues that allowed for the proper exercise of their reason, for the thinkers of the eighteenth century the causal sequence was the reverse and inaugurated not in heaven but on earth: rational self-interest led to the exercise of sociability, and a well-played game of social interaction in turn produced virtues and ethical relationships in its players.

Instead of assuming that nations and cultures were unique and incommensurable, like many of Rousseau's German followers, or following Hegel in believing that the multiplicity of nations and cultures would be subsumed within the universal homogeneous state, the unified Culture of the future, the cosmopolitan philosophers of the Enlightenment believed in an ongoing project of human Civilization, a contact zone or dialogical space between cultures defined by its principled openness to all forms of human difference.[8] The Marquis's repeated emphasis on the openness of his domain—on the fact that he does not believe in walls or fences—is derived from this aspect of the Enlightenment paradigm. The sincerity of his commitment to this ideal is reflected in the diversity of guests at La Colinière, the fact that he integrates pillars of high society such as the General, St. Aubin, and the La Bruyères with other characters who might be classed as marginal or different: the homosexual Dick, the eccentric South American Cava, the obese Charlotte de la Plante, the pedant Berthelin. His commitment to this ideal is also manifest in his act of inviting André to La Colinière against his own self-interest, and we can reasonably infer that the seriousness of his commitment derives from the awareness that his own position as a member of the French nobility is the result of others deciding to include him despite his German-Jewish ancestry.

In contrast to Montaigne's skeptical comparative approach to traditional religious and social categories and Rousseau's radical rejection of such categories, the Enlightenment's game of *sociabilité* was premised on avoiding any discussion of religious and social issues. The *philosophes* recognized that religion and social rank were generally the object of unsociable passions and that bracketing off these topics was thus necessary to orient the players on the main object of the game, enjoyable and productive contact with the other players. This bracketing off laid out two cardinal rules: to never discuss religion and to strive to forget (and to make others forget) one's social rank or eminence, a rule that the Marquis explicitly references in his eulogy for André.[9] In addition to these negative prerequisites, the success of the game of *sociabilité* was also understood to depend on a complex of positive qualities and attitudes, the intelligence and delicacy of feeling one brought to chance encounters, the ineffable fusion of cultivated refinement, sensitivity, and discretion expressed in the phrase *je ne sais quoi*.[10] Though it is impossible to model *je ne sais quoi* in general, we can identify moments when the Marquis displays it and when the comments of others indicate he possesses it.

The Marquis's *je ne sais quoi* is often highlighted through a figure whereby his dialogue retrospectively reveals that he was thinking attentively about the words of others although his facial expression and behavior would have led us to think he was distracted by something else. This figure is enacted in the geometry problems scene with Octave we examined earlier in this chapter; though the Marquis walks away from Octave in order to fiddle with one of his toys, the immediacy and firmness of his decision to invite André to La Colinière indicates that he has not only followed Octave's thinking but has in fact overtaken Octave and taken that thinking to a logical conclusion. This figure is then echoed and emphasized by the comment that closes the scene in which he tells Octave that he is not an idiot but a poet, a dangerous poet; though this comment seems at first to be rather opaque or gratuitous—he makes it after leaving and then reentering the study, where Octave and Lisette are now flirting—we then infer that the comment represents the fruit of his continuing to reflect offscreen on Octave's efforts to make the game at La Colinière interesting.

The Marquis's refinement is also recognized in a speech by the chef that explicitly opposes the values of Civilization to racist conceptions of national culture. In the scene in which the servants have lunch in the chateau's kitchen, the chauffeur, Bob, calls the Marquis a *métèque*, raises the issue of his German-Jewish ancestry, and says he is sure Schumacher agrees with him. The chef's first response to the raising of this issue is to say he used to work in the house of a baron where there were no Jews but everyone ate like pigs and this caused him to quit; race and noble blood are no guarantees of the cultivation and refinement that characterize Civilization. His follow-up comment is that though the Marquis may be a *métèque* he is still a "*homme du monde*." He recalls a recent episode when the potato salad was not prepared in the proper manner and the Marquis spotted it right away and summoned the chef to complain; though he may be a foreigner and a Jew, the Marquis has the cultivated refinement of a "man of the world."

The Marquis's two extended encounters with Marceau—first in the fields of La Colinière and then in an alcove during the fete—constitute the strongest demonstrations of his *je ne sais quoi,* demonstrations that can also serve as illustrations as to how the Enlightenment imagined the exercise of *sociabilité* would address the problem of social inequality. But to fully appreciate what happens during those encounters, it will be useful to first consider Renoir's discussion of how *je ne sais quoi* operated in another context.

In explaining his reasons for making *La grande illusion,* Renoir states that one of these was to represent the survival of a certain social ease within the French military that he belonged to before and during World War I.[11] He begins by noting that the historical existence of this social phenomenon or quality is distorted by the image of the past projected by modernity:

> People think that behavior was much more rigorous, much stiffer before, but it was the complete opposite. There was a kind of ease that seems to have disappeared. The expression or phrase in the military code on which military instructors put the most emphasis was the expression "without affectation or stiffness." Now it seems to me that today, military men carry themselves with a bit of affectation and great deal of stiffness. You can see it, for example, in the way in which arms are presented. What does "Present arms!" mean? It means you show your gun or your rifle to an officer or a superior so that he can see if there is powder in it. And if there is powder in it, he throws you into prison for eight days. That's exactly what "Present arms!" means. It has become a kind of fixed symbol, and in my opinion it makes no sense. It probably relates to some very profound ideas, but in my opinion these very deep ideas are not consistent with the French spirit. The French spirit is an easygoing spirit, a relaxed spirit. It's an aristocratic spirit, whereas this new stiff manner of holding oneself is, in my opinion, more plebeian than aristocratic.[12]

In the French military of the past, embodying *je ne sais quoi* entailed knowing how to forget and make others forget the symbolic value of rank even as rank continued to play a role in a functional sense; the quality of any interaction was defined by the extent to which the superior resisted the temptation to be "stiff" (that is, assert his symbolic authority) and the inferior resisted the temptation to be "affected" (that is, assert his symbolic subordination) as they performed their designated functions of giving and carrying out orders. According to Renoir, in the modern military the original imperative to deemphasize or distance oneself from the abstract symbolism of rank hierarchy has been reversed; the practice of presenting arms has lost its practical value, functioning only as a symbolic demonstration of the stiff sadistic mastery of the officer and the affected masochistic slavery of the subordinate. This demonstration can also be understood as an example of Rousseau's solution to the original political problem of an imbalance of forces—a social hierarchy—created by nature or chance; in order to put this right, to make bondage "legitimate," both officer and subordinate have contracted to be equally slaves to the collectivity, and the act of presenting arms has become nothing more than a ritual reiteration of symbolic roles stipulated in the contract that binds them. It is for this reason that Renoir suggests it represents the triumph of the plebian or slavish spirit.

The aristocratic French spirit that Renoir invokes is linked to the philosophical lineage running from Montaigne to the Enlightenment and offers a very different solution to the same problem. Even as they perform their practical functions as laid out by the existing imbalance of forces, the military hierarchy, each party treats the symbolism of rank with an ironic distance that forges a bond of complicity, trust, and understanding between them. The officer gives orders in a way that indicates his awareness of the extent to which the difference in rank is a product of chance; if the rules of the military game necessarily deprive the subordinate of his faculty of free consent, the behavior of the officer shows that he nonetheless recognizes the existence of this faculty in the subordinate. The subordinate is gratified by this recognition and responds by complying in a way that indicates to the officer that he *chooses* to do so; in this case he freely consents to obey orders that he might otherwise obey only out of necessity or constraint. Though the rules of the military game specify that one commands and the other obeys, the maxim "without affectation or stiffness" indicates that they should perform their functions in a way that shows "they respect the distance which the fact of being two distinct creatures places between them"; even as they act out of necessity, they display a kind of ease that results from a mutual recognition of each other's liberty, a complicity in the understanding that they are both only playing the roles assigned to them. If the behavior of modern military men expresses the fact that they are equally slaves who affirm their common domination by treating the game all too seriously, the behavior of officer and subordinate in this case expresses the fact that they are both equally masters who affirm their

FIGURE 4.8.

Marceau and the Marquis being courteous and complicit.

liberty by treating the military game with a certain playful irony. It is for this reason that Renoir describes the French spirit both as "aristocratic" and as "easy-going" and "relaxed."

This counter-Hegelian model of the master-slave dialectic allows us to appreciate the encounters between the Marquis and Marceau with greater understanding. Like the relationship between Pepel and the Baron, the relationship between these two characters is defined by their immediate attraction to each other and the easy, unaffected courtesy with which they ask for and receive favors. Both of these things are evident in their first meeting on the grounds of the estate. When the Marquis learns from Schumacher that Marceau has been killing rabbits *en flagrant délit*, he exclaims with delight that he is a precious man and orders Schumacher and his subordinates to release him immediately; as soon as Marceau hears this he is emboldened to go on the offensive, call Schumacher a big brute, and try to grab his poached rabbit back. He proclaims the Marquis is an intelligent man who understands him while offering explanations that make his being a poacher understandable (he is really a furniture repairman but the economic crisis has put him out of work, he needs to support his old mother, he just needs to keep busy). The Marquis tells Marceau he likes his face and offers him a job; flabbergasted at this turn of events Schumacher loudly protests, but the Marquis responds to his efforts to malign Marceau by telling him to be quiet, finally ordering him and the other gamekeepers to leave him in peace and continue their rounds. As the three gamekeepers walk off in the background Marceau also starts to walk away, as if reluctant to presume anything further from the man who just rescued him, but immediately responds when the Marquis calls him back to ask, with a bashful and complicit smile, if Marceau would mind showing him one of his snares. Marceau broadly grins and says that since he's now in the Marquis's service he can't refuse; with a very delicate gesture of his arm he indicates the direction of a snare. When they make their way through some bushes and arrive at the snare, Marceau explains that he's made a mistake and put it across a rabbit track that is no longer in use. The Marquis says we all make mistakes, but Marceau insists that if Schumacher saw it he would be embarrassed; the Marquis tells him he can count on his discretion. They then move back into the open field and, in a low-angle medium-close shot that highlights the intimacy and trust between them, have a brief dialogue that contrasts the Marquis's romantic view of Marceau working as his gamekeeper (fresh air, contact with "Nature") with the latter's more pragmatic understanding of what the job would entail (being subordinate to Schumacher) and preference for a job inside the chateau, where he can live out his fantasy of wearing a servant's uniform. The Marquis laughs at this, and they both walk out of the shot as the scene fades out.

In both its initial situation (an aristocrat encounters a thief in the process of stealing from him red-handed) and subsequent development (the aristocrat encourages the thief to steal with his blessing; the aristocrat displays curiosity about the way of life and character of the thief; the thief is gratified by this interest and reveals details of his lifestyle and his feelings in a candid and relaxed manner), the narrative of this sequence reproduces elements that are similar to those in the sequence in *Les bas-fonds* in which the Baron and Pepel first meet. Though the Marquis-Marceau relationship will never be given the time and attention needed for it to develop into a friendship comparable to the one in the earlier film, their first encounter nonetheless projects the possibility of such a friendship. Both characters immediately drop the class-based reflexes that would normally separate them—top-down stiffness and condescension, bottom-up affectation and resentment—and conduct themselves in accordance with the principles and goals of *sociabilité*: the sincere expression of thoughts and feelings; sensitivity and discretion with regard to confidences; the sense of restraint, courtesy, and obligation that implies recognition of the other's liberty; and the smooth progression from practical observations and considerations to a proto-philosophical dialogue about more general principles.

These principles and goals are also on display in their second and final private encounter during the fete. As the disconsolate and confused Marquis walks down a hall in search of Christine, Marceau's arm reaches out from behind a wall to grab and pull him into an alcove filled with tropical plants; the camera tracks into the alcove and frames them in a medium-close shot as the Marquis, amused and curious, turns to follow Marceau's anxious look into the main foyer of the chateau. With instinctive trust and complicity, Marceau tells the Marquis that "you haven't seen me" and explains that Schumacher is after him for fooling around with Lisette; as the Marquis listens and starts to retie his bow tie, Marceau turns his gaze from the foyer toward the Marquis and takes over the task of retying the Marquis's tie, and the conversation takes a more reflective, philosophical turn. Marceau confesses he likes women too much and that they always cause him trouble; the Marquis admits he has the same problem and offers an impromptu plug in favor of the Muslim institution of polygamy, the only logical approach to male-female relations insofar as it allows a man to concentrate on a favorite woman without forcing him to get rid of the others and hurt their feelings. He says he doesn't want to hurt anyone, especially not a woman, and that this is the main cause of the "drama of his life." As Marceau listens to this speech he makes affirming interjections, and when the Marquis finishes, Marceau reminds the Marquis that maintaining a harem takes "means" (that is, money); the Marquis says even with all his money he still hurts everyone—his wife, his mistress,

FIGURE 4.9.

Marceau and the Marquis having a philosophical dialogue.

even himself. He thanks Marceau for tying his tie, and the latter now offers his own wisdom on the topic of women: whether he wants to have a woman, leave her, or hold onto her, he accomplishes his purpose by first making her laugh and disarming her. Marceau suggests the Marquis try this method, but the Marquis ruefully says it requires a certain "talent" (that is, *je ne sais quoi*), something Marceau admits to be obvious.

Throughout this dialogue small camera movements constantly reframe the shot in ways that highlight the frankness and intimacy of their words and actions, tracking back and panning left to follow Marceau's looks out into the foyer, tracking in and panning right to center Marceau's act of tying the tie, panning slightly right or left to focus on the person speaking. Marceau's anxious looks in the direction of the foyer remind us that he is still worried about Schumacher, and the fact that their movements cause the plants in the alcove to move slightly adds to the sense, the subtle sight gag, that they are game hiding in the undergrowth of the chateau. The deft movements of Marceau's hands as he ties the Marquis's tie, the way in which the Marquis yields the job to Marceau without a word from either and holds his head up to make the job easier, and the way in which camera movements echo each movement and shift in the dialogue all accentuate the attentiveness with which they listen to the third person's perspective that their contact has generated. Though each seems distracted or absorbed in a practical task as he listens to the other, their responses to what each other is saying—Marceau's observation about the money he lacks; the Marquis's observation about the talent he lacks—indicate that they have in fact been following the train of the other's thoughts so attentively as to have overtaken them, something that occurs only when the participants in a dialogue are sincerely concerned with the truth about an issue. Though their dialogue does not solve either of their problems, it nonetheless clarifies those problems; each of them is grateful for the rare opportunity to think them through in the company of a friend.

This sense of mutual gratification and gratitude is expressed in the dialogue and action that closes their encounter. Marceau asks if the Marquis would mind doing him a service, and the Marquis says he would gladly do so. Marceau asks the Marquis to make sure that Schumacher is not in the hall so he can sneak out through the kitchen. The Marquis suggests Marceau go out across the terrace, but Marceau says he thinks there's too much light there, and the Marquis agrees to check the hall and walks out to do so; Marceau thanks him. Though the hall seems clear and the Marquis snaps his fingers to indicate this to Marceau, he then catches sight of Schumacher and Lisette coming in the front door and pushes Marceau back behind a wall. With an amused and complicit smile, the Marquis then enacts a diversion on Marceau's behalf; he quickly crosses the hall and summons Schumacher for a dressing down, which allows both Marceau and Lisette to sneak away and escape down the kitchen stairs.

Let us pause to recapitulate some of the story covered so far with respect to the Marquis. The Marquis aspires to personally embody the ideals of Civilization proposed by the ideologues of the French Enlightenment and attempts to run his domain in accordance with those ideals by keeping it open and allowing the game of *sociabilité* to determine whether or not Christine will remain with him or leave with André. Christine's profession of trust challenges him to experiment with the sincerity she represents by keeping the commitment of his marriage vows, something that in principle should be the simplest thing in the world. But though the steps he takes to do so indicate he is sincere in this intention (telling Geneviève he wants to break up with her, consistently trying to avoid her at La Colinière, giving her the farewell embrace that she promises will end their relationship), his actual relations with Christine nonetheless suggest that his love for her is only a fixation on an abstract possibility. His desire for a revolutionary transformation based around his marriage is not grounded in the human contact necessary to give it a real orientation and goal; we are beginning to suspect his project to regenerate his microcosm of Civilization, to wonder whether it is only a kind of fantasy, a game that he plays without really understanding either the stakes or the object.

As we have already examined, the scene in the film in which the Marquis comes to Christine's door after her confession speech underscores her isolation and the lack of connection between them: he congratulates Christine-the-game-player, the real Christine tries in vain to connect, and they say good night and go their separate ways. The conception of this scene in the original script offers an image of what a real connection between the two characters might look like; it offers a utopian image of what the success of the Marquis's project might have looked like that we can use to better understand the failure of that project articulated in the film.[13] In the script, the Marquis knocks on her door "like a conspirator" and says he thinks he has found a disguise for the fete. She opens the door and without a word takes him by the arm and leads him to an open window that presents a view of the chateau's park and the starry night sky. He asks her if she wouldn't like to dress as a dragonfly, a glowworm, or a fairy. She laughs and imagines what the fete would look like as a spectacle of nocturnal enchantment (*une féerie*). They stop talking and contemplate the starry night for a few moments. Christine eventually breaks the silence and says what a beautiful night—the country has never seemed so beautiful to her. The Marquis says that in the end, we know ourselves/each other very little ("en somme, nous nous connaissons très peu"). Christine immediately agrees by repeating "very little." The Marquis says it's true: we conduct an idiotic way of life; we don't do anything, but the work we do is like an assembly-line type of work ("travail à la chaine"). They discuss their future and then embrace as the scene fades out.

The original script imagines Christine and the Marquis coming together as friends through a shared experience of Cytherean enchantment. She silently leads him to the window to contemplate the sky and landscape with her, and this contemplation quickly creates the sense of an intimate and mutual understanding. The fact that his statement about knowing ourselves very little and her affirmation of that statement follows a period of silence indicates that both have been following the thoughts of a third person who can be said to have initiated the dialogue; though we ourselves may not understand what the Marquis's comment is a response to, Christine immediately does. His statement and her agreement acknowledge the fact that that they have not been close and at the same time open onto the prospect of becoming close by embarking on a shared voyage of discovery: by contemplating the infinity of the starry sky (not, like romantics, the moon) they are ready to forget who they have been, what they thought they knew about themselves and each other, in order to become different. The Marquis's blunt characterization of their way of life as an idiotic and unproductive assembly line indicates that he has decisively rejected the circular routines and lies that have hitherto governed his life and is sincerely ready to embark on something new; though the script does not specify what "their future" entails, one can reasonably imagine that it might include the children that Christine so longs for and thus be productive in a way their past way of life was not. This scene in the script gives us a utopian picture of what we might infer the Marquis is aspiring to believe in, what we might imagine he is trying to imagine in order to escape from the ennui of his existence: it gives us a picture of what the other games being played in *La règle du jeu* won't allow him to either imagine or realize.

Second Movement: The Game of Looking-at Others

The scene in which Christine makes a public confession concerning her relationship with André Jurieu represents the beginning of the transition, the invisible dissolve between the first movement of the film and the second; it makes us aware of a second game covertly being played beneath the surface of the official game of *sociabilité* the Marquis thinks he has organized. In contrast to the first game, which most of the guests only pretend to play with little or no conviction, the game of looking-at others is being played in one form or another, and in earnest, by almost all of the characters, guests and servants alike. As in the case of the conversation between the Marquis and Christine discussed above, we can measure the distance between the game the Marquis thinks he has organized and the one that is actually being played by comparing the conception of the confession scene in the original script with the one in the film; the script presents us with what the Marquis *wants* to happen and what he imagines *does happen*, while the scene in the film demonstrates the extent to which this aspiration has already been squelched before Christine even opens her mouth.[14]

In the original script, the scene in which Christine publicly confesses her friendship with André takes place at the end of the first dinner at La Colinière.[15] The General stands up and says that though it is usually his job to make a speech on behalf of the guests expressing their happiness to be once again reunited by the Marquis, their expectations of good hunting, and so on, this year he's going to let André Jurieu begin their celebrations. As André moves to stand up, Christine leans toward him and says she would like to speak in his place. André stands up and says he is so moved that he can't speak; their hostess understands this and has proposed to speak in his place. Christine stands up and says she knows she will greatly annoy André in frankly telling him what she thinks of him. A series of reaction shot close-ups of André, Octave, and the Marquis follows that would, one imagines, have heightened the dramatic impact of this announcement. She then says she thinks he's an exceptional person, he's a hero and he knows it: in his name, she declares the joy of those assembled to have him among them. The guests applaud, and she then continues with the confession speech that occurs in the finished film. After saying she would now like to make a revelation, she claims a small part in the success of his exploit. During the preparations for his flight he often came to see her, and they spent "long, very pleasant hours together..." She pauses, and we are again given close-ups of the guests that heighten the drama of the moment before she finishes the sentence: "... hours spent under the rare sign of friendship." He told her his plans and she listened—it is something rare to be able to listen, and in this case it was not worthless. She is very proud and felt the need to tell them about it this evening. At the end of her speech there is general applause, and the scene ends with another series of close-ups: the General is wildly enthusiastic, André looks completely beaten and paralyzed, Octave genuinely admires her, and the Marquis, who appeared anxious throughout her speech, now seems enchanted.

The scene in the script represents a conception of Christine's confession as a dramatic and completely successful public relations exercise. She deftly intervenes to stop André from speaking and then offers a speech that boldly invokes the suspicion of an illicit affair (long, pleasant hours together) in order to wipe it out with the perfect alibi (a friendship based in her knowing how to listen). She *acts*—and the serious reactions of the other characters to what she says make that action decisive; the scandal inaugurated by André's radio outburst is now over, and the stage is set for Christine and Robert to begin to take their marriage seriously.

Though Christine's actions and speech in the film are more or less the same as in the original script, the mise-en-scène and the reactions of other characters give her act an entirely different meaning and significance. Instead of taking place in the formal context of after-dinner speeches, in the film her confession takes place in the front hall after André and Octave arrive at the chateau and come in out of the rain. Christine comes forward from the kitchen stairs and greets Octave with hugs and kisses and then offers her hand to André, saying it was nice of him to have come. André kisses her hand, saying with abashed sincerity that it is she who is kind while, standing in a doorway behind them, Cava covertly gestures to La Bruyère to come take a look. The Marquis rushes up grinning, shakes André's hand, and, putting an arm around Christine's shoulders and grabbing her hands to create an instant tableau of marital bliss, tells André they are happy and honored to have him with them. André is then besieged by a series of guests who want to shake his hand or kiss him (La Bruyère, his wife, St. Aubin, the General, Cava, Geneviève, Jackie, and Charlotte). Taking her cue from the mass hysteria, Christine says, "And me? I think I have the right [to ask for a kiss]" and boldly comes forward to kiss André on both cheeks. The camera moves to follow Cava and Berthelin walking away and then rapidly tracks into a close-up of the General and St. Aubin as the latter turns and says, "It all stays in the family." The General, startled, asks him, "What's that supposed to mean?!" With an arch smile, St. Aubin says, "Jurieu and Christine"; the General retorts, "What's it to you?! We're here to hunt, not to write our memoirs!" We cut to a close-up of Charlotte and Dick looking on, and the latter asks, "So, did they do it or not?" Charlotte gives Dick a withering look that indicates the answer is obvious and says, "They did"; Dick says, "It's a pity—he's so elegant."

We cut to a close-up of Christine with a nervous-looking André in the background as she looks around, raises her voice to command attention, and launches into her confession speech. As she delivers this, she moves toward André, takes his hand, and looks around at guests with a frank and direct gaze; though the speech is bold and precise in conception, it is delivered with a brittle delicacy that testifies to the difficulty she is having in making it. The Marquis and Octave walk into the center of the background behind and between André and Christine. Octave seems confused and alarmed, his face puckering into a grimace as he tries to understand what Christine is doing, while the Marquis is looking down, concentrating so hard he puts his finger in his mouth like an infant. When she finally arrives at her alibi of friendship, the Marquis smiles, turns to Octave, and tucks his handkerchief into his breast pocket, and they both turn back to the scene with huge grins. Octave seems both ecstatic and baffled by what just happened, his grinning face like a balloon that is always on the verge of deflating into the most abject of frowns, while the Marquis looks around at the guests with a strange, glittering smirk that expresses his delight (and masks whatever confusion he may be feeling). Though most of the audience seem rather noncommittal and uncertain of what to do when she finishes the speech—and both André and Geneviève are clearly pissed off—the General says "Bravo, Christine!" and kisses her hand, while Jackie comes forward to hug her aunt and tell her she's happy. The Marquis moves forward and proposes a party in Jurieu's honor, lurching around among the guests with wild gestures and sputtering out ideas until the form (a masquerade) and time (a week from now, after the hunt) fall into place. He and Christine then drag André off to show him his room.

Since the end of Christine's speech Octave has been desperately trying to connect with a series of characters, first grinning at André as if the speech should have pleased him and then awkwardly grabbing Christine from behind to hug her. As he listens to the party plans taking shape he laughs and stops, laughs and stops, as if pathetically mimicking an enthusiasm he neither feels nor understands. As the group breaks up, the camera

FIGURE 4.10.

Octave devastated by the violation of Christine's innocence.

follows him as he walks over to Geneviève, who is leaning on the railing at the foot of the stairs, pulling out a cigarette, and watching thoughtfully as André, Robert, and Christine go up the stairs. Octave grasps her hands and laughs, then lets her go and looks disconsolate. As she walks away, lighting her cigarette and shaking her head in disbelief, Octave follows her, repeatedly grinning and stopping, and then puts his arm around her waist as if offering himself as a substitute for the Marquis (one of the solutions discussed with Robert in the "geometry problems" scene). We cut to a conversation about André between Madame La Bruyère and Jackie, which ends with a fade-out that concludes the scene.

Though the narrative action of this scene is essentially the same as that envisioned in the original script, the performances and mise-en-scène entirely transform the significance of that action; if the script imagined Christine's confession as a successful public relations exercise, a dramatic

FIGURE 4.11.

Christine as object of a Sadean initiation ritual.

turning point that decisively closes the Pandora's box of scandal opened by André's radio outburst, in the film Renoir's complex deployment of internal and external realism drains Christine's act of its intended effectiveness. To begin with, the dialogue in the two close-ups of Christine's audience (the General and St. Aubin; Dick and Charlotte) suggests that the guests have made up their minds about the affair before her speech even starts. Since they already believe that there was an affair, her performance is received in a very different way than she intends it to be. Rather than accept her story of friendship as an accurate account of what happened, the guests listen to what they believe to be an elaborate lie. Though Christine thinks she is ahead of her audience, boldly acknowledging their suspicions in order to wipe them out, she is in fact behind them on several counts; their minds are already made up about her and André, and they *also* know all about the Marquis's relationship with Geneviève. Knowing what they know, and knowing that she doesn't know what they know, the guests listen to her speech as a group of adults might listen to a child performing a song or dance. Since everyone listening to her speech shares knowledge about her that she doesn't possess, they effectively look-at her with a collective sadism, despite the fact that many of them (Octave, the Marquis, the General) are on her side. This climate of reception turns her speech into a sort of Sadean initiation ritual in which an innocent violates her innocence by presenting her first public lie while nonetheless remaining, in another sense, innocent, ignorant of what everyone else knows. The fact that Christine is not lying but telling the truth makes the sense of violated innocence all the more acute: she is a guileless child who is treated by the adults around her as a guilty child. This sense of genuine innocence exposed to the sadistic gaze and thoughts of others explains the strange behavior of Octave in the scene, for he alone knows and believes in her genuine innocence and can therefore feel the full force of its violation. Though on one level he wants to believe that this speech has solved all the geometry problems, and, taking his cue from the behavior of the Marquis, he attempts to appear ecstatic about it, he can't manage to pull it off; on a deeper level he is devastated by having watched his little girl from Salzburg, his beloved little sister, expose herself in this ritual.

Like Octave's rapid alternation between false enthusiasm and palpable despair, the Marquis's excessive, almost hysterical response to the speech underlines the fact that it has not been successful in anything other than a formal sense, as a well-told lie that the rules of the game of *sociabilité* do not allow one to challenge directly. His spasmodic gestures and sputtering dialogue as he proposes the fete in Jurieu's honor express a desperate eagerness to secure public acceptance of the lie through a ritual celebration of collective complicity, a masquerade. Like that of Octave, his enthusiasm is really an inverted measure of the collective skepticism toward Christine's speech, something that attempts to compensate for the speech's ineffectiveness. If the scene in the script represented the public triumph of Christine's sincerity, in the film the reactions of the other characters transform her speech into a lie she tells unwittingly, a cynical joke at her own expense; if the scene in the script made her sincerity effective and exalted it, setting the stage for a rapprochement between her and the Marquis, the scene in the film makes it the object of collective amusement and rearticulates the gulf between them. While the group indulgently welcomes the entry of Christine-the-neophyte-liar into the game, the real Christine becomes even more separated from the other characters.

From this scene up to the moment at the end of the hunt sequence in which her husband's infidelity is revealed to Christine, the second movement of the film systematically develops the figure of looking-at others. As we saw in chapter 2, we can trace the genealogy of this figure back to the Flaubertian brand of realism as disillusioned romanticism. In what we can call its classic formulation, Flaubert's treatment of Emma in *Madame Bovary*, looking-at others means recognizing the ways in which the historical complex of cultural assumptions an individual uses to interpret the world functions to enclose him or her in a solipsistic bubble. In looking-at other people in this way, one places or reduces them to sets of clichés; one believes that one sees the specific sets of historical circumstances that shape their image of the world, while they are, as Erich Auerbach puts it, too "stupid" to see this context themselves.[16] In a more general formulation, we can say that looking-at others is a figure in which one treats the subjectivity of others as an object; if one knows more about others than they know about themselves, or if one sees them in a different way than they see themselves, one's gaze inevitably has the nonreciprocal, sadistic, objectifying quality we saw at work in the confession scene. The variety and complexity of responses the other characters have to Christine's confession, taken together with the fact that most of them know about her situation as a deceived wife, renders the scene a tour-de-force articulation of looking-at others. If the game of *sociabilité* is a form of productive theatre wherein everyone has the opportunity to develop their own *je ne sais quoi*, recognize it in others, and generate the truths of the third person's perspective, the game of looking-at others is a spectacle of negation that reduces individuals to what others think they know about them. From this point on we start to feel the dangers latent in the gap between what characters think they are saying or doing and the very different ways in which they are viewed by others: we start to sense the potential chaos of unintended consequences. The widening gap between intentions and effects will find its clearest articulation in Christine's misreading of the good-bye kiss between the Marquis and Geneviève, the consequences of which will come to rest only with the final misapprehension of the film in which Marceau and Schumacher kill André.

The figure of Christine's unconscious vulnerability to being looked-at made explicit in the confession scene is developed in the scene that follows in the kitchen, which begins with the Marquis's chauffeur, Bob, inciting a serving girl to criticize Christine's having flouted conventions by placing André on her right at the dinner table. Lisette defends her mistress by saying that Madame doesn't need the serving girl's advice, but the latter persists and says that she still thinks Christine is going a bit far with her aviator. Bob picks up the thread and prompts Corneille into identifying a presumably rare female aristocrat (the Countess de Vaudois) who *did not* take a lover as an example against which to judge Christine. Lisette protests that this is not a good comparison because the woman in question was eighty-five years old and in a wheelchair, but Bob now shifts his aim to his real target and says at least the Comte de Vaudois wasn't a *métèque*. Lisette, clearly upset, asks what that is supposed to mean; Bob refers to the Marquis's German-Jewish ancestry and, as Schumacher appears from above on the stairs, tells Lisette that "I'm sure your husband agrees with me." Schumacher observes that as he's just arrived he doesn't know what Bob is talking about, and the chef intervenes with a story about some pure French aristocrats who ate like pigs and then the potato salad anecdote, which testifies that the Marquis—as much of a *métèque* as he is—is still a "*homme du monde.*"

Despite the diversity of their attitudes, the fact that all the servants discuss their masters in ways those masters would never have imagined makes this scene a further development of the figure of looking-at others established in the preceding scene. Despite their differences, the very fact of their discussion demonstrates that they unite as a class to objectify and look at their masters, who, by taking their servants for granted, are unconsciously exposed and vulnerable. The figure articulated in the confession scene is here extended to lay out a mise-en-abyme structure that Renoir will continue to develop over the course of the film's second movement; the upper-class characters who looked at Christine on the floor above are themselves the unwitting objects of the game of looking-at others being played downstairs. This extension of the figure also subtly reminds us that there is *another* group of characters offscreen we may have forgotten about but who may well be looking-at—interested in, reading newspaper gossip column accounts of—André and Christine at this very moment, the mass media–stimulated general public whom we abandoned at the airport. At this point in the articulation of the figure we have four concentric frames of a mise-en-abyme structure: André and Christine (the individuals at the center), the upper-class spectators of the confession scene (the group looking-at those individuals), the servants downstairs (a group looking-at the illicit couple André and Christine and the group of their masters as a whole), and the general public offscreen (a group looking-at all the characters in the film and in one sense a representation of the film's audience).

There is a specific quality of lethalness and resentment in the way some of the servants look at others, a murderousness-of-the-gaze the recognition of which is crucial to understanding what happens in the next major sequence, the hunt. In terms of their divergent attitudes toward their masters, the servants can be divided into two opposing flanks and a centrist majority. On one flank there are the Loyalists, those who typically step forward to defend the rules of the class hierarchy itself (Corneille) or the individual mistress or master of the upper class whom they serve (Lisette, the chef). The majority in the center are those for whom discussing their masters is an amusement that allows them to relieve the resentment produced by their position without getting too worked up by it. On the opposite flank of this majority from the Loyalists are the Fascists, some of whom display a vicious resentment toward both the individual masters they serve and whole sections of the upper class (Bob, who hates the Marquis, Christine, and all *métèques*) and others who manifest an inchoate resentment against the cosmopolitan complexity of the world upstairs and long for a world of simplicity and order secured by killing anyone who breaks the rules (Schumacher). It is these two Fascists who, in different ways, figure the lethalness of looking-at others and the sharpest, most immediate and political edge of the philosophical danger Renoir and his filmmaking comrades were concerned with.

Bob, whose slicked-back, side-parted haircut clearly alludes to Hitler and who delivers racist comments with an uncanny, glittering knowingness in his eyes and expression, functions to link the world of the servants to the fascist elements of French society. The fact that Bob is the only

FIGURE 4.12.

Schumacher as a frustrated and resentful romantic.

character whose dialogue makes direct topical reference to current tendencies of French politics is significant because it effectively makes him the sole representative of the mob of French society that has remained offscreen since we left it at the airport. The confidence with which he speaks is also manifest in saying he is sure Schumacher agrees with his opinions and is, we infer, derived from knowing, or believing he knows, that the majority of the French population is on his side. He is an amateur ideologue, a man who thinks he sees where his society is headed and who can therefore coolly balance the hatred he feels toward La Chesnaye against the vengeance that will be exacted when the fascist masses come to power. His job as the Marquis's chauffeur offers an apt image of his particular variant of looking-at others; one imagines him driving and looking in the rearview mirror as the Marquis, abstracted, looks out the window and gives him instructions as to where he wants to go next; the Marquis gives him orders and thinks he knows where he is going, but Bob smiles knowingly because he, not the Marquis, knows their ultimate destination.

Schumacher represents a different generation and type of fascist. Rather than a low-grade embodiment of Hitler, he is a low-grade prefiguration of the Pétain of the Occupation. If Hitler and Bob are clear-sighted, forward-looking, fascist revolutionaries, Pétain and Schumacher represent the misty-eyed, backward-looking, conservative tendency within fascism. Like Pétain, Schumacher trades on his status as a World War I veteran and invokes the past as a world of simplicity and order based on zero tolerance, telling the Marquis that during the war he shot men for less than Marceau's crime of poaching. Schumacher's attachment to the ambiguously French-German region of Alsace he comes from is also backward-looking and romantic, a desire for something that is both a kitschy, picture-postcard version of nature (the "great fir trees, snow and storks" listed in Lisette's parodic litany of its attractions) and a culture of order in which (as he tells Lisette) all poachers, crooks, and "Marceaus" are shot in the woods at night. In contrast to the icy cold and clear-sighted version of looking-at others that Bob embodies, Schumacher presents a debilitated version of the figure, for all his loves (order, simplicity, Alsace, Lisette) and hates (disorder, cosmopolitan complexity, Marceau) are represented to be objects of a "blind" romanticism. Though he is the film's most effective embodiment of a lethal hatred—organizing the mass slaughter of the hunt, shooting at Marceau during the fete, shooting and killing André—he is also figured as someone who quite literally can't see the people he shoots at. His character represents the currents of blind but nonetheless lethal romantic resentment that were coursing through the capillaries of French society during the 1930s.

The manifestations of Schumacher's lethal resentment we are presented with prior to the hunt—killing the cat caught in one of his traps, his threatening attitude toward Marceau, and, most important, his mounting frustration with Lisette's coolness toward him—suggest a fuse burning its way to an explosive charge. We have seen this charge being laid early on, in the scene in Christine's Paris bedroom in which the Marquis tells Lisette that Schumacher wants her to join him at La Colinière and she bluntly replies that she would rather divorce than leave Christine's service. Schumacher brings the issue up again when, after the La Chesnayes arrive at their chateau, he is told by the Marquis that Lisette is free to decide where she works and lives, and a moment later we register the difference between the happy ardor of Schumacher's greeting to Lisette and her cool, formulaic response. The next time we see the couple together is in the kitchen. Schumacher walks over to where Lisette is sitting and, bending over her in a way that is possessive and slightly menacing, asks if she will be long. She gives her standard response to any attempt on his part to be with her: she can't say because Madame still needs her. Schumacher, frustrated once again, slowly walks up the stairs, passing Marceau on his way down; a few moments later, Marceau and Lisette will be flirting.

The objects of Schumacher's frustration and resentment identified prior to the hunt—his wife's indifference and paramount loyalty to Christine, and the Marquis, who invites Marceau into his domain and confounds him with contradictory demands (no fences and no rabbits)—function to direct his hatred against the world of the upper-class characters, and, together with the political resentment evoked by Bob, this affect infuses the two frames of the mise-en-abyme structure of looking-at others we need to bear in mind when considering the hunt sequence, the servants looking-at their masters and the mob of mass society looking-at the André-Christine-Robert triangle. Even as each of the upper-class characters imagines that he or she is an invisible spectator, a hunter hidden from view behind his or her blind, the gaze of the camera articulates the characters' exposed vulnerability to the gaze of others who resent them and subtly establishes an analogy between them and the animals they kill.

The events and mise-en-scène of the hunt sequence serve to develop this analogy in a variety of different ways. The early portion of the sequence devoted to the hunt itself takes the mise-en-abyme structure of looking-at others and makes it more explicit, reflexive, and lethal. To appreciate how the figure is developed in this way, we need to consider how the hunt is organized and how the hunted creatures and hunters are represented in the mise-en-scène. Though we know Schumacher is following the Marquis's orders in staging the hunt, in terms of the process itself the hierarchy is inverted, as all the upper-class characters follow Schumacher's orders about where to place themselves and listen to his instructions about what kind and numbers of game they can expect at their assigned spots; from his running of the operation to the presence of his subordinates standing behind each of the upper-class hunters, it is clear that, for the first and last time in the film, Schumacher is in total control of a situation. Though the Marquis may executive produce the ritualized mass murder, Schumacher is the producer-director, the real auteur: the upper-class characters are *his* instruments and carry out *his* intentions. As in Hegel's well-known myth of the master and the slave, this is a moment in the film in which the slave Schumacher expresses his superiority to his master, the Marquis, for here the master understands only part of the situation, has a limited view of the whole, whereas the slave has a synoptic view; the master "attains only a transitory enjoyment" while the slave "attains, through his labor, contemplation of independent being, as well as of himself."[17] Just as Hegel's dialectic posits the slaves to be superior to the masters because they *make* the masters and their world through their labor, Schumacher's staging of the hunt gives the figure of the servants' looking-at their masters a concrete, material embodiment of superiority. By putting themselves in Schumacher's hands, the upper-class characters are in a sense making themselves as vulnerable as the creatures they hunt. The technological method of the hunt in which the animals and birds are flushed from the woods into the jaws of a real danger (the open field and the guns of the hunters) by their apprehension of a false danger (the sound of the beaters' sticks) thus figures as an analogy for the situation of the upper-class characters: they face in one direction and shoot at the defenseless birds and animals while remaining unaware that they themselves are "within the sights" of various others beside or behind them (other upper-class characters, their servants, the mob of mass society).

Schumacher and the beaters start their sweep through the woods, and we get a series of close shots of the frightened animals and birds: rabbits crouch down, trying to hide themselves amid the undergrowth; a pheasant calls out a warning; the line of beaters advances and the creatures start running and flying for their lives. The images of the frightened animals and birds offer a powerful figuration of their vulnerability and, strange as it may seem, their uniqueness or individuality. The absolute conviction with which we register their frightened behavior suddenly makes us aware of the living consciousness inside each one of them. Later, at the conclusion of the hunt, the unforgettable shot of one rabbit's spasmodic gestures as it dies underscores the powerful feeling of pathos this awareness produces; even before the analogy with André's death is established, we feel the personal tragedy of this indelibly real event.

This documentary revelation of the hunted creatures' genuine anxiety, what we take to be their consciousness of their own mortality, which we grasp at the same moment as the equally shocking revelation that the game of the hunt is completely rigged in favor of the hunters, shapes the way we view the series of shots that follow in which the upper-class characters stand waiting in their blinds. When viewed in the context of these intertwined revelations, the main effect of this series of shots is to dramatically reduce the individuality of the characters; their rote participation in the ritual reduces them en masse to the lowest common denominator of a competitive bloodlust. The Marquis, La Bruyère, the General, Geneviève, and St. Aubin are all framed from exactly the same distance and behaving in ways that display a similar readiness and anticipation, taking the gun from the keeper behind them, loading, aiming, or scanning the sky; precisely because we have had a chance to appreciate how different they all are, their similarity in this context is surprising, especially in light of what motivates them to become similar, the prospect of killing birds and animals. When the creatures are flushed from the woods and the slaughter begins, we are given a more rapid series of shots of the same hunters shooting that once again emphasizes their similarity. Each shot is centered on the act of a single rifle gunshot and lasts about the same length of time, and the hunters' hard, intent, vehement expressions as they shoot are almost identical. The similar ways in which the recoil of the rifles acts on their bodies function to equate them with each other and, in the process, reduce them; the behavior of Geneviève, the only woman in the group, is striking not because she behaves differently but because she kills with exactly the same grim determination and vehemence as the others.

To the extent that it upsets our expectations of what a hunt is supposed to be, the technological form of this hunt constitutes a brutal sort of gag, with a lineage going back to the earliest and most violent slapstick and attractions. We know that the activity of hunting has transcended its original utilitarian purposes, but we still expect it to be a display of *sociabilité*, a fair game that gives the hunted animals and hunters a chance to

FIGURE 4.13.

The individuality of the characters negated during the hunt.

demonstrate their individual qualities; in such a fair-game hunt, the hunters would, for example, celebrate the cleverness of the fox or rabbit who got away just as much as they would a particularly good shot from one of them. In the hunt we are presented with we find that the hunted creatures are not given the slightest chance and that instead of the display of *je ne sais quoi* and sportsmanship, the object of the game is simply to kill the greatest number of creatures and thereby demonstrate one's superiority over the other hunters.

The gag aspect of the hunt, the difference between the hunt we expect and the hunt we get, is given a deft, ironic notation in the two brief exchanges between St. Aubin and La Bruyère that frame it. In the first exchange at the start of the sequence we find La Bruyère apologizing to St. Aubin for shooting a pheasant that was rightfully the latter's to shoot; St. Aubin demurs, saying not at all, it was unquestionably La Bruyère's to shoot, and so they continue back and forth, each graciously deferring to the other. After the hunt, they immediately begin arguing over which of them has the right to a dead pheasant; St. Aubin calls La Bruyère a poacher and complains to the other hunters about the injustice being done to him. We now understand that the hunt is a ritual in which each of the masters attempts to demonstrate his or her mastery over the others, one way or another; though they aim at the rabbits and pheasants, they are really looking-at each other: the dead creatures are only the collateral damage of a competition in which the upper-class characters as individuals attempt to negate each other and hence as a group effectively negate themselves. This sense of a collective self-negation is what makes them analogous to the master in Hegel's myth, the figure who by simply reiterating his self-identical unproductive mastery does not develop but instead progressively reduces himself to nothing: it is what makes their slaughtering of the creatures analogous to slaughtering themselves.

After the hunt itself, the lethalness of the figure of looking-at others—the analogy between the gaze of the characters and the destructive power of the guns—is made explicit in the scene in which St. Aubin, Christine, and Berthelin examine a squirrel through Berthelin's field glasses. St. Aubin's offscreen comment that he wishes he had his gun as we watch the squirrel climb up the tree to get away from the people deftly establishes the camera-as-gun equation, an equation that is then developed in Berthelin's offscreen assertion that the field glasses allow one to examine the intimate details of the squirrel's private life without frightening it, an assertion that is ironic insofar as the squirrel we see is clearly frightened out of its wits. The "intimate details of a private life" comment sets up the final figure of looking-at in the sequence in which Christine sees, through the field glasses, her husband and Geneviève embracing. Though we have already considered the pivotal importance of this shot in the film's narrative structure, it is worth noting more specifically how it functions to articulate a cross-fade or invisible dissolve between the last vestiges of the first movement of the film and the third movement to follow.

As already suggested, in the scenes that take place in the aftermath of the hunt it seems as if the Marquis's noble gamble in inviting André to the chateau is about to pay off. From André's comments in discussions with Octave and Jackie, we gather that the week of watching the Marquis and

Christine together has taken its toll and that he is ready to give up the fight. The week has had a similar effect on Geneviève; as she tells the Marquis, she recognizes that she bores him, and she herself is bored watching him and Christine play at being a happily married couple. She offers to leave in exchange for one last embrace that will secure their pre-Christine past together in her memory. The Marquis assents to this request and in embracing her believes he is enacting a gallant transition from his old mode of existence to a new one built around his marriage to Christine. In this sense, the embrace represents the triumph of the aspiration that governed the first movement of the film, the Marquis's faith that if he opened his domain and allowed for the free play of *sociabilité* he could hold onto Christine and with her build a new civilization based in the virtue of sincerity. But when Christine views this embrace through the field glasses, it constitutes something else entirely. The knowledge she gains is false insofar as she interprets the embrace to reveal the current state of the relationship and, at the same time and in another sense, true in revealing a longstanding affair between them. Given the courage and intelligence we have seen in her, we might well imagine Christine swiftly reviewing the events of the past three years and isolating the patterns in her husband's routine that articulate his conduct of the affair while identifying in her memories of the faces of all the people around her (her childhood friend Octave, her husband and Geneviève, her upper-class acquaintances, Lisette and other servants) the specific qualities of their gazes that indicate *they also knew all along*. Rather than the intimate details of the embrace itself, she sees a multiplicity of reverse-angle shots of herself in which her own intimate details were exposed to being looked at for three years. This reversal, in which one shot/example of looking-at others gives way to a multiplicity of other shots/examples of looking-at others, enacts an invisible dissolve between the first movement's attempt at a project of Cytherean enchantment, of being worthy of Christine, and the third movement's exploration of blind passion and instinct. Though Christine's innocence and sincerity had been the ideals around which the first movement's ambiguously modern-romantic-civilized project had been organized, the reverse-angle views of herself she is now given effectively disenchant those ideals for her and make her hate herself for having embodied them. She now wants to abandon the pedestal on which she has been exposed to the pitying or mocking gaze of others and wants to join those others by whatever means necessary. Unbeknownst to any of them, she is now looking-at them all and preparing to play a game of her own.

Third Movement: Christine's Game; or, the Impossibility of Manufactured Desire

Christine inaugurates her game in the scene in which she comes to Geneviève's room for a confidential chat. Christine enters the room, shuts the door, and leans against it as Geneviève continues to pack; she asks if Geneviève is going and, when Geneviève replies yes, tries to persuade her to stay for the fete. Geneviève says, "It's better if I leave," and Christine boldly asks, "Better? Better for whom? You?" Geneviève courteously says no, and Christine then asks, "Well then, better for me?" to which Geneviève, surprised, can only give a dismissive gesture of her hand. Geneviève turns away from Christine and, in a striking two-shot in which both of them face the camera with the latter looking at the back of the former's head, Christine says she wants to speak frankly and asks if she is a "troublesome wife." Geneviève demurs and says she doesn't see how Christine could ever cause her trouble. Despite Geneviève's resistance, Christine continues to pursue the matter until Geneviève is tricked into admitting the relationship. After suggesting she knew about the relationship all along, Christine makes a series of well-chosen observations about the Marquis (his inability to tell a lie, his habit of smoking in bed) that allows her to confirm important facts about his relationship with Geneviève while at the same time developing a sense of complicity with Geneviève that will be useful to her. Christine asks Geneviève to stay and appeals to female comradeship in saying that if the Marquis is busy with Geneviève, that will allow Christine to pursue her own purposes. Geneviève asks, "André Jurieu?" but Christine dismisses him as nice and courageous but too sincere and therefore boring. They drop the topic of men, turn to discussing their costumes for the evening, and then leave the room to find one for Geneviève.

In this scene Christine uses her newly discovered power of looking-at others to achieve her purposes with great precision. She quickly confirms the basic facts of her husband's relationship with Geneviève and goes on to extract information that gives her a better sense of its emotional depth and level of carnality while at the same time presenting Geneviève with a picture of herself as female comrade-in-arms who would be grateful for her assistance in keeping the Marquis occupied. She uses her newfound knowledge of the affair—and the knowledge that nobody but Geneviève knows she knows—to deftly remove herself from the central place in the symbolic economy around which the first movement of the film revolved and sets in motion the chain of events whereby the men who have invested in that economy (Octave, André, the Marquis, St. Aubin) will all try to recoup their investments.

As the curtain closes on a performance at the fete, an intoxicated Geneviève rudely brushes past Christine to give the Marquis a hug; Christine, furious at this, claps her hands as if to say "enough is enough: I'm jumping in" and, grabbing St. Aubin, leads him away. The Marquis, looking this way and that for Christine, is dragged offstage by Geneviève; André, who seems to have found renewed hope in Christine, refuses to help Octave out of his bear suit and rushes off to look for her. Though it would be almost impossible to present a comprehensive description of the multitude of events that follow, fragmented as they are by the constant cross-cutting between locations and by the fact that characters and events are themselves in constant motion between locations, one can nonetheless attempt to characterize what is going on by focusing on certain scenes and isolating certain significant figures in them.

As the "danse macabre" spectacle of skeletons and ghosts begins, it is suddenly clear that the upper-class characters in pursuit of love-objects have lost whatever veneer of *sociabilité* they once displayed; the hunt sequence has demonstrated that those civilized qualities were only a camouflage they projected to cover their blind and potentially lethal instincts, the instincts that we now see governing their behavior. André, St. Aubin, and the Marquis all display their lack of *sociabilité* by refusing to help Octave take off his bear suit, while at the same time they all display a single-minded fixation on finding and getting Christine. The behavior of André and the Marquis when they find Christine with their rivals is telling in this regard. When André discovers Christine in the arms of St. Aubin, the first person he addresses is St. Aubin and his first concern is to put his rival in his place. Despite the efforts of Christine and Jackie to stop them, he and St. Aubin trade insults and threats and begin a fistfight, which ends in St. Aubin being incapacitated. We are subtly reminded of the hunt, where the ostensible object of the game (hunting creatures) was only a means to achieve the real object (expressing one's dominance over other people understood to be rivals). This subtle indication of a certain falseness or self-deception underlying André's love for Christine is immediately reinforced by the fact that, after she says she loves him, he refuses to comply with her request to leave at once and instead asserts that he has to follow the rules by speaking to the Marquis first. Though he himself is blind to the fact, his romantically conceived desire for Christine is starting to look like just another means to get the public recognition that he craves.

Though it ends quite differently, the scene in which the Marquis discovers Christine in the arms of André begins by displaying significant similarities to the one between André and St. Aubin. The Marquis advances into the room toward them with his morose gaze fixed on André and says to him, with only a brief nod of his head in Christine's direction: "Well now, Monsieur Jurieu—it seems you have got what you wanted—you are stealing my wife from me." André tries to slow the Marquis down, asking for five minutes in which to speak to him, but the Marquis's face twists with rage, and he punches André in the face. André falls down, gets up, and punches the Marquis back, causing him to fall. The Marquis gets up, and André grabs him by the throat and challenges him to try another punch as Octave and Geneviève enter the room. Octave drops Geneviève on a couch, grabs Christine, and exits through another door as the Marquis complies with André's request for another punch and sends him tumbling back over the couch. After a moment's hiatus during which we follow Octave and Christine, Marceau, Schumacher and Lisette, we return to the room to find André pushing the Marquis up against a wall, gripping his throat and threatening to break his neck. Their fight is finally stopped by a shot from Schumacher's gun, which shatters a lamp behind them and causes André to notice and observe that Christine has disappeared. The Marquis, exhausted, throws up his arms and hysterically sputters, "Christine has disappeared, that's how it is this evening, Christine has disappeared!" Getting up from the couch, Geneviève launches into a harsh tirade mocking them both for not having seen her leave with Octave, sarcastically telling André he'll find her again some day and, turning to the

Marquis, repeatedly demanding to know in a shrieking voice when they are leaving together. The Marquis flails his arms, hoarsely yelling that it's not the correct moment to discuss this, he's got other things on his mind, and knocks her glass to the ground where it breaks, causing Geneviève to start screaming like a maniac.

In assessing the function and significance of this scene and the earlier one in which André and St. Aubin fight, one has to begin by recognizing their strangeness, the fact that we cannot immediately identify any causes in the preceding film that would explain the violent and irrational behavior of the combatants; precisely because we know that Christine is the formal cause or goal of their combats, the violence and desperation with which those combats are conducted seem excessive, motivated by something other than Christine herself. On one level, these scenes of slapstick violence simply function as crude and predictable gags in which the civilized, sociable personae the characters have projected are now defamiliarized by their real, authentic, instinct-driven selves that alcohol and the excitement of the fete have unveiled and unleashed. But in this case the gags raise (rather than answer) the question as to what those real selves really want; we knew the Marquis and André wanted Christine before, we see them fighting to get her now, but their violent and comical fights to get her seem to take on a life of their own and throw our understanding of their motivation into question. Are the Marquis and André desperate because they really love Christine so much? No. They are desperate because suddenly, deep down, they are unable to locate anything that distinguishes their romantic desire for her from that of their rivals; like the fascist and communist arguing in Simone Weil's anecdote, or like the Greeks and Trojans fighting over Helen, they can no longer remember why they are fighting, what exactly they are fighting for. Having lost the imaginary thread of desire that once grounded their identity, they can maintain that identity only by demonstrating their hatred of their rivals.

Christine's successive attempts to understand and play the game she thinks the others are playing trace a different but complementary exploration of the impossibility of manufacturing desire; just as her husband and André are arriving at the nihilistic end of romantic desire in hate and resentment, she is embarking on the impossible project of generating desire ex nihilo. She begins with the assumption that the game has nothing to do with "romance" and therefore picks the cynical St. Aubin as the logical partner with whom to take her revenge on the Marquis. But even before her attempt to do this is interrupted by André, we can see that it is stalled and infer that she just can't make herself desire St. Aubin in a matter-of-fact carnal way. The fight between André and St. Aubin then deprives her of this first option and presents her with the opportunity to try "too sincere" André. But at the very moment when she attempts to exercise this option, she is startled to discover that his old-fashioned version of romanticism does not offer what it seemed to promise. When she later explains to Octave what she thought would follow her profession of love (an embrace, a kiss, and the two of them immediately leaving together), Octave condescendingly ("poor little Christine") explains to her that his status as a "hero" has to come first. Having renounced her own game of sincerity and having tried and failed to play the games of recreational adultery and romanticism, Christine (and the spectator) is now left bewildered as to what game there is left to play.

Fourth Movement: The End of Romanticism; or, the Rule of Self-Negation

The final movement of the film explores what happens once the Marquis's project of Civilization has completely collapsed. It follows three pairs of people—the Marquis and André, Marceau and Schumacher, Christine and Octave—couples who, in different ways, articulate the ultimate end of romanticism as a reductive negation of the self, a process in which the individual qualities of the characters disappear, contract back into various ideologically determined clichés, and, in effect, die. To understand what happens in this final movement, we will examine the figures that articulate this process in each of these three pairs of characters.

With Christine having disappeared and with a hysterical, shrieking Geneviève breaking everything she can lay her hands on, the exhausted Marquis and André are forced to pause their fight. The Marquis asks for André's assistance in dealing with Geneviève, and they carry her out of the room past Corneille, whom the Marquis orders to stop the Marceau-Lisette-Schumacher "comedy." The Marquis and André work efficiently together to drug Geneviève with sleeping pills and lock her in her room and then collaborate to address the public relations issues at hand, the disappearances of Christine and Geneviève, with expedient lies; André tells the General that Christine has a migraine, while the Marquis tells Charlotte that Geneviève was tired and went to bed. They come downstairs, where the two servant antagonists, Marceau and Schumacher, are awaiting the Marquis's judgment. He deals with them and, turning to André, says, "What an evening! Where were we?" André reminds him of his request for a five-minute talk, the Marquis readily grants his request, and they begin to trade apologies for their behavior during the fight; the Marquis says he behaved like a real peasant, but André protests that he was just as bad. The Marquis says their little exhibition reminds him of certain newspaper reports he has read in which working-class people behaved this way but professes that until now he didn't really believe such things were possible. His comments treat their fight as an accident that happened to them as opposed to something they themselves did, as a brief and anomalous intrusion of working-class phenomena into their domain; he disavows their own responsibility for the fight and displaces it onto peasants and workers. Though André agrees with all this, he steers the conversation back to his goal and says, "But I have an excuse: I love Christine!!" The Marquis responds: "And I don't love her?!—I love her so much—so much—that I want her to leave with you—since her happiness, it seems, resides in this departure." Whether because, like Christine, he misunderstood what he saw when he found his spouse in the arms of another or because he no longer cares, the Marquis gives Christine up to his rival. But even as he does so he feels compelled to tell André that he congratulates himself for the fact that Christine picked someone from their class.

This scene presents us with a breathtaking and chilling figuration of the distance the Marquis has fallen from his own civilized ideals. From being the very embodiment of openness and *je ne sais quoi*, he has now become a man whose every comment reiterates the basest kind of class identification. The bond that now links the Marquis and André is not based on the recognition of each other's individual qualities but is rooted in their complicity in dealing with Geneviève and a class-based concern with appearances. All they really have in common is their class, but this is also all they have left after their otherwise very different projects—the

FIGURE 4.14.

André and the Marquis bond over their upper-class superiority.

Marquis's feeble attempt at Civilization and André's vainglorious attempt to rescue his lady—appear to have collapsed. Though it might seem that André is coming out the winner and has retained the integrity of his own project—childishly repeating "I love Christine!!" with the same vehement intonation we have grown accustomed to—we now appreciate the depth of his narcissistic self-deception and know that Christine is nothing but an empty trophy to him. Having been reduced to the lowest common denominator of their upper-class ideology, both men have effectively become dead, mechanical automatons.

Like the excessive slapstick violence of the fights and André-the-romantic-rebel's surprising comment to Christine about following the rules, the Marquis's sudden concern with class seems at first a rather too-abrupt transformation; the fact that his stiff new class values are so precisely the opposite of the civilized values of inclusion and *je ne sais quoi* we

FIGURE 4.15.

Marceau uses his friend the Marquis as a weapon against his enemy Schumacher.

have seen him display earlier in the film makes his transformation seem almost uncanny in its implausibility, like a gag that overstates its point. But on second thought, as the transformation slowly sinks in, we start to recognize the figure of displaced resentment behind it: the only thing that the Marquis can do with the resentment he feels toward André and himself is to project it onto the people of other classes, whom he now looks at with a feeling of disgust, thankful that he and André—recent demonstrations to the contrary aside—are not *them*. In one sense, and though the act was leavened with a vestige of his characteristic generosity and tact, the Marquis has already taken his revenge on the class he is looking-at by brusquely firing both Marceau and Schumacher. The gag finds its depth in a figure that articulates the dialectical connection between self-loathing and class-consciousness: the end of romanticism as a personal project in hatred of oneself and specific others carries forward into the end of romanticism as a political project whereby the hatred of oneself and one's own group is repressed and displaced onto the members of another group.

The strange rapprochement between Marceau and Schumacher after they are both thrown out of the chateau articulates a similar process in which a self-negating accord between two men of the same class results in a redirecting of resentment toward another social group. So clearly unreciprocated from the outset, Schumacher's love for Lisette is represented to be another example of blind romanticism and makes his role among the group of servants equivalent to the role André plays among the upper-class characters; though on the surface their actions may appear to be opposed rather than complementary (that is, Schumacher is *defending* his marriage to Lisette while André is *challenging* the Marquis's marriage to Christine), they both display a comparable self-righteous hatred of situations they believe to be unjust or impure. Their similarity as types is articulated by their behavior as they search for their love-objects during the fete, rigidly turning their heads and bodies this way and that, their faces glowering with grim resolution. But from the fete on, Schumacher's brand of romanticism is progressively distinguished from André's as being both blinder and potentially more lethal. After discovering Marceau hiding in the kitchen, Schumacher pulls out his gun and the chase begins, with Marceau playing the role of hunted rabbit, scurrying this way and that, clinging to and hiding behind the Marquis and then brutally pushing him at Schumacher (thus brilliantly condensing the entire narrative of the Marceau-Marquis relationship), then pretending to be a waiter, and, as the culmination of this very Chaplinesque series of gags, hiding behind Charlotte de la Plante and hugging her three times in gratitude when the danger has passed. In his role as the hunter, Schumacher is shown to be handicapped by a combination of timing or cognition issues, bad eyesight, and interference from others. Constantly sweeping the field of his vision, he seems to register everything with a two-second delay; his balance and aim thrown off by those who attempt to restrain him, he nonetheless squints and shoots at random. He will obviously need someone to help him if he is ever going to make his resentment more effective.

After they have both been thrown out of the chateau, Marceau discovers Schumacher leaning against a tree, disconsolate and weeping. Suddenly and very strangely, the shared love for Lisette that made them mortal antagonists starts to bring them together. Marceau deftly redirects Schumacher's resentment away from himself and in the direction of the upper-class characters inside the chateau, saying, "I was told [Lisette] was with Madame—with *Madame!*—It's not you she's married to, no—It's *Madame!*" The sarcastic way Marceau pronounces this title is calculated to redirect Schumacher's resentment beyond Christine herself—not just this Madame but all *Madames*, the entire class of Monsieurs and Madames—and remind Schumacher of what they now have in common, a shared resentment against the masters who kicked them out of the chateau. Schumacher asks Marceau what his plans are, and the latter replies that he'll return to poaching, though it shouldn't bother Schumacher now that they've thrown *him* out. He then tries to build on their fresh-minted complicity by suggesting that Schumacher must have poached a few pheasants and rabbits himself. They catch sight of Octave and Christine walking away from the chateau, but because Christine is wearing Lisette's cloak they mistake her for Lisette. Marceau calls Octave a *salaud*, and he and Schumacher follow the couple to the greenhouse. Crouching in the bushes outside the greenhouse they can't see the couple very well, but Marceau suddenly and surprisingly tells Schumacher to let Octave have it with his revolver. Schumacher says he can't as he already fired all his bullets at Marceau. Their bodies glommed together in an embrace so that they look like a two-headed monster, they see Octave and "Lisette" kiss, and Schumacher, now enraged with jealousy, says he's going to fetch his rifle to kill them both. Though Marceau thinks he should stay and keep watch, Schumacher insists Marceau come with him, saying that from this point on they are going to stay together. By the time they return to the greenhouse, Christine is alone, waiting for Octave to return with their coats. Schumacher is about to go speak to her when Marceau hears André running toward the greenhouse and pulls Schumacher back: André runs into view and Schumacher shoots him.

This sequence closely mirrors that of the other pair of reconciled rivals, the Marquis and André. Marceau and Schumacher forge an alliance based on class-based resentment, and, as in the case of the other pair, the character who takes the lead in forging the alliance is the member of the pair who had in the first movement embodied the values of Civilization;

FIGURE 4.16.

Marceau and Schumacher forge an alliance based on resentment of the upper class.

in each sequence the two blind romantics André and Schumacher remain more-or-less true to their types, while the characters who embodied *je ne sais quoi* and seemed to have the potential for a true friendship undergo a breathtaking, chilling disintegration. Though Marceau still retains a vestige of the sentimental weakness for women that links him to the Marquis (feebly objecting when Schumacher asserts he wants to kill Lisette as well as Octave), he, like the Marquis, has lost the mental and physical animation that defined him as a character; like the Marquis, who is reduced to the class identification that unites him with André, Marceau is now reduced to the murderous, class-based resentment he shares with Schumacher.

Schumacher's reinstatement in his position at the chateau, an unintended consequence of his murder of André, constitutes Renoir's final—

FIGURE 4.17.

Schumacher's reinstatement establishes a new order in the chateau.

and incredibly prescient—observation on the political effects of romanticism on France during the 1930s. Though their master, the Marquis, imagined he could simply throw any of them out and be done with them, he was unaware of the resentment among his servants that we have seen building from the second movement of the film on. If the intended act of killing Octave is for Schumacher mainly motivated by personal jealousy, the motivation of his Iago-like accomplice, Marceau, is closer to the more general hatred of an entire class of people embodied in the racist chauffeur, Bob. It is significant that Marceau, not Schumacher, first suggests shooting Octave, and Marceau's motives are perhaps analogous to Bob's insofar as the specific targets of their hate can be viewed as parasites or pretenders to the class and therefore worthy of a double measure of hate. Marceau is thus responsible for giving Schumacher's blind, unfocused resentment a political focus. By reinstating Schumacher in the chateau, the Marquis is making an appeasing gesture analogous to those made by the French ruling class toward the forces of fascism both inside and outside the country; while on one level the reinstatement is only a required corollary of the Marquis's explanation of the murder as an accident, on another level it represents the logical end of the master-slave dialectic that has been at work since the hunt. Stanley Cavell's reading of the film's penultimate tableau, in which Schumacher stands on the stairs above and in front of the guests assembled outside, picks out the salient details of the tableau with great precision: "Schumacher's posture is slightly hunched, turned largely from us but aware of the audience, as over his shoulder, and inflected towards the Marquis. His torsion might present a posture of contrition, but his gamekeeper's shotgun is again in place, strapped across his back, as we have always seen it before the masquerade party. Here the gun happens to be pointing exactly at the Marquis's head."[18] This figure is brilliantly overdetermined. Though Schumacher is perhaps hunched in contrition for killing André, he is also looking-at the upper-class characters—and the film's audience—over his shoulder, the threat in this gaze articulated by his elevated position and the gun on his back. Though on one level his gun "just happens" to be pointing at the Marquis's head, on another it articulates the fact that the Marquis *was forced* to reinstate him in the chateau by Schumacher's use of this very gun; the new order established in the chateau will, we feel, be very much in keeping with the gamekeeper's rule of zero tolerance. The end of *La règle du jeu* gives us an indelible and chilling prefiguration of Vichy.

The sequence of scenes that follow Octave and Christine offers an articulation of the process of self-negation that is more reflexive and reflective than the figures articulated by the two other pairs of characters. In this case the process needs to be broken down into three distinct stages.

In the first stage Octave and Christine escape from the mayhem of the fete by remembering a beautiful moment from their youth, a musical performance conducted by Christine's father, Stiller. Octave reenacts the role of Stiller on a terrace of the chateau, walking out onto the imagined stage and raising his baton to begin. Then he suddenly becomes disconsolate, walks offstage, and sits down on a step; Christine comes over to see what's wrong, but he shakes her off, telling her to leave him alone, and we cut

FIGURE 4.18.

Octave's litany of self-recrimination.

away to other subplots. Several scenes later, we return to Octave spitting in the moat of the chateau, saying it's the only thing he's capable of doing in life, and launching into a monologue to Christine about what a failure and a parasite he is. His performance as Stiller on the terrace reminded him of his youthful ambition to be an artist and to have the same "overwhelming" feeling of contact with an audience that Stiller had. With bitter irony he outlines his attempts to figure out what went wrong and how alcohol offers only an all-too-brief aid to self-deception. He concludes by saying you simply have to live through a bad moment and get used to it.

When compared to that of the Marquis, André, Marceau, or Schumacher, Octave's dejection represents a very different and superior response to the failure of romantic dreams; unlike those others, he is ultimately too honest to direct his resentment at anyone but himself. In addition to measuring his failed career against that of Stiller and his own youthful hopes, his dejection derives from the failure of the game he inaugurated in the Marquis's study, the one he hoped would bring happiness to André and Christine. In contrast to the deft self-deception of the four reconciled rivals, he recognizes that he has in fact "been wrong," though he can't figure out exactly when and why he "went wrong." He is a man who has tried to be a friend to others but who has never had the reciprocated friendships he needed to think things through properly. He has never had such friendships because his aggravated feelings of self-doubt and worthlessness have, probably from an early age, always prevented him from listening to the third person's perspective with real hope and attention. The horrifying abyss of doubt that opened before him in the geometry problems scene exemplifies what happens whenever he tries to think things through, as his thoughts founder on a lack of courage and faith.

The first stage of Octave and Christine's process of self-negation carefully outlines Octave's core problem, that despite his best intentions he lacks the hope, courage, and faith necessary to achieve a true friendship. The second stage of the process is one in which he temporarily gains that hope, courage, and faith. In the greenhouse Octave is telling Christine that she judges other men too harshly against the standard of her father, and she replies, "Not at all, take you for example, you're a good sort." Octave demurs and repeats that he is a failure. Christine says no, he's not a failure, he just needs someone to look after him: she's going to look after him. Looking away, grim, he says that it's too late; "I'm too old." Christine says, "Idiot... you know, it's you I love." Her expression as she says this is radiant and wondrous, completely sincere. She has bravely overcome any moral anxiety she may have had about converting their sibling-like relationship into something else, and the moment is comparable to the end of the geometry problems scene insofar as it reveals that Christine, like the Marquis, has all along been listening to a third person's perspective that Octave himself is oblivious to. He turns back toward her as she asks, "And you—do you love me?" Still grim, he nods and says, "Yes, Christine, I love you." Christine tells him to kiss her, and he kisses her on the cheek. She says, "No, on the lips, like a lover," and he kisses her on the lips. We leave them to focus on Marceau and Schumacher's reactions to this kiss, and when we return Octave is kissing her again and then kissing her hand and running out the door of the greenhouse saying that there is a train at three o'clock in the morning that they're going to try to catch. He runs off jauntily down the path.

The second stage in Octave and Christine's process of self-negation articulates the possibility of their embarking on a true friendship. Though we are also aware of the other possibility—that they are deceiving themselves and embarking on a doomed attempt to convert their romantic attachment to the past into a viable future together—the interplay of intelligence, frankness, and affection we have seen between them in all their scenes together suggests that they would already have considered this possibility and found the courage to stare it down. Despite their frank and affectionate acknowledgment of their differences, their relationship has up till now always had a unidirectional, pedagogical orientation that prevented it from developing into a true friendship; from their chat in Christine's bedroom on, their conversations take the form of Octave pointing out her naïveté and Christine coming to appreciate Octave's worldly wisdom: though she knew how to listen to him, he never really listened to her. Now, staring at her radiant face after she says she loves him, he suddenly realizes that she is no longer the same little girl from Salzburg, and this realization of his blindness in treating her as the same breaks the pattern: he is finally listening to a third person who tells him that he and Christine could both be quite different, and quite possibly happy together regardless of the circumstances (for example, his lack of means, the difference in their ages). Though Octave has been locked in a spell of repetitive self-loathing for as long as he can remember, Christine's profession of love has somehow broken that spell and given Octave the courage to see himself differently; his jaunty schoolboy enthusiasm as he runs off to get their coats testifies to the hope and confidence that now infuse him.

The third and final moment in Octave and Christine's process of self-negation begins when Octave reaches the chateau and meets Lisette. Lisette asks him where Madame is and Octave orders her to go and get Christine's coat for him; Lisette, wary, says, "Huh?" When Octave repeats the request, she immediately grasps the situation and sullenly complies. Octave finds his coat and goes over to a mirror at the corner of which Lisette is now standing, holding Christine's coat. Octave puts on his coat, fiddling with the buttons and pulling at it to make it fit properly. They are now framed in a tight medium shot with Lisette facing the camera and

Octave with his back to us, the mirror giving us occasional glimpses of his face. Lisette tells him he's wrong, he asks "Why's that?," and Lisette lays down her version of the "rules": when it's just for "fun" (flirting, sex) it doesn't matter what you do, but when people live together the old should stick to the old and the young should stick with the young. As she finishes this lesson in moral pragmatism, Octave takes a brief look at his "old" face in the mirror, but her words don't stop him. He asks her if she's found his hat and goes offscreen to find it himself. Lisette goes on to raise the issue of money. Octave doesn't have any, and a woman like Madame needs a lot of things: how will they manage without money? Having found his hat, Octave returns to the mirror to put it on. Lisette has now moved in front of the mirror so that she faces the camera while the back of her head and shoulders are visible in the mirror. Our view of Octave is similarly doubled; we have a view of his profile and a straight-on view of his face in the mirror behind and above Lisette's head. Octave complains about his trampled hat, and Lisette concludes by saying, "I'm just saying what I think: you're making a foolish mistake—Madame won't be happy with you." This comment makes Octave pause; his face becomes heavy and he looks down, pondering, and slowly looks up to meet his own gaze in the mirror. Lisette turns her head, blocking our view of Octave's face in the mirror, and asks: "Will you take me with you?" Octave responds with a hoarse whisper, "Sure—you'll join us later," but the rigid immobility of his body and gaze and the hoarseness all suggest that his old doubts have returned and taken a decisive hold. André's voice is heard over this image asking "Where is Christine?," and the camera pans to frame him standing in the hall, his hands in both pockets, angry and resolute as if he overheard or has guessed what's going on. We cut to a reverse angle of Octave from his point of view, still looking in the mirror. Octave slowly turns, looks at him, and hoarsely says, "She's waiting for you." He then swallows, gathers his resolve, and repeats that Christine is waiting for André in the greenhouse. He grabs Christine's coat and hands it to André, rushing him off, but then calls André back to take his own coat. André thanks and embraces him and rushes out the door as Octave throws his hat to the ground.

Though what happens in this moment is fairly obvious, its figuration and timing is quite complex. At the very moment when Octave has finally

FIGURE 4.19.

Octave looks in the mirror of self-negation.

acquired the hope and faith necessary to imagine a new form of relationship with Christine, Lisette's comments function like those of an Iago or false friend to destroy that faith and hope. Though Octave's first glance in the mirror indicates he can withstand some of this assault—that is, deal with the age issue—the accumulation of other issues such as money and especially her blunt final comment that "Madame won't be happy with you" cuts straight to the heart of his old habit of self-loathing. What we can infer to be happening during his long second look in the mirror is as complex as what we inferred to happen when Christine looked through the field glasses. Viewing once again the string of failures that constitute his past, Octave tries and fails to imagine a future that would be any different; driven by her own self-interest and attachment to Christine, Lisette has destroyed the last possibility of true friendship in the film. Octave inadvertently sends André off to die in his place, and the next time we see

Christine she has already become a dead woman, an automaton, coldly telling Jackie to compose herself because "people are looking at you": Octave's betrayal and André's death have together annihilated every vestige of her innocence, sincerity, and hope.

The ending of *La règle du jeu* represents more than the failure of the film's own aspiration to friendship or Civilization; when the film is given its due weight and value as the capstone of Renoir's decade-long quest to recover the stable bases for meeting and belonging, human communion and community, it presents us with a horrifying expression of despair in the very possibility of friendship or Civilization and an unmistakable portent of the living hell that was about to engulf France and the Jews of Europe.

NOTES

1. Quoted in Spencer and Krauze, *Introducing Hegel*, 54.
2. Renoir, *Renoir on Renoir*, 199–200.
3. Sesonske, *Jean Renoir*, 418.
4. Renoir, *Rules of the Game*, 13.
5. Renoir's casting of Nora Gregor can itself be said to reflect an analogous motivation on his part insofar as the actress and her liberal statesman husband were forced into exile by the Anschluss.
6. Gordon, *Citizens without Sovereignty*.
7. Ibid., 60, 100.
8. Like Montaigne, they often demonstrated their commitment to this ideal by using examples drawn from other cultures to defamiliarize Eurocentric ideas of human nature and society. Montesquieu's *Persian Letters* (1721) and Diderot's *Supplement to the Voyage of Bougainville* (1772) are perhaps the most extended examples of a rhetorical strategy that was in fact quite pervasive.
9. Gordon, *Citizens without Sovereignty*, 65, 76, 80. The second rule is highlighted in the marquis's eulogy for André: "this excellent companion who knew so well how to make us forget that he was a famous man."
10. Ibid., 95, 103.
11. Renoir, *Renoir on Renoir*, 216.
12. Ibid., 216.
13. Renoir, *La règle du jeu*, 161–62.
14. Ibid.
15. Ibid., 156–57.
16. Auerbach, *Mimesis*, 489.
17. Hyppolite, *Genesis and Structure of Hegel's Phenomenology of Spirit*, 176.
18. Cavell, *World Viewed*, 221.

Conclusion:
Why La règle du jeu *Matters*

THERE ARE A FEW LOOSE THREADS that need tying up, implicit phenomenological connections that require explicit conceptual elaboration if this exploration of meeting and belonging in Renoir's 1930s films is to reach a conclusion that is, hopefully, both illuminating and satisfying. What are the defining features of modernity that Renoir is critiquing as detrimental to the achievement of meeting and belonging? What are the defining features of the alternative paradigm he is promoting as beneficial to those aims? How do these two contradictory sets of assumptions work together to structure our experience as modern and postmodern human beings—how do they, considered together, characterize that experience? I'll now try to provide straight-as-possible answers to these intertwined questions, answers that I hope can also serve as a condensed summary of this book's argument. Some enigmatic and provocative comments from Renoir's autobiography can serve to orient our concluding endeavors:

> The separation of mankind into fascists and communists is quite meaningless. Fascism, like communism, believes in progress. The followers of both creeds look to a social order based on technology. Technology is the ruling god, whether in Moscow or New York. But in the last resort one has to take up one's own stand. If I were forced to do so, with my back to the wall, I would opt for communism because it seems to me that those who believe in it have a truer conception of human dignity. But for me, as I have said again and again and shall go on saying, the real enemy is progress, not because it doesn't work but precisely because it does. Aircraft are not dangerous because they

occasionally crash, but because they leave and land on time and carry their passengers in comfort. Progress is dangerous because it is based on perfect technology. It is its success that has distorted the normal values of life and compelled man to live in a world for which he was not intended.[1]

If we take the quote above as directly related to and supportive of this book's argument, what are the defining features of modernity that the author can be said to be critiquing? Perfected technology—airplanes that never crash? The quasi-Luddite crankiness in the quotation above is clearly a kind of ruse on Renoir's part, for the objections to what he seems to be saying appear so obvious. If one takes his condemnation of perfected, humane, and beneficial technology at face value, one is led to assume that the reestablishment of "normal values" and "the world for which man was intended" would logically entail a kind of reversal of progress across the board: much higher infant mortality, much shorter life expectancy, exhausting manual labor, increased human suffering, and of course no planes, trains, automobiles, computers, cell phones, or movies. The manifest absurdity of the position Renoir provokes us to first ascribe to him forces us to ponder the passage more carefully. When we do this we realize that the technological fruits of science (for example, modern medicine, washing machines, airplanes, or movies) are not in themselves the problem; the problem is that we spend too much of our time and spiritual energy adapting to technology, caring about it and investing ourselves in it, when we should, Renoir implies, be doing something else: he believes human beings are "intended," created, to fulfill certain inherent purposes and that our existential identification with technology prevents us from fulfilling these purposes.

The important and, indeed, "inescapable" role played by the figure of looking-at others in Renoir's films during the 1930s is what makes technology, in the Heideggerian sense of a psychological and spiritual orientation, the real, behind-the-scenes villain of this book's story. From its first pronounced manifestations in *La chienne* and *Madame Bovary*, through its ambivalent and contested articulations in the Cytherean, Naturalist, and Revolutionary chronotopes, to its totalization and triumph in *La règle du jeu*—Renoir's final failed attempt to "escape from Flaubert"—the technological figure of looking-at others can be seen to precede and engender the phenomenon of romanticism in the manner that Heidegger's formulations usefully clarify. In contrast to the understanding of technology as applied science, something that appears after and follows from science, Heidegger defines it as "Enframing," a stance of the will that logically precedes the experimental methods of modern science and, one might reasonably add, the assumptions of modern historicism: one stands over and against nature, other people, and historical events as a subject over objects, looking-at them, bracketing off ethical considerations, challenging them to reveal the predictable causes underlying their actions/effects, rendering them in the form of "standing reserve," malleable raw material for the realization of our intentions.[2] Evoking Francis Bacon's infamous characterization of scientific method as "torturing" nature so as to get "her" to reveal her "reasons," Heidegger's analysis illuminates the way in which modern science—and, one might reasonably add, Nietzsche's conception of the historical sense—break with religious notions of all life, but especially human life, as sacred, endowed with value in and of itself. The technological and/or historicist attitude is deliberately blind to the chance or contingent features of phenomena, those features that define their existence as precious-because-unique-and-mortal, parts of Creation, in order to focus on the predictable aspects that turn phenomena into scientific or historical objects, effects-of-which-we-know-the-causes, expendable, replaceable things that we can control and manipulate.

As Leo Strauss explains in "The Three Waves of Modernity," the influence of the modern scientific aspiration to overcome chance or contingency was crucial to the development of modern political philosophy as distinct from classical and religious traditions.[3] In those older traditions, human beings (or "Man") are seen to have an exalted place in Creation as the only part of the whole capable of understanding the whole (Man as "the measure of all things"), and the highest good for individual human beings is to contemplate the whole. By focusing our attention on higher things, the ethical obligations that orient us and illuminate our place in Creation, our fleeting lives can be endowed with transcendent meaning: the kingdom of heaven is within us, primarily a matter of changes in our thinking about the world, not changes in the world itself. In rejecting what can be characterized as a passive or resigned view of human existence, modern philosophy begins with what Strauss calls a "lowering of the sights," dropping ethical questions of how human beings ought to live in favor of scientific observation of how human beings do predictably live and technological proposals as to how they can be made to live, modern political ideals that can be realized by historical action.[4] As we saw in our discussion of Rousseau's concept of the general will, the value of these modern ideals is not something individual human beings can discern, because their achievement is predicated precisely on the negation of our individuality, our blindfolded, submissive willingness to offer ourselves as malleable objects to the collective-as-masterful-subject; as Strauss explains, modern political philosophy entails a masochistic act of assenting to the value or goodness of something one cannot reasonably know or perceive: "Why is the general will necessarily good? The answer is: it is good because it is rational, and it is rational because it is general; it emerges through the generalization of the particular will, the will which as such is not good. It is then the mere generality of a will that vouches for its goodness; it is not necessary to have recourse to any substantive consideration, to any consideration of what man's nature, his natural perfection, requires."[5] The three waves of modern political thinking Strauss associates with Machiavelli, Rousseau, and Nietzsche bring forth a dynamic conception of human nature as standing reserve, corrupted by the accidents of its history but still malleable and capable of being remade: no longer bound by the measure of sacred ethical restraints and his own contingent limitations, the raw or splendid deal dealt by Chance, Fate, or God, "Man" is now the "master of all things," including "Man," in thrall to a self-gratifying faith in technology, the feeling of power we derive from looking-at others and making our mark—"blindly" or irrationally—on/in the realm of time-as-history.

As we saw in our genealogy of the Cytherean chronotope, the phenomenon of romanticism came into being as a reaction to the rise of time-as-history and the waning of traditional belief systems. The inevitable experience of loss and deprival in human life, formerly imbued with transcendent meaning, would now be interpreted in romantic terms as lost in time-as-history and therefore, in principle, recoverable through romantic projects of historical action, personal or political. Despite their apparent differences, the personal projects of Maurice Legrand, Emma Bovary, Toni, Lantier, Henri, Henriette, André, and Schumacher, and the political projects of the revolutionaries in *Le crime de Monsieur Lange* and

La Marseillaise, all share a common set of Rousseau-derived romantic assumptions. Fatal and deeply ambivalent in the best case scenarios of the Revolutionary chronotope, fatal and unambiguously catastrophic in the Flaubertian chronotope, the Naturalist chronotope, and *La règle du jeu*, throughout the French Renoir the net result of holding romantic assumptions illuminates their disastrous effect on Renoir's ideals of meeting and belonging.

We are hopefully now in a position to suggest that technology, time-as-history, and romanticism are just different angles from which to approach modernity as a cohesive system of philosophical assumptions and that it is this system that is the target of Renoir's critique. But having said that, two related qualifications must be made, qualifications that will serve as a transition to considering the alternative paradigm Renoir can be said to be promoting in the films of the Cytherean and Fifth chronotopes. The first qualification is simply to note that certain aspects of the paradigm of modernity we have outlined are not, in principle, modern in the sense of being unprecedented or new: one assumes that human beings have always been (a) open to the temptations of power on the will (technology) and (b) liable to mistake will-gratifying illusions for reality (romanticism). What in practice brought modernity tumbling into history was (a) the extended scientific demonstration of progress, the inexorable steady rise of modern natural science as a power-bestowing force, and, as a kind of corollary, in place of traditional belief systems, (b) the invention and popularization of modern beliefs such as Liberty, Equality, and Fraternity, capital-letter words that are equivocal in their effects, equally capable of inspiring a grassroots development of Civilization or of sanctifying murder and destruction. The second qualification to make is that Renoir is obviously not critical of the life-affirming realizations of modern ideals or technology but would, I think, have understood that those positive realizations happen only when human beings implicitly think and act in accordance with the civilized assumptions manifest in the Fifth chronotope, circumstances when the abstract scaffolding of those ideals is fully fleshed out by the concrete contingencies of living relationships—as when, to take Bazin's example, the concept of Liberty is brought to life by the unforgettable coincidence of Boudu's foot, a bit of grass, white dust, heat, and wind.[6] This is the boldest claim that I would make on Renoir's behalf, and perhaps the key paradox of modernity as an experience rather than a set of ideas: that the modern ideals we explicitly believe in only come into existence when we implicitly think and act in accordance with traditional or countermodern assumptions.

As a means to recapitulate the key principles of the countermodern paradigm that Renoir can be said to be envisioning in the films of the Cytherean and Fifth chronotopes (*Boudu sauvé des eaux, Une partie de campagne, Les bas-fonds, La grande illusion*), I would like to draw on some quotations from Simone Weil that I would ask you, patient reader, to briefly reflect on:

> We have to try to cure our faults by attention and not by will. The poet produces the beautiful by fixing his attention on something real. It is the same with the act of love. To know that this man who is hungry and thirsty really exists as much as I do—that is enough, the rest follows of itself. . . .
>
> Faith is the experience that the intelligence is enlightened by love. It is an act of cowardice to seek from (or wish to give) the people we love any other consolation than that which works of art give us. These help us through the mere fact that they *exist*. To love and be loved only serves mutually to render this existence more concrete, more constantly present to the mind. But it should be present as the source of our thoughts, not as their object. We should have with each person the relationship of one conception of the universe to another conception of the universe, and not to a part of the universe. . . .
>
> To be ever ready to admit that another person is something quite different from what we read in him when he is there (or when we think about him). Or rather, to read in him that he is certainly something different, perhaps something completely different, from what we read in him. What is hidden is more real than what is manifested, and that is true right along the scale leading from what is least hidden to what is most hidden. "That which is not manifest, but by which that which is so is made manifest." One can say that of the cube, in the matter of perception, and so, step by step, right up to God. Analogical utilization of the notion of transfinitude. The seizing hold, the touching of being with the aid of the two pincers of Relation. Cube, cubes of cubes, etc.[7]

Perhaps the most fundamental and clearest contrast we can draw between the two paradigms concerns what they take to be the desirable orientation of the human psyche or spirit. In explicit contrast to the technological/romantic orientation of the will, the faculty of attention crucial to Weil's thought and the Cytherean phenomenology of Renoir's films can be defined negatively as a suspension of the will, an act of looking and waiting on something real—probably, in the final analysis, *someone* real, real in the intuitively-obvious-but-generally-disavowed sense of existing in the same manner, with the same value and importance, as we understand *ourselves* to exist. Truly believing that other people are, like us, "conceptions of the universe"—living, thinking, multidimensional souls, as unfathomable as the infinite universe they look out upon—can be understood as an act of love insofar as it requires us to renounce the illusion that the small part of them we see and understand, the part of them we think we possess as a part of our world, is the whole: in a very precise and concrete sense, we are required to give up or sacrifice a part of ourselves so that the other can exist. Using the metaphor of a cube, wherein we can see three faces (the top and two sides) but logically infer the existence of three other faces (the bottom and two other sides) that are invisible to us, Weil puts forward the general principle that our understanding of reality grows only to the extent that we renounce the gratifying illusion that we already possess it, the extent to which we actively *believe* that what we *can't see* is more real/important than what we *can see* (something we already intuitively *know*): all progress along the axis of thought/attention (understood as perpendicular to the axis of historical action/will) thus depends on *really believing what we already know*.[8] To the extent that we are capable of doing so, the loved existence of other people, the living relationships that connect them to each other and to us, the testimony of works of art and entire ways of life can all function as the life-enhancing source of our thoughts, spiritual illumination that reveals the world to be "different from what anyone supposed, and luckier."[9] Weil's point about other people being the source of our thoughts rather than their object underlines the paradox at the heart of the whole paradigm, the strange Montaignean fusion of skepticism and faith so crucial to the phenomenology of Cythera, which is that we can't see or know what or who we love, can't make them the object of our thoughts, precisely because we can never fathom the depth or quality of our own intentions, the extent to which they illuminate or darken our reasoning (if you don't believe me, try a thought experiment, but don't take it too far). We can never know with any certainty what or who we love because love as attention, as a deliberate suspension of our self-centered romantic willfulness, enacts a kind of radical forgetting, a complete dissolution of the old world with its fixed configurations of subjects and objects.

If my condensed explanation of Weil's cube-of-cubes philosophical method made the sense I intended it to, it should be recognizable both as a down-to-earth version of the Platonic doctrine of Forms and as the operating system of assumptions common to the phenomena of Cythera, true friendship, the Fifth chronotope, Civilization, and so on that we retrieved from Renoir's films. The reader should also be in a position to appreciate my claim that the realizations of the countermodern paradigm are, as a matter of necessity, due to the fact of radical forgetting we just reviewed, invisible and anonymous, not something that could be reconstructed as a historical phenomenon that waxes and wanes. Thus while I needed to draw on the philosophical writings of Plato, Montaigne, Weil, and others in order to reconstruct the paradigm as a system of thought, I have never attempted to represent its articulation in Renoir's films as the direct result of an influence of these thinkers on Renoir, as a historical survival of the premodern past; nor, for that matter, would I ever suggest that the premodern past itself, when the principles of the paradigm were, in a relative and historical sense, ideologically dominant via classical and religious traditions of thought, was a kind of golden age wherein the phenomena of Civilization flourished historically. There has always been an asymmetrical aspect to the book's narrative because it takes place on the border between time-as-history, the world/dimension we share in common as denizens of the modern/postmodern cave, and another, incommensurable, world and dimension of time, perhaps best known via Plato's conception of time ("Becoming") as the moving image of eternity ("Being"). That said, what I hope my reconstruction of Renoir's philosophical journey makes clear is that the new world waiting for us outside the cave of postmodernity is by no means an abstraction or metaphysical nonentity; it is, rather, the palpable, proof-is-in-the-pudding result of a philosophical activity whereby the reality of this world, the one-and-only-here-and-now real world of Creation, flowers into view for those who are, in Renoir's words, capable of being enchanted by it.

The final big question I need to address is how Renoir's films of the 1930s articulate our experience of being simultaneously in thrall to both traditional and modern assumptions; as with the two other questions, I'll assume that the book has already covered, as best it could, how the Cytherean phenomenology works in detail and that what is now needed is a kind of simplified explanation of what is going on behind the scenes, how the metaphysical interface between each paradigm's distinctive radiation produces the effects of that phenomenology.

In the case of the traditional paradigm, the radiation metaphor is derived from Plato's use of the sun's radiation to characterize our natural orientation and growth toward the Good in *The Republic*'s allegory of the Cave. As both the source of all life on earth and the source of all illumination by means of which we see and know all life on earth, the effects of the sun's radiation manifest in, for example, a plant that turns its "face" toward the sun serve as an apt metaphor for the successive stages of philosophical transformation we have considered in the films. From the mysterious germination of Cytherean life and hope out of Flaubertian inertia and sterility—first made visible in the movement from *La chienne* to *Boudu sauvé des eaux* and a recurrent pattern in our story ever after—to the flowering of genuine friendships and wider networks of human meeting and belonging in the Revolutionary and Fifth chronotopes, the countermodern paradigm we have reconstructed functions heuristically, like a kind of time-lapse photography, to make a natural (that is, intended, omnipresent, providential) process visible and audible across eleven films that Jean Renoir made during the 1930s; the paradigm functions to capture and organize details that would otherwise have been too close, too distant, too fast, too slow, too loud, or too soft to perceive. The effects of the sun's radiation on our planet are a metaphor for Creation happening now, in the eternal present, with the growth of our human capacity to love/believe in/know Creation being the effect *we* were intended for.

The implicit contrast between human will–centered clock-time and various nonhuman scales of time and space in this characterization—the size of the sun, the distance the sun's rays span to reach the earth, the microscopic event of a seed's germination, the macroscopic time it takes to become a skyscraping sequoia, the eternal constancy of the sun as efficient cause of all earth's creation, and the manifest sense of intended-ness or Providence, of a plan that works perfectly regardless of human actions or intentions (something that we can neither assist with nor, try as we might, screw up)—allows me to introduce one last distinction between our two philosophical paradigms that will also be an expedient transition to considering the modern paradigm's form of radiation.

In *Religion as Anxiety and Tranquility: An Essay in Comparative Phenomenology of the Spirit*, J. G. Arapura compares "two spiritual spheres," Indian and Western philosophical traditions that share a common starting point in apprehending "the wrongness of existence"—the facts of human suffering, sorrow, mortality, evil, illusions, chance, finitude, and so on—but that differ in their deepest emotional/ethical responses to those facts. In the Indian sphere that Arapura explains with reference to Hindu and Buddhist thought, the core response of "tranquility" is a product of the belief that the phenomenal world of wrongness has no ultimate ontological status, that we and those we love and sorrow over are in fact grounded in an eternal Reality beyond suffering:

> Reality begins where anxiety is terminated. It has been the belief that anxiety itself is the denial of Reality, since it is within the character of the phenomenal world of becoming, to be both contained within its bounds, false as they are, and eventually burnt up along with that world. Every form of anxiety or sorrow is a sign of a *seeming* alienation from Reality—in which in fact painfulness consists—and hence is without depth, because phenomena have no depth or substantiality. The theoretical perception of tranquility will show up the shallow and unsubstantial character of sorrow: what has depth, reality is the tranquility state.[10]

As in the vision of a providential Creation or cosmos sketched above, the philosophical subject oriented by tranquility is profoundly at peace and content, relaxed in the belief that the world and people he or she loves exist, that life has an immutable value and transcendent significance beyond what we can see and grasp and beyond suffering. Arapura's notion of tranquility further refines and clarifies the concept of attention we have borrowed from Weil, because it forces us to recognize the extent to which agonistic qualities associated with the will—resoluteness, stiffness, unyieldingness—can, after the fashion of the Trojan horse, be wrongly smuggled into the concept of attention via connotations derived from "tension," "paying attention," "standing at attention," and so on. Modern as we all are, our thinking is governed by certain unconscious reflexes, and it seems to me that the tranquility hypothesis can help dislodge these defaults and allow us to better understand how the assumptions of the countermodern paradigm cohere, how the calming bliss they generate motivates the philosophical subject. Tranquility arises from the realization that whatever serious problems you yourself have, the cosmos is totally fine, and even better than fine insofar as its "fineness" is diminished by our limited apprehension. It is about identifying with the cosmos, being suffused with joy simply knowing that the cosmos exists, even though you yourself may have good reasons to be unhappy—knowing concretely that, for example, the wonderful country of Brazil exists, even though you yourself have no means of visiting it and might well be sad for that reason. When, as a kind of small surprise or amusing detail, you catch a glimpse of your unhappy Brazil-deprived self from this cosmic reverse angle, you experience only a brief moment of affection and sympathy, because you don't value your own unhappy existence any more than that of the gazillions of happy and unhappy people who have lived on our planet: the tiny drop of your own happiness or unhappiness dissolves into the cosmic ocean of humanity's happiness or unhappiness.

As a fairly obvious corollary of this interpretation as to how and why the subject of the Indian sphere and/or countermodern paradigm is made tranquil by believing in the existence of the cosmos, one can apprehend how and why the contrasting emotion of "anxiety" can be seen to be the effect of doubting or disbelieving in the existence of others and oneself, a kind of fearful and desperate grasping at the surface of phenomena for an epistemological assurance or certainty they are incapable of giving us. Just as we can never *know* whom we really love, we can also never *know* who really loves us (again, if you don't believe me, try a thought experiment, but don't take it too far). If the tranquility sphere is oriented by a reality understood to be beyond our conscious possession, the reality that orients the anxiety sphere that Arapura traces from Saint Paul to modern philosophers such as Kant, Hegel, Kierkegaard, Nietzsche, and Heidegger puts consciousness, in particular self-consciousness and will, at its very center. As Arapura, quoting Kierkegaard, explains, "The more consciousness, the more will; the more will the more self. A man who has no will at all has no self; the more will he has the more conscious of the self he has. The self is the conscious synthesis of infinitude and finitude, which relates itself to itself, whose task it is to become itself."[11] Governed by an encompassing sense of agonistic anxiety, the subject's will and the relation between his or her self-will and the wills of others, issues of freedom and domination, and so on, emerge over time to become the central questions of Western political philosophy, and in a general sense it is the way these questions play out in time-as-history that accounts for the extraordinary dynamism we apprehend in modernity. With the defining emotional response of anxiety in view, we are now in a position to explain exactly how modernity generates that emotional response, how and why it is the inevitable result of the self-contradictory radiation of modern assumptions.

In the case of the modern paradigm, my use of the radiation metaphor is intended to evoke both the pathological effects of nuclear radiation on all forms of life and the way X-radiation and other technologies allow us to look-at-and-through living beings, grasp their reasons or causes, and thereby gain control over them. If the traditional paradigm explains the growth or flowering of life-enhancing beliefs, it should be easy to see how the technological-historicist attitude accounts for the vaporization of those beliefs in nihilism and how the disenchanting experience of nihilism generates both greater anxiety and romantic beliefs/projects whereby we attempt to overcome that anxiety, beliefs/projects that in their turn are threatened by the technological-historicist attitude, the ability of ourselves and others to look-at-and-through them, and so on; and so we go, on and on, deeper and deeper into a quiet, bewildered, anxiety-ridden, almost-impossible-to-articulate desperation.[12]

Writing in 1969, right after the Big Bang of 1968 that inaugurated the long moment of postmodernity (1968–75–89/91), the Canadian philosopher George Grant explains the process whereby the radiation of modern assumptions vaporizes or represses our experiences and even the memory of experiences generated by the traditional paradigm; reading what he writes today, more than two decades after the not-with-a-bang-but-a-whimper end of that moment, I hope it is noncontroversial to suggest, in light of all the ground covered, that postmodernity (the "condition" we still live within today, despite the anachronism of the term) may be nothing more than a form of advanced vaporization, the nihilistic effect of modern radiation on both traditional and modern ideals manifest in, to take my preferred example, the ramped-up love story of Sino-American relations in the wake of Tiananmen Square (wherein the distinction between democracy and dictatorship has for more than twenty-five years been evacuated of any meaning by the hidden-in-plain-sight economic symbiosis between the countries associated with each term):

> It is difficult to think whether we are deprived of anything essential to our happiness, just because the coming to be of the technological society has stripped us above all of the very systems of meaning which disclosed the highest purposes of man, in terms of which, therefore, we could judge whether an absence of something was in fact a deprival. All coherent languages beyond these which serve the drive to unlimited freedom through technique have been broken up in the coming to be what we are. Therefore, it is impossible to articulate publically any suggestion of loss, and perhaps even more frightening, almost impossible to articulate it to ourselves. We have been left with no words which cleave together and summon out of uncertainty the good of which we may sense the dispossession.[13]

What Grant's analysis of technology as a disbelief system should help make clear is that the two forms of philosophical radiation have effects on each other that are similar and symmetrical. Just as adhering to traditional/countermodern assumptions results in a radical dissolution of an old world / birth of a new world via a succession of self-forgetting invisible dissolves, so in Grant's nightmare vision of postmodern technological society we find that we forget everything, both traditional and modern, that we once believed in and can no longer explain, even to ourselves, what we are missing: the world of Creation we once loved has completely vanished and in its place is another world that looks the same but that we dimly, anxiously sense is creation's un-created evil twin, a replicant, a simulacron, or grand pastiche (as was explained by Foucault, Baudrillard, Jameson, and others). If our existential identification with traditional assumptions carries us toward happiness and we are content, trusting, and tranquil in knowing we don't know where it is taking us, our existential identification with the modern assumptions evacuated of meaning by postmodernity makes us anxious: we think we know where we are going, think we know what we have got, but the unspeakable fact remains that the world has slowly, incrementally, inexorably become a much sadder place.[14]

How do the two paradigms of assumptions we have identified in the French Renoir work in tandem to structure our experience as modern and postmodern human beings—how do they, considered together, characterize that experience? This book's contention is that Jean Renoir's 1930s films, through their accidental narrative of consistent rediscoveries, testify to an unchanging set of principles, philosophical bedrock we can trust. We live in two incommensurable dimensions of time, in time-as-history (in both the individual microsense and the conventional big-picture sense) and, at the same time, in the eternal light of an ongoing and inalienable natural process, which I have called Cythera, the Fifth chronotope, or Civilization, but which we should understand as an invisible, anonymous, and ahistorical phenomenon, hopefully clarified by the traditions of thought I have referred to, but in no way contained by or dependent on them. The beautiful new worlds that Renoir's 1930s films encourage us to believe in are not utopian fantasies but are, quite simply, worlds that were and still are possible whenever modern ideals are fleshed out by the positive radiation of the countermodern paradigm's brand of love and belief. They are all originally—and perhaps rather obviously—derived from the world Renoir was born into, the confident late nineteenth-century world of his impressionist father evoked in Eugenio Montale's poem "Boats on the Marne," a work of art that appeared, like *La règle du jeu*, in 1939. If we now return to consider what is going on in this poem more closely, analyzing each stanza in turn, I believe it will illuminate a structure of time common to all our stories, from the invisible dissolves in Watteau's paintings to their embodiment in *Une partie de campagne* and their apotheosis in *La règle du jeu*, the metanarrative of modernity whereby the Cytherean radiation of love and belief (the embarking articulated by "the first invisible dissolve") gives way to the romantic radiation of false belief (the returning articulated by "the second invisible dissolve"), and this in turn gives way to the technological radiation of disbelief and postmodern nihilism:

Boats on the Marne

Bliss of cork bark abandoned
to the current
that melts around bridges upside down,
and the full moon pale in sunlight:
boats on the river, nimble, in summer
and a lazy murmur of city.
You row along the field where the butterfly
catcher comes with his net,
the thicket across the wall where the dragon's
blood repeats itself in cinnabar.

Beginning with the lucky coincidence of the cork in the water, Renoir's signature metaphor for his own "go-with-the-flow" approach to contingency, circumstances, life, and art, the images cohere around the theme of a heightened erotic receptivity manifest in yielding to sensual stimuli—the "bliss" of the cork's utter self-"abandon"-ment to the current, the current yielding in turn by "melting" around the bridges, and the "bridges upside down" establishing a theme of reflections-in-flowing-water as quasi-photographic receptivity, both ongoing like a film or unique and unrepeatable like snapshots. As in our analysis of Watteau's painting, sound also plays a crucial role here, as the "lazy," scarcely audible "murmur of city" deftly establishes the infinitely superior ability of the cosmos to encompass, completely absorb, any project that Man/modernity can come up with.

> Voices from the river, cries from the banks,
> or the rhythmic stroking of canoes
> in the twilight filtering through
> the walnut leaves, but where
> is the slow parade of the seasons
> which was a dawn that never ended, with no roads,
> where is the long expectation, and what is the name
> of the void that invades us?

The contrast between human and cosmic/natural scales of time, space, and action is picked up again in the first two lines, where the vastness of the landscape is accentuated by the way in which sound perspective of the scene absorbs, muffles, and/or echoes human "voices from the river" and "cries from the banks," and the tranquil indifference of natural cycles of time to human projects is made subtly vivid as the falling twilight calmly imposes its implacable deadline on those doing the rhythmic stroking in the canoes. Then we get the first questioning notes in the poem, the bewilderment over an imperceptible turn within modernity, like a sudden chill in the air, a cloud stealthily sliding between us and the sun (my own images, presumably rejected by Montale as banal/obvious). The "slow parade of the seasons," the cyclical narratives of cosmic time recognized as such, were, paradoxically, also "a dawn that never ended," a linear narrative thought to be eternal, because modern time-as-history was fleshed out by a fortunate synchronicity with Cythera, the hidden, unacknowledged source of its "long expectation"; "no roads" simply means that this modern hope was, at its best, completely, all-360-degrees, open, untainted by any sense of romantic fatality. The un-nameable-ness of "the void that invades us" introduces the impossible-to-even-articulate-our-deprival-to-ourselves issue described by Grant above.

> The dream is this: a vast
> unending day, almost motionless,
> that suffuses its splendor between the banks
> and at every bend the good works of man,
> the veiled tomorrow that holds no horror.
> And the dream was more, more, but its reflection
> stilled on the racing water, under
> the oriole's nest, airy, out of reach,
> was one high silence in the noontime's
> rhyming cry, the great turmoil
> great repose.

At first glance it seems that from "The dream is this" to "holds no horror," Montale simply recaps, for emphasis, the synchronized coincidence of Cytherean modernity, the "never-ending dawn" introduced earlier, now putting it in the present tense ("the dream *is* this"), as if that would somehow bring the dream of "suffused splendor" (that is, the possibilities of modernity seeming to overflow the world that contains them) back to life; but by adding "the good works of man," he brings the role of technology into view, like a train crossing a bridge in the background of an impressionist painting, and the painting itself is now seen to be a theatrical backdrop, the false "veiled" promise that tomorrow will be the same as today, only better, when in fact the technologically enabled "horror" of World War I is around the next "bend."[15] But even as the poem/poet points toward the horror, it/he still wants to insist, as if on the verge of remembering something priceless, that there was "more, more" to the dream, and we start to get the sense that the pitched battle between romantic memory (the second invisible dissolve) and Cytherean forgetting (the first invisible dissolve) is something that either (a) happened in the past (the story is over, that is, the romantic version, technological vaporization wins) or (b) is happening within the poet as he writes/speaks (the story is unfinished, that is, the Cytherean version, technological vaporization never wins, it only seems to block an unceasing process of growth the way a cloud bank seems to block the sun).

The answer to this question hinges on our response to the poem, whether we ourselves can remember something priceless that the poet himself can't find the words for or whether the masochist in us finds the sweet fatality of purple twilight and racing water too masterful a turn-on to refuse. The fact that the dream's "reflection stilled on the racing water" and the specific details of that snapshot/reflection from earlier in the day—the oriole's nest being "out of reach," a "high silence" amid the "rhyming cry" of collective birdsong, a "great repose" amid "great turmoil"—all suggest to me that the poet's anxiety-driven romantic attachment to the dream has tacitly severed him from his fellow birds and left him high and lonesome, stuck in the past. Like Henri, Henriette, and romantics in general, he seems to have forgotten what Montale says elsewhere is memory's "first and most urgent task: to forget":[16]

> Here . . . the color that endures
> is the gray of the mouse that leapt
> through the rushes or the starling, a spurt
> of poison metal disappearing
> in mists along the bank.
>   Another day,
> you were saying—what were you saying? And where
> does it take us, this river mouth gathering in a single
> rush?
>   This is the evening. Now we can descend
> downstream where the Great Bear is shining.
>
> (Boats on the Marne, on a Sunday outing
> on your birthday, floating.)[17]

I would like to end this book by making a very simple point. The one quality that I have always found most convincing and beautiful in Renoir's films, the quality that is to my mind his unique signature as an artist, is his absolute fidelity to the contingent Created-ness of the worlds he wishes to express his response to. The audiovisual details of Renoir's films are striking in their singularity and at the same time seem thoroughly saturated by his responses to them. This miracle or paradox of

being loyal to the accidental or chance aspects of the world, to life in all its messiness, and being able to make it all cohere as a whole was the source of the hyperbolic emotions I felt when I first discovered his films in college—infinite, teeming worlds, raging mountain torrents, the light and sounds from long-vanished stars, glistening eyeballs, and so on. Though at the time I did not understand my motives for replaying the magic moments I replayed over and over in a viewing carrel in the university library—Anatole's inane expression of joy as he takes the fishing rods/bait Rodolphe offers him, or the movement of some reeds tumbling into the embrace of Joseph Kosma's score—I now think I was searching for some kind of key to Life that I believed Renoir possessed. Writing this book was an attempt to see if I could find that key by taking the search up another level, to see if Renoir had managed, via a miraculous series of accidents, to make narrative sense of a complicated decade's worth of contingencies, and only you, patient reader, can judge whether I found anything or not. The simple thing I think I learned from Renoir is how deeply calming it

is to see/hear the world through his cherishing eyes/ears, how that non-technological way of perceiving things can really cheer you up, exactly the way the prophet-poet Isaiah does when he describes the encompassing tenderness of "the Lord's servant": "He will not break off a bent reed nor put out a flickering lamp."[18]

NOTES

1. Renoir, *My Life and My Films*, 124.
2. Heidegger, *Question Concerning Technology and Other Essays*, 19–27.
3. Strauss, "The Three Waves of Modernity," in *Political Philosophy*, 81–98.
4. Ibid., 86.
5. Ibid., 91–92.
6. Bazin, *Jean Renoir*, 86.
7. Weil, *Gravity and Grace*, 56–57, 58, 108, 121, 129; Weil, *Notebooks of Simone Weil*, 363.
8. As Weil puts it: "We do not have to understand new things, but by dint of patience, effort and method come to understand with our whole soul the truths which are evident. The most commonplace truth[,] when it floods the whole soul, is like a revelation." Weil, *Gravity and Grace*, 105.

9. Whitman, "Song of Myself," in *Walt Whitman's Leaves of Grass*, 30. Weil provides a compact formula that answers the modern dogma that condemns faith as inherently irrational: "Faith is the experience that intelligence is enlightened by love." Weil, *Gravity and Grace*, 116. As far as I am aware, the most exhaustive examination of the giftedness of human experience in the "Continental" tradition is found in Marion, *Being Given*; the same principles are explored from an "Anglo-American" perspective in Murdoch, *Sovereignty of the Good*. In *Speaking into the Air*, Peters also arrives at an "optimistic" view of human communication by the very different route of comparative historical analysis. He contrasts Plato's account of the close reciprocal relations required for a successful dialogue with Jesus's image of a nonreciprocal dissemination in which the sender is an indiscriminate broadcaster of discursive seed and the receiver is responsible for allowing meaning to sprout, grow, and bear fruit. The parable of the sower reminds us that we manage to successfully communicate before we know how to communicate and focuses our attention on the mysterious providence of earth, rain, and sun that precedes and guarantees the intentions of sender and receiver. While noting the widespread influence of Plato's anxiety over the possibilities of misunderstanding, Peters suggests we take our bearings by the basic nonreciprocality of most human relations and communications, from the asymmetric relations between parents and babies to the primarily unidirectional mediascape we inhabit today. From this angle of approach, the Platonic ideals of mutual communion and justice as reciprocity are underwritten by the more primary sense of indebtedness that puts the economy of human relations in motion, i.e., the nonreciprocal "injustice" of parental love, the providential disposition of nature, and so on. See Peters, "Dialogue and Dissemination," chap. 1 in *Speaking into The Air*, 33–62.

10. Arapura, *Religion as Anxiety and Tranquility*, 77.

11. Ibid., 81.

12. The process whereby nihilism emerges out of modern philosophical assumptions is given a detailed and thorough examination in Rosen, *Nihilism*.

13. Grant, "A Platitude," in *George Grant Reader*, 448, 449–50.

14. If I said that "the entire world has become gloomier incrementally—become sadder without noticing it—since 1989/1991," I would of course be accused of an unconscious but very common nostalgia for the good old days of my own youth; nevertheless, I'm taking a message-in-a-bottle gamble burying that statement in this note and hoping that somebody somewhere might possibly get what I really mean by it.

15. The specific painting I have in mind is Monet's *The Seine at Bougival in the Evening*, 1870, currently in the Smith College Museum of Art, Northampton.

16. Montale, *Poet in Our Time*, 50.

17. Montale, *Occasions*, 115–17. "Boats on the Marne." Copyright © 1957 by Arnoldo Mondadori Editore, Milano. Translation copyright © 1987 by William Arrowsmith., from COLLECTED POEMS OF EUGENIO MONTALE 1925–1977 by Eugenio Montale, edited by Rosanna Warren, translated by William Arrowsmith. Used by permission of W. W. Norton & Company, Inc.

18. Isa. 42:3 (GNT).

BIBLIOGRAPHY

Andrew, Dudley. *Mists of Regret: Culture and Sensibility in Classic French Film.* Princeton, NJ: Princeton University Press, 1995.
Andrew, Dudley, and Steven Ungar. *Popular Front Paris and the Poetics of Culture.* Cambridge, MA: Harvard University Press, 2005.
Arapura, J. G. *Religion as Anxiety and Tranquility: An Essay in Comparative Phenomenology of the Spirit.* The Hague: Mouton, 1972.
Arendt, Hannah. *The Life of the Mind.* New York: Harcourt, Brace, 1978.
Auerbach, Erich. *Mimesis: The Representation of Reality in Western Literature.* Translated by W. R. Trask. Princeton, NJ: Princeton University Press, 1953.
Bakhtin, M. M. *The Dialogic Imagination: Four Essays by M. M. Bakhtin.* Edited by M. Holquist. Translated by C. Emerson and M. Holquist. Austin: University of Texas Press, 1981.
Bann, Stephen. *Romanticism and the Rise of History.* New York: Maxwell Macmillan, 1994.
Barthes, Roland. *Camera Lucida: Reflections on Photography.* Translated by R. Howard. New York: Hill and Wang, 1981.
———. *Mythologies.* Translated by A. Lavers. New York: Hill and Wang, 1995.
Baudelaire, Charles. *Selected Writings on Art and Literature.* Translated by P. E. Charvet. New York: Penguin, 1972.
Bazin, André. *The Cinema of Cruelty: From Buñuel to Hitchcock.* Edited by François Truffaut. Translated by S. d'Estrée. New York: Seaver Books, 1982.
———. *Jean Renoir.* New York: Da Capo, 1992.
———. *Qu'est-ce que le cinéma? I: Ontologie et langage.* Paris: Les Editions Du Cerf, 1958.
———. *What Is Cinema? Essays Selected and Translated by Hugh Gray.* 2 vols. Berkeley: University of California Press, 1967–71.
Benardete, Seth. *The Argument of the Action: Essays on Greek Poetry and Philosophy.* Chicago: University of Chicago Press, 2000.
Benjamin, Walter. *Illuminations.* New York: Schocken Books, 1969.
Berger, John. *Selected Essays.* Edited by Geoff Dyer. New York: Random House, 2001.
Berlin, Isaiah. *The Roots of Romanticism.* Princeton, NJ: Princeton University Press, 2001.
Birnbaum, Pierre. *The Idea of France.* New York: Hill and Wang, 2001.
Bratton, Jacky, Jim Cook, and Christine Gledhill, eds. *Melodrama: Stage, Picture, Screen.* London: British Film Institute, 1994.

Braudy, Leo. *Jean Renoir: The World of His Films*. Garden City, NY: Doubleday, 1972.
Brooks, Peter. *The Melodramatic Imagination: Balzac, Henry James, Melodrama, and the Mode of Excess*. New ed. New York: Columbia University Press, 1995.
Browne, Nick, ed. *Refiguring American Film Genres: History and Theory*. Los Angeles: University of California Press, 1998.
Buchsbaum, Jonathan. *Cinema Engagé: Film in the Popular Front*. Urbana: University of Illinois Press, 1988.
Cavell, Stanley. *The World Viewed: Reflections on the Ontology of Film*. Enlarged ed. Cambridge, MA: Harvard University Press, 1979.
Cook, Patricia, ed. *Philosophical Imagination and Cultural Memory: Appropriating Historical Traditions*. Durham: Duke University Press, 1993.
Deleuze, Gilles. *Cinema 1: The Movement-Image*. Translated by H. Tomlinson and B. Habberjam. Minneapolis: University of Minnesota Press, 1986.
———. *Cinema 2: The Time-Image*. Translated by H. Tomlinson and R. Galeta. Minneapolis: University of Minnesota Press, 1989.
Durgnat, Raymond. *Jean Renoir*. Berkeley: University of California Press, 1974.
Eckstein, Arthur M., and Peter Lehman, eds. *"The Searchers": Essays and Reflections on John Ford's Classic Western*. Detroit: Wayne State University Press, 2004.
Faulkner, Christopher. *The Social Cinema of Jean Renoir*. Princeton, NJ: Princeton University Press, 1986.
Flaubert, Gustave. *Madame Bovary*. Translated by M. Marmur. New York: Signet, 1979.
Fukuyama, Francis. *The End of History and the Last Man*. New York: Maxwell Macmillan, 1992.
Gaines, Jane, ed. *Classical Narrative Revisited: The Paradigm Wars*. Durham: Duke University Press, 1992.
Gordon, Daniel. *Citizens without Sovereignty: Equality and Sociability in French Thought, 1670–1798*. Princeton, NJ: Princeton University Press, 1994.
Grant, George. *The George Grant Reader*. Edited by W. Christian and S. Grant. Toronto: University of Toronto Press, 1998.
Gunning, Tom. "The Whole Town's Gawking: Early Cinema and the Visual Experience of Modernity." *Yale Journal of Criticism* 7, no. 2 (Fall 1994): 189–201.
Hansen, Miriam. "Benjamin, Cinema and Experience: The Blue Flower in the Land of Technology." *New German Critique* 40 (Winter 1987): 179–224.
Harcourt, Peter. *Six European Directors: Essays on the Meaning of Film Style*. New York: Penguin, 1974.
Hartle, Ann. *Michel de Montaigne: Accidental Philosopher*. Cambridge: Cambridge University Press, 2003.
Havel, Vaclav. "The Anatomy of the Gag." *Modern Drama* 23 (Spring 1980): 13–24.
Heidegger, Martin. *Being and Time: A Translation of "Sein und Zeit."* Translated by Joan Stambaugh. Albany: State University of New York Press, 1996.
———. *The Question Concerning Technology and Other Essays*. Translated by W. Lovitt. New York: Harper and Row, 1977.
Hill, John, and Pamela Church Gibson, eds. *The Oxford Guide to Film Studies*. New York: Oxford University Press, 1998.
Hillier, Jim, ed. *Cahiers du Cinéma—The 1950's: Neo-realism, Hollywood, New Wave*. Cambridge, MA: Harvard University Press, 1985.
Hyppolite, Jean. *Genesis and Structure of Hegel's Phenomenology of Spirit*. Evanston: Northwestern University Press, 1974.

Jameson, Fredric. *The Geopolitical Aesthetic: Cinema and Space in the World System.* Bloomington: Indiana University Press, 1995.

———. *Postmodernism; or, The Cultural Logic of Late Capitalism.* Durham, NC: Duke University Press, 1997.

Landy, Marcia, ed. *Imitations of Life: A Reader on Film and Television Melodrama.* Detroit: Wayne State University Press, 1991.

Lourie, Eugene. *My Work in Films.* New York: Harcourt Brace Jovanovich, 1985.

Marion, Jean-Luc. *Being Given: Toward a Phenomenology of Givenness.* Stanford: Stanford University Press, 2002.

Marivaux, Pierre. *Marivaux: Plays.* Introduction by Claude Schumacher. New York: Methuen, 1988.

Mitchell, W. J. T. *Iconology: Image, Text, Ideology.* Chicago: University of Chicago Press, 1987.

Montale, Eugenio. *The Occasions.* Translated by William Arrowsmith. New York: W. W. Norton, 1987.

———. *Poet in Our Time.* New York: Urizen Books, 1976.

Murdoch, Iris. *The Sovereignty of the Good.* New York: Routledge, 1989.

Nichols, Bill, ed. *Movies and Methods: An Anthology.* Los Angeles: University of California Press, 1976.

Nora, Pierre, ed. *Realms of Memory: Rethinking the French Past.* Vol. 1, *Conflicts and Divisions.* New York: Columbia University Press, 1992.

O'Brien, Charles. *Cinema's Conversion to Sound: Technology and Film Style in France and the U.S.* Bloomington: Indiana University Press, 2005.

Panofsky, Erwin. *Early Netherlandish Painting: Its Origins and Character.* Cambridge, MA: Harvard University Press, 1953.

Pascal, Blaise. *Pascal's Pensées.* Translated by W. F. Trotter. London: E. P. Dutton, 1954.

Peters, John Durham. *Speaking into the Air: A History of the Idea of Communication.* Chicago: University of Chicago Press, 1999.

Phillips, Alastair, and Ginette Vincendeau, eds. *A Companion to Jean Renoir.* Oxford: Wiley-Blackwell, 2013.

Plato. *Phaedrus and Letters VII and VIII.* Translated by W. Hamilton. New York: Penguin, 1988.

———. *The Republic.* Translated by G. M. A. Grube. Indianapolis: Hackett, 1974.

Rearick, Charles. *The French in Love and War: Popular Culture in the Era of the World Wars.* New Haven, CT: Yale University Press, 1997.

Renoir, Jean. *Écrits 1926–1971.* Edited by Claude Gauteur. Paris: Pierre Belfond, 1974.

———. *An Interview.* Copenhagen: Green Integer Books, 1998.

———. *Jean Renoir: Letters.* Boston: Faber, 1994.

———. *My Life and My Films.* Translated by N. Denny. New York: Atheneum, 1974.

———. *La règle du jeu: Scénario original de Jean Renoir.* Edited and commentary by O. Curchod and C. Faulkner. Paris: Édition Nathan, 1999.

———. *Renoir on Renoir: Interviews, Essays, and Remarks.* Translated by C. Volk. Cambridge: Cambridge University Press, 1989.

———. *The Rules of the Game: A Film by Jean Renoir.* Translated by J. McGrath and M. Teitelbaum. New York: Lorrimer, 1984.

Rodowick, D. N. *The Crisis of Political Modernism: Criticism and Ideology in Contemporary Film Theory.* Berkeley: University of California Press, 1994.

Rohmer, Eric. *The Taste for Beauty.* New York: Cambridge University Press, 1989.

Rosen, Stanley. *Nihilism: A Philosophical Essay*. South Bend, IN: St. Augustine's, 2000.
Rougemont, Denis de. *Love in the Western World*. Translated by M. Belgion. Princeton, NJ: Princeton University Press, 1983.
Rousseau, Jean-Jacques. *The First and Second Discourses*. Edited by R. D. Masters. Translated by R. D. Masters and J. R. Masters. New York: St. Martin's, 1964.
———. *The Social Contract*. Chicago: Henry Regnery, 1954.
Ruprecht, Louis A. *Symposia: Plato, the Erotic and Moral Value*. Albany: State University of New York Press, 1999.
Schiffman, Zachary Sayre. *On the Threshold of Modernity: Relativism in the French Renaissance*. Baltimore: Johns Hopkins University Press, 1991.
Schneider, Pierre. *The World of Watteau*. New York: Time-Life Books, 1967.
Sesonske, Alexander. *Jean Renoir: The French films, 1924–1939*. Cambridge, MA: Harvard University Press, 1980.
Sims, Bennett. "House-Sitting." *Tin House* 13, no.4 (Summer 2012): 108–109.
Spencer, Lloyd, and Andrzej Krauze. *Introducing Hegel*. New York: Totem Books, 1997.
Strauss, Leo. *Political Philosophy: Six Essays*. Edited by Hilail Gildin. New York: Pegasus-Bobbs-Merrill, 1975.
Weil, Simone. *Gravity and Grace*. Translated by Emma Craufurd. London: Routledge, 1963.
———. *The Need for Roots: Prelude to a Declaration of Duties toward Mankind*. Translated by A. F. Wills. New York: Routledge and Kegan Paul, 1987.
———. *The Notebooks of Simone Weil*. London: Routledge and Kegan Paul, 2004.
———. *The Simone Weil Reader*. London; Moyer Bell, 1977.
———. *Waiting for God*. New York: Harper and Row, 1973.
Whitman, Walt. *Walt Whitman's Leaves of Grass: The First (1855) Edition*. Edited by Malcolm Cowley. New York: Penguin Books, 1977.
Williams, Linda. *Playing the Race Card: Melodramas of Black and White from Uncle Tom to O.J. Simpson*. Princeton, NJ: Princeton University Press, 2001.
Williams, Raymond. *Marxism and Literature*. New York: Oxford University Press, 1977.
Wingrove, Elizabeth Rose. *Rousseau's Republican Romance*. Princeton, NJ: Princeton University Press, 2000.
Wollen, Peter. "The Auteur Theory." In *Signs and Meaning in the Cinema*, 74–115. Bloomington: Indiana University Press, 1972.
Wood, Robin. *Sexual Politics and Narrative Film: Hollywood and Beyond*. New York: Columbia University Press, 1998.
Wright, Gordon. *France in Modern Times: From the Enlightenment to the Present*. New York: Norton, 1981.
Younger, Prakash. "What Is Cinephilosophy? A Bazinian Paradigm, Part One: A Philosophical Preamble, for the Love of Truth." *Offscreen* 13, no. 2 (February 2009).
———. "What Is Cinephilosophy? A Bazinian Paradigm, Part Two: André Bazin or, the Cinephilosophical Heritage of Film Studies." *Offscreen* 13, no. 2 (February 2009).

INDEX

Page numbers in *italics* refer to figures and tables.

abstractions, 17, 21, 108, 127, 132, 143, 170, 182, 190, 194, 239, 242, 246, 302; romantic, 105, 120, 188; Rousseauian, 112

actors, xi, 24, 32, 37, 39, 42, 43, 44, 55, 75n67, 94, 145, 211; direction of, 39, 40, 47, 74n52; individuality of, 34, 36; performances of, 18, 39, 40, 46, 51, 67, 71; voices of, 35, 41, 45, 46, 63

alienation, 2, 26, 34, 64, 74n53, 79, 104, 141, 174, 177, 184, 199, 227, 304; self-alienation, 102

Altman, Rick, 27

anachronism, 19, 20, 84, 116, 126, 137, 157, 180, 226–27, 232, 233, 234, 238, 240, 244, 306; radical, xviii, xix

Andrew, Dudley, 78, 80–81, 122, 144

Anschluss, xiv, 294n5

apertures, 55–56, 57, 58, 60, 62

Arapura, J. G., 304, 305

Arendt, Hannah, xvi, 3

attention, xvi–xvii, 3, 34, 38, 46, 50, 66, 69, 71, 108, 112, 129–30, 137, 153, 155, 156, 167, 174, 176, 200, 242, 290, 297, 300, 301, 304, 314n9; loving, 15, 113; spectator's, 44, 51, 62, 70, 71

Auerbach, Erich, 87, 88–89, 116, 117, 118, 204, 265

Austria, 166, 237, 240, 241

auteurism, xx, 2–3, 4, 29, 31, 33, 44, 66, 72n15, 86, 168, 271; auteur-audience relation, 29; dialogical, 1–4

automatism, 37–38, 39, 90, 130

Bacon, Francis, 75n83, 297

Bakhtin, Mikhail, 5, 6, 19, 77

Balzac, Honoré de, 78, 87, 88–90, 107, 109, 117, 118

Bann, Stephen, 103, 104, 116

Barthes, Roland, xii, 1, 2, 82, 113

Baudrillard, Jean, 307

Bazin, André, xiv, xvi, 10–11, 12–18, 21nn17–18, 21n25, 28, 36, 38, 39, 50, 64, 74n49, 74n64, 76n87, 79–80, 81, 95, 111–13, 161n24, 299

Beaumarchais, Pierre, xiv, 78

belonging, 34, 129, 153, 169, 170, 172–73, 219, 294, 295, 299, 303. *See also* meeting

Benardete, Seth, 84, 85

Benjamin, Walter, xvi, 3, 4, 25, 202

Berger, John, 99, 100

Berlin, Isaiah, 187, 221n30

Berry, Jules, 140, 146, 176

Birnbaum, Pierre, 186–87

Blavette, Charles, 127

blindness, 128, 139, 158, 175, 188, 245, 291; culpable, 92, 123, 174; narcissistic, 122; romantic, 119, 121–22, 129, 175, 269, 284

Blum government, 166

Bordwell, David, 12

Boudu sauvé des eaux, xiv, 19, 94, 106, 107–12, 113, 168, 169, 171–72, 173, 177, 220n10, 299, 300, 303

bourgeoisie, 26, 28, 79, 82–83, 89, 102, 107, 108, 111, 117, 137, 171,176, 189; *grande bour-*

geoisie, 233; *haute bourgeoisie*, 236, 239; *petit bourgeoisie*, 106–107, 134
Brooks, Peter, 27
Brown, Clarence, 72n1
Brunswick Manifesto, 144, 147
Buchsbaum, Jonathan, 165, 220n1

camera, 48, 61, 111, 123, 129, 254, 270, 274, 276, 290, 292; dispassionate, 18, 51, 63–64, 67, 70, 71–72, 85; distance, 63–65; framing, 56, 63–64, 65, 66, 71, 90, 91, 98, 130, 166; movements, xiv, 18, 46, 49, 61, 63–65, 66–67, 69–70, 71, 256, 260, 261; position, 62. *See also* shot
Caprices of Marianne, The, 78
Cavell, Stanley, 12, 35, 36, 288
chance, 6, 81, 107, 147, 182, 184, 203, 204, 251, 297, 298, 304, 312; chance encounters, 128, 133, 199, 200, 248; gift of chance, xiii, 142, 171
Chaplin, Charlie, xx, 18, 23–24, 25, 30, 31, 32, 37, 39, 62, 72n15, 74n49, 76n87, 81, 109, 284
chronotopes, 5–7, 8, 9, 19, 40, 68, 72, 77, 79–80, 81, 82, 83, 84, 85, 86, 99, 162n60. *See also* Cytherean chronotope; Fifth chronotope; Flaubertian chronotope; Naturalist chronotope; Revolutionary chronotope
cinema, 12, 13, 16, 24, 26, 30, 35, 36, 48, 75n83; American, 24–25, 26, 27, 72n15; as art, 10, 16–17, 18, 23; French, xxin7, 23, 24, 72n15, 78, 88; Italian, 24; and language, 12, 16; realistic, 10, 17
civilization, 13, 19, 20, 104, 186, 199, 206, 207, 208, 216, 217, 218–19, 223n62, 228, 230, 231, 232, 233, 234, 242, 246, 248, 256, 257, 280, 282, 294, 299, 302, 308; cosmopolitan, 215; modern, 13, 14; new, 209, 210, 213, 215, 275; values of, 249, 285. *See also* culture
Comédie-Italienne, 42
comedy, xiv, 47, 48, 49, 83, 157, 280; humor, 8, 38, 49; neoclassical, 40, 81; silent, 37, 44; slapstick, 74n64. *See also* Comédie-Italienne; commedia dell'arte; tragicomedy; types, comic

commedia dell'arte, 41–42, 44, 74n64, 94, 128
communism, 164, 165, 181, 188–89, 225, 279, 295
community, xx, 19, 33, 34, 129, 132, 133, 140–42, 144, 146, 147, 153–54, 156, 157, 176, 191, 202, 206–207, 215, 218, 219–20, 223n62, 294
comradeship, 119, 128, 130, 132, 139, 156, 174, 175, 210, 276–77. *See also* friendship
conservatism, political, xviii, 79, 104, 269
contingency, 36, 38, 47, 111, 182, 188, 203–204, 205, 211–12, 219, 297, 309; aural, 46; of nature, 113. *See also* photography: contingency of
Corneille, Pierre, 78
culture, xii, xviii, 5, 16, 19–20, 35, 36, 48, 89, 104, 116, 142, 165, 200, 206, 208, 211, 219, 220, 223n62, 225, 227, 231, 234, 248, 269; bourgeois, 28; global, 105, 226; high, 180, 202, 240; model of, 206, 207, 218; modern, 101, 244; national, 104, 207, 208, 249; popular, 19, 26, 48, 79, 86, 139, 140, 141, 147, 166; traditional, 25. *See also* civilization
Cythera, 94, 101, 108, 113, 171, 177, 178, 220n10, 301, 302, 308, 310; concept of, 103, 115, 116; effect of, 106; experience of, 102, 103, 105–106, 114, 199, 200; memory of, 114, 233; power of, 153; reality of, 115, 172; revolution as, 157. *See also* Cytherean chronotope; Cytherean possibilities; desire, Cytherean; enchantment, Cytherean; modernity, Cytherean; reality, Cytherean; types, Cytherean
Cytherean chronotope, 94, 101, 106, 107, 108, 109, 113, 129, 148, 154, 156, 168, 169, 170, 171, 172, 173, 176–78, 191–92, 194, 298, 299, 300
Cytherean possibilities, 123, 130, 136, 160, 168, 176, 177, 178, 208, 219, 220n10
Czechoslovakia, 166

dandyism, 31, 34–35, 50, 67, 209, 212
Day in the Country, A, xiv, 57, 58, 70, 77, 80, 83, 85, 95, 159, 160, 172

de Maupassant, Guy, 78
defamiliarization, xii, xix, 6, 11, 25, 26, 28, 37, 38, 205, 231, 279, 294n8
Deleuze, Gilles, 12, 117–18, 158–59, 162n60
Deloffre, Frédéric, 42, 43, 44
Depew, David, 87
Descartes, René, 182, 203
desire, xx, 13, 15, 16, 17, 20, 21n25, 58, 60, 89, 90, 101, 102, 115, 145, 170, 171, 173, 174, 184, 185, 191, 197, 206, 225, 228; and blindness, 121, 122–23, 245; carnal, 107, 108, 242; concept of, xvi, 181, 198; Cytherean, 221n27, 242; erotic, 14, 156; negation of, 169, 175; object of, 117, 119, 122, 235; and reason, 103; romantic, 84, 151, 279; and will, xvi
disenchantment, 14, 34, 116, 145, 146, 199, 200, 206, 227, 275, 306
disillusionment, 88, 116, 150. *See also* romanticism: disillusioned
disorientation, 59, 81, 99, 100, 101, 130, 156, 176, 199, 202
dissolve, 111, 112, 172, 192; invisible, 106, 110, 118, 171, 176–77, 178, 191, 215, 217, 234, 258, 274, 275, 307, 308, 310
drama, xix, 48, 169, 259; and comedy, xiv; European, 40; French, 24; psychological, 74n53; social, 47

editing, 18, 59, 63–65, 67, 70–71, 73n23; continuity in, 59, 63, 64, 70, 71
Elena et les hommes, 94
Elsaesser, Thomas, 27
enchantment, 44, 199; Cytherean, 116, 200, 208, 213, 218, 219, 258, 275. *See also* disenchantment
Enlightenment, the, 18, 104, 227, 248, 250, 251; European, 246; French, 186, 256; post-Enlightenment, 20
ethics, xvi, xvii, 11, 13, 14, 15, 16, 100, 123, 167, 173, 185, 196, 197, 200, 228, 297, 298, 304; ethical obligations, 75n83, 186, 188, 193, 198, 202, 221n27, 228, 247, 297
Europe, 30, 51, 53, 105, 113, 160, 165, 180, 181, 190, 202, 203, 209, 228, 294; European politics, 188; European society, 188. *See also* drama: European; Enlightenment, the: European; identity: European; philosophy: European

faith, 87, 116, 173, 196, 199, 200, 201, 204, 209, 218, 225, 230, 290, 293, 300, 301, 314n9; in reality, 13, 17, 115; religious, 190
fascism, 25, 26, 146, 165, 181, 188, 189, 231, 234, 267–69, 279, 288, 295
Faulkner, Christopher, xxn3
fête galante, 94, 106
Fifth chronotope, 18, 19, 191, 192, 219, 299–300, 302, 303, 308
Flaubert, Gustave, xviii, 78, 86–87, 89–90, 158, 170, 296. *See also* Flaubertian chronotope; gaze, Flaubertian; types: Flaubertian
Flaubertian chronotope, 19, 87, 90, 92, 93–94, 106–107, 108, 117, 121, 148, 168, 169, 170, 172, 174, 176–77, 220n10, 299
Foolish Wives, 30–31, 32
Foucault, Michel, 12, 16, 307
France, xix, 5, 24, 30, 41, 45, 103, 145, 146, 160, 165, 166–67, 181, 182, 186, 187, 225, 246, 287, 294; French culture, 18, 26, 41, 72n15, 77, 78, 79, 87, 168
Frank, Nino, 20n2
freedom, xvi, xx, 7, 102, 103, 136, 183, 192, 200, 225, 305, 307
French Revolution, 87, 88, 100, 104, 105, 116, 142, 146, 181, 182, 225
Freud, Sigmund, 74n53, 102, 103, 104, 221n30
friendship, 69, 154–55, 192–93, 195–96, 197, 200, 201–202, 205–206, 207, 208–209, 210–13, 215, 218, 219, 227, 228, 230, 234, 237, 242, 254, 259, 260, 261, 263, 286, 290, 291, 293–94, 302, 303. *See also* comradeship
Fukuyama, Francis, xvii
Furet, François, 181, 182

gags, xx, 20, 38–39, 49, 71, 80, 82, 85, 101, 109, 225, 226, 230, 231, 232, 256, 272, 273, 279, 283, 284; in silent comedy, 37, 44; structure of, 45, 67
Game of Love and Chance, The, 78

gaze, 78, 89, 90, 109, 119, 120, 121–22, 124, 127, 130, 138, 140, 148, 152, 155, 156, 159, 216, 236, 242, 254, 261, 265, 267, 270, 274, 275, 276, 278, 288, 292; Flaubertian, 171; ironic, 158; male, 58, 59; protagonist's, 122; sadistic, 264; spectator's, 53
Germany, 115, 165, 166, 189, 190, 213, 269; German culture, 190; German language, 214, 216, 223n62, 230; Germans, 55, 186, 190, 213, 214, 248
Giraudoux, Jean, 40
globalization, xvi, xvii, xxin6, 105, 137, 226, 227
Golden Coach, The, 94
Gordon, Daniel, 246
Gorky, Maxim, 117
Grant, George, xvi, xvii, xxiv, 306–307, 310
Griffith, D. W., 18, 23, 27, 30, 72n15

Hamann, Johann Georg, 104
Hartle, Ann, 203, 205, 222n61
Havel, Vaclav, 37–38, 39, 74n49, 80
Hawks, Howard, 169
Hegel, Georg Wilhelm Friedrich, xvi, xvii, 102, 104, 126, 136, 144, 147, 158, 175, 203, 225, 226, 227–28, 231, 248, 252, 271, 274, 305
Heidegger, Martin, xvi, xvii, xxn1, 75n83, 102, 170, 205, 296–97, 305
Herder, Johann Gottfried, 104
historicism, 3, 88, 104, 227; micro, 2; modern, 169, 297; radical, 2
Hitler, Adolf, 10, 12, 180, 190, 267, 269
Hitler-Stalin Pact, 166

identity, 43, 127, 155, 190, 191, 199, 200, 206, 279; cultural, 105; European, 202; French, 186, 206; identity crisis, 181; personal, xx, 189; romantic, 83; social, 83
illusion, 11, 13–14, 15, 55, 61, 75n67, 89, 301, 304; and reality, 16, 21n25, 299; representational, 61–62; and truth, 14, 15, 17
intimacy, x, 26, 52, 55, 61, 78, 79, 80, 146, 155, 190, 232, 253, 255, 258, 274, 275
irony, 11, 91, 94, 180, 192, 193, 210, 213, 216, 231, 251, 252, 273, 274, 289; anarchic, 190; comic, 30, 48; ironic amusement, 121, 135, 210. *See also* gaze: ironic

irrationality, 13, 14, 16, 17, 75n83, 78, 88, 89, 118, 119, 123, 125, 180, 181, 182, 228, 244, 279, 298, 314n9. *See also* rationality
isolation, 34, 50, 68, 79, 90, 94, 119, 129, 132, 140, 142, 146, 148, 177, 209, 257
Italian method, 40–41, 44, 45, 46, 71, 74n52
Italy, 52, 74n52, 125, 165; Italian language, 41; Italian Renaissance, 52; Italians, 24. *See also* cinema: Italian; commedia dell'arte; Italian method

Jameson, Fredric, xvi, xxin6, 5
je ne sais quoi, 248–49, 250, 255, 265, 273, 281, 282, 286
Jews, 8, 9, 142, 200, 210, 211, 213, 248, 249, 266, 294
Jouvet, Louis, 40, 42

Kant, Immanuel, xvi, 102, 104, 203, 305
Kierkegaard, Søren, 305
Kojève, Alexandre, xvii

La bête humaine, 19, 60, 61, 63, 116–17, 119–25, 126, 128, 132–35, 136–39, 168, 174, 175, 177, 220, 233, 244, 298
Lacan, Jacques, 104
La chienne, 19, 32, 45, 47–50, 87, 90–91, 93, 168, 169, 177, 220n10, 296, 303
La fille de l'eau, 29
La grande illusion, 19, 54, 61, 63, 168, 191, 206, 209–19, 250, 300
La Marseillaise, 19, 139, 142–45, 146–48, 154–55, 158, 160, 162n60, 165, 168, 175–76, 177, 220, 299
La règle du jeu, ix, xiv–xv, xvii–xviii, xix–xx, xxn5, xxin7, 18, 19, 23, 48, 166, 168, 220, 225–26, 228–31, 232–34, 236–46, 247, 248–49, 252–94, 294n9, 296, 298, 299, 308
La vie est à nous, 165, 168, 220n5
Lawrence, D. H., xvi
Le crime de Monsieur Lange, 19, 64, 139–42, 143–44, 145–46, 148–54, 155, 156–57, 160, 165, 166, 168, 169, 175, 176, 177, 298
Le dejeuner sur l'herbe, 94
Left, the, xx, 104, 164, 165, 166, 167, 186, 188, 190, 220n1, 225. *See also* Right, the

Le jour se lève, 79, 119
Lehman, Peter, xv, xxn5
Les bas-fonds, 19, 54, 65–66, 67–69, 168, 191–96, *197*, 219, 252, 253–54, 300
Levinas, Emmanuel, xvi, 197
looking-at, 121, 148, 169, 170, 174, 176, 177, 187, 259, 271, 274, 276, 283, 288, 297; looking-at oneself, 124; looking-at others, 265, 266–67, 268, 269, 270, 274, 275, 276, 296, 298
Lourie, Eugene, 54, 60–61, 63

Madame Bovary (film), 19, 56, 70, 87, 90, 168, 177, 296
Madame Bovary (novel), 86–87, 90, 169, 265
Maistre, Joseph de, 221n30
Marion, Jean-Luc, 197, 314n9
Marivaux, Pierre de, xiv, 42, 44, 74n57, 78, 115
meeting, 28, 33, 93, 94, 129, 130, 139, 169, 170, 172–73, 178, 191, 192, 200, 208, 219, 228, 294, 295, 299, 303. *See also* belonging
melodrama, 26–28, 49, 51, 88, 90–91, 137, 200, 205; naturalist, 19, 30, 116, 168, 169, 173–74, 175, 176, 177
memories, ix, x, 3, 31, 63, 79, 102, 114, 162n60, 172, 228, 233, 306, 311; cultural, 3; historical, 103; private, 78; romantic, 8, 310
metaphysics, 118, 204, 205, 302, 303
Method acting, 40
mise-en-abyme, 266, 267, 270
mise-en-scène, 31, 34, 39, 55, 56, 57, 60, 61, 64, 71, 76n87, 85, 90, 92, 109, 110, 119, 128, 129, 205, 260, 262, 270
modernity, xvi, xxin6, 31, 75n83, 101, 103, 105, 116, 137, 139, 178, 197, 202, 225, 227, 232, 250, 295, 296, 299–300, 306, 308, 309; capitalist, 137; critique of, 114, 186; Cytherean, 310; history of, 106; nineteenth-century, 9; of modern art, 30; technological, 137. *See also* postmodernity
Molière, 40, 42
Montaigne, Michel de, 18, 196, 197, 202, 203–206, 222n52, 246, 247, 248, 251, 294n8, 301, 302

Montale, Eugenio, xvi, 178, 308, 309, 310, 311
mortality, xii, 20n8, 99, 100, 102, 272, 304
Munich Agreement, 14, 166
Musset, Alfred de, xiv, 78

Nabokov, 170
narcissism, 123, 170, 176, 186, 199, 200, 212, 282. *See also* blindness: narcissistic
nationalism, 19, 105, 206, 207, 213
naturalism, 45, 77, 78, 81, 86, 87, 117–18, 123, 126, 162n49, 193; canonical, 118, 122. *See also* melodrama: naturalist; Naturalist chronotope
Naturalist chronotope/Naturalist melodrama, 19, 67, 78, 116, 128, 155, 156, 168, 169, 173, 174–75, 176, 177, 193, 296, 299
Niblo, Fred, 72n1
Nietzsche, Friedrich, xvi, 102, 104, 158, 159, 160, 170, 297, 298, 305
nihilism, 67, 68, 192, 220n10, 279, 306, 308
Nora, Pierre, 186
nostalgia, xviii, 67, 79, 100–101, 172, 207, 210, 314n14. *See also* memories

obligation, 102, 187–88, 218, 219, 254. *See also* ethics: ethical obligations
O'Brien, Charles, 45
On purge bébé, 29
ontology, x, xv, 10, 12, 16, 17, 21n18, 80, 110, 205, 232, 304

Panicale, Masolino da, 52
Panofsky, Erwin, 51, 52, 53–54, 75n83
Paris, xiv, xvii, 6, 24, 30, 41, 107, 110, 115, 120, 133, 140, 144, 147, 213, 237, 239, 269; Parisians, 81, 82, 107, 147, 241
perspective, 51–52, 53, 54, 59, 75n83; diminishing, 60, 61; forced, 60, 61–62; multiple, 52, 55; single-point, 52, 61. *See also* sound: perspective
Pétain, Phillippe, 167, 269
Peters, John Durham, 314n9
philosophy, xxn1, 10, 11, 12, 18, 85, 182, 206; accidental, 203–204; cinephilosophy, 1, 10, 12, 17; deliberate, 203, 205, 222n61; European, 53, 203; Greek, 20n8; modern, xix, 101, 182, 191, 197, 220n7, 297,

298, 306; political, xvi, xix, 1, 165, 181, 203, 297; Western, 205. *See also* Plato; Socrates

photography, 12, 13–14, 15–16, 17, 25, 54–55, 61, 75n83, 113, 134, 161n44, 303, 309; contingency of, 16, 17, 35; technology of, 10

Plato, xviii, xxiv, 10–11, 12, 16, 18, 21n9, 21n25, 173, 197, 198, 201, 204, 205, 206, 207, 247, 302, 303, 314n9; Platonic dialogues, 84, 85, 205; Platonic models, xvi, 193, 199, 202, 228; Platonic tradition, xvi; Plato's Cave, xix, 17, 233, 302

Poland, 166

Popular Front, 140, 141, 146, 162n55, 165, 166, 220n3

Portugal, 165

postmodernity, xvi, xxin6, 116, 302, 306, 307. *See also* modernity

progress, 99, 225, 227, 236, 295–96, 299

Proust, Marcel, 104

psychoanalysis, 2, 12, 40, 75n83

Quai des brumes, 79, 119

Racine, Jean, 78, 180

racism, 140, 190, 249, 267, 287

radiation, 303, 306, 307, 308

Radical Party, 166

Ram, Radha Shri, 29

rationalism, 20, 182, 221n30

rationality, xvi, 10–11, 13–14, 15, 78, 103, 118, 174, 182, 190, 228, 247, 298. *See also* irrationality; rationalism

realism, 10, 13, 30, 48–49, 80, 87, 89, 150, 175, 265; external, 31–32, 35, 36, 39, 51, 62, 63, 70, 80, 85, 128, 263; French, 30; internal, 31–32, 35, 36, 39, 44, 46, 47, 49, 50, 51, 57, 63, 70, 85, 128, 139, 263; perfect, 55; poetic, 78, 79, 88, 117; pseudorealism, 12, 17, 80; psychological, 28; true, 12, 15, 80. *See also* reality

reality, xvi, 2, 10, 12, 14, 15–16, 21n25, 32, 75n67, 84, 114–16, 137, 139, 149, 158, 159, 173, 188, 199, 200, 234, 236, 299, 302, 304, 305; Cytherean, 118, 172, 175; external, 31, 304; and fantasy, 60; historical, 226; and illusion, 16; internal, 31; simulated, 80;

understanding of, 17, 88, 116, 173, 301. *See also* realism

reason, human, xvi, 11, 15, 102, 103, 191, 197, 198, 203, 247

reflection, process of, 3, 4, 7, 16, 19, 20, 64, 77, 85, 116, 123, 127, 131, 155, 157, 158, 159, 160, 162n60, 167–68, 169, 173, 176, 178, 183–84, 196; self-reflection, 119

rehearsal, 44, 45, 47, 54. *See also* Italian method

relativism, 202, 203

resemblance, 13, 14–15, 16, 17, 21n25

resentment, 67, 138, 170, 176, 211, 212, 231, 254, 267, 270, 279, 283, 287, 289; class-based, 285, 286; political, 270; romantic, 269; social, 136, 284

Resnais, Alain, xiv, xvii

Revolutionary chronotope, 19, 139, 154, 155, 158–59, 168, 169, 175, 176, 193, 296, 299, 303

Right, the, xx, 104, 157, 164, 166, 186, 188, 225

rights, 184, 186, 187–88, 218

River, The, 94

Rivette, Jacques, 173, 237

romanticism, xviii–xix, 27, 67, 77, 104–105, 126, 158, 159, 160, 172, 177, 178, 181, 183, 197, 220, 220n10, 227, 244, 280, 296, 298, 299; and comedy, 40; critique of, 19, 139, 199; disillusioned, 87, 265; effects of, 19, 137, 287; end of, 280, 283–84; genealogy of, 126, 180; habits of, 173, 176, 219; melodramatic, 89; problem of, 19, 116, 180, 183, 190, 192; and rationalism, 20; and time, 103. *See also* blindness: romantic

Rosen, Stanley, xvi, xvii

Rougemont, Denis de, 180–81

Rousseau, Jean-Jacques, xvi, xviii, xix, 18, 19, 77–78, 88, 89, 90, 102–103, 104, 105–106, 112, 118, 137, 161n36, 180, 182–83, 184, 185, 186–87, 189, 191, 197, 199–200, 203, 206, 221n24, 228, 231, 244, 248, 251, 298, 299; *The Social Contract*, 104, 182, 183, 184, 185–86, 187, 200. *See also* abstractions: Rousseauian

Rules of the Game, The, 33, 78, 86, 191

Ruprecht, Louis, 198, 200, 201, 207

Schiffman, Zachary Sayre, 202

Schneider, Pierre, 95, 96, 99
Schumacher, Claude, 43
science, 169, 296–97; faith in, 10; natural, 75n83, 182, 183, 299
Searchers, The, xv, xxn5
self-deception, 90, 123, 166, 170, 190, 278, 282, 289, 290
self-negation, 124, 183, 184, 193, 228, 234, 274, 284, 288, 290, 291, 293
Sennett, Mack, 25
Sesonske, Alexander, 48, 49, 145, 162n57
Shakespeare, William, 40, 180
shot, xi, xiv, 49, 50, 56–59, 61, 69, 70, 71, 81, 92, 106, 123, 127, 129, 131, 132, 215, 220n10, 236, 238, 271–72; close-ups, 49, 55, 59, 65, 80, 81, 84, 90, 106, 111, 135, 176, 215, 259, 260–61, 263; interior, 62; length of, 63–64, 65; long, 49, 56, 58, 60, 65, 90, 92, 97, 98, 129, 130, 168, 176, 181, 213; master, 73n23; medium, 65, 108, 130, 214, 291; medium-close, 56, 65, 92, 253, 254; medium-long, 66; point-of-view, 70, 138; reaction, 92, 139, 259; reverse-angle, 275; shot-reverse shot sequence, 73n23, 93; three shot, 155; tracking, 110, 137, 159, 172; traveling, 81, 83; two shot, 108, 155, 193, 276. *See also* camera
Sims, Bennet, 124
Sirk, Douglas, 27
skepticism, xii, 11, 13, 16, 66, 77, 114, 130, 154, 156, 157, 196, 204, 248, 264, 301; affectionate, 148, 154, 155; radical, 173, 204
sociabilité, 246, 247, 248, 250, 254, 256, 258, 264, 265, 272, 275, 277
Socrates, 10, 12, 22, 85, 173, 204
sound, in film, 6, 18, 32, 45, 55, 59, 62–63, 75n67, 79, 88, 110, 128, 166, 309, 312; direct, 46; natural, 31; perspective, 55, 309; recorded, 35, 45, 46, 139; sound technology, 45
Soviet Union, 165
space, 54, 58–59, 61, 70, 75n83, 111, 148; deep, 46; definition of, 59, 60; diegetic, 6, 56, 62; finite, 61; hybrid, 62–63; infinite, 52, 53, 55, 96; peripheral, 56, 57; pictorial, 18, 51, 53, 55–56, 60, 62, 71; three-dimensional, 52, 55; and time, 5–6, 14, 55, 61, 64, 77, 97, 98, 99, 106, 110, 112, 113, 114, 128, 303, 309. *See also* time: and space
Spain, 166
state of nature, 102, 105, 118, 183, 228
Stavisky affair, 166
Steiner, George, xvi
Stendhal, 87, 90, 180
Stoics, xvi, 158; stoicism, 136, 137, 155, 174, 175
Strauss, Leo, 297, 298

technology, xvi, xvii, 10, 25, 45, 53, 75n83, 137, 166, 182, 183, 202, 203, 226, 227, 236, 244, 295–97, 298, 299, 300, 306, 307, 308, 310–11, 313; faith in, 298; recording, 75n67
theatre, 31, 32; literary, 26
Tiananmen Square, xvii, xxin6
time, xi, xx, 2–3, 5–6, 14, 64, 66, 84, 96, 97–98, 99–100, 102, 103, 105, 127, 158, 159, 160, 191, 196, 197; conceptions of, 100, 118, 302; cosmic, 99, 106, 112, 113, 309; as eternity, 100, 101; historical, xvi, 4, 7, 20, 27, 87, 101, 103–104, 113, 114, 118, 142, 146–47, 158, 160, 162n60, 225, 227, 298, 299, 302, 306, 308, 309; and space, 56, 61, 77, 97, 98–99, 110, 114, 128; structure of, 101, 178, 308; as thought, 7, 232. *See also* space: and time
Tolstoy, Leo, xvi
Toni, 19, 116, 117, 119, 125–32, 137, 139, 156, 168, 169, 174, 175, 177, 244, 298
tragicomedy, 19, 129, 220n10
tranquility, 125, 304, 305, 307, 309
trapdoors, 47, 66, 84, 168, 205
Truffaut, François, 173
truth, xvi, 11, 15, 16, 21n25, 37, 81, 82, 84, 87, 92, 115, 123, 147, 175, 183, 184, 198, 201, 204, 205, 222n61, 256, 313n8; absolute, 10; aesthetic, 17; external, 18, 31, 32, 34; final, 159, 195; and illusion, 14, 15, 17; internal, 18, 31, 32, 34, 39, 41, 45, 47, 80; philosophical, 15, 85
types, 18, 30–31, 34–36, 39, 40, 41–42, 44, 45, 46–47, 48, 49, 50, 52, 60, 74n49, 90, 94, 106, 139, 284, 286; comic, 81; Cytherean, 106–107, 108; Flaubertian, 106–107, 108, 117; Revolutionary, 154, 155; social, 78, 82
Une partie de campagne, 19, 40, 94, 106, 110, 113, 168, 177, 300, 308

Ungar, Steven, 144
utopia, 103, 104, 113, 114, 143, 146, 165, 167, 171, 175, 182, 186, 189, 206, 219, 232, 246, 257, 258, 308

van Eyck, Jan, 52
vaporization, 306, 310–11
von Stroheim, Erich, 18, 23, 30, 31, 72n15, 76n87, 91, 117

Washburn, Gordon, 100
Watteau, Antoine, 94–97, 98–99, 100–101, 106, 108, 109, 110, 113, 171, 308, 309
Weil, Simone, xvi, 51, 187, 188, 189, 190, 192–93, 197, 200, 201–202, 221n27, 221n30, 235, 279, 300, 301, 302, 304, 313n8, 314n9
will, the, xvi, 75n83, 185, 190, 297, 298, 299, 300, 304, 305
Williams, Linda, 27
Williams, Raymond, 5, 7, 20n4
Wingrove, Elizabeth Rose, 184, 185, 221n24
Wollen, Peter, 4
Wood, Robin, xiv, xix
World War I, 23, 26, 178, 180, 250, 269, 310
World War II, 26, 187, 188

Yugoslavia, 105, 165

Zola, Émile, 78, 117

PRAKASH YOUNGER is Associate Professor of English at Trinity College. *Boats on the Marne* is his first book.

www.ingramcontent.com/pod-product-compliance
Lightning Source LLC
Chambersburg PA
CBHW070232240426
43673CB00044B/1764